BILL THILLY

UKRAINE

A Tourist Guide

Second Edition

UKRAINE

A Tourist Guide

Second Edition

Compiled by
Osyp Zinkewych
and Volodymyr Hula

Translated and Edited
by Marta D. Olynyk

SMOLOSKYP Publishers

Kyiv   1995   Baltimore

UKRAINE: *A Tourist Guide*

Second Edition

Compiled by Osyp Zinkewych and Volodymyr Hula

Translated and Edited by Marta D. Olynyk
Partially translated by Yaroslav Lishchynsky
and Tamara Stadnychenko-Cornelison

Cover Photograph: Vitaliy Kuzovkov

Photos by Serhiy Marchenko appear on pages: 31, 32, 33, 34 (bottom), 37, 67, 82, 83, 84 (top), 85, 93, 94, 99, 100, 102, 103, 109, 111, 115 (top), 119, 123, 130, 134, 137, 152, 176 (bottom), 198, 203, 210 (bottom), 213, 214, 215, 233, 242 (top), 243, 262, 259, 263, 301, 305, 306, 319, 335, 346 (bottom), 352, 355, 365 (bottom), 375, 388, 389 (bottom), 403, 405 (bottom).

Photos by Vitaliy Kuzovkov appear on pages: 36 (bottom), 75, 131, 136, 138, 155, 201, 267, 271, 275 (bottom), 295, 313, 339.

Library of Congress Catalog Card Number: 93-84208
ISBN: 0-914834-93-2

Copyright © 1995 SMOLOSKYP Publishers

Maps of cities, and metropolitans of Kyiv and Kharkiv:
Copyright © 1995 SB "Mapa LTD" and Smoloskyp Publishers.

SMOLOSKYP Publishers:

Ukraine: 252053, Kyiv-53   **USA:** P.O. Box 20620
Vul. Artema, 1-5, R. 802   Billings, MT 59104
Tel. & Fax: (044) 212-08-77   Tel. & Fax: (406) 656-0466

Typeset by UKRAPRINT, Inc., P.O. Box 304, Woodstock, MD 21163, USA
Printed and Bound in Ukraine

TABLE OF CONTENTS

11	**WELCOME TO UKRAINE!**

15	**UKRAINE**
15	History
18	Population
19	A Chronology of Ukraine's History

23	**PLANNING A TRIP TO UKRAINE**
	Baggage, Insurance, Social Services, Documents and Visas
24	Currency, Electricity, What to Bring, Customs Regulations
25	The Work Day in Ukraine, Holidays in Ukraine
26	Ukrainian Cuisine, Taxis
27	Tours and Excursions Suggested for Visitors to Ukraine
28	Telephones in Ukraine: How to use them in Hotels, Private Rooms, in the City, International Calls
29	Telephone Services

31	**KYIV — CAPITAL OF UKRAINE**
67	**KYIV REGION**
69	Touring Historic Cities and Villages

75	**CHERKASY REGION**
77	**CHERKASY**
81	Touring Historic Cities and Villages

89	**CHERNIHIV REGION**
93	**CHERNIHIV**
99	Touring Historic Cities and Villages

111	**CHERNIVTSI REGION**
113	**CHERNIVTSI**
118	Touring Historic Cities and Villages

123 **CRIMEAN REPUBLIC**

127 **SIMFEROPOL**

130   Touring Historic Cities And Villages

143 **DNIPROPETROVSK REGION**

145 **DNIPROPETROVSK**

151   Touring Historic Cities And Villages

155 **DONETSK REGION**

157 **DONETSK**

162   Touring Historic Cities And Villages

165 **IVANO-FRANKIVSK REGION**

169 **IVANO-FRANKIVSK**

173   Touring Historic Cities And Villages

179 **KHARKIV REGION**

181 **KHARKIV**

187   Touring Historic Cities And Villages

191 **KHERSON REGION**

193 **KHERSON**

198   Touring Historic Cities And Villages

201 **KHMELNYTSKY REGION**

203 **KHMELNYTSKY**

207   Touring Historic Cities And Villages

219 **KIROVOHRAD REGION**

221 **KIROVOHRAD**

226   Touring Historic Cities And Villages

227 **LUHANSK REGION**

229 **LUHANSK**

232   Touring Historic Cities And Villages

233 **LVIV REGION**

237 **LVIV**

253   Touring Historic Cities And Villages

267 **MYKOLAYIV REGION**

269 **MYKOLAYIV**

274   Touring Historic Cities And Villages

277 **ODESA REGION**

279 **ODESA**

290   Touring Historic Cities And Villages

295 **POLTAVA REGION**

299 **POLTAVA**

305   Touring Historic Cities And Villages

311 **RIVNE REGION**

313 **RIVNE**

317   Touring Historic Cities And Villages

323 **SUMY REGION**

325 **SUMY**

331   Touring Historic Cities And Villages

339 **TERNOPIL REGION**

341 **TERNOPIL**

346   Touring Historic Cities And Villages

355 **VINNYTSYA REGION**

357 **VINNYTSYA**

362   Touring Historic Cities And Villages

---

367 **VOLYN REGION**

369 **LUTSK**

375   Touring Historic Cities And Villages

---

381 **ZAKARPATSKA REGION**

383 **UZHHOROD**

388   Touring Historic Cities And Villages

---

393 **ZAPORIZHZHYA REGION**

395 **ZAPORIZHZHYA**

400   Touring Historic Cities And Villages

---

403 **ZHYTOMYR REGION**

405 **ZHYTOMYR**

410   Touring Historic Cities And Villages

REFERENCE SECTION

417 Government

417   Selected Ministries, Agencies, Commitees

418   State Companies, Selected State Institutions

418 Political Parties of Ukraine

419 Diplomatic Representatives of Ukraine

419 Embassies of Ukraine

422 Consulates of Ukraine

422 Foreign Embassies and Consulates in Kyiv, Ukraine

425 Travel Agencies

425   USA

426   Australia

426   Canada

428   Great Britain

429 Conversion Charts
429   Temperatures
429   Metric System
430   Clothing
431 Telephone Area Codes in Ukraine
438 International Telephone Communications:
         Country and City Codes

444 Index of Cities and Villages

Welcome to Ukraine!

On August 24, 1991 Ukraine declared itself an independent state, taking its rightful place among the countries of the world.

Centuries of economic and political dependence on Moscow have left Ukraine with severe economic, ecological, transportation, communications, and energy problems. In addition, Ukraine's isolation from the Western world was exacerbated by a system of propaganda and censorship, which distorted the actual state of affairs in the republic.

Despite the multitude of problems affecting this newly-independent country, Ukraine is the most stable and peaceful state of all the former republics of the USSR. In an effort to rebuild the country Ukraine has opened her doors to foreign investors, businessmen, and first and foremost to tourists.

Ukraine is an undiscovered treasure — a fascinating, convenient, and inexpensive destination, where visitors can spend their holidays, become acquainted with the history and culture of the Ukrainian people, visit the churches and architectural monuments of a thousand- year-old culture, and explore the many health resorts located throughout Ukraine.

Kyiv and Lviv, Chernihiv and Kamyanets-Podilsky, Ivano-Frankivsk and Chernivtsi, Odesa and the Crimea, the Black Sea and the Carpathian Mountains are just some of the remarkable places awaiting the businessman and tourist. Visitors to Ukraine can enjoy some of the finest cuisine in eastern Europe and every day brings improvements in communications, transportation, services, and hotel accommodations.

Ukraine is fast becoming one of the most enticing destinations in the world. Although tourism was always one of the better developed industries in this country, until recently there was little information available for tourists, who were forced to waste precious time tracking down addresses and telephone numbers to the historical sites and architectural monuments of Ukraine. It is with great pleasure that we offer

ACKNOWLEDGEMENTS

Smoloskyp Publishers and the compilers of this travel guide gratefully acknowledge the assistance of every individual who contributed articles and gathered information for this edition. Without their help and advice, this travel guide could not have been published.

you *Ukraine: A Tourist Guide,* the first complete tourist guide to Ukraine, available in both Ukrainian and English.

This is more than just a travel guide; it is a reference book and a small encyclopedia of historical and current information about Ukraine. New editions will be published annually, with revised information added to provide better service for travellers to Ukraine.

Each of the 24 regions of Ukraine, as well as the autonomous Republic of Crimea, is represented in this easy-to-use guide. There are listings for:

- churches, historical and architectural monuments;
- museums, theatres, philharmonics, publishing houses;
- higher educational institutions, libraries, archives, sports complexes;
- hotels, restaurants, cafes, stores, banks;
- information on tourist agencies, spas and resorts, transportation, auto servicing;
- postal services, telephone, medical services, pharmacies;
- religious denominations and services.

Every section contains information on prominent individuals who were born or deceased in a particular region and sub-sections on selected historical cities and villages of each region. The addresses and telephone numbers of the most important historical and architectural sites (churches, castles, fortresses, and museums) are listed in these sub-sections.

The introductory essay discusses Ukraine: its people, geographic location, and its economic potential. Pertinent information is provided for travellers planning a trip to Ukraine, including: visa requirements, lists of items permitted for import or export, customs regulations, a restaurant and food guide, the telephone system, voltage, currency exchange, tours and excursions.

In addition to addresses, telephone and fax numbers, the reference section of this guide contains listings for:

- Government agencies of Ukraine: political parties and organizations;
- Embassies and consulates of Ukraine abroad;
- Foreign embassies in Ukraine;
- State institutions, ministries, committees, agencies;
- Telephone codes for cities and other populated points in Ukraine;
- Foreign telephone codes (cities & countries);
- Conversion tables for clothing, footwear, the metric system, and temperature charts;
- 95 Travel agencies.

The guide contains maps of 24 regional capitals of Ukraine and the capital of the Republic of Crimea, as well as recent street-name changes, and subway guides for Kyiv and Kharkiv. The English-language travel guide to Ukraine follows the Ukrainian transliteration system for proper names and geographic locations.

The guide does not list current information on costs of hotels, cruises, excursions, airfares, train or bus tickets, because of price fluctuations. But Ukraine is still considerably less expensive than other European countries.

Certain hotels accept Ukrainian currency, while others require payment in foreign currencies. There are three types of hotel rates in Ukraine: individual, business, and group rate.

With this convenient guide travellers to Ukraine can easily create their own itinerary or plan future trips. Tourists are advised to be selective, since it is impossible to see everything in one visit. Take the Andriyivsky Uzviz quarter of Kyiv, a fascinating blend of the historical and the modern: here the tourist will find beautiful architecture, art exhibits and galleries, extraordinary monuments of antiquity, ancient churches, and secluded cafes.

Please be advised that Ukrainian hotels are not on a par with the Sheraton, Marriot, or Holiday Inn chains. But they are comfortable and adhere to accepted standards of accommodation.

Whatever your itinerary, you will find excellent food in Ukraine. Try Ukrainian borshch and varenyky, chicken a la Kyiv, the rolled, filled pancakes, or delicious Ukrainian dark bread. But be prepared for a different style of service in restaurants, where you may have to wait longer for your order. Above all, bring your sense of humor and don't let certain inadequacies of service spoil your visit. We are confident that you will enjoy your visit to Ukraine and come back again and again!

PLEASE NOTE:

At time of publication the most current and reliable listings possible were included by the compilers. However, the names of certain cities, streets, and telephone numbers will be changing in the near future.

The publishers would greatly appreciate being informed about changes in listings which occurred after the publication date.

If readers have any interesting photos of historical churches, architectural monuments, or hotels in Ukraine, please send them to our offices and we will try to include them in our next edition.

We would be grateful to travel agents and tour operators for their suggestions and ideas.

All correspondence should be addressed to:

Smoloskyp	or	Smoloskyp
252001 Kyiv-1,		P.O. Box 20620
Holovposhtamt, A/C 25,		Billings, MT, 59104, USA
Tel. and fax: (044) 212-08-77		Tel. & Fax: (406) 656-0466

Ukraine

Ukraine is a state in Eastern Europe, bounded on the north by Belarus, on the north and east by the Russian Federation, on the west by Poland, Slovakia, on the southwest by Hungary, Rumania, and Moldova, and on the south by the Black Sea and the Sea of Azov.

The total area of Ukraine is 603,700 sq. km (compare the area of France — 551,000 sq. km; Germany — 356,000; Great Britain — 244,000; Italy — 301,000; Spain — 505,000). The population of Ukraine is 52 million (Germany — 78 million; France — 56 million; Great Britain — 58 million; Italy — 59 million; Spain — 40 million). The area spanned in a west-east direction is 1300 km; from north to south — 900 km.

Ukraine's state border extends for a total of 7698 km: with Russia — 2484 km; Belarus — 952 km; Rumania — 608 km; Poland — 542 km; Slovakia — 98 km;

Leonid Kuchma
President of Ukraine

Hungary — 135 km; Moldova — 1194 km. The total length of Ukraine's sea coast is 1758 km (Black Sea — 1533 km; Sea of Azov — 225 km).

The climate of Ukraine is moderate-continental; in the southernmost region of the Crimea the climate is sub-tropical. The largest river of Ukraine is the Dnipro, which is 2201 km in length, of which 981 km flow through Ukraine. The largest mountain system in Ukraine is the Carpathian Mountains which extend for more than 270 km and are 100-110 km wide. The highest peak is the Hoverla (2061 m).

HISTORY

Ukrainians have lived on the territory of present-day Ukraine for millennia. The roots of the Ukrainian nation are found in Trypillian culture which evolved in the Middle Dnipro region in the third millennium B.C., the heritage of the Scythian tribes, and Chernyakhiv culture. More than 1100 years ago Kievan Rus'-Ukraine, a powerful European medieval monarchy, was established on Ukrainian territory. Its lands extended to the Gulf of Finland and the largest lakes of Karelia in the north, to the upper course of the Volga in the east, and to the Syan and Western Buh rivers in the west. The cities of Peremyshl, Sanok, and Kholm in present-day Poland were founded by Ukrainian princes. The rulers of Kievan Rus'-Ukraine controlled the lands above the Tysa and the western most range of the Carpathian Mountains and ruled over the Crimean Peninsula in the south.

The Kievan Rus' state disintegrated in the 12th-13th centuries and some of its territory came under the rule of Muscovy and Byelorussia.

The successor to the Kievan Rus'-Ukraine state was the Galician-Volynian Principality, which was founded by Danylo Halytsky and existed from the 13th to the 15th century.

After a lengthy period of struggle for its independence from Lithuania and Poland, Ukraine re-appeared on the political map of Europe with the emergence of the military organization of the Zaporozhyan Kozak Sich, whose armies, led by Hetman Bohdan Khmelnytsky, waged the national-liberation wars of 1648-1654. However, this brief period of Ukrainian sovereignty was followed by centuries of colonial oppression under the Russian Empire and Poland. After the disintegration of the Polish state in 1772, its Ukrainian lands came under Austrian rule.

As a result of the February and October revolutions of 1917 the Russian monarchy fell and the Empire disintegrated. On January 22, 1918, the independence of the Ukrainian National Republic (UNR) was proclaimed. World War I also hastened the fall of the Austro-Hungarian Empire and the Western Ukrainian National Republic was proclaimed on November 1, 1918. The republic lasted for only eight months: the Polish national minority in Galicia rose up against the Western Ukrainian National Republic and this uprising soon developed into a war of the Polish state against Western Ukraine. Foreign military aid to Poland also had a decisive effect on the outcome of the Ukrainian-Polish conflict and subsequently a council of delegates from the Entente countries recognized Poland's right to occupy Ukrainian territories. The fate of Eastern Galicia was ultimately decided two decades later.

During 1917-1921 Eastern Ukraine (or Greater Ukraine) became the theater of war of six different armies. Neither the government of the Ukrainian Central Rada (M. Hrushevsky and S. Petlyura), the Hetmanate government of Skoropadsky, nor the Directorate were able to secure Ukrainian independence.

National consciousness, which in the past was germane only to a segment of the intelligentsia, began emerging in all strata of Ukrainian society. The events of 1917-1921 thus had a revolutionary significance for the social, economic, and national evolution of Ukraine. For this reason, the Russian Bolsheviks were forced to take into account Ukrainian national sentiment when they established Soviet rule in Ukraine.

Dozens of countries recognized the Ukrainian Soviet Socialist Republic, which was proclaimed in 1921. The new Soviet republic was a signatory of approximately 90 treaties and accords with 15 countries, participated in multilateral diplomatic conferences, and enjoyed consular rights.

The majority of the population wanted the new Ukrainian state to develop independently. But the deceptive promises of the Bolshevik leaders that they would forge a union of equal nations on the territory of the former Russian Empire only resulted in the drafting of the Treaty of the Formation of the USSR, which was signed by Ukraine, Byelorussia, the Trans-Caucasian Federation, and the Russian Federation. Under pressure from the central Communist apparatus, Ukraine was forced to surrender its right to conduct its own external foreign relations to the Union government.

During the early years of the Soviet Ukrainian Republic national consciousness, particularly in the realm of culture, was strengthened by means of an official policy of Ukrainianization. Despite this officially-sanctioned policy, however, Ukrainian national tendencies were widely restricted by the Communist Party, which feared the resurgence of Ukrainian separatism.

The 1930s were a tragic period in the history of Ukraine. The Soviet government of Stalin, Kaganovych, Molotov, and Postyshev pursued a consistent policy which was designed to create an agrarian crisis, i.e. an artificial famine, aimed at destroying the social foundations of Ukrainian national consciousness. The genocidal famine in Ukraine of 1932-1933, news of which was deliberately suppressed by various Western governments, resulted in the deaths of almost eight million Ukrainians living in rural areas. The destruction of such a large segment of the Ukrainian nation, whose biological potential was undermined for an entire century, was accompanied by a ban on the Ukrainian Orthodox Church and the physical liquidation of the Ukrainian intelligentsia.

As a constituent member of the USSR, the Ukrainian republic, in accordance with the Soviet Constitution, formally enjoyed certain rights and features of a sovereign state: territory, organs of state power and administration, budget, state emblem, flag, national anthem, and Constitution.

In 1944, in accordance with a decision of the Supreme Council of the USSR, the Union republics, including the Ukrainian SSR, were granted the right to conduct their own foreign relations. One year later the Ukrainian SSR became a founding member of the United Nations.

Despite its dependence on Union decisions and structures, the international status of Ukraine as a state in its own right increased over the years. During the period of 1944-1990 Ukraine was a signatory of 156 international treaties, was a member of 16 international organizations,

Mykhaylo Hrushevsky,
First President of Ukraine, 1918.

participated in the work of approximately 60 permanent and interim international organs.

On July 16, 1990 the Supreme Rada of Ukraine adopted an important historic document — the Act proclaiming Ukrainian state sovereignty, independence and indivisibility of power within the boundaries of Ukrainian territory, and independence and equality in conducting foreign relations.

On August 24, 1991 the Supreme Rada, in effecting this Declaration and proceeding from the right to self-determination, proclaimed the act of independence of Ukraine. Its territory was proclaimed indivisible and inviolable and the Constitution and laws of Ukraine have exclusive validity. On December 1, 1991 an all-Ukrainian referendum was held. Results of this national referendum indicated that more than 90% of the population favored independence. Leonid Kravchuk, the former head of the Supreme Rada of Ukraine was elected President of Ukraine.

Ukraine is an industrial and agricultural state, rich in coal, iron ore, manganese, nickel, and uranium deposits. Its major industries are: metallurgy (40 million tons of rolled metal), mining (105 million tones of iron ore, up to 165 million tons of coal), energy (500 billion kilowatt-hours), chemical, metal-working, machine-building, food and textile production. Ukraine produces an annual gross yield of 50 million tons of grain, 7 million tons of sugar, and four million tons of meat. Its total sowing area is 32 million hectares. The building and transportation systems are well-developed.

Certain aspects of the Ukrainian economy are weak: its ecology is in a precarious state, there is extensive loss of soil fertility, Ukrainian plants are outfitted with outmoded industrial equipment, there are many structural defects in the national economic complex, the service industries are underdeveloped, and there is an excessive emphasis on heavy industry and production.

These problems may be resolved quickly owing to a highly-trained work-force, well-developed communications and distribution systems, favorable climate, and opportunities to develop tourism, transit systems, and investments.

POPULATION

The population of Ukraine is 52.1 million: 80% of the population are Ukrainians, the remaining 20% are Russians, Byelorussians, Jews, Crimean Tatars, Moldavians, Poles, Hungarians, Rumanians, Greeks, Germans, Bulgarians, and representatives of other numerically-small nationalities. The urban population comprises 66% of the total population. Density: 90 people per sq. km.

Religion. The largest denomination is Christian: Orthodox (two church institutions) and Greek-Catholicism (the Byzantine-rite Ukrainian Catholic Church).

A CHRONOLOGY OF UKRAINE'S HISTORY

8th-9th cent.: —————————————————————————

Creation of the medieval Kievan Rus' state.

988: —————————————————————————————————

Christianity adopted by Grand Prince Volodymyr.

1130's: —————————————————————————————

Beginning of the feudal breakup of the Kievan state.

1187, 1189, 1217: ———————————————————————

First three documented references to the term "Ukraine" appear in the Hypatian Chronicle.

1237-1241: ————————————————————————————

Tatar invasion, the destruction of Kiev.

13th-14th cent.: ————————————————————————

Founding of the Galician-Volynian Principality, which controlled a significant part of the territory of the former Kievan Rus'-Ukraine state.

mid-14th cent.: —————————————————————————

The lands of Rus'-Ukraine are gradually occupied by Lithuania, Poland, and Turkey.

1492: ———————————————————————————————

First documented reference to the Ukrainian Kozaks.

Early 16th cent.: ———————————————————————

Founding of the Zaporozhyan Sich, the military-administrative and political organization of the Ukrainian Kozaks.

1569: ———————————————————————————————

Treaty of Lublin signed by Lithuania and Poland. The beginning of Polish expansion in Right-Bank Ukraine.

1596: ———————————————————————————————

Union of Berestya (between a segment of the Ukrainian Orthodox Church and the Roman Catholic Church).

1648-1654: ————————————————————————————

Ukrainian liberation war against Poland.

1654: ——————————————————————————

Treaty of Pereyaslav, a military and political alliance signed between Ukraine and Russia. (A written agreement was signed in March between Hetman Bohdan Khmelnytsky and the Russian Tsar concerning the status of Ukraine under the protection of the Russian state).

1764-1775: ————————————————————

The Zaporozhyan Sich is suppressed by the Russian Tsarist government.

1792: ——————————————————————————

Ukrainian settlement of the Kuban region begins.

1905-1906: ————————————————————

First revolution in Russia; a Ukrainian movement is galvanized, Ukrainians are permitted to form organizations, the ban on the Ukrainian language is abolished.

1917, March: ——————————————————

The fall of the Russian monarchy and the creation of the Central Rada in Ukraine.

1917, November: —————————————————

The Bolsheviks seize power in Petrograd; the Central Rada proclaims its power in nine provinces with a Ukrainian population and the course toward state autonomy is set.

1918, January 22: ————————————————

Declaration of independence of the Ukrainian National Republic (UNR).

1918, April 29: —————————————————

Mykhaylo Hrushevsky elected President of Ukraine.

1918, November 1: ————————————————

Founding of the Western Ukrainian National Republic (lasted until 1919); war between Western Ukraine and Poland.

1919, January 22: ————————————————

The union of the Western Ukrainian National Republic (ZUNR) with the Ukrainian National Republic (UNR).

1919, December: ——————————————————————————————

The Bolsheviks form the third Soviet Ukrainian government.

1920: ——————————————————————————————————

Symon Petlyura signs the Warsaw Treaty concerning the joint Ukrainian-Polish armed struggle against the Bolsheviks.

1921, November: —————————————————————————————

The Bolsheviks begin consolidating Soviet rule in Ukraine.

1922, December: —————————————————————————————

The formation of the USSR, including the Ukrainian SSR.

1929, January 29: ——————————————————————————

Organization of Ukrainian Nationalists (OUN) under the leadership of Evhen Konovalets was formed.

1929: ——————————————————————————————————

The Soviet authorities launch a campaign of repression directed against the Ukrainian intelligentsia; 45 Ukrainian intellectuals are charged with belonging to the non-existing secret organization "Union for the Liberation of Ukraine"; the persecution of the hierarchies of the independent Ukrainian Autocephalous Orthodox Church begins.

1932-1933: ———————————————————————————————

A genocidal famine, organized by Moscow, results in the deaths of 8 million Ukrainians living in rural areas.

1936-1937: ———————————————————————————————

Mass arrests in Ukraine; hundreds of Ukrainian intellectuals are liquidated.

1938: ——————————————————————————————————

Carpatho-Ukraine is made an autonomous land with its own government within the federated republic of Czechoslovakia; the creation of the military organization "Carpathian Sich."

1939, March 15: —————————————————————————————

The government of Avhustyn Voloshyn proclaims the independence of Carpatho-Ukraine; in accordance with a secret pact signed by Hungary and Germany, the Hungarian armies occupy Carpatho-Ukraine.

1939:
Western Ukrainian lands are annexed to the Ukrainian SSR.

1941-1944:
Germany occupies Ukraine.

1942:
The creation of the Ukrainian Insurgent Army (UPA).

1945:
Together with 50 other nations Ukraine becomes a founding member of the United Nations Organization.

1946:
The Ukrainian Greek-Catholic Church is banned; mass repressions are launched against its clergy and faithful.

Late 1950s-early 1960s:
The period of the so-called Khrushchev's "thaw" in the USSR begins; the emergence of the "sixtyers" movement.

1972:
Arrests of members of the Ukrainian dissident movement.

1989:
The creation of the Popular movement in Ukraine for reconstructuring (RUKH).

1990, July 16:
Declaration of the Supreme Rada of Ukraine proclaims the state sovereignty of Ukraine.

1991, August 24:
The Supreme Rada adopts the Act proclaiming the state independence of Ukraine.

1991, December 1:
A referendum on Ukrainian independence is held; Leonid Kravchuk elected President of Ukraine.

Planning a trip to Ukraine

Trips to Ukraine should be planned in advance, in order to arrange for all pertinent documentation. Travellers are requested to be at the airport at least two hours before flight time in order to arrange all formalities. Failure to do so may delay departure or result in the loss of one's reservation.

In addition to clothing and other articles, visitors to Ukraine should bring non-prescription medication (e.g. Tylenol, aspirin, Advil), toilet paper, feminine napkins, toothpaste, and shampoo.

BAGGAGE

Almost all Ukrainian airlines have a weight allowance of 50 lbs. (23 kg / 2 suitcases), in addition to one piece of carry-on luggage up to 11 lbs. (5 kg) Excess luggage costs $108.00, payable in cash.

Label every piece of luggage or package with your name, address, and phone number.

INSURANCE

Almost every airline provides Travel Insurance in case of death or injury resulting from an air accident, illness during travel, loss of baggage, flight cancellation, etc. For additional information, contact your travel agency.

SOCIAL SERVICES

Your travel agency can arrange the following services in Ukraine: transportation from the airport to the city, train tickets, overnight lodging in the city, transportation to other points in Ukraine or the newly-independent states of the former USSR, food.

DOCUMENTS AND VISAS

Travellers must have a valid passport and Ukrainian visa. Visas may be obtained in Ukrainian embassies and consulates in: Washington, D.C., Chicago, Ottawa, Bonn, Paris, Vienna, Budapest, Athens, Warsaw, Bucharest, Tel-Aviv, London, Teheran, and Prague.

Visas can also be obtained at the international airports of Boryspil (Kyiv), Odesa, Simferopol, Lviv; the seaports of Yalta, Odesa, Illichivsk, Izmayil; at border crossings in Poland, Slovakia, Hungary, and Rumania; entry points in Mostyska, Shegini, Uzhhorod, Chop, Porubne, Vadul-Siret.

Individual visas cost $50.00 (US). Group visas: $25.00 per person. Transit visas: $15.00.

Businessmen and journalists can obtain multiple-entry visas valid for one year at the Ministry of Foreign Affairs of Ukraine.

CURRENCY

Stores, hotels, and travel agencies in Ukraine do not accept travellers' checks or credit cards. Travellers should bring foreign currency (e.g. US dollars) which must be declared upon arrival. Foreign currencies can be exchanged for coupons-karbovantsi in hotels or local Ukrainian banks. Changing currency on the "black market" or by strangers is not advised.

ELECTRICITY

The standard electrical current in Ukraine is 220 volts. You will need an adapter or transformer in order to use North American appliances.

WHAT TO BRING; CUSTOMS REGULATIONS

Travellers to Ukraine may bring all articles, except military weapons and narcotics.

No duty is imposed on articles of artistic, historical, scientific or other value; articles accompanied by permits, pearls; as well as article made of pearls whose weight does not exceed 200 g. per person; food items.

No duty is imposed on goods valued up to $5000.00 US (excluding wine, alcohol, and tobacco products).

Residents of foreign countries can import their own means of transportation for personal use, duty-free, on condition that such articles will be shipped out within one year.

There is no duty and no limit imposed on the quantity and value of gifts.

There is no duty imposed on the importation of foreign currencies. Currency exceeding $200.00 US must be declared at customs.

The following goods are subject to customs declaration and duty: articles and items not intended for personal use by the individual importing them, i.e. items with a commercial designation (e.g. goods, property, equipment, etc.).

There are no restrictions on the amount of articles brought out of Ukraine which have been acquired in specialized establishments and other organizations authorized to conduct trade in foreign currencies (proof of purchase necessary).

Travellers may export souvenirs and gifts (excluding those articles listed below) whose value does not exceed the established minimum wage of Ukraine, per person.

Works of art and cultural-historical treasures may be exported by special permission from the Ministry of Culture of Ukraine.

No duty is imposed on 40-proof alcohol up to 1.5 l.; wine — up to 2 l.; tobacco products — up to 100 cigarettes or 100 g.

Exporting foreign currencies is permitted in the following cases: currency imported from abroad which was registered at customs or currency obtained in the National Bank of Ukraine and other specialized banks authorized to permit its importation abroad; foreign currencies up to $200.00 (US) or its equivalent in other foreign currencies.

Duty is imposed on all articles for export which are designated for exchange, sale, the property of a cooperative, rental, or any personal or other uses resulting in profits.

It is not permitted to export military-type weapons or narcotics, jewelry made of precious metals and gems, gifts included, as well as the following consumer products: household appliances, electronic equipment, tools, building materials, clothing, household items, furs, meat products, or canned dairy products.

Foreign citizens returning abroad after a temporary stay in Ukraine on business, including vacations, are permitted to export no more than one consumer item from each category of the above list during one calendar year.

Restrictions on exporting consumer goods do not apply to articles purchased on the territory of Ukraine with foreign currency.

State Customs Committee of Ukraine: 252005 Kyiv, provulok Politekhnichny, 4-a; tel. 446-51-86; 446-92-41; teletype: 63-17-10; Head: Oleksiy Koval.

Kiev Customs Office: 252034 Kyiv, Reytarska St., 19; tel. 229-51-71; 229-78-92; Director: Oleh Hrabovsky.

Customs Office, Boryspil Airport: tel. 296-70-46; 296-72-16; Director: Stanislav Didenko.

THE WORK DAY IN UKRAINE

The work day lasts eight hours. Most businesses open at 8:00. Ministries, departments, institutions, and organizations begin operating at 9:00. Newspapers, magazines, publishing houses, museums, libraries, educational, cultural, religious, and sports establishments can set their own schedule, depending on their specific needs.

With a few exceptions, restaurants which begin operations at 8:00 begin serving non-stop from 12:00 to 23:00; some close for 1-2 hours between 16:00 and 19:00.

Performances and concerts generally begin at 19:00.

Public transit operates from 6:00-0:00, the metro from 6:00 to 1:00 a.m.

HOLIDAYS IN UKRAINE

January 1 — New Year's Day
January 7 — Christmas Day
March 8 — International Women's Day
May 1 & 2 — International Workers' Solidarity Day
May 9 — Victory Day
August 24 — Independence Day

Easter — one day (Sunday)
Holy Trinity — one day (Sunday)

UKRAINIAN CUISINE

The national cuisine reflects the richness and variety of its traditions which are linked to the customs, culture, spirituality, and folkways of Ukraine. Many dishes are noted for their complexity and variety of cooking methods.

Borshch, an aromatic and appetizing beet-based soup, is the most popular and widely-known Ukrainian dish, containing many ingredients. Besides, meat, standard Ukrainian borshch contains 20 other ingredients. Different versions of borshch are prepared in other regions of Ukraine. The Poltava version, served with halushky (dumplings) contains 18 ingredients, Chernihiv borshch has 16, crucian-carp borshch contains 17 different ingredients. Borshch may be prepared with beef, chicken, meat or mushroom-filled dumplings, baked beets, beans, and mushrooms.

Also popular are the many versions of sauerkraut soup: standard, with buckwheat groats, mushrooms, beans; potato soup, barley soup, and green pea soup.

Many dishes served in Ukraine are prepared in appetizing combinations of meat stuffed in vegetables, e.g. cabbage rolls (holubtsi), stuffed peppers or tomatoes. Skewered roasted meats are also very popular.

Flour-based dishes include the popular varenyky, a type of boiled dumpling stuffed with cheese, potato, cabbage, meat, chopped liver, potato and mushrooms, cabbage and mushrooms, cherries, or plums.

Ukrainian cuisine includes many dairy and cheese dishes: soups, sweet breads, puddings, cheesecakes, pancakes, and fruit soups.

There are many varieties of sweet dough preparations, e.g. doughnuts, crisp fried pastry, etc.

TAXIS

Taxis can be reserved at hotels by notifying the manager, the service bureau, tourist bureau, or the porter. There may be a charge for this service. In certain cases the hotel manager may require a small refundable deposit in Ukrainian currency.

Taxis should be reserved in advance for travel to the airport or the train station. To order a taxi from a private residence, dial 058. Information on rates call 225-03-96.

Rates are usually set by the driver, but a rate can be fixed in advance. Taxi drivers will accept foreign currency from tourists.

Private transportation companies are also available. Rates are exclusively or partially in US dollars or other foreign currencies.

TOURS AND EXCURSIONS SUGGESTED FOR VISITORS TO UKRAINE

Ukraine: The Country and Its People. This tour helps visitors become acquainted with the life of the Ukrainian people. It includes visits to factories, plants, farms, schools, children's daycare centers, and private families, discussions with company directors, economists, political scientists, and encounters with professional colleagues. Witness the building of the democratic process in Ukrainian with your own eyes.

Tours to historical-architectural monuments of Ukrainian culture from the 11th-19th centuries, important sites in Kyiv, Chernihiv, Lviv, Uzhhorod, and other cities are featured.

Rayduha (Rainbow): This tour acquaints tourists with the decorative arts and folklore of Ukraine. Visitors have many opportunities to buy original souvenirs (e.g. embroidered towels or a Ukrainian Easter egg). A unique museum of Ukrainian ornaments is located in the village of Vashkivtsi, 40 km from Chernivtsi. Visit Poltava, celebrated by numerous writers, meet with folk craftspeople, and enjoy a variety of folkloric concerts. Borshch, varenyky, and other wonderful Ukrainian dishes may be sampled in many restaurants.

Take the time to visit at least one art festival:

"Kyiv Spring" (May) and "Golden Autumn" held in Kyiv;
"National Virtuosos" in Lviv (May);
"White Acacia" in Odesa;
"Crimean Stars" in Yalta (August).

Colorful open-air folkloric festivals in Kyiv, Lviv, Uzhhorod, and Chernivtsi are an enchanting way to spend your holiday in Ukraine.

"Kyiv Day" is held on the last Sunday of May. This traditional, picturesque festival celebrating this ancient city attracts thousands of visitors every year. Some of the featured attractions are a carnival, sports shows, theater exhibitions, and markets. Similar festivals are held in other cities of Ukraine.

The Sure Hand: Tourists can try their hand at hunting deer, mountain goats, wild boars, and water fowl in the steppes of southern Ukraine and the Carpathian Mountains. Guides and transportation are supplied, as well as lodging in hunters' cabins.

Dnipro Cruise: Visitors can experience a thrilling 1000-kilometer journey on the Dnipro, the third longest river in Europe, on comfortable, river and seagoing liners. Capacity: 330 persons. Kyiv-Odesa, Odesa-Kyiv. The best months to take this trip are June and September.

Air-conditioned cabins for one to three persons with a refrigerator and other conveniences are available. Ukrainian and European cuisine is offered.

The itinerary includes trips to seven Ukrainian cities, and a visit to the Kyievan

Cave Monastery, the Odesa Opera Theater, which rivals Vienna's Opera House, a visit to Dniprohes, the first hydroelectric station on the Dnipro River, tours of agricultural complexes, folkloric concerts, and visits with Ukrainian families.

This unforgettable journey is also a marvelous opportunity to learn some Ukrainian. Excellent meals of shashlyk and fine Ukrainian wines, a stop-over on a deserted island, and the exciting Neptune Festival are just some of the attractions of this cruise.

Visitors can also tour Ukraine by car, using itineraries set by Inturyst-Ukraine. Visit Uzhhorod, Lviv, Chernivtsi, Kyiv, and Odesa and stay in first-class hotels.

Excursions are arranged to include at least one folkloric concert held in various cultural centers, such as Kyiv, Odesa, Yalta, Lviv, Uzhhorod, Chernivtsi, Kharkiv, and Zaporizhzhya. Ukrainian folk songs and dances are an integral part of these captivating excursions.

Train travel between cities is usually at night and journeys do not exceed 12 hours. Flying time is two hours. Tourists are transported to their hotels in comfortable buses and travel vouchers include the costs of food, lodging, and most excursions.

The service counter of all hotels will help with any problems that may arise during your visit to Ukraine. You can also arrange additional excursions to museums, order your theater or concert tickets, and rent a car by inquiring at the service counter.

Foreign currency can be exchanged at any hotel; some hotels accept credit cards. Foreign currency is accepted at many bars and shops.

For further information, write or call:

Inturyst-Ukraine
Vulytsya Hostpitalna (Hospital St.), 12, Kyiv
Tel.: 225-30-51; 224-42-42

TELEPHONES IN UKRAINE: HOW TO USE THEM IN HOTELS, PRIVATE ROOMS, IN THE CITY. INTERNATIONAL CALLS.

Telephone calls in Kiev hotels can be ordered through the floor attendants, doormen, service bureau, or the hotel manager. Tourists may arrange their own calls in hotels or private residences by dialling 079 (international operator) or 071 (Ukraine and the newly-independent state of the former USSR).

For further information about your long-distance telephone call reservations dial 073 (international) or 072.

To make a telephone call (country and city telephone codes provided in the reference section) dial 8, wait for the dial tone, dial 10 (international service index), then the country code, city code, the telephone number. Pauses after the dialed numbers should not exceed five seconds. If there is no connection after 40 seconds, replace the receiver and dial again.

To call within Ukraine or the newly-independent state dial 8. After the dial tone dial the required code and the telephone number.

There is a reduction of 25% on inter-urban telephone calls made during the weekend, holidays, and business hours between 18:00 and 24:00 and 0:00 to 7:00.

Inter-urban telephone calls in Kyiv are free of charge.

For information about automatic telephone connections and codes, dial 070.

For 24-hour information on Kyiv city numbers, dial 09.

By dialing 009 you can obtain partial information (e.g. the surname of the person you wish to call), Kyiv telephone numbers and information on telephone numbers in all cities of Ukraine or in the newly-independent states. There is a charge for this 24-hour service, payable in Ukrainian currency.

TELEPHONE SERVICES

Long distance and international automatic telephone service
Directories by phone 070

On destinations where Automatic Direct Dialing
is not available, book the call by phone (in Kyiv):

071 — National Calls;
072 — National Directory Service;
079 — International Operator;
073 — International Directory Service.

International calls: Dial 8, wait for a dial tone, dial 10 (international service index), then enter the country code, city code and telephone number.

International integrated long distance (IILD):

Service Division	220-14-10
IILD Complaint Bureau	225-00-01
Billing Center Subscriber Division	513-25-01
Communication Circuits Leasing Division	220-13-08
Conference Call Service	212-45-43
Previously Reserved Long Distance Call Service	225-20-74
Electronic Mail	224-89-06
Bureaufax-CPP	225-51-92
International Automatic Telephone Service	225-31-55

SPECIAL SERVICES

Police: tel. 02
Emergency: tel. 03

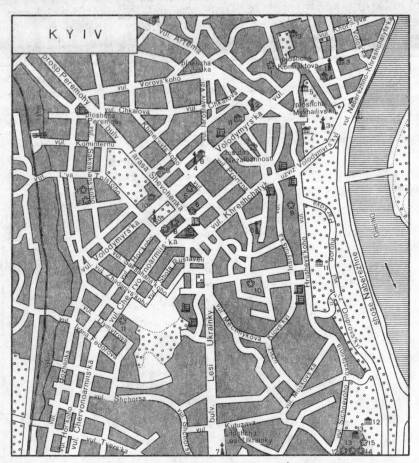

KYIV

📖 Hotels

🏛 Monuments:
1 Hryhoriy Skovoroda
2 Bohdan Khmelnytskyi
3 Prince Volodymyr
4 Mykola Lysenko
5 Taras Shevchenko
6 Ivan Franko
7 Lesia Ukraïnka

🏛 Architectural monuments:
1 Intercession Monastery, turn of the 20th c.
2 St. Florus' Monastery, 18th—19th cc. 3 Kyïv-Mohyla Academy, 1703—1740. 4 Trade Rows, 1809, reconstr. 1990. 5 St. Andrew's Church, 1747—1753. 6 St. Sophia Museum, 10th—19th cc. 7 Refectory of St. Michael's Monastery of the Golden Domes, 1712. 8 Golden Gates, 11th c., reconstr. 1982. 9 St. Vladimir's Cathedral, 1862—1886. 10 Shevchenko University, 1837. 11 Mariïns'kyi Palace, 1750—1870. 12 Church of the Savior at Berestove, 1113—1125. 13 Kiev-Pechersk Lavra, 11th—19th cc.

🏛 Museums:
1 History. 2 T. Shevchenko Literary-Memorial. 3 L. Ukraïnka Literary-Memorial. 4 M. Lysenko Memorial. 5 Natural History museums of Ukrainian Academy of Sciences. 6 Taras Shevchenko. 7 Russian Art. 8 Western and Oriental Art. 9 Ukrainian Fine Arts. 10 History of Kiev. 11 Planetarium. 12 Theater, Music and Cinema Art. 13 Historic Treasures of Ukraine. 14 Books and Bookprinting. 15 Ukrainian Folk Decorative Art.

Kyiv — Capital of Ukraine

The capital of Ukraine and its most important cultural, scientific, and industrial center.

Kyiv was the capital city of the mighty state of Kyivan Rus'-Ukraine and the seat of the Ukrainian Orthodox Metropolitanate.

It is situated on the banks of the Dnipro River, below the mouth of the Desna River. Population: 2,654,000.

Telephone code: 044.

History

The oldest human traces on the territory of Kyiv date from the Stone Age (40-10 B.C.). In the 1890s the Ukrainian archaeologist, V. Khvoyko, uncovered remains of these settlements and those known as the Kyrylivsky dwellings. According to archaeological data, the emergence of the ancient Slavic settlements should be traced to no later than 2-1 cent. B.C. The officially accepted date of the "birth" of Kyiv is 482. Kyy, the prince of the Slavic tribe of Polyans, is considered the city founder. According to a widely-known legend, Kyiv was founded by three brothers, Kyy,

St. Sophia Cathedral,
1017-37.

Building of Hetman I. Mazepa.

Shchek, Khorev, and their sister, Lybid, whose names today are part of the toponomy of Kyiv.

In the 9th century Kyiv became an important political, religious, crafts and trading center of Kyivan Rus'-Ukraine. In 988 Prince Volodymyr introduced Christianity as the official state religion. The most important architectural construction of this period is the Desyatynna Church (Church of the Tithes, 989-996).

In 1019 Prince Yaroslav, called the Wise, ascended to the throne and vigorously began promoting the cultural and educational development of the city. Construction of St. Sophia's Cathedral began in 1037; in 1051 the Kyivan Cave Monastery, which became the most important religious and cultural center in Kyivan Rus, was built. Rus'ka Pravda (Rus' Law), the first code of laws, was compiled in Kyiv.

After the death of Yaroslav the Wise internecine battles for the throne of Kyiv ensued. The state, partitioned into separate principalities, fell prey to the attacks of the Tatar-Mongols. In 1240 Kyiv was almost completely destroyed.

In 1362 the city came under the control of the Lithuanian state. During the 14th-15th centuries Kyiv was rebuilt and in 1484 it adopted the Magdeburg law.

After the Treaty of Lublin (1569) and the Treaty of Berestya (1596) the position of the Catholic and Greek-Catholic churches was consolidated and a period of Polish expansion began. The residents of Kyiv actively participated in the national-liberation war waged by Hetman B. Khmelnytsky against Poland. In January 1654, after the signing of the Treaty of Pereyaslav, Kyiv came under Moscow control. Ukraine and, simultaneously Kyiv, gradually lost its rights and privileges and the population was de-nationalized.

The Kyiv guberniya (province) was created in 1708. After the great fire of 1811 the straight-road system was changed to a regular one and urban reconstruction was begun in earnest.

The consolidation of pro-Russian positions continued. In 1834 Kyiv's right of Magdeburg law was officially rescinded and in 1840 the Lithuanian statute was abolished. The Ukrainian language and culture were subject to stringent restrictions by various Tsarist ukazes (decrees).

In 1846-47 a secret political organization, the Cyril and Methodius Brotherhood was active. Its members were representatives of the Ukrainian intelligentsia. Among them were M. Kostomarov, P. Kulish, T. Shevchenko, V. Bilozersky, M. Hulak, and O. Markovych. An important role in the civic-political movement of Kyiv in 1863-79 was played by the Hromada (M. Drahomanov, M. Lysenko, V. Antonovych, M. Starytsky et al.).

At the beginning of the 20th century publishing activities intensified and several

Ukrainian political parties were established. Encouraged by the collapse of the Tsarist Empire, on 4 March 1917 the Central Rada, headed by M. Hrushevsky, S. Yefremov, V. Vynnychenko, and S. Petlyura, was created. On 5-7 April 1917 the All-Ukrainian National Congress took place, during which the goal of Ukrainian autonomy was proclaimed and power officially transferred to the Central Rada. On 22 January 1918 the independence of the Ukrainian National Republic was proclaimed. During this period a highly unstable situation emerged in Ukraine, caused by the Civil War and the actions of several hostile armies, particularly the Bolshevik Army and the White Guards.

After the dissolution of the Central Rada, Hetman P. Skoropadsky, with German support, became the head of the Ukrainian state on 28 April 1918. In December of that year power was seized by the Directory, headed by V. Vynnychenko and S. Petlyura.

In the summer of 1920 Kyiv was occupied by Bolshevik Russia. During the period of Soviet power, which was forcibly introduced in Ukraine, many important architectural and historical monuments were destroyed in the 1930s: the Bratsky (Brotherhood) Monastery and the Mykhaylivsky (St. Michael's) Golden-Domed Monastery, St. Nicholas' Military Cathedral, the Stritennya (Presentation of Christ at the Temple) Church, the Nativity of Christ and the St. Nicholas Prytysko Churches, SS. Peter and Paul in Podil, the Zalizna (Iron) Church and St. Constantine's, the bell tower of Kyrylivska Church (St. Cyril's), the Pustynno-Mykhaylivsky Monastery in Pechersk, and many others.

World War II caused much destruction in Kyiv. The Nazi Germans conducted numerous mass executions of the civilian population. Among those executed in Babyn Yar (Jews, Ukrainians, Russians) were several Ukrainian nationalists, including the poetess, O. Teliha. Thousands of people were transported to Germany to perform forced labor.

Shortly after the Soviet Army's retreat, Soviet agents detonated a bomb under the Uspensky (Dormition) Cathedral of the Kyivan Cave Monastery, one of the oldest monuments of Ukrainian culture, and destroyed part of the Khreshchatyk, the central street of Kyiv.

Kyiv was one of the centers of the Ukrainian national and religious renaissance and resistance movement during the period of Soviet totalitarianism. During the 1920s-30s the Ukrainian Autocephalous Orthodox Church, headed by Metropolitan V. Lypkivsky, was restored here. A number of literary organizations were created and the Berezil Theater was founded. The Soviet authorities executed many Ukrainian writers and important cultural activists in Kyiv. In the 1960s and

"Kyivan Mohyla Academy"
University.

St. Andrew's Church, 1747-53.

1970s Kyiv was the base for many members of the Ukrainian intelligentsia who protested against Russification and other aspects of Soviet dictatorship.

The Ukrainian Helsinki Monitoring Group was founded in Kyiv in 1976. In the late 1980s the national-democratic rebirth of Ukraine intensified in Kyiv and several civic-political and cultural organizations, including the Rukh Movement of Ukraine, were established. The Act of Independence of Ukraine was proclaimed in Kyiv on 24 August 1992.

PROMINENT INDIVIDUALS

BORN IN KYIV:

A. Archipenko (1887-1964), sculptor, artist. • **D. Bahaliy** (1857-1932), historian, academician. • **M. Bulgakov** (1891-1940), Russian writer. • **F. Ernst** (1891-1949), German art expert; executed. • **I. Hryhorovych-Barsky** (1713-85), architect. • **O. Murashko** (1875-1919), painter. • **A. Petrytsky** (1895-1964), painter. • **S. Pylypenko** (1891-1934), writer, executed. • **M. Rylsky** (1895-1964), writer, art expert, academician. • **Yu. Shcherbak** (1934), writer, political activist, legislator. • **L. Starytska-Chernyakhivska** (1868-1941), writer, died in prison.

BURIED IN KYIV:

See, Baykove, Lukyanivka, Zvirynets cemeteries; see, also entries on the Vydubychi Monastery, the Kyivan Bratsky (Brotherhood) Monastery, Kyivan Cave Monastery.

Churches of the Kyivan Cave Monastery.

CHURCHES, HISTORICAL AND ARCHITECTURAL MONUMENTS

ANDRIYIVSKA (ST. ANDREW'S) CHURCH, 1747-53. Architect: I. Michurin, designed by V. Rastrelli. Built in the Baroque style. Constructed on the site of the 13th century Khrestovozdvy-

zhenska (Elevation of the Holy Cross)
Church. The iconostasis is embellished
with carved, gilded ornamentation,
sculptures, and paintings. The church
was restored several times. (Andriyivsky Uzviz, 23. Metro: Poshtova
Ploshcha Station; funicular).
**BRATSKY (BROTHERHOOD)
MONASTERY,** 1616. The complex
includes the academic building (1704-
40), refectory-type church and Holy
Spirit Church (Svyatoho Dukha) (17th-
19th cent.), a sundial (late 18th cent.).
All the 18th century architectural structures were built in the Ukrainian Baroque style. At one time the Brotherhood school, Kyivan Mohyla Academy, and Kyivan Theological Academy
were located here. Today the work of
the Mohyla Academy has resumed.
Hetman P. Sahaydachny (d. 1622) and

Vydubychi Monastery, 11th cent.

the writer and traveller, V. Hryhorovych-Barsky (1701-47) are buried on monastery
land. Among the graduates and lecturers of the monastery were H. Skovoroda and
the architect I. Hryhorovych-Barsky. The architectural style of the structure tends
toward Classicism. (Skovoroda St., 2. Metro: Kontraktova Ploshcha).

VOLODYMYRSKY (ST. VOLODYMYR'S) CATHEDRAL, 1862-96. De-
signed by I. Shtrom and P. Sparro, additional designs by O. Beretti. Built in the
pseudo-Byzantine style. Of considerable artistic merit are the interior wall paintings,
executed in 1885-96 by V. Vasnetsov, M. Nesterov, M. Vrubel, V. Zamyraylo, S.
Kostenko, M. Pymonenko, and others under the direction of A. Prakhov. (Shevchenko Blvd., 20. Trolleybus 5, 8, 9, 17).

VOSKRESENSKA (RESURRECTION) CHURCH, 1701-05. Built in the
Ukrainian Baroque style, the church is part of an 18th century ensemble of buildings
adjoining the Kyivan Cave Monastery. (Sichneve Povstannya St., 27. Trolleybus 20).

VYDUBYCHI MONASTERY, 11th cent. Founded by Grand Prince Vsevolod
Yaroslavovych as his ancestral monastery. Many distinguished individuals are buried
here: Ya. Handzyuk (1873-1918), General-Major of St. George's Cavalry and Commander of the First Ukrainian Corps (1918), executed by Muravyov in Kyiv; B.
Khanenko (1848-1917) collector, patron of the arts, and co-founder with his wife,
Barbara, of the Kyiv Art Museum; K. Ushynsky (1823-71), pedagogue, founder of a
school in Russia, advocate of teaching in the Ukrainian language. (Vydubytska St.,
40. Trolleybus 14, 15).

*Golden Gate, 1037
(restored 1982).*

THE MONASTERY COMPLEX INCLUDES:

MYKHAYLIVSKY (ST. MICHAEL'S) CATHEDRAL, 1070-88. Destroyed several times. After its reconstruction in 1767-69 the cathedral acquired a Baroque appearance. Eleventh century frescoes and paintings from the 18th-19th centuries have been preserved.

HEORHIYIVSKY (ST. GEORGE'S) CATHEDRAL, 1696-1701. The slender proportions of the building and the masterfully executed molding of the facade gives the church a picturesque and artistic distinctness.

REFECTORY, 1696-1701. Distinguished by its refined molding, in sections similar in character to wood folk carving.

BELL TOWER, 1727-33. Erected by Hetman D. Apostol; built in the Ukrainian Baroque style.

DMYTRIVSKA (SS. CONSTANTINE AND HELEN'S) CHURCH, 1734. The original building has not been preserved. In the 1750s the architect I. Hryhorovych-Barsky built a refectory for it in the Baroque style, decorated with pilasters and lavish sculptural molding. The present brick church was built in 1865. The forms of this monument reflect the tradition of 18th century Ukrainian architecture. (Frunze St., 8/6. Trolleybus 18).

DORMITORY (Castle of Richard the Lionhearted), 1902. Built in the modernized English Gothic style. The monumental facades are decorated with architectural elements typical of fortresses and castles. (Andriyivsky Uzviz, 15. Trolleybus 16, 18).

DORMITORY (Horodetsky), 1902-03. Architect: V. Horodetsky. Built in the shape of a cube and characterized by the eclectic utilization of various styles typical of the Art Nouveau period. The facades are embellished with sculptural cement decorations based on mythological and hunting themes (Italian sculptor E. Salia). The interior paintings depict the sea floor. (Bankivska St., 10. Metro: Khreshchatyk).

DORMITORY, 1911. Designed by the architect P. Alyoshyn. The facades are noted for the creative interpretation of Romanesque architectural forms and un-

*Horodetsky Building,
1902-03.*

usual detail. Renaissance motifs predominate in the interior decorations. (Orlyk St., 1/15. Metro: Khreshchatyk).

DORMITORY, late 19th cent. Built in the palatial style. The facade is bevelled and the interior is decorated in marble, carvings, and incrustation. Of considerable value are the Dutch tiled stoves. In 1888-96 the building was rented by the Kyivan Governor-General. Today it houses the Union of Writers of Ukraine. (Bankivska St., 2. Metro: Khreshchatyk).

GOLDEN GATE, 1017-24. The main triumphal entrance of ancient Kyiv. Its construction is mentioned in the chronicle for the year 1037. Was part of the urban defense system created by Yaroslav the

Kyivan Cave Monastery.
Refectory, 1696-1701.

Wise. Destroyed in 1240 during the Tatar-Mongol raids. In 1648 the residents of Kyiv greeted B. Khmelnytsky's Kozak regiments near the Golden Gate. In 1750 the gate's remains were covered with earth. The ruins were excavated and reinforced in 1837. In 1982 a pavilion was erected above the Golden Gate which recreates the original appearance of this monument. (Volodymyrska St., 35. Metro: Zoloti Vorota).

ILLINSKA (ST. ELIAS') CHURCH, 1692. A tripartite, one-storied structure with a high cupola. At the beginning of the 18th century a small bell tower with a tent-shaped top and a Baroque gate were built next to it. In the first half of the 19th century a portico and chapel were added on. Fragments of 18th century paintings have been uncovered. (Pochaynynska St., 2. Bus 62).

INSTITUTE FOR YOUNG NOBLEWOMEN, 1838-42. Designed by the architect V. Beretti in the late Classical style. Until 1917 it housed an educational institution. During the Soviet period various institutions were located here, particularly the NKVD, where many Ukrainian cultural activists and scholars were murdered. Today it houses the International Center of Culture and Art. (Bankivska St., 1. Metro: Maydan Nezalezhnosti).

KYYEVO-PECHERSKA LAVRA (KYIVAN CAVE MONASTERY). A Ukrainian Orthodox monastery founded in 1051 by the monks Antoniy and Feodosiy. In the 11th century it became the center for the expansion and consolidation of Christianity in Kyivan Rus'-Ukraine. The chroniclers Nykon, Nestor, Sylvester, the artists Alimpiy, Hryhoriy, and the healer, Ahapit, at one time worked in the monastery. In 1240 it was looted and destroyed by the Tatar-Mongol armies of Khan Baty. The monastery was again destroyed in 1480. In 1615 an imprimery was located at the monastery. In the late 16th century it was designated a Lavra (monastery). The architectural ensemble attained completion in the mid-18th century. The majority of the structures is built in the Ukrainian Baroque style. The ensemble is organically linked to the relief and forms a beautiful and majestic silhouette of Kyiv from the Dnipro River side. In 1926 the Kyivan Cave Historical-Cultural Preserve was established on the premises of the monastery.

V. Kochubey, I. Iskra, P. Stolypin (1862-1911), the notorious head of the Council of Ministers of the Tsarist Russia, the archaeologist D. Shcherbakivsky (1877-1927), and various distinguished church figures are buried here. (Sichnevoho Povstannya St., 21, 25. Trolleybus 20).

BUILDINGS OF THE CAVE MONASTERY COMPLEX

USPENSKY (DORMITION) CATHEDRAL (ruins), 1073-78. The first stone structure of the monastery; the main monastic church. During its lengthy history the cathedral was damaged, rebuilt, and enlarged several times. In November 1941 the church was destroyed by mines laid by Soviet forces retreating from the German advance.

GREAT BELL TOWER, 1731-44. The highest monumental structure in Ukraine (96 m) and the compositional center of the monastery. Built in Classical forms by the architect J. Schaedel. Consists of four stories. A library was located on the first two stories; 13 bells were once located on the third story, of which only three remain. A clock was located on the fourth story.

TROYITSKA NADBRAMNA (HOLY TRINITY) CHURCH, 1106-08. Located above the main gate of the monastery. After the destruction of the Dormition Cathedral in 1240 it became the main monastery church. A unique monument of 18th century Ukrainian architecture. Contains brilliant wall paintings, rich in local scenery, historical-ethnographic material, and folk traditions. The church floor is covered with molded cast-iron tiles.

MYKOLAYIVSKA (ST. NICHOLAS') CHURCH, late 17th cent. Built in the Ukrainian Baroque style. In the second half of the 19th century a second floor was added. The church was part of St. Michael's Hospital Monastery, founded in the 12th century by Svyatoslav Davydovych, called Svyatosha, the former prince of Chernihiv, (monk's name: Mykola) to house ailing monks. Later it was a hospice for aged Kozaks.

VSIKHSVYATSKA (ALL-SAINTS') CHURCH, 1696-98. Located above the Economic Gate in the Ukrainian Baroque style. At the beginning of the 20th century the interior was decorated with pictorial and ornamental oil paintings. Fragments of 17th century paintings have been uncovered. Contains a carved and gilded wood iconostasis from the 18th century. One of the finest monuments of Ukrainian Baroque architecture.

RIZDVA BOHORODYTSI (NATIVITY OF THE HOLY MOTHER OF GOD) CHURCH, 1696. Built on the site of an earlier church of the same name. In 1784 a wood iconostasis was built in the Rococo style. The engraved silver Royal Doors were designed by the artist H. Chyzhevsky. The artist I. Kvyatkovsky painted the interior in 1817.

KHRESTOVOZDVYZHENSKA (ELEVATION OF THE HOLY CROSS) CHURCH, 1700. Erected on the site of a wood church. In 1769 a carved and gilded iconostasis was installed (artist: K. Shverin). A refectory was added in 1839. The interior was painted in the 18th century and in 1816. Paintings by the artist D. Davydov were completed in 1894. The main southern entrance was lavishly decorated with molded garlands in the spirit of 17th century decorative folk art.

BELL TOWER OF THE FAR CAVES, 1754-61. Erected by the master builder S. Kovnir. A brick structure in the Ukrainian Baroque style. Forty-one m high. Lavishly decorated with molded foliate ornaments.

ANNOZACHATIYIVSKA (CONCEPTION OF ST. ANNE) CHURCH, 1679. Located above the upper entrance to the Far Caves. In 1796 the roof was covered with iron and the cupola was gilded. The church was rebuilt in 1810-1819 and the pear-shaped cupola was replaced by a new, tent-shaped cupola. In the 19th century the interior was decorated with pictorial and ornamental paintings. The oak iconostasis is carved.

REFECTORY PALACE WITH SS. ANTONIY AND FEODOSIY (SS. AN-THONY'S AND THEODOSIUS') CHURCH, 1893-95. Designed by Academician V. Nikolayev in the old Byzantine style. A two-storied structure adjoined by a church with a large, spherical cupola and five gilded cupolas. At the beginning of the 20th century the refectory and church interiors were painted by the artists I. Yizhakevych and H. Popov, following I. Shchusev's designs.

NEAR CAVES, 1051. So-called because of their proximity to the Dormition Cathedral. First mentioned in the Tale of Bygone Years for the year 1051. Also called Anthony's Caves in honor of the monastery's founder. The caves measure 228 m in length, with a depth of 5-20 m. In the 1760s the floor was covered with cast-iron tiles. The caves were first used to house monks and later as burial places. The unique geological structure of the soil and constant temperature resulted in the natural mummification of some of the interred remains. There are 75 burial niches in the caves, including the remains of Antoniy, the artists Alimpiy and Hryhoriy, and the healers Ahapit and Damian, Nestor the Chronicler, the religious and political leader Nykon, Bishop Simeon, and others. In the Near Caves three crypt churches have been preserved: Vvedenska (Presentation at the Temple) Church, Antoniyivska (St. Anthony's) Church (11th cent.), and Varlaamska (St. Varlaam's) Church (1641). All of them have gilded bronze iconostasis which were executed by the Kyiv master builders F. Korobka and Z. and Yu. Bryzhunov (1813-19).

FAR CAVES, 1051. First mentioned in the Tale of Bygone Years for the year 1051. Also known as the caves of Theodosius, in honor of the saint. They measure 280 m in length and are 5-20 m deep. In 1826 the floor was covered with cast-iron tiles. They contain 45 burial niches and three churches: Rizdva (Nativity), Feodosiyivska (St. Theodosius'), both of which have 18th century bronze iconostasis, and the Blahovishchenska (Annunciation) Church, which has a wood iconostasis, built in this century.

Besides these monuments, the Kyivan Cave Monastery contains many examples

Ukrainian Greek-Catholic Chapel-Church in the Podil.

of civil architecture of the 18th-20th centuries and fortification structures from 1698-1701.

KYRYLIVSKA (ST. CYRIL'S) CHURCH, mid-12th cent. Built by Maria, the wife of the Chernihiv prince, Vsevolod Olhovych, as the cathedral of an ancestral monastery. In the 12th-13th centuries the church was a royal burial place. Originally the church was a structure with cupolas in a cruciform design crowned with one cupola. It acquired its present appearance, with its Ukrainian baroque features, in the mid-18th century as a result of reconstruction undertaken by I. Hryhorovych-Barsky. Twelfth century fresco paintings (approximately 800 sq. m) embellish the interior. Of particular interest are the compositions executed by M. Vrubel. (Frunze St., 103. Trolleybus 18).

KLOV PALACE, 1752-56. Designed by J. Schaedel and built by P. Neyelov. Construction was completed by S. Kovnir, who introduced elements of Ukrainian folk architecture. The interior was painted in 1757. (Orlyk St., 8. Metro: Khreshchatyk).

MARIYINSKY PALACE, 1745-52. The architects I. Michurin, P. Neyelov, and I. Hyrhorovych-Barsky collaborated on the construction. Noted for the remarkable beauty of the interior decor and facades. Was named in honor of Tsar Alexander III's wife, the Empress Maria. Today it is used for official state functions. (Hrushevsky St., 5. Trolleybus 20; Bus 15, 62).

BUILDING OF THE UKRAINIAN ART MUSEUM (formerly the Museum of Ancient Artifacts and Art), 1897-99. Architects: V. Horodetsky and H. Boytsov. Built in the style of an ancient Greek temple. (Hrushevsky St., 6. Trolleybus 20).

TEACHERS' BUILDING (formerly the Pedagogical Museum), 1911. Enlarged in 1935-37 by the architect P. Alyoshyn. Built in the Neoclassical style. The Central Rada of the Ukrainian National Republic was located here in 1917-18. On 22 January 1918 the Central Rada proclaimed the independence of Ukraine in this building. (Volodymyrska St., 57. Trolleybus 12).

MYKOLAYIVSKY (ST. NICHOLAS') ROMAN CATHOLIC CHURCH, 1899-1909. Designed by S. Valovsky and built by the architect V. Horodetsky. Has the structure and decor of a medieval Gothic cathedral. Today it houses the Republican Building of Organ and Chamber Music. Church services for Ukrainian Roman Catholics are conducted here. (Chervonoarmiyska St., 61. Trolleybus 11, 12).

CHURCH OF MYKOLA DOBRY (ST. NICHOLAS THE GOOD) (BELL TOWER), 1716. Has not been preserved. This monument is an important part of the historic Podil district of Kyiv. (Zelinsky St., 6. Metro: Poshtova Ploshcha).

NABEREZHNO-MYKILSKA (ST. NICHOLAS' NABEREZHNA) CHURCH,

1772-75. Designed by the architect I. Hryhorovych-Barsky in the Ukrainian Baroque style on the site of a wood church. Noted for the elegance of its facades and interior. Of considerable artistic interest is the iconostasis built in the late Classical style. In 1863 a bell tower with a church designed by the architect M. Ikonnykov was built next to the church. (Skovoroda St., 12. Metro: Kontraktova Ploshcha Station).

POKROVSKY (PROTECTION OF THE BLESSED VIRGIN MARY) CONVENT, 1889. The main cathedral (1899) was built by the architect V. Nikolayev. The complex includes cells, a refectory, hospital, and gate. (Bekhterivsky Provulok, 15. Trolleybus 16, 18).

POKROVSKA (PROTECTION OF THE BLESSED VIRGIN MARY) CHURCH AND BELL TOWER, 1766. Designed by I. Hryhorovych-Barsky in the Ukrainian Baroque style. The iconostasis was built in the mid-19th century by the architect I. Shtrom. The bell tower was erected in the mid-18th century and rebuilt in the 19th century. (Zelinsky St., 7. Metro: Poshtova Ploshcha).

CHURCH OF MYKOLA PRYTYSKO (ST. NICHOLAS PRYTYSKO), 1631. Built with funds provided by the Kyiv burgher P. Zalizny Hrish on the site of a wood church of the same name. A cruciform structure with one cupola built in the Ukrainian Baroque style. Was rebuilt several times. A chapel was built on to the church in 1868. (Metro: Kontraktova Ploshcha).

OLEKSANDRIVSKY (ST. ALEXANDER'S) ROMAN CATHOLIC CHURCH, 1817-42. Built in the Classical style. Designed and built by F. Myechovych. (Kostelna St., 17. Metro: Maydan Nezalezhnosti).

SOFIYSKY (ST. SOPHIA'S) MONASTERY. The ensemble was built over a period of nine centuries. The complex includes:

SOFIYSKY (ST. SOPHIA'S) CATHEDRAL. Constructed in 1017-31 in honor of Prince Yaroslav the Wise's victory over the Pecheneg tribe. Was the main metropolitan church of Kyivan Rus'-Ukraine. Ceremonies to designate envoys, public meetings, and the writing of chronicles took place here. The first library in Kyivan Rus was located here. The cathedral bears a resemblance to Byzantine constructions, but there is no direct analogy. The original forms of the Romanesque style were preserved until the 17th century. The church facades were not plastered and were embellished with decorative niches, ornaments, and paintings. The interior reveals the harmonious union of mosaics and fresco paintings in a style similar to the Byzantine capital style. Religious and secular themes predominate. Of great value are the decorative works of the 11th century: the Metropolitan's chair, choir loft. The interior of the cathedral is also embel-

Kyivan Cave Monastery. Far Caves.

lished with fresco ornamentation, mosaic pavement, marble decorations, etc. The cathedral contained the tomb of the Grand Kyivan Princes: Yaroslav the Wise, Vsevolod, Rostyslav, and Volodymyr Monomakh were buried here (only the sarcophagus of Yaroslav the Wise has been preserved). After the Tatar-Mongol invasion of 1240, the cathedral gradually fell into ruins. In the 16th century Greek Catholic priests served Mass here. In the 1630s-40s the Kyivan Metropolitan P. Mohyla founded a monastery in the cathedral. He engaged the Italian architect O. Mancini to work on its restoration. In 1685-1707 the cathedral was rebuilt in the Ukrainian Baroque style. A Baroque iconostasis was built in 1731-47. St. Sophia's Cathedral is a masterpiece of world architecture. (Volodymyrska St., 24. Trolleybus 2, 12, 16, 18).

BELL TOWER, 18th-19th cent. A four-storied structure, with a height of 76 m The first story shows features of Ukrainian architecture of the late 17th-early 18th centuries; the second and third stories are embellished with molded decorations in the Ukrainian Baroque style. Ornaments in the pseudo-Byzantine style are featured in the fourth story.

TRAPEZNA (REFECTORY WITH A CHURCH or SMALL SOPHIA'S CHURCH), 1722-30. Rebuilt several times, acquiring Baroque forms in the process.

The monastery complex includes several examples of 18th century civil and defense architecture.

SPASA (OUR SAVIOR) CHURCH IN BERESTIV, 1113-25. (Sichnevoho Povstannya St., 15. Trolleybus 20).

TRAPEZNA (REFECTORY-TYPE) CHURCH OF THE MYKHAYLIVSKY (ST. NICHOLAS) MONASTERY, 1712. Built in the Ukrainian Baroque style on the site of a wood church. The interior is decorated with 19th century paintings. (Heroyiv Revolyutsiyi St., 2. Trolleybus 9).

TROYITSKA (HOLY TRINITY) CHURCH, 1763-68. Built by the architect S. Kovnir in the Ukrainian Baroque style. In the church courtyard in the 19th century a bell tower, residential buildings, and a refectory were built in the Classical style. (Kytayivska St., 15. Trolleybus 1).

FEODOSIYA PECHERSKOHO (ST. THEODOSIUS OF THE CAVES) CHURCH, 1698-1702. Built in the Ukrainian Baroque style with funds provided by K. Mokyyivsky, the Kyiv colonel of the Zaporozhyan Army. A tripartite church with three cupolas. (Sichnevoho Povstannya St., 32/1. Trolleybus 20).

FLORIVSKY (ST. FLOR'S) MONASTERY. Fifteenth century women's monastery. The architectural ensemble has been preserved. (Florivska St., 6/8. Metro: Kontraktova Ploshcha).

THE MONASTERY COMPLEX INCLUDES:

VOZNESENSKA (ASCENSION) CHURCH, 1722-32. The main monastery church. A six-columned structure with three apses and three cupolas. The pediments show obvious traces of wood folk architecture. Interior paintings of the 19th-20th centuries have been preserved.

TRAPEZNA (REFECTORY) CHURCH, 17th cent. The first brick monastery structure. The interior is decorated with 20th century paintings.

VOSKRESENSKA (RESURRECTION) CHURCH, rotunda, 1824. Built in the Classical style. Has refined proportions and forms and is one of the finest works of the architect A. Melensky.

BELL TOWER, 1740. Rebuilt in 1824. A rectangular, three-storied structure with Classical features.

The St. Flor's Convent complex also includes a number of dormitories dating to the first half of the 19th century. It is a functioning monastery.

HOSTYNNY DVIR (MANSION), 1809. Built by the architect L. Ruska in the Classical style on the site of a wood structure. Only the first floor was completed. Once held 50 shops. (Kontraktova Ploshcha, 4. Metro: Kontraktova Ploshcha).

STATE BANK. The first two floors were built in 1902-05 by the architects O. Kobelyev and O. Verbytsky. The third and fourth floors were built in 1934 by the architects O. Kobelyev and V. Rykov. It is one of the finest structures of the early-20th century. (Bankivska St., 9. Metro: Khreshchatyk).

GOVERNOR'S BUILDING, 1780. A monument of early Classicism. (Sichneve Povstannya St., 29. Trolleybus 20).

BUILDING OF THE T. SHEVCHENKO MUSEUM, 1841. Was substantially rebuilt in the 1870s and subsequently acquired Renaissance features. Owned by P. Demydov, head of the city committee and later by M. Tereshchenko, a businessman and patron of the arts. Since 1949 it has housed the T. Shevchenko Museum. (Shevchenko Blvd., 12. Trolleybus 9).

UNIVERSITY, 1837-43. Built in the late Classical style by the architect V. Beretti. Completed by O. Beretti. (Volodymyrska St., 60. Metro: Universytet Station; Trolleybus 12).

CEMETERIES

BAYKOVE

Established in December 1833 as a burial site for members of the Orthodox, Lutheran, and Roman Catholic faiths (in separate sections). Every section had its own chapel. In 1884 a brick church was built by the architect V. Nikolayev, which is still in operation today. The Old Cemetery is located on the left side of the road, and the New Cemetery (1880s) is on the right side. The latter is surrounded by a brick wall with a gate.

Vaults designed by the architects V. Horodetsky, V. Nikolayev, and others have been preserved. Also preserved are tombstones designed by the sculptors and architects V. Boroday, I. Honchar, H. Kalchenko, K. Kuznetsov, V. Hnyezdylov, A. Ihnashchenko, E. Bilostotsky, B. Dovhan, O. Skoblykov, A. Fuzhenko and others. A crematorium located beyond Baykove Cemetery has been in operation since 1875. (Baykova St. Streetcar 9, 10).

Askoldova Mohyla, 1810 (Askold's Grave).

PROMINENT INDIVIDUALS BURIED IN THE CEMETERY:

O. Antonov (1906-84), aviation designer, academician. • V. Antonovych (1834-1908), historian, archaeologist, archeographer, ethnographer. Founder of a school of Ukrainian historiography. • V. Beretti (1781-1842) and O. Beretti (1816-95), father and son, 19th century architects. • K. Dankevych (1905-1984), composer. • P. Demutsky (1860-1927), composer. • B. Hrinchenko (1863-1910), writer, civic activist. • M. Hrushevsky (1866-1934), historian-academician, head of the Ukrainian Central Rada, first president of Ukraine. • V. Kasiyan (1896-1976), painter-graphics artist, academician. • I. Kavaleridze (1887-1978), sculptor, film director, playwright. • O. Konysky (1836-1900), writer, historian. • B. Lyatoshynsky (1895-1968), composer. • M. Lysenko (1842-1912), distinguished Ukrainian composer. • Yu. Lytvyn (1934-84), poet, human rights activist, died in a Soviet labor camp. • P. Mayboroda (1918-89), composer. • H. Narbut (1886-1920), graphics artist. • I. Nechuy-Levytsky (1838-1918), writer. • Ye. Paton (1870-1953), scholar, academician. • A. Petrytsky (1895-1964), artist. • L. Revutsky (1889-1977), composer, academician. • M. Rylsky (1895-1964), poet, academician, civic activist. • I. Svitlychny (1928-92), poet, human rights activist; was imprisoned. • V. Sosyura (1898-1965), poet. • M. Starytsky (1840-1904), writer, playwright. • V. Stus (1938-85), poet; died in a Soviet labor camp. • P. Tychyna (1891-1967), poet, academician, civic activist. • O. Tykhy (1927-84), teacher, human rights defender; died in a Soviet labor camp. • Lesya Ukrayinka-Kosach (1871-1913), poetess and dramatist. • N. Uzhviy (1898-1986), actress. • H. Veryovka (1895-1964), founder and director of the Ukrainian Folk Choir. • P. Virsky (1905-75), founder and director of the Ukrainian Dance Ensemble. • I. Yizhakevych (1864-1962), artist, icon-painter. • M. Zankovetska (1854-1934), actress.

LUKIYANIVKA

The main cemetery in the 1870s. Many representatives of Kozak officers' families, associates of the Ukrainian National Republic, and deceased prisoners from Lukyanivka Prison are buried here. In the 1930s executed victims of the Stalinist purges were buried on the paths between sections at the end of the cemetery. (Shamrylo St., 7. Trolleybus No. 16).

PROMINENT INDIVIDUALS BURIED IN THE CEMETERY:

F. Krychevsky (1879-1947), artist, teacher. • **O. Murashko** (1875-1919), artist, civic activist. • **M. Pymonenko** (1862-1912), artist. • **M. Strazhesko** (1876-1952), therapist, academician. • **M. Vasylenko** (1877-1935), linguist, academician, second president of the All-Ukrainian Academy of Sciences

ZVIRYNETS

Verkhnya St., 21. Trolleybus No. 10, 24.

V. Tarnovsky, Jr. (1837-99), a collector of antiquities and Shevchenkiana is buried here.

BABYN YAR

Between Teliha, Melnykov, and Dorohózhytsky Streets.

O. Teliha (1907-42), a poetess and a leading activist of the Melnyk faction of the Organization of Ukrainian Nationalists, executed by the Germans, is buried here.

MONUMENTS

ASKOLDOVA MOHYLA (ASKOLD'S GRAVE). Part of a nature and architectural preserve on the right bank of the Dnipro River. According to the chronicle, the Kyivan Princes Askold and Dir, died here. In 1810 a brick church-rotunda designed by the architect A. Melensky was built here. In January of 1918, 18 soldiers from a students' unit who died in battle against Bolshevik forces near Kruty were buried here. A second story designed by the architect P. Yurchenko was built in 1935. Since the end of the 18th century it has been considered one of the most beautiful cemeteries in Europe. Demolished in 1934 by order of the People's Commissar V. Zatonsky. (Trolleybus 20).

Memorial ceiling (stele) in the library of St. Sophia's Cathedral, 1969. Sculptor: I. Kavaleridze. On the grounds of St. Sophia's Cathedral. Volodymyrska St., 24 (Trolleybus 16 and 18 from Maydan Nezalezhnosti; Trolleybus 2).

St. Volodymyr, 1853. Sculptors: V. Demut-Malynovsky and P. Klodt. Architect: O. Thon. On the terrace of Volodymyr's Hill. (Trolleybus 20; Bus 62, 71).

T. Shevchenko, 1939. Sculptor: M. Manizer. Architect: Ye. Levinson. In Shevchenko Park. (Metro: Universytet or Ploshcha Lva Tolstoho).

N. Glinka, 1904. Architect: V. Nikola-

Monument to St. Volodymyr the Great, 1853.

T. Shevchenko Monument 1939.

yev. In the City Garden. (Trolleybus 20; Bus 62).

O. Dovzhenko, 1964. Designed by A. Kozub and P. Orlov. On the grounds of the O. Dovzhenko Feature Film Studio. (Metro: Shulyavska).

M. Zankovetska, 1974. Sculptor: H. Kalchenko. Architect: A. Ihnashchenko. In the City Garden. (Metro: Khreshchatyk; Trolleybus 20; Bus 62).

I. Kotlyarevsky, 1957. Sculptor: H. Kalchenko. Architect: A. Ihnashchenko. On the corner of Melnykov and Herzen Streets. (Trolleybus 16, 18 or 19).

M. Lysenko, 1965. Sculptor: O. Kovalyov. Architect: V. Hnyezdylov. Teatralna Ploshcha. (Metro: Teatralna or Zoloti Vorota).

Monument to Magdeburg Law, 1802-08. Considered the lower monument to the baptizm of Rus'-Ukraine and the return of the Magdeburg Law to Kyiv. Architect: A. Melensky. On the banks of the Dnipro River near Naberezhne shosse. Metro: Poshtova Ploshcha; Streetcar 21, 31, 32, 34).

Monument to the victims of Babyn Yar, 1976. Collective work. Between Teliha, Melnykov, and Dorohozhytsky Streets. (Trolleybus 16 from Maydan Nezalezhnosti).

M. Rylsky, 1968. Sculptor: O. Kovalyov. Architect: V. Kostin. On the grounds of the M. Rylsky Museum. (Metro: Lybidska and Trolleybus 4, 11, 12).

H. Skovoroda, 1976. Sculptor: I. Kavaleridze. Architect: V. Hnyezdylov. Kontraktova Ploshcha. (Metro: Kontraktova Ploshcha; Streetcar 21, 31, 32, 34).

Lesya Ukrayinka, 1973. Sculptor: H. Kalchenko. Architect: A. Ihnashchenko. Lesya Ukrayinka Square. (Metro: Palats Sportu and Trolleybus 14 or 15).

Lesya Ukrayinka, 1965. Sculptor: V. Boroday. Architect: A. Ihnashchenko. In City Garden. ().

K. Ushynsky, 1974. Sculptor: O. Skoblykov. Architect: A. Ihnashchenko. (On the corner of Chokolivsky Blvd. and Piterska St.).

Monument to the victims of Babyn Yar, 1976.

I. Franko, 1956. Sculptors: O. Suprun and A. Bilostotsky. Architect: M. Ivanchenko. Franko Square. (etro: Khreshchatyk).

B. Khmelnytsky, 1888. Sculptor: M. Mykeshyn. Architect: V. Nikolayev. Sofiyivsky Square. (Metro: Zoloti Vorota; Trolleybus 16 or 18 from Maydan Nezalezhnosti).

Nestor-Litopysets, 1988. Sculptor: F. Sohoyan. Architect: M. Kysly. On the ground of the Kyivan Cave Monastery. (Metro: Arsenalna and Trolleybus 20).

O. Pushkin, 1962. Sculptor: O. Kovalyov. Architect V. Hnyezdylov. Pushkin Park. (Metro: Shulyavska or Politekhnichny Instytut).

Hryhoriy Skovoroda Monument, 1976.

MUSEUMS

Andriyivska (St. Andrew's) Church Museum: Andriyivsky Uzviz, 23; tel. 228-58-61 (Metro: Poshtova Ploshcha and Funicular). • **Archeological Museum:** Khmelnytsky St., 15; tel. 225-62-86 (Metro: Universytet). • **Botanical Museum:** Khmelnytsky St., 15; tel. 225-03-74 (Metro: Universytet). • **Historical Museum of Ukraine:** Volodymyrska St., 2; tel. 228-29-24 (Metro: Poshtova Ploshcha and Funicular). • **Museum of the Book and Book Printing:** Sichneve Povstannya St., 21; tel. 290-22-10 (Trolleybus 20). • **Literature of Ukraine Museum:** Khmelnytsky St., 52; tel. 225-13-09 (Metro: Teatralna). • **Theater and Cinema Arts Museum:** Sichnevoho povstannya St., 21; tel. 290-51-31 (Trolleybus 20). • **Ukrainian Art Museum:** Hrushevsky St., 6; tel. 228-64-82 (Trolleybus 20). • **Ukrainian Decorative Folk Art Museum:** Sichneve Povstannya St., 21; tel. 290-13-43 (Trolleybus 20). • **T. Shevchenko Museum:** Shevchenko Blvd., 12; tel. 224-25-56 (Metro: Teatralna). • **Western and Eastern Art Museum:** Tereshchenkivska St., 15; tel. 225-02-06 (Metro: Teatralna). • **Zoloti Vorota (Golden Gate):** Yaroslaviv Val; tel. 225-82-65 (Metro: Zoloti Vorota). • **Zoological Museum:** Khmelnytsky St., 15; tel. 224-16-13 (Metro: Universytet). • **Museum of Veterinary History:** Volynska St., 12; tel. 272-21-53. • **Museum of Army History:** Hrushevsky St., 30/1; tel. 293-27-50 (Trolleybus 20). • **History of Kyiv Museum:**

Lesya Ukrayinka Monument, 1973.

T. Shevchenko Museum.

Orlyk St., 8; tel. 293-13-44 (Trolleybus 20). • **Museum of Historic Treasures of Ukraine:** Sichneve Povstannya St., 21; tel. 290-13-96. • **Kyivan-Cave-Monastery Historical-Cultural Preserve:** Sichneve Povstannya St., 21; tel. 290-30-71 (Trolleybus 20). • **Kyrylivska (St. Cyril's) Church Museum:** Frunze St., 103; tel. 435-21-23 (Trolleybus 18 from Maydan Nezalezhnosti). • **Kosyi Kaponir:** Hospitalna St., 24-a; tel. 225-01-46 (Metro: Palats Sportu). • **T. Shevchenko Literary-Memorial Museum Building:** provulok Shevchenka, 8-a; tel. 228-35-11 (Metro: Maydan Nezalezhnosti). • **Lesya Ukrayinka Literary-Memorial Museum:** Saksahansky St., 97; tel. 220-16-51 (Metro: Ploshcha Lesi Ukrayinky). • **M. Rylsky Literary-Memorial Museum:** Rylsky St., 7; tel. 265-24-71 (Trolleybus 11 or 12 from metro Respublikansky Stadion). • **P. Tychyna Literary-Memorial Museum-Residence:** Tereshchenkivska St., 5, apt. 1 (Metro: Teatralna). • **Museum of Medicine of Ukraine:** Khmelnytsky St., 37; tel. 225-20-46 (Metro: Teatralna). • **M. Lysenko Building and Museum:** Saksahansky St., 95; tel. 220-02-85 (Streetcar 5 or 35 from metro Ploshcha Lva Tolstoho). • **Museum of Folk Architecture and Folkways of Ukraine:** village of Pyrohovo; tel. 266-24-16 (Bus 84 from metro Lybidska). • **Museum of Paleontology:** Khmelnytsky St., 15; tel. 225-60-53 (Metro: Universytet). • **Pedagogical Museum:** Volodymyrska St., 57; tel. 224-25-90 (Trolleybus 8 or 17 from metro Ploshcha Lva Tolstoho; Metro: Teatralna). • **Russian Art Museum:** Tereshchenkivska St., 9; tel. 224-62-18 (Metro: Teatralna). • **St. Sophia State Architectural-Historical Preserve and Museum:** Volodymyrska St., 24; tel. 228-61-52 (Metro: Zoloti Vorota or trolleybus 16 and 18 from Maydan Nezalezhnosti). • **Ukrainian Distinction in Sports Museum:** Esplanadna St., 42; tel. 220-93-96 (Metro: Respublikansky Stadion). • **History of the Great Patriotic War Museum (1941-1945):** Sichneve Povstannya St., 33; tel. 295-09-60 (Trolleybus 20). • **Central Natural Science Museum:** Khmelnytsky St., 15; tel. 224-93-83 (Metro: Universytet). • **V. Kosenko Memorial Museum:** Kotsyubynsky St., 9, apt. 4; tel. 224-44-74 (Streetcar 2 from metro Vokzalna). • **M. Bulgakov Literary-Memorial Museum and Building:** Andriyivsky Uzviz, 13; tel. 416-31-88 (Metro: Kon-

Museum of Folk Architecture and Folkways of Ukraine.

traktova Ploshcha). • **Central Archive-Museum of Literature and Art of Ukraine:** Volodymyrska St., 22-a; tel. 228-07-24 (Metro: Zoloti Vorota).

PUBLISHING HOUSES

Veselka: Melnykov St., 63; tel. 213-96-01. • **Dnipro:** Volodymyrska St., 42; tel. 224-31-82. • **Lybid:** Khreshchatyk St., 10; tel. 229-11-71. • **Mystetstvo:** Zolotovoritska St., 11; tel. 225-53-92. • **Naukova Dumka:** Repin St., 3; tel. 224-40-68. • **Ukrayinsky Pysmennyk:** Chkalov St., 52; tel. 216-25-92. • **Budivelnyk:** Observatorna St.; tel 212-10-90. • **Hlobus:** A. Barbyus St., 51/2; tel. 269-25-41. • **Berehy:** Turhenyevska St., 46; tel. 216-63-10. • **Osvita:** Yu. Kotsyubynsky St. 5; tel. 216-58-02. • **Smoloskyp:** Artem St., 1-5, Room 802; tel. & Fax: 212-08-77. • **Abrys:** Tryokhsvyatytelska St., 4; tel. 228-40-37; Fax: 228-48-55. • **Sonyashnyk:** Turhenyevska St., 46; tel. 216-63-10.

NEWSPAPERS

Vechirniy Kyiv: Marshal Hrechko St., 13; tel. 434-65-67; Fax: 443-96-09. • **Visti z Ukrayiny:** Zolotovoritska St., 4; tel. 228-56-42; Fax: 228-08-04. • **Holos Ukrayiny:** Nesterov St., 4; tel. 446-92-11; Fax: 224-72-54.. • **Kultura i Zhyttya:** Observatorna St., 6; tel. 216-88-44. • **Literaturna Ukrayina:** Lesya Ukrayinka Blvd., 20; tel. 296-36-39. • **Molod Ukrayiny:** prospekt Peremohy, 50; tel. 441-83-83. • **Osvita:** Khmelnytsky St., 44; tel. 225-53-66. • **Ukrayina Moloda:** prospekt Peremohy, 50; tel. 441-83-00. • **Uryadovy Kuryer:** Sadova St., 1; tel. 293-55-09. • **Dilova Ukrayina:** Kutuzov St., 18/9; tel. 294-91-89; Fax: 294-91-84. • **Narodna Armiya:** Artem St., 24; tel. & fax: 216-17-27. • **Narodna Hazeta:** Saksahansky St., 61/17; tel. 220-45-54; Fax: 220-42-92. • **News From Ukraine:** Artem St., 91; tel. 244-58-98. • **Zeleny Svit:** Dehtyarivska St., 38-44; tel. 213-07-92; Fax: 213-62-53. • **Ukrayinska Hazeta:** Observatorna St., 11/1; tel. 216-14-16; Fax: 417-82-82. • **Khreshchatyk:** B. Khmelnytsky St., 26-h; tel. 225-32-60. • **Demokratychna Ukrayina:** prospekt Peremohy, 50; tel. 441-86-29. • **Ukrayinske Slovo:** Sichneve Povstannya St., 6; tel. 290-70-59. • **Samostiyna Ukrayina:** Prorizna St., 27; tel. 229-47-72. • **Nasha Vira:** T. Shevchenko Bulv., 12, kv. 6; tel. 268-73-26. • **Robitnycha Hazeta:** prospekt Peremohy, 50; tel. 441-83-33; Fax: 446-68-85.

JOURNALS

Arkhivy Ukrayiny: Solomyanska St., 24; tel. 277-82-44. • **Vitchyzna:** Hrushevsky St., 34/1; tel. 293-28-51. • **Vsesvit:** Hrushevsky St., 34/1; tel. 293-13-18. • **Dnipro:** Dehtyarivska St., 38-44; tel 213-98-79. • **Kyiv:** Desyatynna St., 11; tel. 229-02-80. • **Nauka i Suspilstvo:** Rylsky Provulok, 10; tel. 228-23-87. • **Ukrayina:** prospekt Peremohy, 50; tel. 446-63-16. • **Ukrayinska kultura:** Rylsky Provulok, 10; tel. 228-00-16. • **Vidomosti Verkhovnoyi Rady Ukrayiny:** ploshcha L. Ukrayinky, 1;

T. Shevchenko Theater of Opera and Ballet.

tel. 296-82-97. • **Visnyk Akademiyi Ukrayiny:** Tryokhsvyatytelska St., 4. • **Ekonomika Ukrayiny:** Tsytadelna, 4/7; tel. 290-52-75. • **Polityka i Chas:** Desyatynna, 4/6; tel. 229-75-73. • **Ukrayina:** prospekt Peremohy, 50; tel. 446-63-16. • **Sonyashnyk:** Turhenyevska St., 46; tel. 216-63-10. • **Zhinka:** prospekt Peremohy, 50; tel. 441-86-16. • **Ukrayinsky Teatr:** Velyka Zhytomyrska St., 6/11; tel. 229-19-75. • **Obrazotvorche Mystetstvo:** Artem St., 1-5, k. 513; tel. 212-02-86. • **Lyudyna i Svit:** Observatorna St., 11/1; tel. 216-78-17. • **Muzyka:** Khreshchatyk, 48; tel. 225-60-72. • **Ranok:** Dehtyarivska St., 38-44; tel. 211-02-29. • **Viche:** prospekt Peremohy, 50; tel. 441-82-76. • **Starozhytnosti:** Chervonoarmiyska, 57/3; tel. 227-37-75. • **Suchasnist:** Kostyantynivska St., 5; tel. 225-02-40. • **Zoloti Vorota:** Zolotovoritska St., 6; tel. 225-02-40. • **Perets:** prospekt Peremohy, 50; tel. 441-82-14. • **Barvinok:** Dehtyarivska St., 38-44; tel. 213-99-13. • **Malyatko:** Dehtyarivska St., 38-44; tel. 213-98-91. • **State Television and Radio Company of Ukraine:** Khreshchatyk St., 26; tel. 228-33-33; 229-12-85.

THEATERS, PHILHARMONIC, CIRCUS

T. Shevchenko Theater of Opera and Ballet: Volodymyrska St., 50 (Metro: Teatralna). • **I. Franko Ukrainian Drama Theater:** ploshcha Franka, 3 (Metro: Khreshchatyk). • **Lesya Ukrayinka Russian Drama Theater:** Khmelnytsky St., 5 (Metro: Teatralna). • **Theater of Drama and Comedy (left bank of the Dnipro):** prospekt Brovarsky, 25 (Metro: Livoberezhna) . • **Operetta:** Chervonoarmiyska St., 53/3 (Metro: Respublikansky Stadion). • **Youth Theater:** Prorizna St., 17 (Metro: Khreshchatyk or Zoloti Vorota). • **Young Spectator's Theater:** Lypska St., 15/17 (Metro: Arsenalna; Trolleybus 20; Streetcar 27, 53; Bus 62). • **Children's Musical Theater:** Mykhaylivska Ploshcha, 2 (Trolleybus 16, 18 from Maydan Nezalezhnosti). • **Variety Theater:** Kontraktova Ploshcha, 1 (Metro: Kontraktova Ploshcha; Streetcar: 21, 31, 32, 34). • **Puppet Theater:** Rustaveli St., 13 (Metro: Ploshcha Lva Tolstoho; Streetcar 1, 5, 35). • **Municipal Puppet Theater:** Lunacharsky St., 1-b (Metro: Chernihivska; Streetcar 22, 29, 31). • **Philharmonic:** Volodymyrsky Uzviz, 2

I. Franko Ukrainian Drama Theater.

(Metro: Maydan Nezalezhnosti). • **Circus:** Ploshcha Peremohy (Metro: Universytet; Trolleybus 5, 8, 9, 17). • **Suzirya:** Yaroslaviv Val, 14-a (Metro: Zoloti Vorota). • **Koleso:** Andriyivsky Uzviz, 8 (Metro: Kontraktova Ploshcha). • **Na Podoli:** Kontraktova Ploshcha, 4 (Metro: Kontraktova Ploshcha).

ART EXHIBITIONS

Budynok Khudozhnykiv: Artema St., 1-5 (Trolleybus 16, 18 from Maydan Nezalezhnosti). • **Vystavochny Pavilion:** Instytutska St. (Metro: Maydan Nezalezhnosti; Bus 71; Trolleybus 20). • **Vystavochny Zal of Kyiv Artists' Union of Ukraine:** Chervonoarmiyska St., 12 (Metro: Ploshcha Lva Tolstoho).

HIGHER EDUCATIONAL INSTITUTIONS

Automobile and Roads Institute: Suvorov St., 1 (Metro: Arsenalna; Trolleybus 20). • **Civil-Engineering Institute:** Povitroflotsky Prospekt, 31; tel. 272-95-80, 276-53-30 (Metro: Universytet and Trollybus 8, 9). • **Conservatory:** Marx St., 1/3; tel. 229-07-92 (Metro: Khreshchatyk or Maydan Nezalezhnosti). • **Institute of Civil-Aviation Engineers:** prospekt Komarova, 1; tel. 484-93-33 (Metro: Politekhnichny Instytut; Streetcar 1, 3). • **Institute of Culture:** Shchors St., 36; tel. 269-98-44 (Metro: Palats Sportu; Trolleybus 14, 15). • **Kyiv University of the National Economy:** prospekt Peremohy, 54/1; tel. 441-20-33, 446-50-55 (Metro: Shulyavska; Trolleybus 5). • **Institute of Physical Education:** Fizkulturna St., 1; tel. 227-54-52 (Metro: Respublikansky Stadion). • **Institute of Theater Arts:** Yaroslaviv Val, 40; tel. 212-10-32 (Metro: Zoloti Vorota or Trolleybus 16, 18 from Maydan Nezalezhnosti). • **O. Bohomolets Medical Institute:** Shevchenko Blvd., 13; tel. 244-40-62 (Metro: Teatralna). • **M. Drahomanov Pedagogical University:** Pyrohov St., 9; tel. 221-99-33, 224-11-08 (Metro: Universytet). • **Pedagogical Institute of Foreign Languages:** Chervonoarmiyska St., 73; tel. 227-33-72 (Metro: Ploshcha Lva Tolstoho). • **Polytechnical Institute:** prospekt Peremohy, 37; tel. 274-79-89, 274-69-13 (Metro: Politekhnichny Instytut). • **T. Shevchenko University:** Volodymyrska St., 64; tel. 221-02-33, 220-86-91 (Metro: Universytet or Ploshcha Lva Tolstoho). • **Technological Institute of the Food Industry:** Volodymyrska St., 68 (Metro: Ploshcha Lva Tolstoho). • **Technological Institute of Light Industry:** Nemyrovych-Danchenko St., 2 (Metro: Streetcar 35, 27; Bus 62; Trolleybus 14, 15). • **Trade and Eco-**

Building of Kyiv University, 1837-43.

nomics Institute: Kioto St., 19; tel. 513-23-09, 513-33-48 (Metro: Lisova) . •
Ukrainian Agricultural University: Heroyiv Oborony St., 15; tel.263-92-33, 263-
51-75 (Metro: Lybidska; Trolleybus 4, 11, 12). • University "Kyievo-Mohylanska
Akademia": Kontraktova Ploshcha; tel. 416-45-15; Fax: 417-84-61 (Metro: Kontraktova Ploshcha). • Ukrainian Academy of Art: Smyrnov-Lastochkin St., 20; tel.
212-15-40; Fax: 212-19-46 (Trolleybus 16, 18 from Maydan Nezalezhnosti).

LIBRARIES

State Library of Ukraine: Hrushevsky St., 1; tel. 228-85-12 (Metro: Khreshchatyk or Maydan Nezalezhnosti). • State History Library: Sichneve Povstannya
St., 21, bldg. 24; tel. 290-46-17 (Metro: Arsenalna and Trolleybus 20). • Library of
Ukrainian Diaspora: Velyka Zhytomyrska St., 4; tel. 228-02-76 (Trolleybus 16, 18
from Maydan Nezalezhnosti). • Regional Library of Music and Theater: Mykhaylivska St., 9; tel. 228-36-41 (Metro: Maydan Nezalezhnosti). • V. Vernadsky Central Scientific Library: prospekt Zhovtnya, 3; tel. 265-81-04. • University Library: Volodymyrska St., 58; tel. 229-70-98 (Metro: Universytet or Ploshcha Lva Tolstoho). • State Medical Library: Tolstoy St., 7; tel. 220-14-40 (Metro: Ploshcha
Lva Tolstoho).. • State Agricultural Library: Heroyiv Oborony St., 10; tel. 266-05-
09. • State Scientific-Technical Library: Gorky St., 180; tel.269-42-04 (Trollyebus
1, 11, 12 from metro Respublikansky Stadion). • Divisional Republican Scientific-
Technical Library: Kontraktova Ploshcha, 4; tel. 416-03-10 (Metro: Kontraktova
Ploshcha). • Library of the Litterateurs' Building: Bankova St., 2; tel. 293-84-12
(Metro: Khreshchatyk) . • Library of the Officers' Building: Hrushevsky St., 30/1;
tel. 293-73-83 (Metro: Arsenalna and Trolleybus 20) . • Library of the P. Tchaikovsky Conservatory: Marx St., 1/3; tel. 229-28-56 (Metro: Khreshchatyk). • Medical Institute Library: Zoolohichna St., 1; tel. 213-95-56.

ARCHIVES

Regional Executive Committee Archive of the Kyiv Region: Frunze St., 113;
tel. 435-00-19 (Metro: Kontraktova Ploshcha; Streetcar 11, 12, 19). • Kyiv Municipal Executive Committee Archive: Teliha St., 23; tel. 440-63-50 (Metro: Shulyavska; Trolleybus 27). • Kyiv Regional Archive: Melnykov St., 38; tel. 213-19-10
(Trollybus 16 from Maydan Nezalezhnosti). • Central State Archive of Administration of Ukraine: Solomyanska St., 24; tel. 277-12-33 (Metro: Universytet; Trolleybus 8, 9). • Historical Archive: Solomyanska St., 24; tel. 277-12-33 (Metro: Universytet; Trolleybus 8, 9). • Archive of Cinema, Photography, and Phonography
Documents: Solomyanska St., 24; tel. 277-37-77 (Metro: Universytet; Trolleybus 8,
9). • Archive-Museum of Literature and Art: Volodymyrska St., 22-a; tel. 228-25-
38.

PARKS, ZOOLOGICAL AND BOTANICAL GARDENS, PLANETARIUM

Hydropark. Branch: prospekt Heroyiv Stalinhrada, 10. • **M. Rylsky Holosiyivsky Park:** prospekt Sorokrichchya Zhovtnya; Zhovtnevy Park: Lepse Blvd., 9-v. • **A. Pushkin Park:** prospekt Peremohy, 40. • **M. Frunze Park:** Frunze St., 134. • **Nyvky Park:** prospekt Peremohy, 82. • **Partyzanskoyi Slavy (Partisan Glory) Park:** Rosiyska St., 28/1. • **Peremoha (Victory) Park:** Perov Blvd., 2. • **Pushcha Vodytsya:** Chervonoflotska St., 26. • **Tsentralny (Central) Park:** Volodymyrsky Uzviz, 2. • **Yunist (Youth) Park:** Koltsov Blvd., 20. • **Zoological Garden:** prospekt Peremohy, 32. • **Central Republican Botanical Gardens of the Academy of Sciences of Ukraine:** Timiryazyevska St., 1. • **A. Fomin State University Botanical Gardens:** Komintern St., 1. • **Planetarium:** Chervonoarmiyska St., 57/3.

SPORTS COMPLEXES

Republican Stadium: Chervonoarmiyska St., 55; tel. 224-43-07; 220-02-10. • **Tennis Courts of the Republican Stadium:** Esplanadna St., 42; tel. 221-57-64; 221-59-27. • **Sports Palace:** Sportyvna Ploshcha, 1; tel. 224-16-46; 221-52-12. • **Central Training Base for Skating (Ice stadium):** prospekt Hlushkova, 9; tel. 266-37-08; 266-61-64. • **Olympic Sports Training Base in Koncha-Zaspa:** village of Chapayivka; tel. 261-26-64; 261-26-23. • **Dynamo Stadium:** Hrushevsky St., 3; tel. 229-52-52. The stadium complex consists of a soccer field, light athletics nucleus, tennis courts, an open-air swimming pool, sports gymnasiums and fields. • **Nauka Sports Complex:** prospekt Vernadskoho, 32; tel. 444-02-02; 444-03-72. • **Tennis Courts of the Antey Sports Complex:** Vitruk St., 8; tel. 444-24-24; 444-24-23. • **Light Athletics Manege:** Tychyna St., 18; tel. 550-42-59; 550-41-28. • **Central Hippodrome:** prospekt Hlushkova, 10; tel. 266-15-64. • **Sokil Sports Training Center:** Melnykov St., 46; tel. 213-33-55; 213-34-78. • **Spartak Stadium:** Frunze St., 105; 435-10-96. The stadium complex includes a rugby field, track and field nucleus, a swimming pool, and sports fields.

HOTELS

Ukrayina: Shevchenko Blvd., 5; tel. 229-43-03, 229-28-07. • **Natsionalny:** Luxemburg St., 3; tel. 291-87-77, 291-88-88, 291-87-10. • **Kyiv:** Hrushevsky St., 26/1; 293-01-55, 293-01-10, 293-00-42. • **Khreshchatyk:** Khreshchatyk St., 14; tel. 229-73-39; 229-71-93. • **Rus':** Hospital-

Kyiv Hotel.

Rus' Hotel.

na St., 4; tel. 220-42-55, 220-42-26, 220-52-33; Fax: 220-45-68. • **Kyivsky:** Hospitalna St., 12; tel. 227-95-55, 220-40-44; fax: 220-45-68. • **Lybid:** ploshcha Peremohy; tel. 274-00-63, 224-32-06; Fax: 224-05-78. • **Dnipro:** Khreshchatyk St., 1/2; tel. 229-81-79, 229-82-87; 228-65-69; Fax: 229-82-13. • **Bratyslava:** Malyshko St., 1; tel. 551-76-44; 559-72-80. • **Moskva:** Instytutska St., 4; tel. 228-28-04, 229-03-47, 228-28-04. • **Sport:** Chervonoarmiyska St., 55; tel. 220-03-27, 220-02-52, 220-00-16; Fax: 220-02-57. • **Slavutych:** Entuziastiv St., 1; tel. 555-38-59, 555-09-11, 555-19-22. • **"St. Peterburg":** Shevchenko Blvd., 4; tel. 229-74-53, 229-73-64; Building 3: Volodymyrska St., 36; tel. 229-59-43. • **Zoloty Kolos:** prospekt Sorokrichchya Zhovtnya, 95; tel. 261-40-01, 263-11-87. • **Teatralny:** Holosiyivska St., 7; tel. 265-89-88, 265-74-27. • **Turyst:** Okipna St., 2; tel. 517-88-32; 517-88-30. • **Myr:** prospekt Sorokrichchya Zhovtnya, 70; tel. 268-53-83, 263-33-81. • **Holosiyivsky:** prospekt Sorokrichchya Zhovtnya, 93; tel. 261-42-68, 261-42-74, 261-41-63. • **Salyut:** Sichneve Povstannya St., 11-a; tel. 290-61-30, 290-21-03; Fax: 290-72-70. • **Kozatsky:** Mykhaylivska St., 1/3; tel. 229-48-25, 228-27-86. • **Kooperator:** Saksahansky St., 53/80; tel. 227-24-63; 227-25-69. • **Feofaniya:** Metrolohichna St., 14-b; tel. 266-53-22, 266-52-15. • **Akademichny:** Perovska St., 6/11; tel. 446-64-53; 446-90-31. • **Prolisok (summer camping):** prospekt Peremohy, 139; tel. 444-14-90; 444-12-93.

RESTAURANTS, CAFES, BARS

Kyivsky: Hospitalna St., 12. • **Lybid:** ploshcha Peremohy, 1. • **Rus':** Hospitalna St., 4. • **Prolisok:** prospekt Peremohy, 139. • **Apollon (Currency Service):** Khreshchatyk St., 15. • **Moskva:** Instytutska St., 4. • **Ukrayina:** Shevchenko Blvd., 5/7. • **Dnipro:** Khreshchatyk St., 1/2. • **Kyiv:** Hrushevsky St., 26/1. • **Kozatsky:** Mykhaylivska St., 1/3. • **Kooperator:** Saksahansky St., 53/80. • **Bratyslava:** Malyshko St., 1. • **Holosiyivsky:** prospekt Sorokrichchya Zhovtnya, 93. • **Desna:** Mylyutenko St., 46. • **Druzhba:** Druzhby Narodiv Blvd., 5. • **Zoloty Kolos:**

Lybid Hotel.

prospekt Sorokrichchya Zhovtnya, 95. • **Myr:** prospekt Sorokrichchya Zhovtnya, 70. • **Salyut:** Sichneve Povstannya St., 11-a. • **Turyst:** Okipna St., 2. • **Slavutych:** Entuziastiv St., 1. • **Feofaniya:** Metrolohichna St., 14-b. • **Dubky:** Stetsenko St., 1. • **Verkhovyna:** prospekt Peremohy, 135. • **St. Peterburg:** Shevchenko Blvd., 4. • **Mlyn:** Hydropark. • **Zoloti Vorota:** Lvivska Ploshcha., 8. • **Maksym:** Khmelnytsky St., 21. • **Sport:** Chervonoarmiyska St., 55. • **Yaroslaviv Dvir:** prospekt Peremohy, 139. • **Ekspres:** Pryvokzalna Ploshcha. • **Vitryak:** prospekt Hlushkova, 11. • **Rus':** Yura St., 7. • **Holosiyivske:** prospekt Sorokrichchya Zhovtnya, 87-a. • **Odesa:** Chervonoarmiyska St., 114. • **Sonyachny Hrot:** Chervonoarmiyska St., 12. • **Artcafe:** Andriyivsky Uzviz, 11. • **Zamkove:** Andriyivska St., 24. • **Albena:** Komandarm Kamenyev St., 2. • **Bilya Kaminu:** Chervonoarmiyska St., 95. • **Hostynny Dvir:** Kontraktova Ploshcha. • **Evryka:** Lesya Ukrayinka Blvd., 30-a. • **Ekspres:** Saksahansky St., 42. • **Lavanda:** Vasylkivska St., 11. • **Lavra:** Sichneve Povstannya St., 21. • **Orfey:** Rustaveli St., 36. • **Retro:** Vorovsky St., 31-a. • **Trembita:** Khmelnytsky St., 44. • **Yaroslavna:** Kostyantynivska St., 12/28. • **Cherkasy:** Chervonoarmiyska St., 85/87. • **Khreshchatyk:** Khreshchatyk St., 28. • **Grill-bar:** prospekt Chubarya., 16. • **Zaporizhzhya:** Sahaydachny St., 27-a. • **Khreshchatyk:** Chervonoarmiyska St., 103. • **Pinhvin:** Chervonoarmiyska St., 23. • **Morozyvo:** Khreshchatyk St., 50. • **Morozyvo:** Khreshchatyk St., 17. • **Ararat Cafe-shashlychna:** Ushynsky St., 1.

STORES

Tsentralny Hastronom (Food): prospekt Peremohy, 4. • **Tsentralny Hastronom (Food):** Khreshchatyk St., 46. • **Yuvileyny Hastronom (Food):** prospekt Peremohy, 20. • **Kooperator:** Besarabska Ploshcha., 2. • **Nika (Currency):** Shevchenko Blvd., 4. • **Kashtan (Currency):** Lesya Ukrayinka Blvd., 26. • **Varshava (Currency):** Hospitalna St., 10. • **Tsentralny Univermah (Central Department Store):** Khmelnytsky St., 2. • **Ukrayina univermah (Department Store):** ploshcha Peremohy. • **Pechersky Market Center:** Suvorov St., 4. • **Darnytsky Univermah (Department Store):** prospekt Myru, 1. • **Podilsky Univermah (department store):** Sahaydachny St., 24. • **Moskovsky Univermah (Department Store):** prospekt Sorokrichchya

View of Rusanivka.
Slavutych Hotel.

Zhovtnya, 104. • Zaliznychny Univermah (Department Store): Povitryanoflotsky Prospekt, 44. • Kvity Ukrayiny (Flowers): Artem St., 49. • Kashtan: Shevchenko Blvd., 2. • Budynok Odyahu (Clothing): Lvivska Ploshcha, 8. • Budynok Radio: Lesya Ukrayinka Blvd., 3. • Budynok Podarunkiv (Gifts): Lesya Ukrayinka Blvd., 5. • Podarunky (Gifts): Khreshchatyk St., 15. • Charivna Skrynka: Khreshchatyk St., 15.

BANKS

Natsionalny Bank Ukrayiny (National Bank of Ukraine): Zhovtnevoyi revolyutsiyi St., 9; tel. 226-29-14, 293-59-73. • Regional branch: Andriyivska St., 1; tel. 226-29-32, 417-80-62. • Ukrayinsky aktsionerny komertsiyny promyslovo-investytsiyny bank (Ukrainian Joint-Stock Commercial Industrial-Investment Bank): provulok Shevchenka, 12; tel. 226-20-32, 229-37-87. • Respublikansky aktsionerno-komertsiyny ahropromyslovy bank "Ukrayina" ("Ukraine" Republican Joint-Stock Commercial Agro-Industrial Bank): provulok Rylskoho, 8; tel. 228-97-46, 293-07-11. • Respublikansky aktsionerno-komertsiyny bank sotsialnoho rozvytku "Ukrsotsbank" ("Ukrsotsbank" — Republican Joint-Stock Commercial Bank for Social Development): Kovpak St., 29; tel. 269-13-26, 269-24-81. • Derzhavny spetsializovany komertsiyny oshchadny bank Ukrayiny (State Specialized Commercial Savings Bank of Ukraine): prospekt Nauky, 7; tel. 265-31-50, 265-37-36. • Derzhavny eksportno-importny bank Ukrayiny (State Export-Import Bank of Ukraine): Khreshchatyk St., 8; tel. 226-09-10, 226-27-45. • Ukrayinsky aktsionerny inovatsiyny bank "Ukrinbank" ("Ukrinbank" — Ukrainian Joint-Stock Innovations Bank): Zhovtneva Revolyutsiya St., 12a; tel. 229-38-04, 229-77-50. • Komertsiyny bank rozvytku promyslovosti budivelnykh materialiv Ukrayiny "Budmbank" ("Budmbank" — Commercial Development Bank for the Building Materials Industry of Ukraine): Artem St., 74; tel. 216-75-95, 211-37-01, 211-35-85. • "AZh 10" Aktsionerny bank ("AZh 10" Joint-Stock Bank): Leskov St., 9; tel. 295-31-61, 294-81-10. • Kyivsky Narodny Bank (Kyiv National Bank): Zolotovorotska St., 11; tel. 228-74-51. • Aktsionerny komertsiyny bank "Personalny Komputer" ("Personal Computer" Joint-Stock Commercial Bank): Sahaydachny St., 17; tel. 225-22-29, 291-86-20, 291-86-85. • Aktsionerny komertsiyny bank "Lehbank" ("Lehbank" — Joint-Stock Commercial Bank): Kuybyshev St., 8/10; tel. 220-87-29, 227-41-32. • Komertsiyny bank "Brokbiznes Bank" ("Brokbiznes" — Commercial Bank): Rustaveli St., 3; tel. 294-64-40, 227-32-68. • Haluzevy komertsiyny bank "Ukrmontazhspetsbank" (Branch of the "Ukrmontazhspetsbank" Commercial Bank): Stelmakh St., 10a; tel. 263-03-03, 263-32-09. • Aktsionerny bank "Inko" ("Inko" — Joint-Stock Bank): Mechnykov St., 18; tel. 294-92-19, 294-69-86, 290-71-30. • Ukrayinsky komertsiyny bank "Vidrodzhennya" ("Vidrodzhennya" — Ukrainian Commercial Bank): Kotsyubynsky St., 7-a; tel. 224-85-74, 221-30-40. • Kyivsky komertsiyny shlyakhovy bank "Kyivshlyakhbank" ("Kyivshlyakhbank" — Kyiv Commercial Roads Bank):

Andriyivsky uzviz. Old building.

Fizkulturna St., 9; 227-27-83, 227-24-74. • Aktsionerny komertsiyny "Hradobank" ("Hradobank" — Joint-Stock Commercial Bank): Barbyus St., 9a; tel. 268-84-93, 227-55-10. • Kyivsky aktsionerny komertsiyny "Birzhovy Bank" (Kyiv Joint-Stock Commercial Exchange Bank): Khoryv St., 1; tel. 416-31-20, 417-53-90. • Komertsiyny bank "Bank Dilovoho Spivrobitnytstva" (Commercial Bank of Business Cooperation): Rylsky St., 10; tel. 229-06-84, 229-73-82. • Haluzevy komertsiyny bank "Enerhobank" (Branch of the "Energy" Commercial Bank): Zankovetska St., 9/9; tel. 229-50-64, 291-75-36. • Aktsionerny komertsiyny inovatsiyny bank "Intelekt" ("Intelekt" Joint-Stock Commercial Innovation Bank): Osvita St., 4; tel. 245-42-01. • Aktsionerny komertsiyny bank "Ukrainska Finansova Hrupa" ("Ukrainian Financial Group" Joint-Stock Commercial Bank): Vokzalna St., 7; tel. 245-45-60. • Komertsiyny bank Kredytno-finansova spilka "Ekspobank" ("Expobank" Credit-Financial Union Commercial Bank): Volodarsky St., 2/4; tel. 212-24-49, 216-09-10, 216-16-76. • Komertsiyny poshtovo-oshchadny bank "Poshtabank" ("Poshtabank" — Commercial Postal-Savings Bank): Mykilsko-Botanichna St., 6/8; tel. 220-45-04, 229-69-71. • Komertsiyny bank "Mebliprombank" ("Mebliprombank" — Commercial Furniture Industry Bank): Khreshchatyk St., 34; tel. 225-61-85, 225-21-06. • Komertsiyny bank "Kontynent" ("Kontynent" — Commercial Bank): Hrushevsky St., 10; tel. 293-58-72. • Komertsiyny aktsionerny bank "Alyanskredytbank" ("Alliance Credit" Commercial Joint-Stock Bank): Saksahansky St., 93; tel. 220-95-40, 220-64-15. • Komertsiyny bank "Sana" ("Sana" Commercial Bank): Sahaydachny St., 37-a; tel. 416-40-84. • Aktsionerno-komertsiyny bank "Interbank" ("Interbank" Joint-Stock Commercial Bank): Yaroslaviv Val, 36; tel. 212-40-20, 212-45-15. • Aktsionerno-komertsiyny bank "Aval" ("Aval" Joint-Stock Commercial Bank): Leskov St., 9; tel. 294-96-91, 295-04-31. • Aktsionerny bank "Antek" ("Antek" Joint-Stock Bank): Povitroflotsky Prospekt, 94; tel. 271-71-54. • Aktsionerny komertsiyny bank "Slavutych" ("Slavutych" Joint-Stock Commercial Bank): Frunze St., 47; tel. 417-30-88, 417-01-91. • Vseukrayinsky aktsionerny bank "Vabank" ("Vabank" All-Ukrainian Joint-Stock Bank): Pavlivska St., 4/8; tel. 216-01-57, 216-65-16. • Komertsiyny bank "Aleks" ("Alex" Commercial Bank): Gorky St., 114; tel. 268-76-24. • Komertsiyny bank "Edland" ("Edland" Commercial Bank): Vorovsky St., 22; tel. 224-21-76. • Kyivsky pryvatny bank "Kyivpryvatbank" ("Kyivpryvatbank" Kyiv Private Bank): Kotovsky St., 27; tel. 244-64-80. • Aktsionerno-komertsiyny bank "Mriya"

("Mriya" Joint-Stock Commercial Bank): Hoholivska St., 22/24; tel. 216-63-35, 216-68-37. • Ukrayinsky bank ekolohiyi ta medytsyny "Ekomedbank" ("Ekomedbank" Ukrainian Bank of Ecology and Medicine): Vorovsky St., 20; tel. 216-06-86. • Aktsionerny komertsiyny bank "Heosantris" ("Heosantris" Joint-Stock Commercial Bank): Pirohovsky St., 19/2; tel. 261-90-20, 261-99-12. • Aktsionerny komertsiyny bank "Liha" ("Liha" Joint-Stock Commercial Bank): Hrushevsky St., 30/1; tel. 290-67-48, 290-17-71. • Komertsiyny bank "Universalny" ("Universalny" Commercial Bank): Frunze St., 61; tel. 417-37-35. • Aktsionerny komertsiyny bank "Praveks-Bank" ("Praveks-Bank" Joint-Stock Commercial Bank): Klovsky Uzviz, 9/2.

CURRENCY EXCHANGE

Budbank, Shevchenkivsky Univermah: O. Teliha St., 17. (Metro; Shulyavska; Trolleybus 27). • "Azhio" Bank, "Escom" Store: M. Zankovetska St., 3/1. (Metro: Khreshchatyk). • "Yunist" Store: prospekt Peremohy, 3. (Metro: Vokzalna). • Kyiv Narodny Bank: T. Shevchenko Blvd., 38/40. (Metro: Universytet). • "Lehbank", "Dilova Moda" Store: O. Pushkin St., 9. (Metro: Teatralna). • "Perlyna" Store: Khreshchatyk, 21. (Metro: Khreshchatyk). • Brokbiznes Bank, Hotel "Dnipro": Khreshchatyk, 1/2. (Metro: Maydan Nezalezhnosti; Trolleybus 20). • Airline Cash Registers: prospekt Peremohy, 2 (Metro: Vokzalna and Sreetcar 2 or metro Universytet and Trolleybus 5, 8, 9, 17). • Bank "Inco", Hotel "Kyiv": M. Hrushevsky St., 26/1. (Metro: Arsenalna; Trolleybus 20). • Movie Theater "Kyivska Rus'": Artem St., 93. (Metro: Beresteyska; Trolleybus 14, 15). • Zaliznychny Vokzal (Train Station): Pryvokzalna Ploshcha, 3. (Metro: Vokzalna). • Bank "Vidrodzhennya", Airline Cash Registers: K. Marx St., 6. (Metro: Maydan Nezalezhnosti). • Hotel "Lybid": ploshcha Peremohy, 1 (Metro: Vokzalna and Streetcar 2 or metro Universytet and Trolleybus 5, 8, 9, 17). • "Ukrayinska Finansova Hrupa": Respublikansky Stadion. (Metro: Respublikansky Stadion). • Univermah "Ukrayina": ploshcha Peremohy. (Metro Vokzalna and Streetcar 2 or Trolleybus 5, 8, 9, 17). • Hradobank, Hotel "Sport": Chervonoarmiyska St., 55. (Metro: Respublikansky Stadion or Trolleybus 9, 17). • "Ukrayinsky Dim": Khreshchatyk, 2. (Metro: Maydan Nezalezhnosti). • Interbank, "Yulia" Store: Yaroslaviv Val, 26. (Metro: Zoloti Vorota).

Besarabian Market.

Ukrayina Palace of Culture.

BOOKSTORES

Lileya: Khreshchatyk St., 5. • **Zmina:** Khreshchatyk St., 15. • **Akademknyha:** Khmelnytsky St., 42. • **Knyhy:** prospekt Peremohy, 74. • **Suchasnyk:** prospekt Peremohy, 29. • **Yuvileyny:** prospekt Sorokrichchya Zhovtnya, 17. • **Mystetstvo:** Khreshchatyk St., 26. • **Syayvo:** Chervonoarmiyska St., 6. • **Inozemna Knyha:** Chervonoarmiyska St., 48.

TOURISM

Tourism State Committee of Ukraine: Hospitalna St., 12; tel. 225-30-51; Fax: 224-59-76.

Tours: Kyiv-Lviv-Uzhhorod-Chernivtsi-Odesa-Kyiv; Kyiv-Lviv-Chernivtsi-Vinnytsya-Kyiv; Kyiv-Odesa-Lviv-Uzhhorod-Mukacheve-Lviv-Kyiv; Kyiv-Kaniv-Cherkasy-Moryntsi-Shevchenkove-Kyiv; Kyiv-Cherkasy-Mizhhirrya-Kaniv-Zolotonosha-Cherkasy-Pereyaslav-Khmelnytsky-Kyiv; Kyiv-Zaporizhzhya-Dnipropetrovsk-Kharkiv-Poltava-Kyiv.

Ukrintur: Yaroslaviv Val, 36; tel. 212-58-14, 212-59-30; Fax: 212-58-40.

"Suputnyk": prospekt Sorokrichchya Zhovtnya, 70; tel. 263-71-24, 263-42-79; Fax: 264-95-34.

"Ukrzarubizhturservice": B. Khmelnycky St., 26; tel. 224-72-58, 224-69-58; Fax: 224-69-58.

"Ukrproftur": Velyka Zhytomyrska St., 15; tel. 517-60-56, 226-27-78; Fax: 244-37-17.

Kyiv Tourism Bureau: Volodymyrska St., 17; tel. 229-39-97.

Association of Commercial Tourists Organizations: Desyatynna St., 4/6; tel. 228-88-46, 220-51-55; Fax: 212-20-43.

POST OFFICES, TELEPHONES, FAX

Kyiv Main Post Office: Khreshchatyk St., 22; tel. 065. • General Director, Serhiy M. Sklyarenko: tel. 226-21-32; 229-20-29. • Chief Engineer, Mykola I. Lisovenko: tel. 228-03-75.

Communications branches: (the main ones, by No.):

No. 1: Khreshchatyk St., 22; tel. 228-17-93. • **No. 22:** Vasylkivska St., 38; tel. 263-40-48. • **No. 35:** Urytsky St., 23; tel. 276-32-71. • **No. 105:** prospekt Vozzyednannya, 6; tel. 552-81-52. • **No. 195:** Lesya Ukrayinka Blvd., 28-a; tel. 296-57-15. • **No. 211:** Zalka St., 2/12; tel. 419-76-88. • **No. 215:** prospekt Svobody, 26; tel. 434-95-31.

Telegraph Offices (24-hours): Suvorov St., 18/20; tel. 290-84-20. • Train station; tel. 224-09-94. • Puhachov St., 6/29; tel. 213-33-10. • Prospekt Peremohy, 128/2; tel. 444-20-36. • Prospekt Sorokrichchya Zhovtnya, 110; tel. 263-33-12. • Kharkivske shosse, 2; tel. 552-61-22. • Aviakonstruktor Antonov St., 7; tel. 276-73-14. • Prospekt Obolonsky, 14; tel. 418-79-68. • Prospekt Mayakovskoho, 45; tel. 515-45-32.

TELEGRAM SERVICE: tel. 066. 24-hour service, seven days a week, including holidays. Telegrams sent to all points in Ukraine and to the newly-independent states from residential phones on credit.

Businesses, organizations, institutions, embassies, etc. may sign a contract with the telegram service (tel. 228-79-54) to obtain a special telephone number for 24-hour service.

INTERNATIONAL EXPRESS MAIL EMS: Khreshchatyk St., 22 (entrance on Maydan Nezalezhnosti). Service to 50 countries: tel. 228-33-52. Maximum mailing weight: 10 kg.; books: 3 kg., payable in Ukrainian currency.

Similar services are offered at the Communications point in the Intouryst Hotel: Hospitalna St., 12; tel. 220-70-54, payable in foreign currency; Prolisok motel-camping site: prospekt Peremohy, 139; tel. 44-87-90, payable in foreign currency.

EXPRESS MAIL: To 39 population points in Ukraine, cities in Belarus, Moscow. Packages (to 8 kg.) and letters are delivered the following day. Mail for delivery must be brought in by the designated time to Communications branch No. 32, Saksahansky St., 88; tel. 225-23-10. (Streetcar No. 1, 5, 9, 10, 35; trolleybus No. 2).

Packages and letters for delivery in Ukraine are delivered the following day.

10:00: For delivery to Chernivtsi and Simferopol;

12:30: For delivery to Cherkasy, Kherson, Ivano-Frankivsk, Kirovohrad, Mykolayiv, Odesa, Uzhhorod;

15:00: For delivery to Bila Tserkva, Dnipropetrovsk, Donetsk, Ivankiv, Kaharlyk, Kryvy Rih, Luhansk, Lviv, Makariv, Poltava, Rokytne, Kvyr, Stavyshche, Ternopil, Tarashcha, Tetiyiv, Volodarka, Zaporizhzhya, Yahotyn.

19:00: For delivery to Chernihiv, Kharkiv, Khmelnytsky, Kremenchuh, Konotop, Kovel, Lutsk, Rivne, Sumy, Vinnytsya, Zhytomyr.

Building of the Supreme Rada of Ukraine.

Building of the Cabinet of Ministers of Ukraine.

Delivery to Belarus:

10:00: For delivery to Minsk; 12:30: Brest; 19:00: Homel, Mohylyov, Vitebsk.

Delivery to the Russian Federation:

15:00: For delivery to Moscow (only packages accepted; delivery on the third day).

Fax: Main post office (operations hall), Khreshchatyk St., 22; tel. 228-12-91.

To obtain information (letters, etc.), citizens of foreign countries can use the fax No.: 228-72-72. They must first register their names at this service point: TELEFAX. Payable in Ukrainian currency.

MEDICAL SERVICES

Emergency: tel. 03.

Kyiv Emergency Station: Khmelnytsky St., 17-b. Chief physician: Anatoliy V. Vershyhora; tel. 224-51-86; Senior physician: tel. 225-41-42; Physician on duty of the Main Territorial Medical Association of the City of Kyiv: tel. 228-46-40.

Emergency Hospital: Bratyslavska St., 3. Chief physician: Heorhiy H. Roshchyn; tel. 518-03-35; Physician on duty: tel. 518-04-96.

Central Scientific-Practical Medical Association of the City of Kyiv:

Clinical Hospital for Adults: Liebknecht St., 39/1; information: tel. 224-20-22; Chief physician: Kateryna S. Palamarchuk: tel. 224-53-52; Physician on duty: 225-11-53.

Clinical-Diagnostic Center (Polyclinic): Mechnikov St., 1. Patient registration: tel. 224-73-64; Director: 227-67-97; the stomatologist and ophthalmologist provide 24-hour care, 7 days a week, including holidays.

Clinical Hospital: Pidvysotsky St., 4-a. Provides service to foreign citizens with injuries and illnesses of the muscular-skeletal system (fractures and joint dislocations, etc.) Registration: tel. 286-40-14; trauma and orthopedics division: tel. 268-35-32, 268-35-14. Service 24-hours, 7 days a week, including holidays.

Pharmacies: No. 1: Volodymyrska St., 51/53; Director: Klavdiya H. Yevtushenko; tel. 224-81-66. • **No. 7:** Artem St., 10; tel. 212-11-28; Director: Tetyana P. Pereverzyeva; tel. 212-10-00. • **No. 24:** Chervonoarmiyska St., 10; tel. drug prescriptions payable in currency; Director: Vira H. Mala; tel. 224-14-33. • **No. 70:** Chervonoarmiyska St., 81; Director: Halyna H. Zasukha; tel. 269-62-21.

Farma Company: Prorizna St., 3; drug prescriptions payable in currency only; Director: Ihor V. Budko; tel. 228-28-71.

Farmatsiya Pharmaceutical Association: Franko St., 38-b. General Director: Anatoliy L. Boyko; tel. 224-91-41; vice-director: Valentyna H. Babyak; tel. 224-69-19; vice-director: Volodymyr V. Rudenko; tel. 224-92-03.

Ministry of Health: Hrushevsky St., 7. Minister Yuriy P. Spizhenko; Reception: tel. 226-22-05; fax: 293-69-75.

Main Territorial Medical Association of the City of Kyiv: Prorizna St., 19. General Director: Volodymyr D. Yurchenko; Reception: tel. 228-40-41; fax: 228-01-03.

TRANSPORTATION

Train Station: Vokzalna Ploshcha (Metro: Vokzalna Station); tel. 005; Station chief: tel. 265-30-53.

Advance train tickets: Shevchenko Blvd., 38/40.

Train tickets for international travel: train station (2nd floor), 24-hour service, except between 2-3, 7-8, 14-15, 19-20 hrs.

Boryspil Airport. International Flights: tel. 296-72-43; Airport Director: tel. 296-74-99; 296-74-21; information: tel. 296-76-09. Airport buses depart from prospekt Peremohy.

Zhulyany Airport. Information: tel. 272-12-01; Airport Director: tel. 276-81-38.

Zonal Agency for Connecting Flights: Menzhynsky St., 1. Ticket reservation office open until 18:00; Sundays — 15:00; tel. 274-42-33, 224-05-01, 225-32-17. Agency branches: Mayakovsky St., 22; tel. 515-06-33; information and ticket reservations for national flights and to the newly independent states of the former USSR: tel. 062; information on international flights of Ukrainian airlines and airlines of the newly-independent states, ticket reservations: tel. 052.

Central Bus Terminus: Moskovska Ploshcha, 3; tel. 265-04-30; Director: tel. 265-57-74.

Advance bus tickets (all destinations): Lesya Ukrayinka Blvd., 14; tel. 225-50-15, 224-14-01.

Other bus depots:

Polissya: ploshcha Shevchenka,; tel. 430-35-35, 430-35-54; Pivdenna: prospekt Hlushkova, 3; tel. 263-12-51; 263-40-04.

Darnytsya: prospekt Gagarina, 1; tel. 559-64-95, 559-46-18.

Dachna: prospekt Peremohy, 172; tel. 444-14-03.

Podil: Nyzhniy Val, 15-a; tel. 417-37-20, 417-35-42.

Ferry Station: Poshtova Ploshcha, 3 (Metro: Poshtova Ploshcha Station). Information office: tel. 416-73-72; Manager on duty: tel. 416-75-61. Crossings

Khreshchatyk.

from April to October. Express Dnipro river crossings available on the "Meteor" and "Voskhod" motor vessels. The most popular river crossings are to Kaniv and to Shevchenko's grave on Tarasova Hora. Tickets may be purchased 1-5 days in advance at the Kyiv ferry station.

Ukrrichflot Inter-Branch State Association: Nyzhniy Val, 51. Director of Passenger and Tourist Service: Anatoliy I. Shyty; tel. 417-44-35; fax: 417-15-93; telex: 131-423.

Trolleybus and streetcar service from 6:00-24:00 daily; information on routes, lost and found department: tel. 446-71-51.

As a rule bus service is available from 6:00-24:00; irregular times for some routes. Central Dispatcher Service: tel. 225-03-06.

Kyiv metro (subway) service from 6:00-13:00 a.m., daily. Kyiv Metro Administration: prospekt Peremohy, 35. Director: Mykola Balatsky; tel. 228-90-00; lost and found: tel. 226-38-09. In case of emergency, contact manager of next metro station.

AUTO SERVICING

Avtoservis: Tsyvilnoyi oborony St., 4; tel. 263-53-75; Kharkivske shose, 179; tel. 556-81-83.

Road Service Complex: Hurovshchyna, Kyiv-Svyatoshynsky district, 34 km a/d E-40, Kyiv-Chop.

Winner Ford-Kyiv: Natodnoho Opolchennya St., 16-a; tel. 271-79-93; Fax: 220-01-81. Ford.

Ilta-Kyiv: Zaliznychne Shosse, 25; tel. 268-40-01. Peugeot.

"Mercedes": Zroshuvalna St., 7; tel. 556-00-21. Mercedes.

"Fiat": L. Ukrayinka Blvd., 17; tel. 219-24-45, 219-24-55. Fiat.

"BMW": Mykhaylivska St., 18; tel. 228-38-61, 268-21-49. BMW.

"Honda": prospekt Peremohy, 57; tel. 442-20-19. Honda.

Ukraina-Motors: Chervonoarmiyska St., 13; tel. 224-89-33. Cadillac, Chevrolet.

"Citroyen": prospekt Peremohy, 139; tel. 444-24-97. Citroyen.

"Minolta Trading Ukraine": Bereznyakivska St., 28; tel. 550-02-03. Mazda.

Transservice LTD.: Osvity St. 4; tel. 276-40-04. Towing, gasoline.

"Druzhba": Tovarna St., 10; tel. 269-34-70. (HAZ, VAZ, ZAZ).

"Pechersky": amyshna St., 4; tel. 295-23-32. (HAZ, VAZ, ZAZ).

Servicing and towing: prospekt Vozyednannya, 7-b; tel. 558-47-71. Luhova St., 15; tel. 410-24-52.

SERVICE STATIONS

Kharkivske Chosse, 179; tel. 556-91-83. (Toyota, VAZ). • Prov. Perspektyvny, 4; tel. 269-90-45. (Reneau, VAZ, Moskvich). • Heroyiv Oborony St., 4; tel. 263-53-75. (Nissan, VAZ, ZAZ). • Stolychne Shosse, 90; tel. 296-04-10 (HAZ, VAZ, Moskvich). • Murmansk St., tel. 559-18-44. (Moskvich, VAZ). • Prospekt Chervonykh

Kozakiv, 22; tel. 419-98-16. (Moskvich, VAZ). • Tupolyev St., 19; tel. 442-72-75. (HAZ, VAZ, Moskvich). • Hlushkov St., 67; tel. 266-37-23. (VAZ, Moskvich).

DENOMINATIONS

Ukrainian Orthodox Church — Kyivan Patriarchate. His Holiness Volodymyr, Patriarch of Kyiv and Ukraine; Metropolitan Filaret, assistant to the Patriarch of Kyiv and Ukraine. Office of the Patriarchate: Pushkinska St., 36; tel. 224-10-96. Volodymyrsky (St. Volodymyr's) Cathedral: Shevchenko Blvd., 20; tel. 225-03-62; Masses served daily at 9:00, 18:00; Sundays and holy days: 7:00, 10:00.

Ukrainian Greek-Catholic Church: Pokrovska St., 6; tel. 416-14-77, 416-11-80. Father Valeriy Shkarubsky, tel. 477-88-84. Religious services daily at 9:00, 19:00; Sundays and holy days: 10:00. Masses are served also at Askoldova Mohyla.

Metropolitanate of the Ukrainian Orthodox Church (Moscow Patriarchate): Sichnevoho povstannya St., 25; tel. 290-15-08. Metropolitan Volodymyr of Kyiv and Ukraine. **Trapezna (Refectory) Church of the Kyivan Cave Monastery:** Sichnevoho povstanny St., 25; tel. 290-15-08; Masses served daily at 9:00, 16:30; Saturdays: 16:30.

Union of Evangelical Christians-Baptists of Ukraine: Tolstoy St., 3-a; tel. 224-82-41. **Main church:** Yamska St., 70; tel. 268-52-65; religious services on Tuesdays at 19:00, Thursdays at 19:00, Sundays at 10:00, 17:00.

Eparchy of the Rus' Orthodox Old-Rite Church of Kyiv and Ukraine (Treaty of Bila Krynytsya): Bishop Ioann of Kyiv and Ukraine. **Old-Rite Church:** Pochaynynska St., 26; tel. 416-42-28; Masses served on holy days and pre-holy day period from 8:00-10:00, 16:00; daily from 8:00-10:00.

Union of Christians of the Evangelical Faith of Ukraine: Vitryani Hory, 6-b; tel. 444-25-80. Head: Mykola A. Melnyk. **Prayer meetings:** Bilshovyk Building of Culture: prospekt Peremohy, 38; tel. 446-25-80; religious services: Sundays at 10:00, 14:00; Thursdays at 19:00; separate schedule for holy days. Karyerna St., 44; tel. 484-08-81; religious services: Sundays at 10:00, 18:00; Saturdays at 18:00; Wednesdays at 19:00.

Ukrainian Union Conference of Seventh Day Adventist Churches: Lukyanivska St., 9-b; tel. 417-56-88. President: Mykola A. Zhykalyuk. **Main church:** Yamska St., 70; tel. 268-52-65; religious services: Wednesdays and Fridays at 19:00; Saturdays at 10:00, 18:00; separate schedule for holy days.

German Evangelical-Lutheran Church of Ukraine. Church of St. Kateryna (St. Catherine's): Lyuteranska St., 22; tel. 293-63-19. Pastor: Akhim Rays. Religious services every Sunday and holy days at 10:00, 19:00.

Union of Jewish Religious Communities of Ukraine: Mayakovsky St., 49-a, apt. 18; tel. 543-90-55. President: Noyakh M. Dubynsky. **Kyiv Jewish Religious Community:** services in the Kyiv Choral Synagogue: Shchekavytska St., 29; tel.

416-13-83. Services daily at 8:00, 15:30; holy days of the Jewish calendar, every prayer on the appropriate day at 8:00.

Main Muslim Administration of Ukraine: Dehtyarivska St., 58, apt. 156; tel. 446-17-70. Chief: Imam-Mukhtasyb Akhmed Tamym. Services held every Friday at 13:00; other days (winter) at 6:30, 12:00, 15:00, 17:00, 18:30 at Yaroslavska St., 31-b; tel. 416-03-53.

Union of the Sons and Daughters of the Native Ukrainian National Faith (RUN Faith): Koltsov Blvd., apt. 184; tel. 475-60-16. Vice-head: Valeriy V. Korobin. Times and place of services change: Saturdays and Sundays at 10:00, Wednesdays and Thursdays at 18:00, 19:00.

Union of Churches of the Seventh Day Adventist Reform Movement in Ukraine: Stelmakh St., 22; tel. 263-90-14. Vice-head: Anatoliy H. Bohatov. Religious services: prospekt Druzhby Narodiv, 5 (in the concert hall of the Druzhba Hotel); tel. 263-90-14; every Saturday at 10:00.

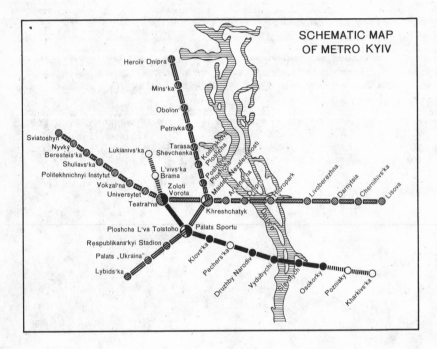

Kyiv Region

It is situated in north-central Ukraine in the forest and forest-steppe zone. The climate is temperate-continental. The Dnipro River and its tributaries, the Prypyat, Irpin, Desna, Ros, and others, are the principle rivers.

Created in 1932. Population (excluding Kyiv): 1,938,000. Area: 28,900 sq. km.

History

The territory of the Kyiv region was first populated in the Paleolithic era. A nucleus of Eastern Slavic tribes was formed during the first millennium. The Kyivan Rus'-Ukraine state was established in the 4th century; its principle cities were Pereyaslav, Bilhorod, Vyshhorod, and Vasyliv. The state culture was highly-developed, particularly in such centers as the Kyivan Cave Monastery and St. Sophia's Cathedral, where the first library in Kyivan Rus' was established.

The term "Ukraine" as applied to the Kyiv territory was first used in 1187. The Kyivan Principality was greatly weakened by the Tatar-Mongol invasions and in 1362 it came under the rule of Lithuania. In 1471 Kyiv became a voivodeship (palatinate). After the Treaty of Lublin, uniting Lithuania and Poland, Polish rule in the Kyiv region intensified.

The second half of the 15th century saw the emergence of the Zaporozhyan Kozaks. The entire Kyiv region was affected by the major peasant-Kozak uprisings and

Kyiv. B. Khmelnytsky Square.

events of the national-liberation war of 1648-54. Kozak regiments were formed in Kyiv, Bila Tserkva, and Pereyaslav. As a result of the Treaty of Pereyaslav, which united Ukraine with Muscovy, Right-Bank Ukraine was annexed by the Russian Empire, whose policies led to the abolition of the Hetmanate in 1764 and of the Kozak regimental administration in 1781. Kyiv then became a viceregency and later a guberniya (province).

The Kyiv region was the arena of the Ukrainian struggle for independence during 1917-20. Alternately active in this region were the armies of the Ukrainian National Republic, the Ukrainian Hetman State, and the Directory.

The most ancient monuments of the material culture which have been excavated in this region are 15 to 20 thousand years old. Among them are 50 settlements of Trypillian culture, 90 ancient towns and graves mounds dating to the Scythian period.

The chief monuments of Zarubynetsky Chernyakhiv cultures have been Ukrainian scholars' main focus of study. Dozens of monumental stone and wooden structures and fortifications, e.g. the Dnipro River bridge (1015) attest to the advanced development of building technology in Kyivan Rus'-Ukraine.

The region is also rich in architectural structures of the 18th-19th centuries, some of which reflect the significant influence of folk architecture.

PROMINENT INDIVIDUALS

BORN IN THE REGION:

Sholom Aleichem-Rabynovych (1859-1916), Yiddish writer; Pereyaslav (now Pereyaslav-Khmelnytsky). • **K. Bilokur** (1900-61), artist; village of Bohdanivka in the Yahotynsky district. • **P. Chubynsky** (1839-84), ethnographer; Boryspil. • **P. Demutsky** (1860-1927), composer; village of Yanyshivka (now Ivanivka) in the Stavyshchensky district. • **I. Drach** (1936), writer, political and civic activist; village of Telizhentsi in the Tetiyivsky district. • **O. Koshyts** (1875-1944), conductor, composer; village of Romashky in the Myronivsky district. • **L. Kostenko** (1930), poetess; village of Rzhyshchiv in the Kaharlytsky district. • **H. Kosynka-Strilets** (1899-1934), writer, executed; village of Shcherbakivka in the Obukhivsky district. • **I. Mazepa** (1644-1709), Hetman; village of Mazepyntsi in the Bila Tserkva district. • **P. Popovych** (1930), first Ukrainian cosmonaut, civic activist; Uzyn. • **I. Soshenko** (1807-76), painter; Bohuslav. • **D. Tuptalo** (1651-1709), writer, religious and cultural figure; Makariv. • **Yaroslav Mudry (the Wise)** (978-1054), Grand Prince of Kyivan Rus'-Ukraine; Vyshhorod.

BURIED IN THE REGION:

K. Bilokur (1900-61), artist; village of Bohdanivka in the Yahotynsky district. • **P. Chubynsky** (1839-84), ethnographer; Boryspil. • **V. Samiylenko** (1864-1925), writer; Boyarka. • **K. Stetsenko** (1882-1922), composer; village of Vepryk in the Fastiv district.

TOURING HISTORIC CITIES AND VILLAGES

ANTONIVKA

Village in the Stavyshchensky district, 25 km from the Zhashkiv railway station.

RIZDVA BOHORODYTSI (NATIVITY OF THE MOTHER OF GOD) CHURCH, 1777. An example of traditional wood architecture of Right-Bank Ukraine. Fragments of wall paintings have been preserved. Near the village are ruins of an ancient Ukrainian city of the 10th-12th centuries.

BYKIVNYANSKY FOREST, Brovary district, 1.5 km from the village of Bykivnya on the Kyiv-Chernihiv Highway near Kyiv.

The site of mass graves of victims of the Stalinist purges, executed between 1929-41. Approximate number of victims: 200,000, among them thousands of Ukrainian intellectuals. A monument is located on the gravesite.

BILA TSERKVA

City on the Ros River, 87 km from Kyiv. Population: 181,000. Bila Tserkva is located on the site of Yuryev, a city founded in 1032 by Grand Prince Yaroslav the Wise. The present name first appeared in 1334. After being destroyed by the Tatar-Mongols, Bila Tserkva was rebuilt and came under the rule of Lithuania and later, the Lithuanian-Polish state. In the late 16th century the population of Bila Tserkva took an active part in the uprisings led by K. Kosynsky and S. Nalyvayko. The city's history is closely intertwined with the national-liberation struggle of 1648-54. In 1651 B. Khmelnytsky signed the Treaty of Bila Tserkva in this city.

Units of free Kozaks and the Sichovi Striltsi (Sich Sharpshooters), who fought against the Bolsheviks, were formed here in 1917.

Bila Tserkva. Cathedral of the Transfiguration, 1833-39.

OLEKSANDRIYA TREE PARK, 1793-99. Located between Skvyrsky Road and the Ros river. Architect: D. Botani; landscape artist: A. Stanhe. An example of a landscaped park of the 18th-19th centuries. More than 600 species of exotic trees and shrubs grow in the park.

PREOBRAZHENSKY (TRANSFIGURATION) CATHEDRAL, 1833-39. Built in the Classical style. (Gagarin St.).

MYKOLAYIVSKA (ST. NICHOLAS') CHURCH, 1706. Completed in 1852. Has an unusual asymmetrical structure. (Gagarin St.).

ST. IOAN PREDTECHA (ST. JOHN THE

*Fastiv. Pokrovska Church,
1779-81.*

BAPTIST) ROMAN CATHOLIC CHURCH, 1812. Situated on Zamkova Hora, on the site of a cathedral of the city of Yuryev. A classical Roman Catholic church with Corinthian porticos.

Bila Tserkva also has an Ethnographic Museum and a monument to B. Khmelnytsky.

BOHUSLAV

City on the Ros river, 183 km from Kyiv; railway station. Population: 20,000.

In the period of Rus'-Ukraine it was one of the largest fortified cities on the southern border. The original name of Bohuslavl was first mentioned in the chronicle in 1195. In 1240 it was destroyed by the Tatar-Mongols. Bohuslav came under Lithuanian rule in 1362 and from 1569 was part of the Lithuanian-Polish state. B. Khmelnytsky assembled his armies here in 1648, 1651, 1654, and 1655. Bohuslav once again came under Polish rule in 1667 and was the site of popular uprisings led by Hetman S. Samus and later, M. Zaliznyak, M. Shvachka, and others. Came under Russian imperial rule in 1793.

Bohuslav was visited several times by T. Shevchenko, who incorporated historical events connected to this city into his poetry. The city was also an important center of decorative weaving.

TROYITSKA (HOLY TRINITY) CHURCH, 1862. Built in the late Classical style. (Marx St.).

Also located in the city: Villa-Museum of the artist I. Soshenko, a monument to Marusya Bohuslavka, two historical-ethnographic museums, and an art museum.

BUSHEVE

Village in the Rokytnyansky district, 12 km from the district center.

TROYITSKA (HOLY TRINITY) CHURCH, 1750. The refined composition of the central section of the structure and unique wooden porticos make this one of the finest examples of wood architecture of Right-Bank Ukraine.

The ruins of an ancient Slavic city of the 6th-9th centuries and the period of Kyivan Rus'-Ukraine are located near the village.

FASTIV

City on the Unava River, 64 km from Kyiv; a railway station. Population: 55,000.

First documented references to the city appear in 1390. Was devastated by Tatar invasions in the 15th century. Settlement commenced in the early part of the 16th century and Fastiv's rise to prominence is associated with the activities of S. Paliy. In 1768 the Haydamaky leaders M. Shvachka and A. Zhurba made their base in Fastiv.

POKROVSKA (PROTECTION OF THE BLESSED VIRGIN MARY) CHURCH, 1779-81. Celebrated for its unusually harmonious proportions and refinement of forms. Considered a masterpiece of Ukrainian wood architecture.

ROMAN CATHOLIC CHURCH, 1903-11. Built in the city center by the architect V. Dombrovsky.

KOZHANKA

Village in the Fastiv district, 3 km from the Kozhanka railway station.

POKROVSKA (PROTECTION OF THE BLESSED VIRGIN MARY) CHURCH, 1761. Has a unique structure; a fine example of wood architecture of Right-Bank Ukraine.

KRENYCHI

Village in the Obukhivsky district, 18 km from the district center.

POKROVSKA (PROTECTION OF THE BLESSED VIRGIN MARY) CHURCH, 1761. A wooden bell tower was built next to the church in 1850. Has unique archaic features and is a rare example of the most ancient traditions of Ukrainian wood architecture.

PARKHOMIVKA

Village in the Volodarsky district, 25 km from the Bila Tserkva railway station.

POKROVSKA (PROTECTION OF THE BLESSED VIRGIN MARY) CHURCH, 1903-06. Designed by V. Pokrovsky. The monumental mosaics, designed by M. Rerikh, are remarkable for their harmonious proportions and use of color.

Parkhomivka. Pokrovska Church, 1903-06.

PEREYASLAV-KHMELNYTSKY (until 1943 — Pereyaslav)

City on the shores of the Trubizh and Alta Rivers, 28 km from the Pereyaslav railway station and 9 km from the port of Pereyaslav on the Dnipro river. Population: 24,000.

The city is first mentioned in the treaty signed by Rus' and Byzantium in 907 as one of the three largest cities in the Kyivan state. It was a fortress on the southern border and an important crafts and trading center. From the second half of the 12th century the city was the center of a large independent principalities ruled by the Princes Volodymyr Monomakh, Yuriy Dolhoruky, Volodymyr Hlibovych, and others. After the introduction of Christianity it became the base of the Pereyaslav eparchy. The city suffered extensive damage during the 13th-15th centuries and played an important role in the formation of the Kozaks during the 15th-16th centuries. The Treaty of Pereyaslav, by which Ukraine was united as an equal partner with Muscovy, was signed here in 1654.

A collegium was established in Pereyaslav in 1738. The philosopher H. Skovoroda taught here in 1753. The Ukrainian poet T. Shevchenko lived here in 1845 and 1859.

BORYSOHLIBSKA (BORYS' AND HLIB'S) CHURCH, 1839. Built in the late Classical style with features of provincial architecture.

VOZNESENSKY (ASCENSION) MONASTERY, 17th-18th cent. The monastery complex is one of the finest examples of Ukrainian architecture. Each of its structures is of great historic and artistic worth. (Ploshcha Vozyednannya)

VOZNESENSKY (ASCENSION) CATHEDRAL, 1695-1700. Built with funds provided by Hetman I. Mazepa. Features of Baroque architecture are brilliantly reflected in its spacious composition. (Skovoroda St.).

Pereyaslav-Khmelnytsky. Bell tower of St. Nicholas' Church, 1745.

BELL TOWER, 1770-76. Built in the Baroque style.

COLLEGIUM, 1753-57.

THE EARTHEN RAMPARTS OF THE DYTYNETS (FORTRESS) AND CITY, 11th-12th cent. The castle is surrounded by trenches and 17-18 m-high walls; 18 m wide. (Corner of Gorky and Velyka Pidvalna Streets).

MYKHAYLIVSKA (ST. MICHAEL'S) CHURCH, 1646-66; **BELL TOWER,** 1745. Interior wall paintings executed in the 18th-19th centuries by artists of the Kyivan school have been preserved. Today it houses the Ethnography Division of the municipal Historical Museum. The church structure is a rare example of Ukrainian architecture of the first half of the 18th century. (Moskovska St., 34).

Monuments to T. Shevchenko and H. Skovoroda are located in Pereyaslav-Khmelnytsky. The Historical-Cultural Preserve includes the Historical, Folk Architecture and Folkways museums; the H. Skovoroda Memorial Museum; the building in which T. Shevchenko stayed in 1845 and 1859; and a museum dedicated to the Yiddish writer Sholom-Aleichem.

Sulymivka. Pokrovska Church, 1622-29.

SULYMIVKA

Village in the Baryshivsky district, 4 km from the Sulymivka railway station.

Founded by Hetman I. Sulyma in the early 17th century.

POKROVSKA (PROTECTION OF THE BLESSED VIRGIN MARY) CHURCH, 1622-29. Built in the style of tripartite Ukrainian churches with funds provided by Hetman I. Sulyma.

TARHAN

Village in the Volodarsky district, 30 km from the Bila Tserkva railway station.

A monument to the victims of the famine-genocide of 1932-33 is located in the village cemetery.

VASYLKIV

City on the Stuhna River, 36 km from Kyiv; a railway station. Population: 36,000.

Vasylkiv was founded in 988 by Prince Volodymyr the Great and until 1157 was known as Vasyliv, in honor of the Prince's Christian appellation. Was an important base of defense and one of the trading and crafts centers of Kyivan Rus'-Ukraine. For a period of time this city was also the center of an independent principality. Was destroyed by the Tatar-Mongols in 1240. During the second half of the 13th century Vasylkiv administered the affairs of the Kyivan Cave Monastery. Scholars speculate that Feodosiy Pechersky (Theodosius of the Caves), the abbot of the Kyivan Cave Monastery, was born in Vasylkiv (ca. 1036-74). From the mid-14th century the city was under Lithuanian rule and from 1654 — under Russia. Vasylkiv became the county center in 1797. In 1918-19 the city was wrested from Bolshevik control several times by Ukrainian armies.

*Vasylkiv. St. Nicholas'
Church, 1792.*

CATHEDRAL OF SS. ANTHONY AND THEODOSIUS', 1756-58. Architect: S. Kovnir. Its architectural forms and decor are typical of Ukrainian Baroque architecture. (Marx St.).

MYKOLAYIVSKA (ST. NICHOLAS') CHURCH, 1792. Combines features of the Classical style with typical Baroque elements. (Shevchenko St.)

ZHYTNI HORY

Village in the Rokytnyansky district, 4 km from the Rokytne railway station.

YOSYFIVSKA (ST. JOSEPH'S) CHURCH, 1766. Nineteenth century paintings have been preserved. This monument is renowned for the picturesqueness of its forms and slender proportions of its central section.

Remnants of six early Slav settlements of Chernyakhiv culture, as well as ancient cities dating back to the period of Kyivan Rus'-Ukraine, have been excavated in the vicinity of this village.

Cherkasy Region

Lies on both banks of the Dnipro River in the forest-steppe belt of central Ukraine. The right-bank part of the region lies in the Dnipro Upland; this part is an undulating plateau. The left-bank part of the region lies in the Dnipro Lowland. The climate is temperate-continental. Area: 20,900 sq. km. Population: 1,540,000. Created in 1954.

History

The earliest traces of human settlement date to the 7th-3rd cent. B.C. At the beginning of the new era Slavic tribes settled the territory which later became part of Kyivan Rus'-Ukraine. In 1239-40 these lands were devastated by the Tatars. In the second half of the 14th cent. they came under Lithuanian rule.

The history of Cherkasy region is tightly interwoven with the anti-Polish struggle of the Zaporozhian Kozaks in the years 1648-54 and the peasant uprisings known as Koliyivshchyna and the Haydamaky Movement. During the years 1648-60 the city of Chyhyryn was the Hetman's residence and an important political center in Ukraine. After the Treaty of Zboriv in 1649 six administrative-territorial units (regiments) were created here. In 1764 the Tsarist government abolished the Hetmanate and in 1781, the regimental administration.

*Monument
to T. Shevchenko in Kaniv.*

PROMINENT INDIVIDUALS

BORN IN THE REGION:

V. Chornovil (1937), human rights activist, publicist, political figure; in Yerky, Katerynopilsky district. • M. Dray-Khmara (1889-1937), writer; Mali Kanivtsi, Chornobayiv district; died in a Soviet prison. • P. Fylypovych (1891-1937), poet; in Kaytanivka, Katerynopil district; executed. • P. Hulak-Artemovsky (1790-1865), poet-fabulist; in Horodyshche. • S. Hulak-Artemovsky (1813-73), composer; in Horodyshche. • A. Livytsky (1879-1954), political figure, president of the Ukrainian National Rada-in-Exile; in Lipnyava, Zolotonosha district; died in Germany. • M. Maksymovych (1804-73), scholar, first dean of Kyiv University; in the settlement of Tymkivshchyna, now Bohuslavets, Zolotonosha district. • I. Nechuy-Levytsky (1838-1918), writer; in Stebliv. • T. Shevchenko (1814-61), the greatest poet of Ukraine, artist, political figure; in Moryntsi. • M. Starytsky (1840-1904), playwright; in Klishchyntsi, Chornobayiv district. • K. Szymanowski (1882-1937), Polish composer; in Tymoshivka, Mankivka district. • S. Yefremov (1876-1937), literary scholar, political figure; in Palchyk, now in Katerynopil district; died in a Soviet prison. • I. Yizhakevych (1864-1962), painter, graphics artist; in Vyzhnopil.

BURIED IN THE REGION:

B. Khmelnytsky (1595-1657), Hetman of Ukraine; in Subotiv. • M. Maksymovych (1804-73), historian; in Mykhaylova Hora. • T. Shevchenko (1814-61), the greatest poet of Ukraine; in Kaniv. • I. Soshenko (1807-76), artist; in Korsyn-Shevchenkivsky. • N. Surovtseva (1896-1985), writer, journalist, political figure; in Uman. • L. Symerenko (1855-1920), fruit plant scientist; in Mliyiv. • V. Symonenko (1935-63), poet; in Cherkasy.

CHERKASY

City and port on the Dnipro River, on the right bank of the Kremenchuk Reservoir, 240 km from Kyiv. Population: 305,000. Telephone code: 0472.

First mentioned in historical documents dating to 1384. In the late 15th cent. it was an important strong-point against the invading Tatars. In the early 16th cent. the majority of its population was comprised of Zaporozhian Kozaks. In 1648 it became a regimental city and in 1793 was annexed to the Russian Empire.

MONUMENTS

T. Shevchenko, 1964. Architects: M. Voronsky, S. Oliynyk, and V. Hnyezdilov. (Teatralna Ploshcha).

Old building.

B. Khmelnytsky, 1957. (Pershotravnevy Park).

I. Pidkova, 1986. Architects: I. Kulyk and V. Blushchuk. (Komsomolsky Skver.).

V. Symonenko, 1963. Architects: S. Hrabovsky and M. Kyrylenko. The monument is located at the poet's grave-site in the Odeska St. cemetery.

MUSEUMS

Regional Ethnography Museum: Slavy St., 1; tel. 45-11-46. • **Kobzar Book Museum:** Khreshchatyk St., 219; tel. 45-52-11. • **Art Museum:** Khreshchatyk St., 259; tel. 47-29-49.

THEATERS, PHILHARMONIC

Music and Drama Theater: Shevchenko St., 234; tel. 47-44-18. • **Puppet Theater:** Lenin St., 4; tel. 47-47-20. • **Philharmonic:** Khreshchatyk St., 194; tel. 47-30-56.

HIGHER EDUCATIONAL INSTITUTIONS

Pedagogical Institute: Shevchenko Blvd., 81. • **Scientific Research Institute of Technical-Economics Research:** Shevchenko Blvd., 460.

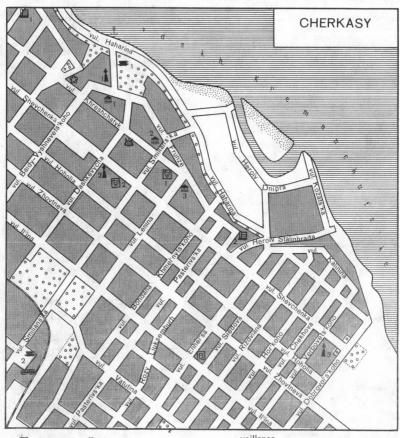

CHERKASY

B   Excursion office

▤   Hotels:
      1 Turyst
      2 Zhovtnevyi

🍴   Restaurants:
      1 Chaika
      2 Zustrich
      Note. Restaurants Turyst and
      Zhovtnevyi are attached to the
      hotels of the same names

🚃   Railway Station

⚓   River Station

▮   Monuments:
      1 Memorial plate on the house
      where in 1859 Taras. Shev-
      chenko lived under police sur-
veillance
      2 Taras Shevchenko
      3 Boian, legendary bard at the
turn of the 12th c.

🏛   Architectural monuments:
      1 Building of the former Slo-
vianskyi Hotel, early 20th c.
      2 Building of the former Com-
mercial Bank, 1914
      3 Building of the former Zemstvo
council, 1907—1912

✿   Museum of Local Lore

▣   Theaters:
      1 Puppet
      2 Taras Shevchenko Theater of Mu-
sic and Drama

🎵   Philharmonic Society

LIBRARIES, ARCHIVES

Scientific Library: Bayda-Vyshnevetsky St., 8. • Youth Library: Ilyin St., 285. • Children's Library: Kirov St., 24. • Regional Archive: Zhovtneva St., 244-a. • Municipal Archive: Hromov St., 12.

SPORTS COMPLEXES

Light Athletics Complex: Pasterovska St., 102; tel. 63-85-45. • Budivelnyk Sports Palace: Khimiky St., 50/1; tel. 64-74-34. • Swimming Pool: Komsomolska St., 78; tel. 7-62-73.

HOTELS

Rosava: Frunze St., 29; tel. 45-03-21. • Dnipro: Frunze St., 13; tel. 47-23-60.

RESTAURANTS, CAFES

Rosava: Frunze St., 29; tel. 11-32-91. • Tsentralny: Trydsyatyrichchya Peremohy St., 36; tel. 66-55-21. • Slavutych: Lisova St., 1; tel. 47-08-00. • Cherkasy: Lazarev St., 6; tel. 47-05-30. • Chayka: Parkovy Spusk, 3; tel. 47-45-26. • Yaroslavna: Bayda-Vyshnevetsky St., 26; tel. 45-51-25. • Roksolyana Pyvny Bar: Hromov St., 146; tel. 63-94-81; 63-89-74. • Astra Casino: Lisova St., 1; tel. 47-08-00.

STORES

Budynok Torhivli (Trade Building): Shevchenko Blvd., 207. • Univermah (Department Store): Hohol St., 274. • Sosnyak: Dakhnivska St., 23. • Yunist: Shevchenko Blvd., 224. • Dytyachy Svit (Children's Store): Dashkevych St., 26. • Khudozhniy Salon (Art): Bayda-Vyshnevetsky St., 28. • Vyshyvanka: Khreshchatyk St., 219. • Knyhy (Books): Khreshchatyk St., 200. • Kobzar: Krupska St., 50. • Druzhba (Foreign-Language Books): Lazarev St., 2. • Komersant: Ordzhonikidze St., 43.

BANKS

National Bank of Ukraine (regional branch): Dashkevych St., 23; tel. 47-30-42.

TOURISM

Inturyst-Cherkasy: Lazarev St., 1; tel. 47-51-38; 47-31-01.

Local excursions: "In the Footsteps of Shevchenko" (Zvenyhorod district; Kaniv); "Kozak and Haydamaky Districts" (Chyhyryn, Subotiv).

Literary-Memorial excursion: To sites associated with the poet V. Symonenko (Cherkasy-Biyivtsi).

POST OFFICE, TELEPHONE

Main post office: Bayda-Vyshnevetsky St., 34; tel. 069; 47-23-36; 45-28-70. **Fax:** 47-53-30; 47-55-72.

MEDICAL SERVICES

Emergency: tel. 03.
Pharmacies: tel. 067. • No. 3: Shevchenko Blvd., 398; tel. 43-65-71. • No. 10: Ilyin St., 204; tel. 45-33-22.

TRANSPORTATION

Railway station: Krupska St., 1; tel. 63-87-87.
Bus station (suburban): Krupska St., 3; tel. 63-89-37.
Bus station (inter-city): Smilyanska St., 164; tel. 63-44-33.
Airport: Smilyanske shose, 168; tel. 63-06-06.
Airline Connections Agency: Dashkevych St., 30; tel. 45-32-86.
River station: Heroyi Stalinhrada St., 1; tel. 45-27-27.
Taxi reservations: tel. 002.

AUTO SERVICING

Avtoservis: Smilyanske shosse 8 km; tel. 63-58-69.

TOURING HISTORIC CITIES AND VILLAGES

CHYHYRYN

City located 63 km from Cherkasy, 45 km from the Fundukliyivka railway station, 8 km from Adamivka harbor.

During the first half of the 16th cent. it was a fortified winter Kozak settlement. In 1592 it came under Magdeburg Law. In 1638-47 Head of Chyhyryn county was B. Khmelnytsky, who resided here from 1648 to 1657. Later it became the capital of the Hetman state, until 1676. After it was sacked by the Tatars in 1678 and the capital was moved to Baturyn, the town declined. Sections of the Kozak fortifications on Zamkova Hora have been preserved. T. Shevchenko visited Chyhyryn in 1843 and 1845, which was the subject of several of his paintings and poems.

A museum dedicated to Hetman B. Khmelnytsky and a Historical-Ethnographic Museum are located here.

DRABIVTSI

Village, Zolotonosha district, 8 km from the Palmyra railway station.

MYKOLAYIVSKA (ST. NICHOLAS') CHURCH. This wood church built in the 18th cent. is an example of folk architecture incorporating elements of Classicism. Paintings of the 19th cent. have been preserved.

DUMANTSI

Village, Cherkasy district, 20 km from the Bilozirya railway station.

MYKOLAYIVSKA (ST. NICHOLAS') CHURCH, 1789. This wood church is an original monument of folk architecture.

HELMYAZIV

Village, Zolotonosha district, on the Supiy River, 12 km from the Hladkivshchyna railway station.

Kyiv to Kaniv cruise.

TROYITSKA (HOLY TRINITY) CHURCH. Built in 1841 in the late Classical style. Fragments of monumental paintings have been preserved.

HORODYSHCHE

City on the Vilshanka River.

MYKHAYLIVSKA (ST. MICHAEL'S) CHURCH. Built in 1844 in the neo-Gothic style. A 100 sq. m painting of the "Last Judgment" has been preserved.

MUSEUM AND MONUMENT to S. Hulak-Artemovsky, 1971. Sculptor: H. Kalchenko.

OBELISK. Erected at the birthplace of the brothers Semen and Petro Hulak-Artemovsky.

KANIV

City on the right bank of the Dnipro River, 64 km from Cherkasy, 7 km from the Liplyava railway station.

First mentioned in the Chronicle for the year 1144. Three ancient settlements, a burial mound, and treasures of the 10th-12th cent. have been uncovered here. The city was ruled successively by the Tatars, Lithuanians, Poles, Turks, and Russians.

Kaniv. Heorhiyivsky Uspensky (St. George's Dormition) Cathedral, 1144.

During the national-liberation war of 1648-54 the residents of Kaniv distinguished themselves in the Battles of Zboriv and Berestechko.

Grave of T. Shevchenko Museum and Preserve, 1939. Tarasova Hora; tel. 2-23-65.

T. Shevchenko Literary-Memorial Museum.

T. Shevchenko Monument, 1923. Sculptor: K. Tereshchenko.

T. Shevchenko Monument, 1939. Sculptor: M. Manizer.

Museum of Ukrainian Decorative and Applied Art. Lenin St., 64; tel. 2-23-91.

HEORHIYIVSKY USPENSKY (ST. GEORGE'S DORMITION) CATHEDRAL,

1144. This church, erected by Prince Vsevolod, is one of the few remaining churches built in the Kyiv style. Shevchenko's coffin lay in state here before its interment.

KANIV PRESERVE. Located 4 km south of Kaniv. Area: approx. 2000 ha. Unique historical, architectural, geological, and paleontological monuments are masterfully incorporated into the natural surroundings. There are more than 5000 different plant species of the steppe-forest belt in this preserve.

Kaniv. T. Shevchenko Literary-Memorial Museum.

KORSUN-SHEVCHENKIVSKY

City on the Ros River, 3 km from the Korsun railway station.

LOPUKHIN ESTATE, 18th cent. Architect: J. Muentz. One of the finest estate and park complexes in Ukraine built in the Romantic style. Area: 97 ha. The complex includes: a palace (1787, architect: Lindsay). Built in the Romantic style, with elements of Byzantine civil and church architecture and neo-Gothic features; entrance gates (1780s, architect: Lindsay), built in the Romantic style incorporating medieval architectural elements; wing (1786), built in the Early Classical style with Romantic elements; door-keeper's building (1783, architect: J. Muentz).

Located in the city are: I. Soshenko Monument, at the grave-site; a Kozak burial mound (17th cent.); a Scythian tumulus; a Kozak observation point; B. Khmelnytsky monument (bust); T. Shevchenko's chestnut tree in the arboretum.

KVITKY

Village, Korsun-Shevchenkivsky district, 15 km from the Korsun railway station.

K. Stetsenko Museum and Monument (1882-1922). Dedicated to the Ukrainian composer, conductor, and civic activist.

Chernyakhiv culture settlements (4th-2nd cent. B.C.)

LEBEDYN

Village, Shpola district.

PREOBRAZHENSKA (TRANSFIG-URATION) CHURCH, 1826. A rare structure built in the Late Classical style. A monumental painting of the 19th cent. has been preserved.

BELL TOWER OF THE LEBEDYN MONASTERY, 1833. Located on the grounds of the former monastery. By its monumental form and design this bell tower is a unique structure built in the Late Classical style.

Melnyky. Troyitska (Holy Trinity) Church of the Motronynsky Monastery, 1804.

MATUSIV

Village, Shpola district, 4 km from the Syhnayivka railway station.

VOZNESENSKA (ASCENSION) CHURCH, 1812-18. Built in the Late Classical style. Interior paintings of the 1900s have been preserved.

MELNYKY

Village located along Kholodny Yar, on both banks of the Sriblyanka river, 40 km from Chyhyryn, 30 km from the Fundukliyivka railway station.

TROYITSKA (HOLY TRINITY) CHURCH OF THE MOTRONYNSKY MONASTERY, 1804. Founded in 1568 in Kholodny Yar at the site of an ancient Ukrainian settlement. In the 18th cent. it became the center of the Haydamaky movement (Koliyivshchyna) led by M. Zaliznyak. The church was built on the site of a wood church and was later rebuilt in the Baroque style. T. Shevchenko visited the village in 1843 and 1845; this historical site was the subject of several poems and paintings: "Kholodny Yar," "Haydamaky" and a painting of the Motronynsky Monastery.

Memorial marker of the Ukrainian National Republic, 1992. Erected in Kholodny Yar at the site of the army

Moryntsi. T. Shevchenko Museum.

Moshny.
Preobrazhenska (Transfiguration)
Church, 1830-40.

headquarters of the Ukrainian National Republic.

MLIYIV

Village, Horodyshche district, on the Vilshanka river, 10 km from the Horodyshche railway station.

Building-Museum and Monument to L. Semyrenko (1855-1920). Dedicated to the scientist and founder of the Mliyiv Fruit-Culture Research Station.

L. Semyrenko Scientific Fruit-Culture Institute of the Ukrainian Forest-Steppe Belt (tel. 2-24-90).

MORYNTSI

Village, Zvenyhorod district.

Taras Shevchenko, the greatest poet of Ukraine, was born in this village. A museum dedicated to the poet is located here.

MOSHNY

Village on the right bank of the Dnipro River, 35 km from Cherkasy.

First mentioned in a document issued by the grand Lithuanian Prince Alexander. From 1649 it was a Kozak company town.

PREOBRAZHENSKA (TRANSFIG-URATION) CHURCH, 1830-40. Built by the Italian architect Toricelli in the Romantic style incorporating Gothic and Eclectic elements.

CHERKASKY BIR (FOREST). Area: 40,000 ha. A unique forest in the Dnipro river region and the only remaining forest-steppe belt in Ukraine. The Moshnohirya Preserve and sanatoriums open year-round are located in the forest.

Subotiv.
Illinska (St. Elias')
Church, 1653.

Uman.
Sofiyivka Arboretum.

SUBOTIV

Village, Chyhyryn region, on the Tyas-myn River, 21 km from Adamivka harbor on the Dnipro, 38 km from the Fundukli-yivka railway station.

ILLINSKA (ST. ELIAS') CHURCH, 1653. Built in the Ukrainian Baroque style at the request of Hetman Khmelnytsky; designed as his ancestral tomb. Today it houses a museum devoted to the Hetman.
B. Khmelnytsky Monument, 1954.

TALNE

City on the Hirsky Tikych and Talyan-ka Rivers, 141 km from Cherkasy.

HUNTERS' CASTLE, 1896-1903. Built in the Renaissance style of French country castles.

MUSEUM OF AGRICULTURAL HISTORY. Houses remnants of a gigantic settlement of the earliest farmers in Ukraine who lived here 6000 years ago. This farming civilization, uncovered in the city, preceded the civilization of the Egyptian Pharaohs. (tel. 2-34-64).

UMAN

City on the Umanka river, 188 km from Cherkasy.

First mentioned in historical documents dating to 1609. In 1648 it became the administrative center of the Uman regiment. Following the Treaty of Andrusiv in 1667 it was annexed by Poland. In the early 1670s the city was frequently attacked by the Tatars. From 1762 to 1832 it was ruled by the Potocki family which built Catholic schools and a monastery here, and in 1761 a fortress. After 1860 it became part of the Kyiv Guberniya (province).

SOFIYIVKA ARBORETUM, 1796. Built by the Belgian engineer L. Metletz at the request of Count S. Potocki and named in honor of his wife Sofiya. The park occupied 150 ha of land and included the Great Waterfall with an iron bridge, the Amsterdam sluice carved out of a cliff, the Lion's Grotto, the Grotto of Venus with waterfall, Rybka pool, Hippocrene's Well, Upper and Lower ponds, the subterranean river Styx, etc. Restored in 1966-72.

Architectural structures of the Arboretum: entrance gates (1850-52); floral pavilion (1842-44); the Grotto of Venus (1796-1800) built in the shape of an ancient Roman temple with a statue of Venus de Milo; the pink Renaissance-style pavilion on the Island of Love (1850-52); the Chinese Pavilion (1841). (Provulok Kyivsky, 12-a; tel. 5-61-11).

Regional Ethnography Museum, 1924.

Autoroute Service Complex: 1406 km on the E-93 autoroute Sankt-Peterburg-Kyiv-Odesa; tel. 5-20-79.

ZOLOTONOSHA

City on the Zolotonosha River, 30 km from Cherkasy.

PREOBRAZHENSKA (TRANSFIGURATION) CHURCH of the Krasnohirsky Monastery, 1767-71. Built by I. Hryhorovych-Barsky in the Ukrainian Baroque style.

Chernihiv Region

Located in northeastern Ukraine, on the border with Russia and Belarus. The region encompasses the Dnipro and Polissya Lowlands. The climate is temperate-continental. The principal river is the Desna, a tributary of the Dnipro. Created in 1932. Area: 31,900 sq. km. Population: 1,390,000.

History

The first traces of human existence in Chernihiv region date to the Paleolithic period. In the 7th-8th cent. the territory was occupied by the East Slavic Siveryany tribe (Siverians). In the 9th cent. the Chernihiv-Siversk territory was part of Kyivan Rus'-Ukraine. This territory became the Chernihiv Principality in the 11th cent. and its inhabitants were forced to defend their lands against constant Polovtsian aggression. The best known crusade against the Polovtsian tribes was led by Prince Ihor Svyatoslavovych in 1185; the crusade is chronicled in the epic poem "The Tale of Ihor's Host."

During the 11th-12th cent. the Chernihiv principality was divided into three smaller principalities: Novhorod-Siversk, Putyvl, and Rylsk. In 1239 the area was invaded by the Tatars.

For many centuries the Chernihiv lands were under the occupation of Lithuania (1356), Muscovy (1503), and Poland (1618). After the national liberation war (1648-54), the territory was divided into four administrative districts. These lasted until the liquidation of Kozak autonomy by Catherine II in 1775.

*Boryso-Hlibsky
(SS. Borys and Hlib)
Cathedral, 12th cent.*

The Ukrainian people resisted foreign domination of their lands. Best exemplifying this resistance are the anti-Polish national-liberation war and the war against Russia. During the latter the residents of Chernihiv sided with Hetman Ivan Mazepa and the Swedish King Charles XII against Tsarist forces. In 1708 Russian forces under Menshikov retaliated by burning down Baturyn, the Ukrainian Hetman's residence.

In January 1918, near Kruty, heavily-outnumbered Ukrainian students fought against the regular forces of the Bolshevik army.

The culture of the Chernihiv Principality was rich, varied, and highly evolved. Its architectural monuments, together with the churches of Kyiv, represented the golden era of ancient Ukrainian architecture in Kyivan Rus'-Ukraine . Of great interest are the architectural monuments of the Hetman era which reflect the Ukrainian Baroque style.

PROMINENT INDIVIDUALS

BORN IN THE REGION:

V. Blakytny-Ellansky (1894-1925), writer; in Kozel (now Mykhaylo-Kotsiubynske). • **O. Bodyansky** (1808-77), philologist, historian; in Varva, Sribnyansk district. • **V. Chumak** (1901-19), poet; in Ichnya, executed by Denikin supporters. • **O. Dovzhenko** (1894-1956), cinematographer and essayist; in Sosnytsya. • **V. Hantsov** (1892-1979), linguist and cultural activist, persecuted. • **M. Ivchenko** (1890-1939), writer; in Nykonivka, Sribnyansk district. • **A. Kazka** (1890-1929), writer; in Sedniv, died in prison. • **I. Kocherha** (1881-1952), dramatist; in Nosivka. • **H. Kochur** (1908), writer and translator; in Feskivtsi, Mena district, persecuted. • **B. Kovalenko** (1903-38), writer and critic; in Khetunychy, Shchors district, executed. • **L. Lukyanenko** (1927), political prisoner, political figure; in Khrebtivka, Horodnya district. • **O. Markevych** (1847-1903), historian; in Smoshchi, Pryluky district. • **I. Martos** (1754-1835), sculptor; in Ichnya. • **Yu. Mushketyk** (1929), writer; in Vertiyivka, Nizhyn district. • **S. Paliy** (17th cent.), Zaporozhian colonel; in Borzna. • **M. Ptukha** (1884-1961), academician and demographer; in Oster, Kozelets district, persecuted. • **L. Revutsky** (1889-1977), composer; in Irzhavets. • **V. Revutsky** (1911), theater critic; in Irzhavets, lives in Canada. • **K. Rozumovsky** (1728-1803), last Hetman of Ukraine; in Lemeshi. • **H. Sachenko** (1905-37?), writer; in Hayenky, Ichnya region, died in prison. • **M. Samokysh** (1860-1944), artist; in Nizhyn. • **V. Sedlyar** (1889-1937), artist; in Lyubech, executed. • **P. Tychyna** (1891-1961), poet; in Pisky, Bobrovytsya district. • **S. Vasylchenko-Panasenko** (1878-1932), writer; in Ichnya. • **O. Veresay** (1803-90), bard, in Kalyuzhyntsi. • **H. Veryovka** (1895-1964), choreographer, composer; in Borzna. • **M. Vorony** (1904-37), poet; in Chernihiv, executed. • **V. Zabila** (1808-96), poet; in Kukurikivshchyna (now Zabilivshchyna), Borzna district. • **M. Zankovetska-Adasovska** (1854-1934), actress; in Zanky, Nizhyn district.

BURIED IN THE REGION:

L. Baranovych (1620-93), church scholar, religious leader; in Chernihiv. • **H. Barvinok** (1828-1911), writer; in Motronivka. • **L. Hlibov** (1827-93), poet, writer; in Chernihiv. • **M. Kotsyubynsky** (1864-1913), writer; in Chernihiv. • **P. Kulish** (1819-97), writer; in Motronivka. • **O. Markovych** (1822-67), ethnographer; in Chernihiv. • **K. Rozumovsky** (1728-1803), Hetman of Left-Bank Ukraine; in Baturyn. • **M. Sespel-Kuzmin** (1899-1922), first writer in the Chuvash language; in Oster, Kozelets district. • **O. Veresay** (1803-90), bard; in Sokyryntsi. • **V. Zabila** (1808-96), poet; in Borzna.

Katerynynska Church (St. Catherine's), 1715.

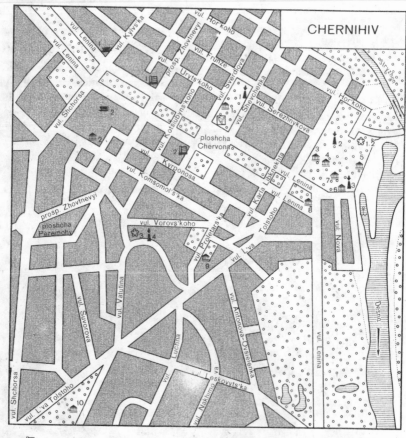

CHERNIHIV

Hotels:
  1 Ukraïna
  2 Desna

Restaurants:
  1 Druzhba
  2 Polissia
  Note. Restaurants Ukraïna and Desna are attached to the hotels of the same names

River Station

Monuments:
  1 Bohdan Khmelnytskyi
  2 A. S. Pushkin
  3 Taras Shevchenko
  4 Mykhaïlo Kotsiubynskyi

Architectural monuments:
  1 St. Parasceve's Church, 12th—13th cc.
  2 Resurrection Church, 18th c.
  3 Building of the former Collegium, 1701

4 Sts. Boris and Gleb's Cathedral, 12th c.
5 Transfiguration of the Savior Cathedral, 11th c.
6 Chernihiv Fortress, 16th—18th cc.
7 17th-century building (former Cossack regiment office)
8 St. Catherine's Church, 17th—18th cc.
9 Yeletsky Monastery of Dormition, complex of buildings of 12th—17th century buildings
10 Trinity-St. Elijah's Monastery, complex of buildings of the 11th, 17th and 18th cc.

Museums:
  1 History
  2 Art department of the History Museum
  3 M. Kotsiubynskyi Literary-Memorial

Taras Shevchenko Theater of Music and Drama

CHERNIHIV

City and regional center on the right bank of the Desna River, approximately 150 km from Kyiv, one of the oldest cities in Ukraine. Population: 300,000. Telephone code: 046.

Established at the end of the 7th cent. In the 9th cent. it was the capital of the Slavic Siverian tribes. In the late 9th cent. the city became part of Kyivan Rus'-Ukraine. First historical reference dates to 907. In 1024 the city became the capital of the Chernihiv Principality, and was destroyed in 1239 by the Tatars. In the 14th cent. the city was captured by Lithuanian princes who built a fortress in the city. In 1618 it passed from Lithuanian to Polish rule.

CHURCHES, HISTORICAL AND ARCHITECTURAL MONUMENTS

DYTYNETS (FORTRESS). Located on the site of settlements dating to the beginning of the first millennium. From the 7th cent. these early settlements grew into a succession of fortified towns. By the early 12th cent. Dytynets was a mighty fortress containing royal chambers and living quarters of the boyars. Twelve cast-iron cannons, dating to the 17th-18th cent. were stationed on the fortress ramparts. There are numerous well-preserved churches in the area. Today the Dytynets is called the M. Kotsyubynsky Central Park of Culture and Recreation.

SPASO-PREOBRAZHENSKY (TRANSFIGURATION) CATHEDRAL. 11th cent. One of the oldest churches of Kyivan-Rus'-Ukraine. Built by Prince Mstyslav Volodymyrovych Khorobry (the Brave). The prince, his wife Anastasiya, and his son Yevstafiy are buried in the cathedral. It is also the burial place of Prince Svyatoslav Yaroslavych and, probably, Ihor Svyatoslavych, the hero of "The Tale of Ihor's Host." In 1239 the cathedral was partially damaged. It was reconstructed and renovated in the 17th-19th cent. The iconostasis was the work of Nizhyn masters S.

Chernihiv Collegium, 1700.

Voloshenko and S. Bilopolsky (1795-98). The cathedral was closed in 1926 and re-opened from 1942 to 1961. (Pidvalna St. in Dytynets).

BORYSO-HLIBSKY SOBOR (SS. BORYS AND HLIB'S CATHEDRAL), 12th cent. Built by Prince Davyd-Hlib Svyatoslavych on the remains of an 11th cent. stone structure. The "Royal Doors" (part of the iconostasis), built in the 18th cent., are still standing inside the cathedral. They were commissioned by Hetman Ivan Mazepa and portray the first Ukrainian saints, Borys and Hlib. The first rector of the Kyivan-Mohyla Academy, archbishop Lazar Baranovych (1620-93), is buried in the cathedral. During the Second World War the cathedral was damaged in fires. It was renovated in 1952-58 by M. Kholostenko in the style of ancient Ukrainian architecture. It is now open to the faithful. (In Dytynets. Trolley-bus No. 8).

CHERNIHIV COLLEGIUM, 1700. Established by archbishop L. Baranovych in the former Borysohlibsky Monastery. Destroyed by fire during the Second World War. Restored in 1952-54. (In Dytynets).

KATERYNYNSKA CHURCH (ST. CATHERINE'S). Built in the Ukrainian baroque style on the site of an earlier church from the Rus'-Ukraine era. The church now houses a museum of national decorative art of the Chernihiv area. (On a hill facing Dytynets).

CHORNA MOHYLA (BLACK GRAVE). According to legend, it is the burial site of Prince Chorny, the founder of Chernihiv. During excavations in 1872-73, many 10th cent. artifacts were unearthed in the area. In 1873 a monument was erected at the grave site. (At the corner of Proletarska and Vorovsky Streets. Trolley-bus No. 8).

YELETSKY USPENSKY (DORMITION) MONASTERY, 11th cent. Founded by Chernihiv Prince Svyatoslav Yaroslavovych (1027-76). Burned down by the Tatars in 1239, it was renovated in 1445-95. In 1646 Ukrainian writer K. Stavrovetsky printed *Perlo Mnohotsennoye (The Precious Pearl),* the first book published in Chernihiv region. The archimandrites of the monastery, Lazar Baranovych and Ioanikiy Halyatovsky, were important Ukrainian cultural figures. The architecture of the monastery is Ukrainian Baroque. On the grounds of the monastery are the 12th cent. Uspensky (Dormition) Cathedral, a 36 m bell tower over the entrance gate, and the Petropavlivska (SS Peter and Paul) church with a refectory, monks' cells, and the burial vault of the Chernihiv Colonel Yakiv Lyzohub and his family. (Proletarska St. Bus No. 4, 7).

*Katerynynska Church
(St. Catherine's), 1715.*

TROYITSKO-ILLINSKY (HOLY TRINITY AND ST. ELIAS') MONASTERY, 1069. Founded by Antoniy Pechersky. On the grounds of the monastery are Antoniy's caves, 315 m in length, with underground wood churches connected by a system of subterranean galleries. Destroyed in 1239; rebuilt in 1649. It includes the Troyitsky (Holy Trinity) Cathedral (1679), Vvedenska (Presentation of the Holy Virgin) Church with a refectory (1677), a 58 m bell tower, and monks' cells. During the second half of the 17th cent. the monastery was a center of Ukrainian chronicle-writing. L. Hlibov is buried near the south wall of the Troitsky (Trinity) Cathedral. Several distinguished writers of the 19th cent. are buried here. (Tolstoy St., 92. Trolley-bus No. 8).

PYATNYTSKA CHURCH, 12th-13th cent. Named after the patroness saint of commerce, St. Paraskeva Pyatnytsya. Until 1786 it was the main building of the Pyatnytsky Monastery. Rebuilt and renovated several times, most recently in 1962 by P. Baranovsky and M. Kholostenko. In 1972 it was converted to a museum. Today it has reverted to the faithful. (B. Khmelnytsky Sq. Bus No. 4, 7, 10).

Pyatnytska Church,
12th-13th cent.

VOSKRESENSKA (RESURRECTION) CHURCH, 1772-75. Built in the Ukrainian Baroque style. (Komsomolska St., 36).

YAKIV LYZOHUB BUILDING, 17th cent. The building served as the private offices of the Chernihiv Colonel Y. Lyzohub. A unique example of 17th century civil architecture. (In Dytynets).

MONUMENTS

B. Khmelnytsky, 1956. Sculptors: I. Kavaleridze and H. Petrashevych. Architect: A. Kornabid. (Khmelnytsky Sq.) .

T. Shevchenko, 1950. At the entrance to Chernihiv from the Sedniv side. In 1964 it was relocated to the Dytynets.

M. Kotsyubynsky, 1939. Sculptor: I. Ginsburg. (Kotsyubynsky St., 3).

MUSEUMS

M. Kotsyubynsky Memorial Museum: Founded in 1935 on the estate where the writer lived from 1898 to 1913. Kotsyubynsky St., 3; tel. 4-04-59. • **State Historical Museum:** Gorky St., 4; tel. 7-26-50. Located in the former residence of the governor

Hradetsky Hotel.

(1804). • **Art Museum:** Gorky St., 6; tel. 7-27-15. • **Chernihiv Historical-Architectural Preserve:** Marx St., 1; tel. 7-01-45. • **Museum of Folk Decorative and Applied Arts of Chernihiv:** Aleya Heroyiv, Katerynynska (St. Catherine's) Church; tel. 4-32-36.

THEATERS, PHILHARMONIC

T. Shevchenko Ukrainian Music and Drama Theater: Chervona Ploshcha. • **Philharmonic:** Lenin St., 15. • **Puppet Theater:** Komsomolska St., 11.

HIGHER EDUCATIONAL INSTITUTIONS

Branch of the Kyiv Polytechnical Institute: Shevchenko St., 95. • **T. Shevchenko Pedagogical Institute:** Sverdlov St., 53.

LIBRARIES, ARCHIVES

V. Korolenko Regional General Library: Lenin St., 41. • **Main Library:** Kyrponis St., 22. • **Regional Medical-Scientific Library:** Lyubetska St., 7. • **O. Dovzhenko Central Children's Library:** Kyrponis St., 22. • **Regional Archive:** Frunze St., 2.

SPORTS COMPLEXES

Gagarin Stadium: Shevchenko St., 31; tel. 3-37-64. • **Avanhard Swimming Pool:** prospekt Zhovtnevoyi revolyutsiyi, 34; tel. 7-19-68. • **Sports Complex:** Sverdlov St., 53. • **Yunist Stadium:** prospekt Zhovtnevoyi revolyutsiyi, 110. • **Spartak House of Physical Education:** Gorky St., 1. • **Lokomotyv Stadium:** Vokzalny Provulok, 19.

HOTELS

Ukrayina: Lenin St., 33; tel. 7-46-04. • **Hradetsky:** Lenin St., 68; tel. 4-50-25. • **Prydesnyansky:** Shevchenko St., 99a; tel. 95-48-02. • **Desna:** Kuybyshev St., 1;

tel. 7-70-00. • **Sport:** Shevchenko St., 61; tel. 3-06-74. • **Kolos:** Chervonohvardiyska St., 17. • **Nyva:** Paytdesyat Rokiv SRSR, 5; tel. 3-90-67.

RESTAURANTS, CAFES

Siversky: Rokosovsky St., 15. • **Stary Chernihiv:** prospekt Zhovtnevoyi revolyutsiyi, 137. • **Bryansk:** Shevchenko St., 103. • **Druzhba:** Lenin St., 49. • **Polissya:** Lenin St., 32. • **Vokzalny:** ploshcha Vokzalna. • **Ukrayina:** Lenin St., 32. • **Hradetsky:** Lenin St., 68. • **Desna:** Lenin St., 20. • **Ukrayinski Varenyky:** Lenin St., 54. • **Teatralne:** Kuybyshev St., 1-a. • **Diyetychne:** Odyntsov St., 5. • **Lakomka:** Rokosovsky St., 35. • **Yunist:** Pyatdesyat Rokiv VLKSM. • **Molochne:** Shevchenko St., 11. • **Ogonyok:** Marx St., 16. • **Desna:** Kuybyshev St., 1. • **Molodizhne:** prospekt Zhovtnevoyi Revolyutsiyi, 75. • **Vesna:** Tolstoy St., 108. • **"Prokholoda" Pyvny Bar:** prospekt Zhovtnevoyi revolyutsiyi, 106.

STORES

Druzhba Commercial Center: Lenin St., 49. • **Siversky Univermah (Department Store):** Rokosovsky St., 35. • **Turyst:** Rokosovsky St., 10. • **Homelsky Universam (Department Store):** Lenin St., 54. • **Sport and Tourism:** prospekt Zhovtnevoyi revolyutsiyi, 96. • **Budynok Knyhy (Books):** Lenin St., 45. • **Khudozhniy (Art) Salon:** prospekt Zhovtnevoyi revolyutsiyi, 90. • **Podarunky (Gifts):** Lenin St., 35. • **Dytyachy Svit (Children's):** Lenin St., 30. • **Universam (Department Store):** Vokzalna Ploshcha. • **Yantar:** Lenin St., 19. • **Akord (Retail Store of a musical instruments factory):** Muzychna St., 1. • **Markets: Nyva:** Pyatdesyat Rokiv SRSR.; Central, Rynkova Ploshcha.

BANKS

National Bank of Ukraine (Regional Branch): Kyrponis St., 16; tel. 7-68-11. • **Commercial Bank "Chernihivbank":** Seryozhnykov St., 6; tel. 7-24-86, 7-32-51. • **Commercial Joint-Stock Bank "Demark":** Shchors St., 66; tel. 14-24-57, 14-22-67. • **Joint Stock Investment Rural Bank "Ahroinvestbank":** Shevchenko St., 42.

TYPICAL SOUVENIRS OF CHERNIHIV REGION

Krolevets weavings, embroidered runners and blouses, wood carving, porcelain and pottery.

TOURISM

Chernihivturyst: Shevchenko St., 103-a; tel. 3-06-82; 3-81-56.

Chernihiv Travel and Excursion Agency: Shevchenko St., 103-a; tel. 3-81-69; 3-81-55.

The following excursions are available: "Thirteen Centuries of Chernihiv History," "Architectural Monuments of Chernihiv" (visits to SS. Borys and Hlib Cathedral and Antoniy's Caves).

Tours of neighboring vicinities: to Novhorod-Siversky, including visits to the museum "The Tale of Ihor's Host"; Sosnytsya, including a visit to the O. Dovzhenko Memorial Museum.

POST OFFICE, TELEGRAPH

Main post office: Lenin St., 28; tel. 7-35-1.
Inter-urban calling point: Lenin St., 28; tel. 071.
Fax: Lenin St., 28.
Central telegraph: Lenin St., 28; tel. 7-20-15.

MEDICAL SERVICES

Emergency: tel. 03.
Pharmaceutical kiosks are located in hotel lobbies.
Pharmacy No. 25: Kuybyshev St., 1; tel. 7-33-47; 7-49-77.

TRANSPORTATION

Railway station: Vokzalna Ploshcha; tel. 005, 7-43-76; tickets: tel. 055.
Bus Terminus: prospekt Zhovtnevoyi revolyutsiyi, 3; tel. 004; tickets: tel. 054; 4-52-91.
Airport: tel. 1-14-32, 1-14-60.
Ukrainian Airlines: Lenin St., 65; tel. 5-34-84; tickets: 5-34-76.
River port: Pidvalna St., 23; tel.7-51-30, 11-83-01.
Taxi reservations: tel. 058.

AUTO SERVICING

Avtoservis: Lenin St., 33; tel. 5-91-52.

TOURING HISTORIC CITIES AND VILLAGES

BATURYN

Village, Bakhmach district, on the Seym River, 24 km from the Bakhmach railway station.

Former capital of the Ukrainian Hetmans. First mentioned in documents dating to 1625. In 1669-1708 and 1750-64, Baturyn was the residence of the Ukrainian Hetmans Danylo Mnohohrishny, Ivan Samoylovych, Ivan Mazepa, and Kyrylo Rozumovsky, the last Hetman of Ukraine. In November 1708, by order of Tsar Peter I, Russian forces under the command of 0. Menshikov destroyed the city, murdering all the inhabitants, including children. In 1750 Kyrylo Rozumovsky was given permission to rebuild the Hetman's capital. Taras Shevchenko visited Baturyn in May 1843.

POKROVSKY (PROTECTION OF THE BLESSED VIRGIN MARY) CATHEDRAL, 1789.

VOSKRESENSKA (RESURRECTION) CHURCH, 1803.

HETMAN K. ROZUMOVSKY PALACE, 1799-1803. Built in the Classical style by the Italian architect Antonio Rinaldi based on sketches of Charles Cameron.

V. KOCHUBEY BUILDING, 17th-18th cent. The building now houses a national museum.

DANIVKA

Village on the Oster river, Kozelets district, 25 km from the Bobrovytsya railway station.

HEORHIYIVSKY SOBOR (ST. GEORGE'S CATHEDRAL), 1741-70. The main structure of the Kozelets Heorhiyivsky Monastery. One of the finest examples of Ukrainian Baroque.

VOSKRESENSKA (RESURRECTION) CHURCH, 1851. Wood.

DIHTYARIVKA

Village on the Desna river, Novhorod-Siversky district, 21 km from the Vitemlya railway station.

POKROVSKA (PROTECTION OF THE BLESSED VIRGIN MARY) CHURCH, 1709-10. Funded by Hetman Ivan Mazepa. An outstanding example of monumental stone architecture of the Ukrainian Baroque era.

Baturyn. Hetman K. Rozumovsky Palace, 1799-1803.

4*

HORODNYA

City on the Chebryzh River, 4 km from the Chebryzh railway station. Visited by T. Shevchenko in 1846.

TROYITSKA (HOLY TRINITY) CHURCH, 18th cent. Artwork by H. Stetsenko.
TROYITSKY (HOLY TRINITY) CATHEDRAL, 1874.
Monument on grave of S. Nis (1829-1900). Ukrainian writer, ethnographer, folklorist, and physician. After returning from exile in 1886, Nis lived in Horodnya until his death. The monument was reconstructed in 1971.
T. Shevchenko Monument. Built in 1982.

HUSTYNYA

Village, Pryluky district, 10 km from the Pryluky railway station.

HUSTYNSKY MONASTERY, 17th cent. A unique architectural complex built in the Baroque style. The original wood structures were destroyed by fire in 1636 and 1671. In 1799 it was closed. Restored and renovated by the Repin princes. In 1845 the monastery was visited by T. Shevchenko.
TROYITSKY (HOLY TRINITY) CATHEDRAL, 1672-76. Commissioned by Hetman I. Samoylovych and built in the Baroque style. The Hustynsky Chronicle was written here.
VOSKRESENSKA (RESURRECTION) CHURCH, 1695. Since 1845 it has been used as a burial vault.
PETROPAVLIVSKA (SS. PETER AND PAUL) CHURCH, 1693-1708.

ICHNYA

City on the Ichenka River, at the junction of the Kruty-Ichnya-Pryluky railway lines.

Famous for its pottery and embroidery. The city was the administrative center of the Ichnya Kozak regiment. A castle was built here in the 17th cent.

S. Vasylchenko Monument, 1974. Sculptor: I. Honchar.

Hustynsky Monastery, 17th cent.

V. Chumak Building. The poet was born and spent his childhood and youth here..

V. Chumak Monument, 1975. Sculptor: V. Lutsak.

IRZHAVETS

Village, Ichnya district, 18 km from the Ichnya railway station.

Best known for its miraculous icon of the Mother of God. T. Shevchenko, who visited the village in 1843, based his poem "Irzhavets" (written in exile) on the legend of this icon.

T. Shevchenko Monument, 1959.

L. Revutsky Monument, 1989.

L. Revutsky Memorial Estate-Museum, 1989.

KACHANIVKA

Village, Ichnya district; a garden-park architectural ensemble.

In 1770 the village was owned by Governor-General P. Rumyantsev-Zadunaysky who initiated construction of a garden-palace complex. In the 18th cent. a palace in the pseudo-Gothic style was built by the architect K. Blank. Until 1982 the palace housed a sanatorium. In 1980 the partially destroyed palace, the T. Shevchenko monument, the park, the Heorhiyivska (St. George's) Church, and the Russian composer M. Glinka's arbor were incorporated into the Kachanivka Historical-Cultural Preserve. Open from May to September.

The village houses V. Tarnovsky's collection of documents and other memorabilia associated with the life and work of T. Shevchenko, who visited the area in 1843 and 1859.

KOROP

Village, 26 km from the Altynivka railway station.

First mentioned in 1153. In the late 17th cent. and early 18th cent. it was, together with Hlukhiv, a center of the Kozak artillery. The revolutionary populist M. Kybalchych (1853-81) was born in the village.

ILLINSKA (ST. ELIAS') CHURCH, 1750-60. A defensive structure with 2 m deep walls.

VOZNESENSKA (ASCENSION) CHURCH, 1764. Funded by the Kozak chieftain P. Yurkevych.

M. Kybalchych Monument. Member of the revolutionary organization "Zemlya i Volya," scholar, and inventor, who was sentenced to death for his participation in a plot to assassinate the Russian Tsar Alexander II. While in prison he designed a jet-propelled flying apparatus.

M. Kybalchych Memorial Museum. (Provulok Kybalchycha, 18; tel. 2-17-07).

DARAHAN ESTATE, 18th cent. Belonged to the sister of Hetman K. Rozumovsky.

KOZELETS

Village on the Oster River, 40 km from the Bobrovytsya railway station, on the Kyiv-Chernihiv autoroute. Population: 10,000.

The former base of Kozak regiments. In 1662 it was the site of a Kozak officers' council which elected Y. Somko Hetman of the Kozaks. In 1669 the village was destroyed by the Tatars. T. Shevchenko stayed here in 1846.

SOBOR RIZDVA BOHORODYTSI (NATIVITY OF THE MOTHER OF GOD CATHEDRAL), 1752-63; **BELL TOWER,** 1766-70. Built by N. Rozumykha, mother of Kozak O. Rozum who later became Count Rozumovsky. Architects: I. Hryhorovych-Barsky and A. Kvasov. Icon artist: H. Stetsenko. Woodcarvings: S. Shalmatov.

VOZNESENSKA (ASCENSION) CHURCH, 1866-74. A unique example of a five-domed, crucifiction in plan.

MYKILSKA (ST. NICHOLAS') CHURCH, 1781-84. Built in the late Baroque style.

REGIMENTAL OFFICE BUILDING, 1756-60. Architects: I. Hryhorovych-Barsky and A. Kvasov.

Auto Servicing: Autoservis — 1123 km a/d E-93 Sankt Peterburg-Kyiv-Odesa; tel. 2-10-02.

Kozelets. Sobor Rizdva Bohorodytsi (Nativity of the Mother of God Cathedral), 1752-63.

KRUTY

Village, Nizhyn district, 3 km from the Nizhyn railway station, on the Kyiv-Bakhmach-Moscow line.

BATTLE OF KRUTY. On 29 January 1918, at the Kruty railway station, a battle was fought between the 4,000-strong Bolshevik forces and a small Ukrainian contingent of approximately 600 men, consisting of a company of the Student Kurin of Striltsi, a company of the Khmelnytsky Cadet School, and a Haydamaky detachment. The Ukrainian contingent attempted to block the Bolshevik advance on Kyiv at the Kruty railway station. Nearly half of the Ukrainian soldiers were killed. The Battle of Kruty has endured as a symbol of patriotic self-sacrifice and an example for many generations of Ukrainian youth. Numerous literary works have been dedicated to the fallen heroes, some of whom were buried at the site of Askold's Grave in Kyiv.

LADAN

Village, Pryluky district, on the Uday River, 18 km from the Pryluky railway station.

LADAN POKROVSKY (PROTECTION OF THE BLESSED VIRGIN MARY) MONASTERY, 1603. Established as a monastery. In 1619 it was converted to a convent. The monastery complex includes the Baroque-style Pokrovsky

Lemeshi. Tryokhsvyatytelska (Three Saints') Church, 1755.

(Protection) Cathedral (1763), the 19th cent. Mykolayivska (St. Nicholas's) Church, monks' cells, sections of the convent walls. In 1928 the convent was closed by the Soviet authorities. Until 1938 it housed a commune for juvenile delinquents.

LEMESHI

Village, Kozelets district, 8 km from the Kozelets railway station.

TRYOKHSVYATYTELSKA (THREE SAINTS') CHURCH, 1755. Funded by O. Rozumovsky and built on the grave-site of his father H. Rozum. Architect: S. Kutsevych.

ZEMSKA (COUNTY) SCHOOL BUILDING, 1909-10. Funded by K. Rozumovsky, the last Hetman of Left-Bank Ukraine, to commemorate his mother N. Rozum. Designed by I. Yakubovych. An example of Ukrainian folk architectural style of the early 20th cent.

LYUBECH

City on the left bank of the Dnipro River, 28 km from the Nedanychi railway station. Population: 3700.

One of the oldest cities of the Kyivan Rus'-Ukraine era, Lyubech was a defensive fortress and was first mentioned in the chronicles for the year 882. Near Lyubech Prince Yaroslav Mudry (the Wise) defeated the forces of Prince Svyatopolk Okayanny (the Damned), who had ordered his brothers Borys, Hlib, and Svyatopolk to be killed. At an assembly of Kyivan princes convened in 1097, including Volodymyr Monomakh (Monomackus) and Vasylko Rostyslavych, an agreement was reached to end their internecine quarrels and unite to fight the Polovtsians. In the 11th cent. the Antoniyivsky (St. Anthony's) Monastery was built in Lyubech. In the 12th cent. the town was twice destroyed by fire and plundered by the Polovtsians. From the 14th cent. Lyubech was under the control of Lithuania, Russia, and Poland. In 1654 it became a military garrison of the Chernihiv Kozak regiment.

ANTONIYIVSKY (ST. ANTHONY'S) MONASTERY, 11th cent. Originally a cave dug out by Antoniy Pechersky. The monastery was destroyed in the 13th cent. and restored in 1694. The monastery was closed in 1786. Only the original cave remains.

PREOBRAZHENSKA (TRANSFIGURATION) CHURCH, 1811-17. Built in the Empire style. It was commissioned by H. Myloradovych and served as a family burial-vault.

POLUBOTOK STONE BUILDING, 18th cent. Commissioned by Hetman I. Mazepa. Was owned by Hetman P. Polubotok from 1709. Ownership later passed to the Myloradovych family.

MEZYN (MIZYN)

Village, Korop district, on the Desna River, 35 km from the Voronizh railway station. The site of the oldest settlement in Ukraine (15th cent. B.C.)

MEZYN STOYANKA, 1908. A late Paleolithic Age settlement unearthed by the Ukrainian anthropologist F. Vovk. During the excavations, 4,000 flint utensils, agricultural tools, and sculptures made of mammoth tusk were uncovered.

MEZYN MUSEUM, 1965. Housed in an 18th cent. wood building on the grounds of the Mezyn Stoyanka. The collection includes 41,000 artifacts assembled by V. Kurylenko.

NIZHYN

City on the Oster River, 83 km from Chernihiv and 126 km from Kyiv. Population: 100,000. Telephone code: 231.

Nizhyn (formerly Unenezh) was first mentioned in written sources in 1147. In the 12th cent. it was a fortress of the Chernihiv principality, and was destroyed by the Tatars in 1239. A new settlement and fortifications were built in 1625. Led by Colonels Balylovets (1631), Pavluk (1637), and Ostryanytsya (1638), the residents of

Nizhyn took part in uprisings against the Polish magnate M. Potocki. These uprisings were cruelly suppressed; at the Katedralny Maydan (now Hohol Square) and along the roads leading to it, gallows and stakes were erected where the rebels were tortured to death. After the liberation war of 1648-54, the city became the Nizhyn regiment's administrative center. In 1633 a "Chorna Rada" (Black Council) was held in Nizhyn and I. Bryukhovetsky was elected Hetman of Left-Bank Ukraine. He immediately surrendered all of Ukraine to the Muscovite Tsar. In the second half of the 17th cent. Nizhyn became one of the largest commercial centers in Ukraine. In 1918 Nizhyn's inhabitants joined the Ukrainian National Republic's troops fighting against the Bolsheviks.

Nizhyn. Mykolayivsky (St. Nicholas') Cathedral, 1668-70.

Travel and Excursion Agency: Lenin St., 15; tel. 2-45-49.

MYKOLAYIVSKY (ST. NICHOLAS') CATHEDRAL, 1668-70. Has five cupolas and is cruciform in plan. Restored 1980-86.

BLAHOVISHCHENSKY (ANNUNCIATION) CATHEDRAL, 1702. Architect: H. Ustynov. Restored in 1969.(Hohol St., 10).

BOHOYAVLENSKA (EPIPHANY) CHURCH, 1721.

VVEDENSKY (PRESENTATION IN THE TEMPLE) CATHEDRAL, 1775; **BELL TOWER,** 1814. Built in the Ukrainian Baroque style.

MYKHAYLIVSKA (ST. MICHAEL'S) CHURCH, 1719-29. Greek.

VSIKH SVYATYKH (ALL SAINTS') CHURCH, 1780. Greek.

TROYITSKA (HOLY TRINITY) CHURCH, 1733. Built in the Neo-classical style.

YOANA BOHOSLOVA (ST. JOHN THE THEOLOGIAN'S) CHURCH, 1752. (Hohol St., 4).

POKROVSKA (PROTECTION) CHURCH, 1765.

PREOBRAZHENSKA (TRANSFIGURATION) CHURCH, 1757. Built in the Ukrainian Baroque style. (Chervony Partyzany St., 14).

MYKOLAYIVSKA (ST. NICHOLAS') CHURCH, 1873. Architect: L. Sadovsky. (Podvoysky St., 23-a).

Nizhyn Gymnasium of Higher Education, 1805-17. Architect: A. Rusko.

SVYATOHO VASYLIYA (ST. BASIL'S) CHURCH, 18th cent.

SPASA (REDEEMER) CHURCH, 1757. Ruins.

Oster. Yuryeva Bozhnytsya (St. George's Temple), 10th-11th cent.

M. Hohol Monument, 1881. Sculptor: P. Zabila.

Regional Museum: Batyuk St., 14; tel. 2-31-28.

Commercial Bank "Partner": Hohol St., 15-a; tel. 2-44-52, 2-22-81.

NOVHOROD-SIVERSKY

City on the Desna river, 176 km from Chernihiv. Population:. 15,300. Telephone code: 258.

From 1097 Novhorod-Siversky was the capital of the Chernihiv principality. Remains of dwellings dating to the late Paleolithic Age, Neolithic, and Bronze-age settlements have been unearthed in the area. The city, founded in the 10th cent. as one of the fortresses of Kyivan Rus'-Ukraine, was first mentioned in the chronicle for the year 1078. Prince Ihor Svyatoslavych (1180-98), the hero of "The Tale of Ihor's Host" was a Siverian Prince. Colonel Ivan Bohun was slain near the city in a battle against the Poles in 1664.

Travel and Excursion Agency: Marx St., 10; tel. 2-15-86.

SPASO-PREOBRAZHENSKY (TRANSFIGURATION) CATHEDRAL, 1785-87. Designed by J. Quarenti. The cathedral houses an exhibit on "The Tale of Ihor's Host."

SPASO-PREOBRAZHENSKY (TRANSFIGURATION OF OUR SAVIOUR) MONASTERY, 12th cent. Within the monastic complex are SS. Peter and Paul Church (17th cent.), St. Elias' Church (1787), and a seminary (1657-67).

PREDTECHENSKA (ST. JOHN THE BAPTIST CHURCH), 1746.

MYKILSKA (ST. NICHOLAS') CHURCH, 18th cent.

MYKHAYLIVSKA (ST. MICHAEL'S) CHURCH, 1814.

OSTER

City, Kozelets district, on the Desna River, 43 km from the Bobryk railway station.

YURYEVA BOZHNYTSYA (ST. GEORGE'S TEMPLE), 10th-11th cent. The ruins are an example of the architecture of Kyivan Rus'-Ukraine.

Regional Museum.

PISKY

Village, Bobrovytsya district, 25 km from the Bobrovytsya railway station.
The renowned Ukrainian poet P. Tychyna (1891-1967) was born in the village.

TROYITSKA (HOLY TRINITY) CHURCH, 1887. Wood.
P. Tychyna Museum, 1981. Located in the restored building where the poet lived.
P. Tychyna Monument, 1981. Sculptors: A. Kushch, A. Redko, and V. Shevtsov.
(In the courtyard of the poet's family home).

POLONKY

Village, Pryluky district.

MYKHAYLIVSKA (ST. MICHAEL'S) CHURCH, 1777-79. One of the oldest
Ukrainian Baroque churches.

PRYLUKY

City on the Uday River, 170 km from Chernihiv. Population: approx. 100,000.
City-fortress of the Kyivan Rus'-Ukraine and Kozak eras. First mentioned in the
chronicles for the year 1092. The inhabitants participated in Kozak uprisings led by
S. Nalyvayko (1596) and Y. Ostryanyn (1637-38), and in the national-liberation war
of 1648-54. A mighty fortress was built here in the late 18th cent. Four Kozak
schools were established at this time. A gymnasium for women was opened in 1911
and a teacher's college was established in 1915.

Travel and Excursion Agency: Lenin St., 203; tel. 5-39-98; 5-30-17.
Regional Museum: Ordzhonikidze St., 39; tel. 3-12-48.
SPASO-PREOBRAZHENSKY (TRANSFIGURATION) CATHEDRAL, 1710-
20. Built in the Ukrainian Baroque style, on the grounds of the Pryluky Fortress.
**RIZDVA BOHORODYTSI (NATIVITY OF THE MOTHER OF GOD) CA-
THEDRAL,** 1806-15. Built in the Classical style.
MYKOLAYIVSKA (ST. NICHOLAS') CHURCH, 1720. Built in the Baroque
style. After reconstruction in 1817, the decor was changed to the Classical style.
Today it houses the art department of the Pryluky Regional Museum.
IVANIVSKA (ST. JOHN'S) CHURCH, 1865.
TRYOKHSVYATYTELSKA (THREE SAINTS') CHURCH, 1878.
SRETENSKA CHURCH, 1889. Houses the Pryluky Regional Museum.
PANTELEYMONIVSKA (ST. PANTELEYMON'S) CHURCH, 19th-20th cent.
PRYLUKY FORTRESS, 18th cent. On the right bank of Uday River, built on
the site of an ancient Rus'-Ukraine city. Only sections of the ramparts have been
preserved. (At Hohol St., near Tsentralna Ploshcha).

POLKOVA SKARBNYTSYA (REGIMENTAL TREASURY), Halahan's Arsenal, 18th cent. One of the few Baroque-style civil buildings in Ukraine still standing. It once housed Kozak treasures and weapons.

T. Shevchenko Monument, 1961. Sculptor: A. Hayday. (Square near Lenin St.).

T. Shevchenko Monument, 1959. (Marx St., 36).

T. Shevchenko Monument, 1963. (Dzerzhynsky St., 19).

RADKIVKA

Village, Pryluky district.

VOZNESENSKA (ASCENSION) CHURCH, 1797-1805. Built in the Classical style.

SEDNIV

Village on the Snov River, 25 km from Chernihiv.

Historic city from the Kyivan Rus'-Ukraine era. Former estate of the Ukrainian philanthropists, the Lyzohub family. First mentioned in written sources as the fortified city of Snovsk; in 1234 it was ruled by King Danylo Halytsky.

HEORHIYIVSKA (ST. GEORGE'S) CHURCH, 1715-47. Built on the site of an ancient city, in the traditional style of Ukrainian monumental wood architecture.

VOSKRESENSKA (RESURRECTION) CHURCH, 1690. One of the oldest churches of the Baroque era. Built by Yakiv Lyzohub as a family burial vault.

USPENSKA (DORMITION) CHURCH, WITH BELL TOWER, 1860.

SADYBA LYZOHUBIV (LYZOHUB ESTATE), 17th cent. Converted to a picturesque architectural complex.

KAMYANYTSYA LYZOHUBIV (LYZOHUB MANSION), 1690. With a two-storied serrated tower and buttresses.

SHEVCHENKOVA LYPA (SHEVCHENKO'S LINDEN TREE). In the garden of the Lyzohub estate; this 600 year-old tree was a favorite resting place of Shevchenko when he visited Sedniv in 1846 and 1847.

ALTANKA L. HLIBOVA (HLIBOV'S ARBOR), 19th cent. Built in the Classical style; located on the Lyzohub estate.

T. Shevchenko Monument, 1957. Near Shevchenko's Linden Tree. Architect: H. Bystrovsky. Another Shevchenko monument, erected in 1976, is located in front of the secondary school on Shevchenko Street.

SOKYRYNTSI

Village, Sribne district, 5 km from the Kyiv-Sumy autoroute.

First mentioned in the chronicles for the year 1092. From 1717 it belonged to the Halahan family.

HALAHAN PALACE, 19th cent. Built in the Empire style. Architect: P. Dubrovsky.

O. Veresay Museum, 1959. The Ukrainian kobzar (bard) was born in this house.

O. Veresay Monument, 1971. (In Sokyryntsi Park).

Sokyryntsi. Halahan Palace, 19th cent.

SOSNYTSYA

Village on the Ubid River, 16 km from the Mena railway station.
First mentioned in the chronicles for the year 1234.

O. Dovzhenko (1894-1956), world-renowned film producer and writer was born in the village.

POKROVSKA (PROTECTION) CHURCH, 1847. Wood.

O. Dovzhenko Memorial Museum, 1960, 1964: Dovzhenko St., 2; tel. 2-15-90.

Young Sashko (Dovzhenko) Monument, 1975. Erected opposite the house where the film producer was born. Sculptor: A. Fuzhenko. Architect: A. Ihnatenko.

O. Dovzhenko Monument, 1965. On the museum grounds. Sculptor: L. Kozub.

STOLNE

Village, Mena district, 24 km from the Mena railway station.

ANDRIYIVSKA (ST. ANDREW'S) CHURCH, 1782. Built in the Classical style.

SYNYAVKA

Village, Mena district, 9 km from the Nyzivka railway station.

POKROVSKA (PROTECTION OF THE BLESSED VIRGIN MARY) CHURCH, 1775. This wood church was built in the Ukrainian Baroque style.

TROSTYANETS

Village on the Trostyanets River, Ichnya district, 24 km from the Kachanivka railway station.

Arboretum Park. In 1834 I. Skoropadsky, a descendant of I. Skoropadsky, Hetman of Left-Bank Ukraine, established a dendrological park. In 1983 the park was designated a nature preserve, renowned for its 1700 varieties trees and shrubs, and 250 species decorative flowering plants.

In 1964 a monument to T. Shevchenko was erected there.

VOLOSKIVTSI

Village on the Tyahova River, Mena region, 15 km from the Mena railway station.

USPENSKA (DORMITION) CHURCH, 1765. A wood church connected with a bell tower in the mid-19th cent.

The grave of T. Parkhomenko, a Ukrainian kobzar (bard). Located in the village cemetery.

VYSHENKY

Village, Korop district, 32 km from the Krolevets railway station.

Belonged to Hetmans I. Samoylovych, I. Mazepa, and P. Polubotok.

USPENSKA (DORMITION) CHURCH, 1728-87. Built in the Classical style.

P. RUMYANTSEV-ZADUNAYSKY PALACE, 1782-87. On the left bank of the Desna river. Now partially disassembled. Architect: M. Mostsepanov.

ZANKY

Village, Nizhyn district, 18 km from Nizhyn.

MYKOLAYIVSKA (ST. NICHOLAS') CHURCH, 18th cent.

M. Zankovetska Museum, 1964. This Ukrainian actress was born and spent her childhood years in this building.

M. Zankovetska Monument, 1984. On the museum grounds. Architect: Yu. Stanetsky.

ZHUKLYA

Village, Koryukivka district, 40 km from the Koryukivka railway station.

POKROVSKA (PROTECTION OF THE BLESSED VIRGIN MARY) CHURCH, 1913-14. Combines the traditions of ancient Ukrainian architecture, folk wood construction, and innovative architectural features of the 19th cent.

Chernivtsi Region

The region lies in southwestern Ukraine, bordering on Rumania and Moldova. It has a large variety of landforms: the Carpathian Mountains and picturesque hills at the foot of the mountains gradually change to a broad plain situated between the Dnister and Prut Rivers.

The Chernivtsi region, known by its ethnographic name of "Bukovyna," was created in June 1940. Population: 944,000. Area: 8,100 sq. km.

History

Human settlements in this region date back to the Paleolithic Age. The remains of more than 100 settlements, from 15,000 to 40,000 years old, have been uncovered.

The northern part of Bukovyna, which comprises the territory of the present region, was part of Kyivan Rus'-Ukraine in the 10th-12th centuries. In the 12th-13th centuries it was part of the Galician-Volynian Principality, which was later conquered by the Golden Horde. In 1345, when Hungarian armies expelled the Tatars from the Right-Bank of the Dnister River, northern Bukovyna fell under Hungarian rule. In the mid-14th century it was conquered by Moldova and in 1514 by Turkey.

During the Russo-Turkish war of 1768-74, Bukovyna became part of Austria, under whose control it remained until 1918. After the dissolution of the Austro-Hungarian Empire, in November 1918 the Bukovynian population opted for annexation to Ukraine. In response the Rumanian army occupied Bukovyna, which remained under Rumanian control for 22 years.

During the years of foreign occupation, which were particularly harsh under Soviet rule with its policy of total Russification, the Ukrainian population was able to preserve its language, customs, and traditions.

Chernivtsi Region. Dnister river forms the boundary of the region.

The Bukovynian land is rich in monuments from the ancient past. Remnants of the Trypillian culture have been excavated in 300 sites. Materials uncovered near the villages of Moldove and Komarove, and in Polyvany Yar in the Sokyryansky district, have led scholars to conclude that these settlers were a nomadic people, rather than a group tribes.

During archaeological excavations more than 50 different objects made by the Scythians in the early Iron Age were unearthed. The unity of the tribes inhabiting the upper regions of the Dnipro and Dnister Rivers is attested by numerous remnants unearthed in the villages of Lenkivtsi, Kruhlyk, and Ostrytsi in the Kelmenetsky, Khotyn, and Novoselytsky districts, respectively. These remains portray the evolution of the early Slavic Chernyakhiv culture in Bukovyna. (6th-6nd century B.C.).

PROMINENT INDIVIDUALS

BORN IN THE REGION:

Yu. Fedkovych (1834-88), writer, civic activist; village of Storonets-Putyliv (now the village of Putyla). • **V. Ivasyuk** (1949-79), poet, composer; Kitsman. • **P. Mehyk** (1899-1992), painter; died in the US. • **I. Vilde (Polotnyuk)** (1907-82), writer; Chernivtsi. • **H. Vorobkevych** (1838-84), poet; Chernivtsi. • **S. Vorobkevych** (1836-1903), writer, composer; Chernivtsi. • **Ye. Yaroshynska** (1868-1904), writer; village of Chunkiv in the Kitsman district. • **D. Zahul** (1890-1944), writer; village of Miliyeve in the Vyzhnytsya district; died in imprisonment.

BURIED IN THE REGION:

Yu. Fedkovych (1834-88), writer, civic activist; Chernivtsi. • **O. Kobylyanska** (1863-1942), writer, civic activist; Chernivtsi. • **H. Vorobkevych** (1838-84), poet; Chernivtsi. • **S. Vorobkevych** (1836-1903), writer, composer; Chernivtsi. • **Ye. Yaroshynska** (1868-1904), writer, teacher, civic activist.

CHERNIVTSI

The regional civic-political and cultural center of Bukovyna, 650 km from Kyiv, situated on both shores of the Prut River. Population: 260,000. Telephone code: 0372.

The city was first mentioned in 12th century chronicles which described a fortress built on the banks of the Prut river to protect the Galician-Volynian Principality from attacks by migrating steppe tribes.

The complex history of the city is uniquely reflected in the city's old quarter, with its buildings of various architectural styles: Byzantine, Gothic, Baroque, and others.

Mykolayivska (St. Nicholas') Cathedral, 1939.

CHURCHES, HISTORICAL AND ARCHITECTURAL MONUMENTS

THE RESIDENCE OF THE BUKOVYN-IAN METROPOLITANS, 1864-82. The architectural complex was built by the Czech architect Y. Hlavka. It consists of three separate buildings linked by the same design: the main building and two side ones, which form a large inner courtyard. All the architectural details are characterized by perfection of form and structural harmony.

During World War II the complex was looted. A fire destroyed the right wing and the Marble, Red, and Blue halls suffered damages; part of the library was destroyed. The residence has been restored and today houses the Yu. Fedkovych University of Chernivtsi. (Kotsyubynsky St., 2).

ARMENIAN CHURCH, 1869-1975. Built by the architect Y. Hlavka. Since 1922 the church, with its excellent acoustic hall, has been used for concerts of classical and chamber music. (Ukrayinska St., 30).

Chernivtsi University.

O. Kobylyanska Theater of Music and Drama, 1904-05. Built by the Viennese architects F. Felner and H. Helmer. The facade is embellished with sculptural compositions based on ancient Greek mythology. Side niches contain the marble busts of famous Ukrainian and world cultural figures. Melpomene, the muse of theater arts, is depicted above the theater's cupola. The balconies and foyer of the theater are built in the Baroque style.

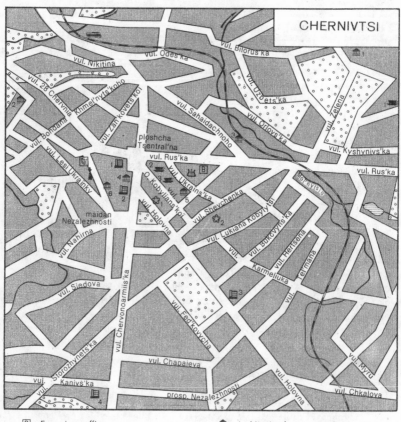

B	Excursion office
▤	Hotels: 1 Verkhovyna 2 Kyїv 3 Bukovyna 4 Turyst
🝙	Restaurants: 1 Prolisok 2 Dnister 3 Chernivchanka Note. Restaurants Verkhovyna, Kyїv, Bukovyna and Turyst are attached to the hotels of the same names
🚋	Railway Station
♟	Monument to writer Olha Kobylianska
🏛	Architectural monuments: 1 Dormition Church and bell-tower, 1783 2 Building of the former residence of Bukovyna Metropolitans, 1866—1878 3 St. Nicholas' Church, 1607 4 Town Hall, 1847 5 Armenian Church, 1860 6 Palace of Justice, 1906
✿	Museums: 1 Local Lore 2 O. Kobylianska Literary-Memorial
▣	Olha Kobylianska Theater of Music and Drama
🎼	Philharmonic Society

MYKOLAYIVSKA (ST. NICHO-LAS') CHURCH, 1607. A wood structure rebuilt in the 18th century. Built in the archaic "house" style typical of Bukovyna. Restored in 1954. The oldest building in the Chernivtsi region.

RIZDVA BOHORODYTSI (NATI-VITY OF THE HOLY MOTHER OF GOD) CHURCH, BELL TOWER, 1767. Built on the site of an earlier wood church in Horech. Was used as a fortress. The Baroque style, combined with Ukrai-

O. Kobylyanska Regional Theater of Music and Drama.

nian and Moldavian architectural traditions of the 18th century, is reflected in the structure. Eighteenth century frescos have been preserved. (Troyanovska St., 1).

VOZNESENSKA (ASCENSION) CHURCH AND BELL TOWER, 16th cent. Wood. Built in the village of Haryachy Urban, which is part of the municipal zone. (Boryspilska St., 13).

MONUMENTS

O. Kobylyanska, 1980. Sculptors: M. Miroshnychenko and A. Skyba. Architect: O. Taratuta. (Teatralna Ploshcha).

S. Vorobkevych, 1986. Sculptor: M. Miroshnychenko. (28 Chervnya St.).

Y. Hlavka, 1936. Sculptor: A. Severyn. (Kotsyubynsky St., 2).

P. Celan, 1992. A gift from the people of Austria (corner of Holovna and Bohomolets Streets).

MUSEUMS

Museum of Architecture and Folkways: Svitlovodska St., 2. • Museum of Regional Ethnography: Kobylyanska St., 1. • O. Kobylyanska Literary-Memorial Museum: Dymytrov St., 5. • Yu. Fedkovych Literary-Memorial Museum: Kobylyanska St., 28. • Museum of the Ukrainian Diaspora: Zhukovsky St., 1-a. • Art Museum: Tsentralna Ploshcha, 1.

THEATERS, PHILHARMONIC

Voznesenska (Ascension) Church, 16 cent.

O. Kobylyanska Regional Theater of Music and Drama: Teatralna Ploshcha, 1. •

Turyst Hotel.

Puppet Theater: Holovna St., 22. • **Philharmonic:** ploshcha Filarmoniyi, 10; tel. 2-61-82.

HIGHER EDUCATIONAL INSTITUTIONS

Yu. Fedkovych University: Kotsyubynsky St., 2. • **Medical Institute:** Teatralna Ploshcha, 2. • **Chernivtsi Campus of the Kyiv Trade and Economics Institute:** Holovna St., 91.

LIBRARIES

Regional Library: Kobylyanska St., 47. • **Central Municipal Library:** Holovna St., 162. • **Scientific Library:** Ukrayinka St., 23.

PARKS

T. Shevchenko Central Park of Culture and Recreation: Holovna St. • **University Botanical Gardens,** 1877: Fedkovych St.

SPORTS COMPLEXES

Bukovyna Stadium: Leninhradska St., 1; tel. 3-83-18; 3-85-11. • **University Sports Complex:** Stasyuk St.

HOTELS

Kyiv: Holovna St., 46; tel. 2-24-83; 2-08-48. • **Bukovyna:** Holovna St., 141; tel. 3-86-15; 3-06-38. • **Verkhovyna:** Tsentralna Ploshcha, 7; tel. 2-27-23; 2-45-73. • **Turyst:** Chervonoarmiyska St., 184; tel. 4-39-11; 4-39-10. • **Cheremosh:** Komarov St., 13-a; tel. 4-84-00, 4-87-77; fax: 4-13-14.

RESTAURANTS, CAFES, BARS

Bukovyna: Holovna St., 141; tel. 3-48-05. • **Turyst:** Chervonoarmiyska St., 184; tel. 4-39-08. • **Cheremosh:** Komarov St., 13-a; tel. 4-86-00. • **Teatralny:** Kotlyarevsky St., 6; tel. 2-23-05. • **Dnister:** Kobylyanska St., 5; tel. 2-70-71. • **Kyiv:** Holovna St., 46; tel. 2-28-51. • **Nazaret:** Chervonoarmiyska St., 194; tel. 3-60-96. • **Smerichka:** Holovna St., 63; tel. 2-27-34. • **Edelweis:** Komarov St., 9; tel. 4-59-12. • **Chernivchanka:** Kobylyanska St., 11; tel. 2-58-61. • **Davnya Kazka:** Shevchenko St., 64; tel. 3-04-83.

STORES

Rubin: Kobylyanska St., 10. • Suveniry: Holovna St., 38. • Khudozhniy Salon: Kobylyanska St., 23. • Ryazan: Chervonoarmiyska St., 56. • Optyka: Polyetayev St., 11. • Filateliya: Holovna St., 48.

BANKS

Natsionalny bank Ukrayiny (Regional Branch of the National Bank of Ukraine): Tsentralna Ploshcha, 3; tel. 2-68-11. • Komertsiyny bank "Bukovyna" ("Bukovyna" Commercial Bank): Beethoven St., 5; tel. 2-60-02; 2-38-82.

TOURISM

Bukovyna Regional Tourism and Excursion Association: Chervonoarmiyska St., 184; tel. 4-39-10.
Travel and Excursion Agency: Marx St., 34; tel. 2-53-34.
Cheremosh International Tourism Company of Chernivtsi: Komarov St., 13-a; tel. 4-87-77.
International Youth Tourism Association: Chervonoarmiyska St., 5; tel. 2-95-43.

POST OFFICES, TELEPHONES

Main post office: Khudyakov St., 6; tel. 2-66-54.
Central calling-point: Ryazanska St., 5.

MEDICAL SERVICES

Emergency: tel. 03.
Pharmacies: Central municipal pharmacy: prospekt Nezalezhnosti, 91-a; tel. 4-11-26. • Central pharmacy: Pivdenno-Okruzhna St., 31; tel. 4-33-98.

TRANSPORTATION

Central Inter-Urban Bus Depot: Holovna St., 219; tel. 4-16-35.
Train station: Gagarin St., 38; tel. 005, 9-21-90; ticket reservations: tel. 055, 4-29-24.
Aeroflot: Holovna St., 128; tel. 006.
Airport: Chkalov St., 30; tel. 4-32-21.

TOURING HISTORIC CITIES AND VILLAGES

BAYRAKY

Village located 28 km from the district center of Hlyboka, 25 km from the Novoselytsya railway station. First mentioned in the 17th century.

RIZDVA BOHORODYTSI (NATIVITY OF THE HOLY MOTHER OF GOD) CHURCH, 1646. This building is one of the finer examples of 17th century Bukovynian architecture, which reflects the Baroque style and the Galician school of church architecture.

BILA KRYNYTSYA

Village in the Hlyboka district, 12 km from the regional center, near the Vadul-Siret railway station on the border.

Founded in the late 17th century by Russian old-believers, descriptions of whom appear in the writings of L. Tolstoy, V. Korolenko, and A. Herzen.

OLD BELIEVERS' USPENSKY (DORMITION) CATHEDRAL, 1900-1908. A celebrated architectural monument, featuring architectural details typical of the 16th-17th century Russian building style. A museum of the history of Old Believers is located here.

KOSMODAMIANIVSKA (SS. COSMAS' AND DAMIAN'S) CHURCH, 18th-19th cent. Built in the Ukrainian church style of the 18th-19th centuries.

Dubivtsi. Uspenska (Dormition) Church, 17th cent.

CHORTORYYA

Village in the Kitsman district, on the banks of the Cheremosh River, 20 km from the district center.

Museum-Estate of I. Mykolaychuk.

DUBIVTSI

Village in the Kitsman district.

USPENSKA (DORMITION) CHURCH, BELL TOWER, 17th cent. Rebuilt in 1792, this church is one of the finest examples of Hutsul architecture. The construction of the bell tower is typical of Ukrainian folk architecture. Architecture, carvings, and paintings are organically unified in the church.

KHOTYN

City and center of the Khotyn district, located on the right bank of the Dnister River, 74 km from Chernivtsi. Population: 11,000.

Rich in archaeological, historical, and cultural monuments.

KHOTYN FORTRESS, 12th-16th cent. Was rebuilt and altered several times. For a long period of time the fortress was a stronghold of the Galician-Volynian Principality on the Dnister River. It is situated on the slopes of the steep right

Khotyn. Khotyn Fortress, 12th-16th cent.

bank of the Dnister, at the crossroads of several trading routes. Was an important defensive location in the Dnister region. In the mid-13th century the wood fortifications were replaced by stone and in the 15th century they were completely rebuilt. Ukrainian and Moldovian ornamental decorations have remained in places. In 1538 the fortress was captured by the Poles and partially destroyed. Rebuilt in 1540-44. In the 16th century the fortress was one of Turkey's advanced posts, and was reinforced by the Turks in the 18th century. In 1812 the fortress belonged to Russia; destroyed in 1856. The fortress complex includes four defensive towers (1480); commandant's palace; a church with fragments of paintings preserved from the 16 century; a Russian church (1835), now housing the Khotyn Ethnographic Museum. Many pitched battles were fought below the fortress walls. One of the greatest battles was fought in Khotyn in September 1621, when unified Slavic units won a victory over the 150,000-strong Turkish army, then considered unvanquishable. As a result of this victory, Western Europe was saved from Turkish domination. The Ukrainian Kozak army of 40,000 fighters led by Hetman P. Sahaydachny played a decisive part in the victory. The heroism of the Zaporozhyan Kozaks was celebrated by the Croatian poet I. Hundulych (1589-1638) in his poem entitled "Osman."

KONYATYN

Village in the Prytulsky district, on the right bank of the Cheremosh River, 30 km from the district center, 48 km from the Vyzhnytsya railway station.

VASYLIVSKA (ST. BASIL'S) CHURCH, 1790. One of the finest examples of wood church architecture of Right-Bank Ukraine in the 17th-18th centuries. Nineteenth century carvings have been preserved. The structure is noted for its monumental appearance and distinctive construction.

LUZHANY

Village in the Kitsman district, 8 km from the district center.

USPENSKA (DORMITION) CHURCH, 15th cent. Built by the local boyar F. Vityuk, this church is one of the oldest in the region. The frescos are a priceless monument of Bukovynian painting.

NOVODNISTROVSK

City, the most recent settled area in the region. Chartered in 1975.

A resort area has been established near Novodnistrovsk, on the shores of an artificial sea which extends for 80 km along the upper current of the Dnister River. Wood cabins, boats, pedal-boats, fishing, scuba-diving, and hunting gear available. This town is the last stop of a tourist excursion by cutters along the Dnister, which begins in the village of Kadubivtsi in the Zastavna district.

PETRASHIVKA

Village in the Hlybotsky district.

ARKHANHELSKA (ARCHANGELS') CHURCH, 1663. This wood structure is uniquely constructed and is an important work of 17th century Bukovynian architecture.

PODVIRNE

Village in the Novoselytsky district, 36 km from the district center, on the Moldavian border.

POPELYUSHKA CAVE. A unique natural formation; its entrance begins at the Kryva landmark, near Podvirne. The three-levelled subterranean galleries are 150 km long. The cave contains many strange rock formations, unique to Europe. A popular tourist attraction.

PUTYLA

City and center of the Putyla district, located beyond the Carpathian ravine in the picturesque Putyla River valley (a small tributary of the Cheremosh), 115 km from Chernivtsi. Population: 3,500.

A wood carving school founded by M. Klyuchan (1894-1957) is located here. Souvenirs made by Hutsul craftsmen were exhibited at the International Fair in Leipzig in 1967, where they were purchased by collectors and museums from around the world.

MYKOLAYIVSKA (ST. NICHOLAS') CHURCH, 1885. This wood structure is one of the finest churches with three cupolas in mountainous Bukovyna.

The Yu. Fedkovych Literary-Memorial Museum is located in the city.

STOROZHYNETS

City and center of the Storozhynets district, on the left bank of the Siret River, near the Carpathian foothills, 20 km from Chernivtsi.

Storozhynets Arboretum. A state nature preserve featuring trees and shrubbery from many countries. Open to tourists.

VASHKIVTSI

City on the right bank of the Cheremosh River, 32 km from Vyzhnytsiya.

Founded in the first half of the 15th century. The remains of three early Slavic settlements of the Chernyakhiv culture have been excavated nearby in Monastyryshche. The ancestral land of Ray Hnatyshyn, the Governor-General of Canada, who visited here in October 1992.

The H. Haras Museum-Estate (1901-72), self-taught master-craftsman, artist-ornamentalist.

VELYKA BUDA

Village located 35 km from the district center of Hlyboka and 13 km from the Kosmyn railway station. First mentioned in documents dating to 1461.

USPENSKA (DORMITION) CHURCH, 1794. A combination of Byzantine and Galician-Volynian architectural traditions. One of the finest examples of Bukovynian church architecture of the 18th-19th centuries.

VIKNO

Village located 16 km from the district center of Zastavna and 4 km south of the Dnister River.

PALACE, 1809. Its complex design gives this building a Romantic appearance. Unique in Bukovyna.

IOANIVSKA (ST. JOHN'S) CHURCH, 1826. A church without a cupola typi-

cal of early 19th century Bukovynian structures. Baroque paintings have been preserved.

VYZHNYTSYA

City located on the right bank of the Cheremosh River, 86 km from Chernivtsi.
Noted for its folk crafts.

Applied Arts Building. Founded at the turn of the century to teach wood carving; a training center for weavers, embroiderers, and designers.

Cheremosh Tourist Resort. Open year-round. Two itineraries available: by bus
through the picturesque mountain roads of the Carpathians and a walking tour in the
footsteps of Oleksa Dovbush, the Ukrainian Robin Hood.

Crimean Republic

Situated on the Crimean Peninsula, between the Black Sea and the Sea of Azov. Its landform is of two different types: the larger part is a plain in the north, while the smaller, southern part of the peninsula is occupied by the Crimean Mountains.

Restored as an independent state within the boundaries of Ukraine in February, 1991. Area: 27.0 thousand sq. km. Population: 2,642,000. Russians: 68.4%, Ukrainians: 25.6%. In the last three years large numbers of the Crimean Tatars have returned to the Crimea. One in 12 residents is a member of this nation.

History

The Crimean territory was first settled in the Early Paleolithic period. Its earliest settlers, the Cimmerians, lived on the peninsula in 15-7 B.C. The coastal and mountainous regions were inhabited by the Taurians, after whom the peninsula was named Taurica. In 7 B.C. the Cimmerians were forced out by the Iranian-speaking Scythian tribes who had come from Asia.

In 4 B.C. the Scythian kingdom was established in the steppes of the Crimea. Its capital became Neapolis, which was situated in the southeastern part of present-day Simferopol. Nearby were ancient Greek colonies. The Greeks founded Panticapaeum, Tipitaca, Nimfei, Cimmeric, Mirmeci, which in 5 B.C. were united in the Bosporan Kingdom. The great colony of Chersonese (Kherson) was established in the district of present-day Sevastopol. In 1 B.C. Chersonese became a vassal state of the Roman

Haspra near Yalta.
"Lastivchyne Hnizdo"
(Swallow's Nest).

Empire. Later it served as the main base of the Roman army and its garrison was located in the fortress of Kharaks, 9 km from present-day Yalta.

At the beginning of the new era the Scythian kingdom was conquered by the Germanic tribes of Goths. In the 4th c. the Crimea was invaded by the Huns who destroyed the greater part of the peninsula's population. Later the Khazar tribes, whose descendants are considered the Karaims, appeared on the restored lands. They were eventually ousted by the Pechenegs (Patzinaks), and later, by the Polovtsians. The Greek colonies on the coast were under the control of Byzantium.

In the 3rd c. Christianity arrived in the Crimea. It played a significant role here during the 8th-9th c. After waging a campaign against Chersonese, Grand Prince Volodymyr began to propagate Christianity from the Crimea throughout Rus'-Ukraine. His military campaigns helped the Slavs to gain a foothold in the Crimean Peninsula, where in the 10th c. they established the principality of Tmutorokan.

In the 13th c. some of the coastal lands were captured by Italian traders from the city-republics of Venice and Genoa. During this century Taurica was captured by the Mongols who gave the peninsula its present name — Kyrym (Krym). For two centuries the Crimea was the seat of the Golden Horde. In the 15th c. the Crimean Khanate was established and significantly enriched by its campaigns against Ukraine and Russia. The Crimea became one of the largest slave-trading markets. The Ukrainian Kozaks resisted the occupiers courageously. During their campaigns against the peninsula they captured Ghezlev (present-day Yevpatoria) in 1589 and in 1616 they stormed Kafa (present-day Feodosiya).

After winning a decisive victory in the Russo-Turkish War of 1768-1774, Russia annexed the Crimea. It was settled by Ukrainians and Russians, as well as by Bulgarians and Germans. In 1854-1855 the peninsula became the main theater of the Crimean War between England, France, and Russia.

In 1918 the Crimea became a part of the Ukrainian Peoples' Republic. In 1920 the Bolsheviks occupied the Crimea. In 1921 the Crimean ARSR was established. During World War II its territory was the arena of savage battles between the Soviets and the Germans. In 1944, after being unjustly accused of collaborating with the Germans, the Crimean Tatars were deported from the peninsula. In 1954 the Crimea became a part of the Ukrainian SSR.

The first Neanderthal relics were uncovered in the Crimea in 1924 by the archaeologist H. Bonch-Osmolovsky, who discovered skeletal parts of an adult and a child in the Kiik-Koba grotto. There are 25 monuments of Mousterian culture on the peninsula. The largest of them is the Ak-Kaya (White Cliff) near Bilohorsk, which consists of 17 dwellings and settlements. A large number of Neolithic dwellings was unearthed on the main range of the Crimean Mountains.

More than 170 burial sites of Kemi-Obinsk culture of the Neolithic period have been uncovered. Approximately 100 Taurian settlements were found, as well as the ruins of 34 ancient cities, 20 fortified settlements, many villages and burial mounds. A large number of monuments of antiquity and of the Middle Ages, particularly the "cave cities" of Manhup, Eski-Kermen, Chufut-Kale, Kyz-Kermen, the feudal castles of Tepe-Kermen, Kyz-Kule, as well as cave monasteries have been unearthed.

The Crimea has a long-standing reputation as a balneological (therapeutic baths) resort. Of particular renown are the mudbaths of the Saky resort, founded more than 150 years ago. Besides mudbaths, the local thermal and mineral waters are widely used. The main therapeutic remedies are the local air, sun, and sea.

There are a total of 330 sanatoriums in the Crimea and one of the finest is the "Ukrayina" sanatorium in Yalta.

PROMINENT INDIVIDUALS

BORN IN THE REGION:

I. Ayvazovsky (1817-1900), seascape artist, Feodosiya. • A. Horska (1929-1970), artist, human rights defender, Yalta.

BURIED IN THE REGION:

S. Rudansky (1833-1873), poet, Yalta.

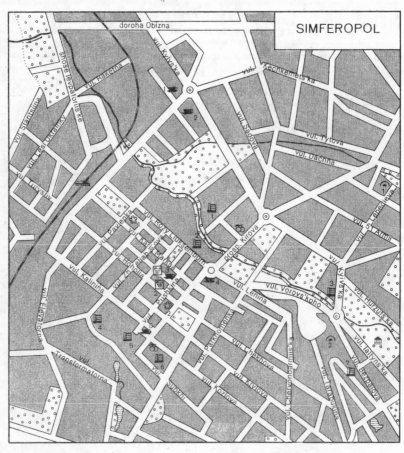

SIMFEROPOL

Hotels:
1 Dynamo
2 Ukraïna
3 Moskva
4 Sportyvnyi
5 Lokomotyv
6 Kolos
7 Tavriia Tourist Lodge

Restaurants:
1 Kechkemet
2 Selena
3 Astoriia
4 Okean
5 Simferopol'

Markets

Railway Station

Palace complex, 1827

Archæological monuments:
1 Chokurcha site (Paleolithic Age)
2 Neapolis of Scythia, capital of
the late Scythian state, 3rd c.
B. C. — 4th c. A. D.

Museums:
1 Art
2 Local Lore

Theaters:
1 Maxim Gorky Russian Theater
of Drama
2 Ukrainian Theater of Music and
Drama

SIMFEROPOL

The administrative and cultural center of the Crimea. Population: approximately 400,000. Telephone code: 0652.

The Tatar settlement of Ak Mechet (White Mosque) was established here in the 15th c. In 1784 the Taurian guberniya (province) was established, with its center in Simferopol. In 1850 there were 16 educational institutions in Simferopol; among them was the Provincial Crown Gymnasium for men (K. Marx St., 23).

SCYTHIAN NEAPOLIS, 3 B.C. Lasted until the 4th c. An excavated site, in the center of which is a large public building with columns. An archeological expedition investigated the mausoleum, which led to the discovery of more than 70 burial sites of Scythian noblemen. One of the skeletons belonged to King Skylur. Another burial site was that of a Scythian queen. (Vorovsky St.)

MUSEUMS

Crimean Museum of Regional Ethnography: Pushkin St., 8; tel. 27-63-64. • **Art Museum:** Liebknecht St., 35; tel. 17-54-04.

THEATERS, PHILHARMONIC

Ukrainian Musical Theater: Kirov St., 17. • **Crimean-Tatar Musical-Drama Theater:** Mendeleyev St., 3. • **Puppet Theater:** Gorky St., 9. • **Philharmonic:** Pushkin St., 3.

HIGHER EDUCATIONAL INSTITUTIONS

Medical Institute: Lenin Blvd., 5/7. • **Agricultural Institute:** Moskovske Shosse, 9th km. • **Institute of Architecture and Resort Construction:** Pavlenko St., 5. • **University of Simferopol:** Yaltynska St., 4.

LIBRARIES

Childrens' Republican Library: Turgenev St., 16. • **I. Franko General Research Library:** Gorky St., 10. • **Scientific-Medical Library:** Gorky St., 5. • **Central Scientific-Technical Library:** Yaltynska St., 20. • **Youth Library:** Kechkemetska St., 94-a.

Simferopol. Station square.

PARKS

SALHIRKA PARK, 18th c. The building, erected in the gardens in 1826, is an architectural monument. Of interest are the interior paintings and kitchen complex, styled to resemble a Bakhchysarai palace. (Yaltynska St., 2).

HOTELS

Kolos: Subkhy St., 4; tel. 27-23-84. • **Moskva:** Kyivska St., 2; tel. 23-20-12, 23-20-00. • **Sportyvny:** Zhelyabov St., 48; tel. 27-93-81. • **Ukrayina:** Luxemburg St., 9; tel. 27-55-73, 27-61-95. • **Airport Hotel:** tel. 29-53-37; information: tel. 29-53-08. • **Apartment office of the Synteks Company:** tel. 24-32-48.

RESTAURANTS, CAFES, BARS

Kechkemet: Gagarin St., 22; tel. 22-03-57. • **Moskva:** Kyivska St., 2; tel. 23-20-83. • **Okean:** Kirov prospekt, 27; tel. 29-56-64. • **Selena:** Kyivska St., 90; tel. 22-12-70. • **Simferopol:** Pionersky Prospekt, 3; tel. 27-33-29. • **Desert:** Gorky St., 1; tel. 25-44-56. • **Ogonyok:** Kirov Prospekt, 24; tel. 27-88-30. • **Ruse:** Naberezhna St., 1-a; tel. 22-98-18. • **Desserts:** Kyivska St., 2; tel. 39-22-77. • **Coffee:** Kirov Prospekt, 46. • **Moskva:** Kyivska St., 2; tel. 39-22-68.

STORES

Knyha: Kirov prospekt, 28. • **Druzhba:** Gorky St., 8. • **Filateliya:** Sevastopolska St., 26. • **Univermahs (Department Stores): Tsentralny:** Kirov Prospekt, 19; **Krym:** Kechkemetska St., 1; **Univermah "Dytyachy Svit":** Marx St., 1/40.

BANKS

Crimea Cooperative Bank "Krym-Bank:" Krylov St., 37; tel. 25-25-02, 25-00-18. • **Commercial Bank "Interkontbank:"** Hohol St., 7; tel. 25-63-54, 27-91-58. • **Commercial Stockholding Bank "Krym-Kredyt:"** Kuybyshev St., 61; tel. 27-26-91, 27-94-25.

TOURISM

Foreign Tourists' Bureau: Luxemburg St., 9; tel. 27-46-71.
Simferopol Travel and Excursion Bureau: Shmidt St., 9; tel. 27-42-46, 27-05-33.

POST OFFICE, TELEPHONE

Main post office: Luxemburg St., 1; tel. 27-20-11, 27-04-22.

24-hour telegram service: tel. 066.
Inter-urban telephone booths: Luxemburg St., 1; Gorky St., 5; Lenin Blvd., 2-a.

MEDICAL SERVICES

Emergency: tel. 03; 22-23-23.
Pharmacies: Pushkin St., 13; tel. 27-40-67; Samokysh St., 2/3; tel. 27-31-35; Marx St., 6; tel. 27-54-60.

TRANSPORTATION

Offices of Avialiniyi Ukrayiny (Airlines of Ukraine): Sevastopolska St., 22/2; tel. 27-21-16, 29-53-08.
Ticket reservations: tel. 056.
International shipping dispatcher: tel. 27-23-77.
International flights sector: tel. 27-22-88.
Railway tickets: Sevastopolska St., 22; tel. 27-33-16.
Bus tickets: Kyivska St., 4, bus station; tel. 27-52-11, 27-23-02.
Inter-urban trolleybus tickets: train station, cashiers' pavilion; tel. 27-34-30.
Taxi reservations: tel. 058.

AUTO SERVICING

Autoservice: Kyivska St., 148; tel. 22-34-22.

TOURING HISTORIC CITIES AND VILLAGES

ALUPKA PALACE

City, Yaltynsky district, resort, 17 km from Yalta and 97 km from Simferopol, 75 km from the Sevastopol railway station. Population: 12,000.
Ai-Petri, the most beautiful peak in the Crimea, looms over the city.

grossly under-stated

VORONTSOV'S PALACE AND PARK, 1830-1846. One of the finest palaces and parks in Ukraine. Built in the Late English Gothic style with Moorish motifs. The palace complex includes: Main building (1830-1837), Shuvalivsky wing (1830-1834), park structures (1829-1848), "Fountain of Tears" et al. Works of famous landscape artists, examples of applied art, rare books, and notes are displayed in the palace halls.

BAKHCHYSARAI

City, 32 km from Simferopol. Population exceeds 20,000.
The territory of the city was settled more than 40,000 years ago. In the 15th c. the capital of the Crimean Khanate was established here. The city was constructed by local master builders, Ukrainian and Russian captives, as well as by master builders from Iran, Italy, and Turkey. In 1628 the Ukrainian Hetman M. Doroshenko led a campaign against the Crimea and routed the army of Khan Kan-Temir at Bakhchysarai. In 1648 a delegation headed by B. Khmelnytsky arrived in Bakhchysarai. Preparing for war against Poland, he concluded an alliance with the khan and obtained a detachment of Tatar cavalry. By the terms of this alliance, Hetman B. Khmelnytsky was forced to leave his son and several distinguished Kozaks as hostages in Bakhchysarai. In 1675 the Kozaks, under the command of the Zaporozhyan chieftain I. Sirko, re-captured Bakhchysarai and liberated many captives.

HISTORICAL AND ARCHITECTURAL MONUMENTS

KHAN'S PALACE, 16th-18th c. The palace complex includes: the main building, Sokolyny Tower, a garden with a harem building, the khan's mosque (1740), a cemetery, rotonda, tombs (dyurbe), which are the most prevalent architectural mon-

Bakhchysarai. "Chufut-Kale."

ument in the Crimea. Since 1955 the Bakhchysarai Historical-Archaeological Museum has been housed in the palace buildings. (Richkov St., 129).

USPENSKY (DORMITION) CAVE MONASTERY, 7th-19th c. The monastery complex includes the Uspensky (Dormition) church dating to the 8th c., which is hewn out of a cliff. Located near the Chufut-Kale road.

MOSQUE OF TOKHTALA-DZHA-MA, 1707. Sixteen-sided minaret. (Luxemburg St., 7).

Bakhchysarai. Khan's Palace.

FORTRESS OF "CHUFUT-KALE" AND CAVE CITY, 10th-18th c. Built in the Crimean Mountains, 3.5 km from Bakhchysarai, on a precipice. The "Dyurbe Dzhanike-Khanyn" tomb (1437), the eastern wall of the fortress (1396-1433), Karaim kenases (temples) (14th and 18th c.), and the cave city have been preserved.

TOMBS, 14th-17th c. "Ancient dyurbe", 14th-15th c., "Eski-dyurbe," (15th c., "Dyurbe of Khandzha-Ghirei," (1501), "Small octagonal dyurbe," (16th c.), "Kubovydne dyurbe," (16th c.), and mimber (pulpit) (16th-17th c.). (Frunze St., 10/1).

FEODOSIYA

City on the shores of Feodosiya Bay, 116 km from Simferopol, a railway station. Population: approximately 80,000.

Founded in 6 B.C. Was destroyed by the Huns in the 4th c. and by the Alans in the 5th-6th c. Was the main slave-trading market during the 16th-17th c. In 1616 Ukrainian Kozaks, under the command of Hetman Petro Konashevych-Sahaydachny, attacked Kafa, destroyed the Turkish fleet, and liberated many captives. In 1667 a similar attack was led by Kozak chieftain I. Sirko.

HISTORICAL AND ARCHITECTURAL MONUMENTS

ARMENIAN CHURCH OF ARCHANGELS MYKHAYIL AND HAVRYIL (MICHAEL AND GABRIEL), 1408. Built in the style of Armenian church architecture. Restored in 1967-1970. (Timiryazyev St., 9).

GENOESE FORTRESS, 14th c. Located in the northern part of the city, above Feodosiya Bay. Was a citadel of ancient Kafa's (Feodosiya) city fortifications. In the 18th and 19th c. most of the structures were dismantled. The following structures are located on the territory of the fortress: Tower of Klyment (1348), Tower of Krisko (14th c.), Armenian church of Ioann Predtecha (John the Baptist) (1348), St. Ioan

Bohoslov (St. John the Divine) (14th c.), St. Heorhiy (St. George) (14th c.), St. Stefan (14th c.), et al. Many structures have been restored.

CITY FORTRESS, 14th c. Located in the old part of the city. In 1266 the Genoese wrested control over Kafa from the Golden Horde. In the 14th c. they began to build the fortress. Located on its territory are the fortress walls (14th c.), tower of St. Konstantyn (Constantine) (1382-1448), tower of St. Foma (St. Thomas) (1373), tower of G. di Scaffa (1342).

Monument to I. Ayvazovsky, 1970.

MUSEUMS

I. Ayvazovsky Art Gallery: Halereyna St., 2. • Ethnographic Museum: Lenin Prospekt, 11.

BANKS

Stockholding Commercial Bank "Tavria:" Korobkov St., 9; tel. 3-05-70; 3-51-15. • Azov-Chornomorsky (Black Sea) Commercial Bank "Azchorkombank:" Luxemburg St., 4; tel. 3-50-56; 3-22-25.

KERCH

City on the shores of Kerchenska Strait, 210 km from Simferopol, a railway junction and important seaport on the Black Sea and Sea of Azov. Population exceeds 150,000.

On this site in 6 B.C. the Greeks founded the city of Panticapaeum, which later became the capital of the Bosporan Kingdom. It ceased to exist after the invasion of the Huns in the 5th c. In the 8th c. known as Krch in the Chronicle. Was part of the principality of Tmutorokan. For 150 years the city, known as Cerccio, was one of the Genoan colonies. During the 16th-18th c. the Ukrainian Kozaks made frequent campaigns against the city, as evidenced by several historical sites: Haydamaky caves and cliffs, the Kozak fortress Borzovka.

HISTORICAL AND ARCHITECTURAL MONUMENTS

MELEK-CHESMENSKY KURHAN (GRAVE MOUND), 4 B.C. One of the oldest structures of antiquity on the territory of Ukraine, it was a mausoleum for the Bosporan nobilities. (Haydar St.).

TSARSKY KURHAN (TSAR'S GRAVE MOUND), 4 B.C. Tomb of the Bosporan nobilities, 17 m high, with a corridor and a burial chamber. Restored in 1885-1886.

CHURCH OF ST. IOAN PREDTECHA (ST. JOHN THE BAPTIST) CHURCH, 8th-14th c., structures added in the 19th c. The oldest part of the church

Kerch. Sv. Ioan Predtecha
(St. John the Baptist)
Church, 8th-14th cent.

is built in the Byzantine style. Original frescoes have been preserved. Restored in 1980. Since 1960 it has housed the gemological exhibit of the Kerchensky Histori-cal-Archaeological Museum.

FORTRESS OF ENI-KALE, 1703. Built by the Turks with the help of French engineers. The only monument of military-defense architecture in Ukraine reflecting the superior level of Western European fortifications construction.

MUSEUMS

Archaeological Museum: Sverdlov St., 22. • **Ichthyological Museum:** Sverdlov St., 2. • **Art Gallery:** Teatralna St., 36.

KRASNY MAK

Village in the Belbek River valley, 8 km from the Syren railway station. Population: 11,000.

CAVE CITY OF "ESKI-KERMEN" (Old Fortress), 5th-6th c. Ruins. Located on a mountain with precipices, founded by the Scythian-Sarmatians, occupied an area of 10 ha. and contains almost 350 caves. In the 13th c. the cave city was destroyed by the Tatar-Mongols.

CRYPT CHURCH OF THE BENEFACTORS, 10th-15th c. Hewn out of a cliff. Some frescoes dating to the 12th-14th c. have been preserved. They are a unique monument of Medieval artistic culture in the Crimea.

KUDRYNE

Village, Bakhchysaraisky district, 16 km from the Bakhchysarai railway station.

CAVE CITY OF "KYZ-KERMEN" (Divycha fortetsya - Maiden's Fortress), 8th-9th c. Measures 100 by 200 m, located on the shores of the river Kacha. Life in the city ceased to exist in the 9th c.

CRYPT CHURCH OF "TEPE-KERMEN" (Hillside Stronghold), 8th-9th c. Ruins of the church and some of its structures have been preserved.

SS. HAVRYYIL AND MYKHAYIL CHURCH (SS. GABRIEL AND MICHAEL), 1328. Ruins. Some interior paintings have been preserved.

SADOVE

Village, Kuybyshevsky district, 22 km from the Bakhchysarai railway station.

CAVE MONASTERY OF "CHELTER-KOBA" (Cave screen), 8th c. The church, cells, refectory, and defense caves, hewn out of a cliff, have been preserved.

SYURENSKA TURRET AND RAMPARTS, 8th c. Built by the Byzantines to defend the approaches to Chersonese. Was destroyed by the Tatar-Mongols in 1299.

SEVASTOPOL

One of the best-known cities in the Crimea. Seaport and an industrial, scientific, and cultural center of Ukraine. Population exceeds 300,000. Telephone code: 0692.

The ruins of the ancient Greek colony of Chersonese Taurica, founded in 5 B.C., have been preserved. During the 5th-6th c. the city was the bastion of the Byzantine Empire on the northern shore of the Black Sea. During the 9th-10th c. it played an important role in the economic and political relations between Byzantine and Kyiv. In 988 the Kyivan Grand Prince Volodymyr Svyatoslavovych captured Sevastopol, where he was converted to Christianity.

In May 1783 the first 17 ships of the Black Sea fleet cast anchors in present-day Akhtiarsky harbor. Construction of the port and military settlement was begun.

The city sustained considerable damage during the Russo-Turkish War of 1854-1855 and during the Soviet-German War of 1941-1944.

Sevastopol. Chersonese ruins, 5th cent. B.C.

HISTORICAL AND ARCHITECTURAL MONUMENTS

THE CITY OF CHERSONESE TAURICA (TAURIAN PENINSULA), 5 B.C. Ruins, located in the western part of Sevastopol on the Heraclian Peninsula. An important political and cultural center of the Black Sea region. Founded by Greeks in 422-421 B.C. From 5-1 B.C. was a city-state with democratic self-government. In 3-2 B.C. the first defense structures consisting of 24 towers, 10-15 m high, were built. More than 30 streets and a large number of gardens were laid in the city. The city center contains an acropolis and an agora (place of public meetings), a theater, and a temple. During the 1st-4th c. Chersonese became an aristocratic republic under the control of Rome. Later it fell under Byzantine rule and in the 4th c. converted to Christianity. In the 5th-6th c. a mighty defense system was constructed. In 988 Prince Volodymyr the Great captured Chersonese. In 1299 it was captured and destroyed by the Tatar-Mongols.

CHERSONESE HISTORICAL-ARCHEOLOGICAL PRESERVE. Organized in 1978 with the branches of "Cembalo Fortress", "Kalamita Fortress," including the ruins of Chersonese and a museum.

KALAMYTA STRONGHOLD (ruins), 15th c. Built on the monastery cliff at the mouth of the Chorna River. Founded by the Byzantines in the 5th-6th c. In the 15th c. a new fortress was built on the site of the old. Destroyed by the Genoans in 1433. Captured by the Turks in 1475 who renamed it Inkerman.

CAVE MONASTERY, 7th-9th c. The monastery complex included 8 land and crypt churches linked by passageways and stairs, among which is the church of St. Klyment (St. Clement).

MUSEUMS

Art Museum: Nakhimov Prospekt, 9. • Aquarium-Museum: Nakhimov Prospekt, 2. • Chornomorskoho Flota (Black Sea Fleet Museum): Lenin St., 11; tel. 52-22-89. • Archeological: Chersonese Preserve; tel. 54-14-15.

THEATERS

Chornomorskoho Flota: Ushakov St., 1; tel. 52-45-67. • Russian Drama Theater: prospekt Nakhimova, 6; tel. 52-43-28.

HOTELS

Ukrayina: Ushakova St.; tel. 52-21-27. • Krym: Bastyonna St., 46; tel. 52-31-81. • Sevastopol: Nakhimov St., 8; tel. 52-36-82.

Sudak. Genoese Fortress.

RESTAURANTS

Bryhantyna: prospekt Nakhimova, 8; tel. 52-43-01. • **Viktoria:** prospekt Peremohy, 40; tel. 56-26-30. • **Krym:** Rabocha St., 13; tel. 56-61-62.

BANKS

Sevastopol Innovation Commercial Bank "CIHK:" Ostryakova Prospekt, 61; tel. 57-02-69, 57-71-04. • **Commercial Stockholding "Nevykon Bank:"** Nakhimov St., 2; tel. 52-54-68, 59-33-84. • Crimea Commercial Church Bank "KKCB:" Lenin St., 25; tel. 52-53-73, 52-24-43. • Innovation Bank "Tavryka:" Hohol St., 8; tel. 59-17-33.

TRANSPORTATION

Bus Station: Repin St., 1; tel. 56-63-32.
Maritime Station: Nakhimov St., 5; tel. 52-40-82.

AUTO SERVICING

Autoservice: Horpyshchenka St., 138; tel. 36-70-48.

STARY KRYM

City, Kirovsk district, in the Churuk-Su River Valley, 10 km from the Kirovsk railway station. Population: 10,000.

MOSQUE OF KHAN UZBEK, 1314. The oldest mosque in the Crimea. Rebuilt many times. (Khalturin St., 5).

COMPLEX OF THE ARMENIAN MONASTERY OF "SURP-KHACH", 14th-18th c. The complex includes: the church of "Surp-Khach" (1338), cells (1719). Some of the structures have been restored.

SUDAK

City on the shores of the Black Sea, 57 km from the Theodosia railway station. Population: 15,000.

Founded in the 3rd c. In early written sources it is referred to as the fortress of Sugdaea, a trading city on the Great Silk Road. The Venetian consulate was maintained here from 1287. At this time the Black Sea was called Sudak. The "Great Silk Road" festival-market takes place here every summer.

GENOESE FORTRESS, 14th-15th c. Situated on a mountain 150 m high; its southern coastal side is a precipice. Occupies an area of 29.5 ha. The fortress was built in 1371-1469. The territory of the fortress includes: Sentry Tower (14th-15th c.), Tower of Torsello (1385), bridge fortification (1385-1414), Tower of di Pagano (1414), Tower of Giudice (1392), Circular Tower (14th-15th c.), Tower of Cicalo (1404) Tower of L. de F. Lavani (1409),

Yalta. View from the sea.

Tower of G. Marione (1388), Tower of H. Rumbaldo (1394), Tower of Astahvera (1386), Church of the Twelve Apostles (14th-15th c.), Consul's Tower (13th-15th c.), Heorhiyivska Tower (St. George) (14th-15th c.), Mosque (13th c.), Underground structures (14th c.) et al. Many structures have been repaired and restored.

YALTA

City, located 79 km south of Simferopol. Population: approximately 150,000.

In the 12th c. the Arabic geographer Idrizi mentions Dzhalita, i.e. Yalta, as the city of the Polovtsians. At first the southern shore of the Crimea was part of the kingdom of Feodoro. Later it came under the control of the Genoese. On Italian maps of the 14th c. it is called Healita, or Etalita. In the 15th c. the city was levelled by an earthquake. The Greeks and Armenians settled the district only 70 years later. Since then the settlement has been known as Yalta.

Together with neighboring villages and cities, Yalta is the largest international resort in the Crimea. It began to develop as a resort in the 19th c. Today there are 144 therapeutic resort establishments. The main one is the I. Syechenov Yalta Scientific-Research Institute of Physical Therapeutic Methods and Medical Climatology.

The young Mark Twain spent time in Yalta. The poet, S. Rudansky (1834-1873), lived here. A memorial plaque has been hung on the building where he lived and died (Ihnatenko St., 18). The renowned Ukrainian poetess, Lesya Ukrayinka, came here for a cure. A. Horska (1929-1970), a Ukrainian painter who died under tragic circumstances, was born in Yalta.

HISTORICAL AND ARCHITECTURAL MONUMENTS

"LASTIVCHYNE HNIZDO" (SWALLOW'S NEST), 1911-1912. Built in Haspra above Aurora's Cliff according to the designs of the architect A. Sherwood.

Yalta. Livadiyan Palace.

Designed as a medieval castle. Beside it are the ruins of an ancient Roman fortress of the 1st-3rd c. On the site of the Ai-Todorsky lighthouse is a collection of lighthouse bells.

ARMENIAN CHURCH, 1909-1917. Built by the architect H. Ter-Mikelov. Modelled on the church of St. Rypsyme in Echmiadzyn, a masterpiece of medieval architecture. The paintings were executed by the Armenian artist, V. Sureniants, whose grave is nearby.

PALACE, 1831-1836. Built in the Gothic style by the architect V. Hunta. One of the first structures in the Crimea featuring Romantic motifs. Today it houses the "Yasna Polyana" Sanatorium for Mothers and Children.

VILLA OF "KICHKINE", 1908-1911. Built in the Moorish style with decorative cupolas and a minaret-shaped tower. designed by the architect I. Tarasova. A park with exotic flowers encircles the villa. Used as a tourist base.

POLUKOROVSKY HILL. The burial site of distinguished historical and cultural figures. S. Rudansky is buried here (1873).

COMPLEX OF PALACE STRUCTURES, 19th-20th c. Located in Livadiya on the coast, on Mt. Mohabi. The former summer residence of the Russian Tsars. Consists of 60 buildings. The most important structure is the Great Palace (1910-1911), built in the Italian Renaissance style with elements of Byzantine, Gothic, and Arabic architecture. The Yalta Conference of February 4-11, 1945, during which Roosevelt, Churchill, and Stalin completed plans for Germany's defeat, was held here.

"POLYANA KAZOK" (MEADOW OF FAIRY TALES). Open-air museum, containing a collection of more than 200 sculptures drawn from fairy tale motifs and designed by Crimean artists, wood carvers, and stone-cutters. A branch of the local historical museum, 5 km from Yalta. Tel. 39-53-03.

MUSEUMS

Alupka Palace Museum: Dvortsove Shosse, 10; tel. 72-10-30. • **A. Chekhov Estate Museum:** Kirov St., 112; tel. 32-44-42. • **Museum of Regional Ethnography:** Pushkin St., 25; tel. 32-24-65. • **Livadiya Palace Museum:** tel. 31-55-81.

Yalta. Nikitsky Botanical Gardens.

THEATERS, PHILHARMONIC

A. Chekhov Theater: Litkens St., 11. • Yalta Branch of the Crimean Philharmonic: Litkens St., 13.

LIBRARIES

A. Chekhov Library: Morska St., 8.

RECREATION SITES

Hurzuf. A Crimean sanatorium.

NIKITSKY BOTANICAL GARDENS, 1812. Contains almost 28,000 types and species of plants. Founded by the botanist Kh. Steven. Occupies an area of approximately 1000 ha. Has A large collection of roses — more than 2000 varieties.

ARTEK, 1925. Formerly a well-known Pioneers' camp, now re-organized as the International Childrens' and Youth Center.

HOTELS

Office of the Hotel Union: Roosevelt St., 10; tel. 32-78-73. • Avanhard: Pyrohovska St., 2/4; tel. 32-87-77. • Adalary, Hurzuf: Leninhradska St., 37; tel. 36-33-79. • Alupka: Kirov St., 6; tel. 72-22-97. • Khvylya: Sadova St., 4; tel. 32-39-40. • Krym: Moskovska St., 1; tel. 32-60-01. • Livadiya: Baturyn St., 28; tel. 31-59-58. • Mahnoliya, Alupka: Lyotchyky St., 25; tel. 72-23-89. • Massandra: Drazhynsky St., 50; tel. 32-78-00. • Morska: pereulok Matrosky; tel. 32-31-21. • Tavrida: Lenin St., 13-3; tel. 32-77-84. • Ukrayina: Botkinska St., 13; tel. 32-57-61.

RESTAURANTS, CAFES, BARS

Oreanda: Lenin St., 35/2; tel. 35-83-24. • Riyeka: Drazhynsky St., 50; tel. 35-00-02. • Yalta in the Yalta Hotel: Drazhynsky St., 50; tel. 35-01-14. • Yaltynsky Bereh (in the Yalta Hotel). • Dzhalita: Moskovska St., 8; tel. 32-55-48. • Lastivchyne Hnizdo: Miskhor; tel. 74-14-71; 74-12-52. • Nitstsa: Moskovska St., 1; tel. 32-57-33. • Espanyola: Lenin St., 35/2; tel. 32-00-43. • Tavrida: Lenin St., 13/3; tel. 32-88-92.

STORES

Trade building: ploshcha Radyanska, 1. • Kashtan: Lenin St., 5. • Budynok Knyhy (books): Moskovska St., 9-a.

TOURISM

Intourist: Drazhynsky St., 50; tel. 35-02-86.
International Youth Tourism Bureau: K. Marx St., 7; tel. 32-83-82.

POST OFFICE, TELEPHONES

Main post office: Lenin St., 1
Telegram service: tel. 066; 32-97-64.

MEDICAL SERVICES

Emergency: tel. 03.
Pharmacy: Botkinska St., 3; tel. 32-15-54.

TRANSPORTATION

Airline agency; International shipping department: Moskovska St., 37; tel. 32-00-92.
Bus station: Moskovska St., 8; tel. 34-20-65.
Inter-city bus station: Moskovska St., 8; tel. 32-56-58, 32-79-94.
Marine station: Roosevelt St., 5; tel. 32-75-35.
Taxi reservations: tel. 058.
Inter-city taxis: tel. 34-33-33.
Funicular, lower station: Miskhor, Lenin St., 15.
Autoservice: Moskovska St., 33; tel. 32-25-40.

Yevpatoriya. Tavriya Sanatorium.

YEVPATORIYA

City on the shores of Kalamita Bay, 78 km from Simferopol; a railway station and seaport. Population: 90,000.

During the period of Greek colonization in 6-5 B.C. the ancient city of Kyrkynytyda was founded here. During the 10-12th c. this district was settled by emigrants from Kyivan Rus'-Ukraine. In the 15th c. the Turks founded the city-fortress of Ghezlev, which became one of the largest slave-trading markets in this region. In 1784 the city was renamed Yevpatoriya.

The famous All-Ukrainian Childrens' Health Resort is located in Yevpatoriya, which has more than 70 therapeutic establishments.

MONASTERY OF TEKIYE DERVISHES, 11th c. Has ascetic structures and pentagonal cells. (Karavayev St., 2).

DZHUMA-DZHAMI MOSQUE, 1552-1564. Built by Khodzha Sinan in the Turkish Classical style. Restored together with the mihrab (prayer niche), mimber (pulpit), and eastern minaret in 1976.

ENSEMBLE OF KARAIM KENASES (TEMPLES), 19th c. The complex includes the Great kenasa (1807), Small kenasa (1815), small doors with arcades (1835).

Ethnographic Museum: Sverdlov St., 11; tel. 3-12-80.

ZALISNE

Village, Bakhchysaraisky district, 8 km from the Syren railway station.

FORTRESS AND CAVE CITY OF "MANHUP-KALE", 6th-15th c. The largest cave city in the Crimea. Was designed to be the fortifications for the approaches to Chersonese. The fortress and city fell into ruins in the 18th c. Archaeological excavations uncovered the palace of the kings of Feodoro (14th c.), a basilica (10th c.), Karaim temples (14th c.), Church of St. Heorhiy (St. George) (10th c.), and a mosque (15th c.).

NATURAL "SPHINXES". The Karalezka Valley (strange rock formations).

Dnipropetrovsk Region

Located in the steppe belt, in the middle and lower basin of the Dnipro River, which bisects the region from the north to the south. The principal rivers are the Oril, Samara, Vovcha, Bazavluk, Mokra Sura, and the Inhulets, all tributaries of the Dnipro river. The territory of the region is a rolling flatland. The climate is temperate-continental, with hot summers and cold winters. Area: 31,900 sq. km. Population: 3,940,000. Established in 1932.

History

The first known settlements date to the early Paleolithic era. Archaeologists have uncovered settlements and burial mounds of the Copper-Bronze Age. Remains of the Scythian (e.g. Chortomlytsky burial mound), Sarmatian, and Chernyakhiv cultures have been excavated. The first Slavic settlements appeared in the 6th-7th cent. In the Kyivan-Rus' period the Oril River formed a border between the nomads' lands and the Polovtsian steppe. The Tatars devastated the lands near the Dnipro river. In the 1540s these lands were settled by Kozaks who established a fortified outpost known as the Zaporozhian Sich along the Dnipro River. In retaliation for attacks made by the Turks and Tatars, the Zaporozhian Kozaks waged campaigns on land and sea against Turkey and the Crimea. The Kozaks also played a significant part in the national-liberation war against Poland in the 17th cent.

In 1709 Tsar Peter I ordered the liquidation of the Zaporozhian Sich (Stara Sich, or the Chortomlytska Sich). In 1734 the Zaporozhian Kozaks were allowed to establish the New Sich along the Pidpilna river (near the present village of Pokrovsk, in the Nikopol district). The territory of the Sich was divided into "palanky," (districts).

*Dnipropetrovsk
hydroelectric plant.*

The Kozaks took an active part in the rebel peasant movement known as Koliyiv-shchyna (1768), led by M. Zaliznyak. In 1775 the Tsarist army, by the order of Catherine II, occupied and destroyed the Sich and its lands were annexed to the Azov and Novorosiysk gubernias.

TYPICAL SOUVENIRS OF THE REGION

China, plates, vases, and boxes brilliantly decorated in the Petrykivka folk style developed in the 18th cent. Examples of this folk art are exhibited in many museums around the world.

The soft dolls and brightly decorated samovars are very popular with tourists.

NOTABLE PERSONALITIES

BORN IN THE REGION:

O. Blavatsky (1831-1940), Theosophist, writer; in Katerynoslav. • **V. Pidmohyl-ny** (1901-37), writer; in Chapli, executed. • **A. Shtoharenko** (1902), composer; in Novi Kaydaky. • **I. Sokulsky** (1940-92), poet; in Chervonoyarsk, Synelnykove district. • **M. Vorony** (1871-1938), poet; in the Katerynoslav district; executed.

BURIED IN THE REGION:

I. Sirko (1610-80), Kozak chieftain; in Kapulivka, Nikopol district. • **D. Yavor-nytsky** (1855-1940), historian, academician; in Dnipropetrovsk.

DNIPROPETROVSK
(until 1918 — Sicheslav; until 1926 — Katerynoslav)

City, railroad center, airport and capital of the region, on the Dnipro River, 592 km from Kyiv. Population: 1,153,000. Telephone code: 0562.

Founded by Prince H. Potyomkin in 1787 on the site of the Zaporozhian village of Polovytsya, and named in honor of Empress Catherine II; renamed Novorosiysk by Peter I (1796-1802). The intensive development of the city began in the 1870s when a railroad line was built linking the town with the Kryvy Rih and Donets Basin.

In 1917-20 the city was occupied several times by the anarchist army of Nestor Makhno.

CHURCHES, HISTORICAL AND ARCHITECTURAL MONUMENTS

BRYANSKA MYKOLAYIVSKA (ST. NICHOLAS') CHURCH, 1913-15. A typical 20th cent. brick church.

MYKOLAYIVSKA (ST. NICHOLAS') CHURCH, 19th cent. Combines features of Classical and eparchial architecture of the second half of the 19th cent. Twentieth cent. paintings have been preserved. (Romanovsky St., 92).

MYKOLAYIVSKA (ST. NICHOLAS') CHURCH, 1807. Built in the Classical style near the earlier wood church of St. Nicholas in the town of Novy Kodak. Paintings from the 20th cent. have been preserved. (Zhovtenyata St., 108).

PREOBRAZHENSKY (TRANSFIGURATION OF OUR SAVIOR) CATHEDRAL, 1830-35. Built by the architect O. Zakharov in the Classical style. Renovated in 1975.

POTYOMKIN PALACE, 1786. Reconstructed in 1952 by the architects A. Baransky, S. Hlushkov, and M. Muchnyk. In 1961 it was designated a Culture Palace for students. (In Shevchenko Park).

View of Dnipropetrovsk.
In center — Preobrazhensky
Transfiguration of Our Savior
Cathedral, 1830-35.

DNIPROPETROVSK

Hotels:
1 Teatral'nyi
2 Ukraïna
3 Tsentral'nyi
4 Sverdlovs'k
5 Sport
6 Svitanok

Restaurants:
1 Poplavok
2 Zustrich
3 Liuks
4 Teatral'nyi
5 Iuvileinyi
6 Maiak
7 Ural

Railway Stations:
1 Dnipropetrovsk
2 Dnipropetrovsk-Pivdennyi

River Station

Markets

Monuments:
1 Taras Shevchenko
2 Alexander Pushkin
3 Nikolai Gogol
4 Mikhail Lomonosov
5 Bohdan Khmelnytskyi
6 At the grave of famous chemist
L. V. Pysarzhevskyi

Museums:
1 Dmytro Yavornytskyi Memorial Museum
2 Yavornytskyi Museum of History

Theaters:
1 Opera and Ballet
2 Young Spectators'
3 Shevchenko Ukrainian Theater of Music and Drama
4 Maxim Gorky Russian Drama Theater

Circus

MONUMENTS

T. Shevchenko: In Shevchenko Park. (Ploshcha Shevchenka).

B. Khmelnytsky: In B. Khmelnytsky Park. (Heroyi Stalinhrada St.).

L. Hloba (Kozak chieftain): In L. Hloba Park; Sculptor: N. Kurylov. (Prospekt Marksa, 95).

MUSEUMS

D. Yavornytsky Historical Museum: prospekt Marksa, 18. • **D. Yavornytsky Memorial Building-Museum:** ploshcha Shevchenka, 5. • **Cultural Preserve:** ploshcha Zhovtneva, 15. • **Art Museum:** Shevchenko St., 21.

THEATERS, PHILHARMONIC, CIRCUS, PLANETARIUM

Theater of Opera and Ballet: prospekt Marksa, 72-a; tel. 44-03-26. • **T. Shevchenko Ukrainian Music and Drama Theater:** Lenin St., 5; tel. 44-52-26. • **M. Gorky Russian Drama Theater:** prospekt Marksa, 97; tel. 45-34-92. • **Youth Theater:** Lenin St., 6; tel. 45-30-14. • **Puppet Theater:** Plekhanov St., 7; tel. 45-24-11. • **Philharmonic:** prospekt Kalinina, 47; tel. 52-60-94. • **Organ Music Hall:** prospekt Kalinina, 66; tel. 52-41-08. • **Circus:** Lenin Naberazhna St., 33; tel. 44-86-79. • **Planetarium:** Rohalyov St., 10; tel. 44-14-05.

Monument to T. Shevchenko.

HIGHER EDUCATIONAL INSTITUTIONS

University: prospekt Gagarina, 42. • **Agronomy University:** Voroshylov St., 25. • **Mining Institute:** prospekt Marksa, 19. • **Railway Transport Institute:** Universytetska St., 2. • **Construction Institute:** Chernyshevsky St., 24-a. • **Medical Institute:** Dzerzhynsky St., 9. • **Metallurgical Institute:** prospekt Gagarina, 4. • **Chemical Technology Institute:** prospekt Gagarina, 8.

LIBRARIES, ARCHIVES

Regional Scientific Library: Savchenko St., 10. • **Main Municipal Library:** Moskovska St., 1. • **Library of Foreign Literature:** Rohalyov St., 9. • **Arts Library:** prospekt Pushkina, 1. • **Regional Children's Library:** Voroshylov St., 9. •

Hotel Ukraina.

Regional Youth Library: Komsomolska St., 60. • **Regional Archive:** Liebknekht St., 89. • **Municipal Archive:** prospekt Marksa, 47.

PARKS, GARDENS

Yu. Gagarin Park: prospekt Gagarina, 72. • **Sevastopol Park:** Lotsmansky spusk, 2. • **B. Khmelnytsky Park:** Heroyiv Stalinhrada St. • **L. Hloba Park:** One of the oldest parks in the city, established by L. Hloba, where he was buried in 1793. There is a lake in the park. (Prospekt Marksa, 95). • **T. Shevchenko Park:** Established in the 18th cent. by the Zaporozhian Chieftain L. Hloba. Prince Potyomkin built a palace here in 1787. (Ploshcha Shevchenka). • **Botanical Gardens:** prospekt Gagarina, 72. • **Aquarium:** Komsomolsky Ostriv.

HOTELS

Ukraina: Korolenko St., 2; tel. 45-24-54, 45-22-83. • **Dnipropetrovsk:** Lenin Naberezhna St., 33; tel. 45-53-27; 44-10-74. • **Zhovtnevy:** ploshcha Shevchenka, 4-a; tel. 44-88-03, 45-52-20. • **Astoria:** prospekt Marksa, 66; tel. 44-23-04; 44-24-94. • **Svitanok:** Fuchyk St., 30; tel. 47-05-05, 47-07-38. • **Sport:** Shchors St.,4; tel. 45-02-09, 45-24-85. • **Sverdlovsk:** Sverdlov St., 6; tel. 42-88-07, 42-88-06. • **Tsentralny:** prospekt Marksa, 50; tel. 44-54-74, 45-03-47. • **Aeroflot:** Zaporizke shosse, 42; tel. 99-54-11, 99-55-84.

RESTAURANTS, CAFES, BARS

Astoria: prospekt Marksa, 66; tel. 44-82-42. • **Dnipropetrovsk:** Lenin Naberezhna St., 33; tel. 41-61-62, 44-88-07. • **Dnipro:** kosmonavt Volkov St., 8; tel. 95-33-32. • **Dniprovski Khvyli:** prospekt Pravdy, 109-a; tel. 27-00-97. • **Dorozhny:** stantsiya Dnipropetrovsk; tel. 42-30-77. • **Zustrich:** ploshcha Petrovskoho, 1; tel. 42-30-77. • **Kolos:** Teplychna St., 5; tel. 27-59-51. • **Luks:** prospekt Marksa, 72; tel. 45-22-02. • **Okean:** prospekt Pravdy, 68; tel. 27-50-35. • **Polumya:** prospekt Petrovskoho, 1-a; tel. 45-22-25. • **Poplavok:** Lenin Naberezhna St.; tel. 41-31-47. • **Svitanok:** Fuchyk St., 30; tel. 47-06-65. • **Rubin:** Yanhel St., 30; tel. 96-30-80. • **Stara vezha:** prospekt Gagarina, 104; tel. 39-17-08. • **Stary Lotsman:** prospekt Heroyiv, 28; tel. 68-42-47. • **Teatralny:** Lenin St., 10; tel. 45-31-65. • **Ukraina:** Korolenko St., 2; tel. 45-44-20. • **Ural:** Sverdlov St., 12; tel. 42-88-30. • **Ekspres:** Voronezka St., 1; tel. 27-39-43. • **Aurika:** Chkalov St., 2; tel. 44-45-31. • **Vechir:** prospekt Marksa, 99; tel. 52-12-69. • **Vechirne:** prospekt Marksa, 50; tel. 45-31-81. • **Viktoria: Naberezhna Peremohy St., 44; tel. 41-75-62. • **Druzhba:** prospekt Marksa, 46; tel. 44-86-24. • **Lavash:** Bobrov St., 7; tel. 42-36-09. • **Metro:** prospekt Kalinina, 37; tel. 52-52-33. • **Molodizhne:** prospekt Petrovskoho, 3; tel. 52-89-22. • **Pizzeria:** Myronov St., 3; tel. 44-35-71. • **Poltavski Halushky:** prospekt Marksa, 119; tel. 42-01-93. • **Sokil:** bulvar Slavy, 46; tel. 68-42-66. • **Sonyachne:** Marshal Malynovsky St., 8; tel. 23-40-04. • **Ukrayinski Stravy:** prospekt Pravdy, 37; tel. 23-80-97. • **Krasny Koral Cocktail Bar:** Lenin Naberezhna St., 11; tel. 42-49-71. • **Retro:** prospekt Marksa, 72; tel. 44-31-49. • **Pyvny Bar:** Budyonny St., 12; tel. 58-40-98. • **Shokoladny:** Shmidt St., 3; tel. 42-69-19. • **Nektar:** Liebknekht St., 1; tel. 44-12-54. • **Casino:** Fuchyk St., 30; tel. 47-07-65.

STORES

Tsentralny Univermah (Department Store): prospekt Marksa, 52. • **Dytyachy Svit:** prospekt Marksa, 48. • **Slavutych:** prospekt Kirova, 104-a. • **Topolyok:** Zaporizke shosse, 56. • **Budynok Torhivli:** prospekt Pravdy, 51. • **Kolos:** Teplychna St., 5. • **Zhemchuh Jewelry Store:** prospekt Kirova, 90. • **Izumrud Jewelry Store:** prospekt Marksa, 67. • **Yuvileyny:** prospekt Kirova, 42. • **Tysyacha Dribnyts:** prospekt Marksa, 92. • **Antykvar:** Mechnykov St., 4. • **Kylymy (Rugs):** prospekt Gagarina, 127. • **Podarunky:** prospekt Marksa, 81. • **Yunist:** prospekt Kirova, 78. • **Ukrayinski Suveniry:** prospekt Marksa, 49. • **Khudozhny (Art) Salon:** prospekt Marksa, 46. • **Myslyvstvo:** prospekt Marksa, 44.

BANKS

National Bank of Ukraine (Regional Branch): Lenin St., 13; tel. 45-42-15. • **Dnipropetrovsk Commercial,' Joint-Stock, Investment and Innovations Bank "Pivden-Kominbank":** Tytov St., 21; tel. 42-23-20, 42-39-02. • **Joint-Stock Commercial Bank of Technical Progress "Dnipro":** Lenin Naberezhna St., 29-a; tel. 42-39-02, 41-60-90. • **Commercial Joint-Stock Bank "Samara-Ahro":** Radyanska St., 12; tel. 2-35-80; 2-35-81. • **Commercial Bank "Pryvat-Bank":** Serov Naberezhna St., 5-a; tel. 41-20-01; 41-22-84. • **Joint-Stock Commercial Bank "Novy":** Marx St., 93; tel. 44-50-55, 45-42-68. • **Economic Joint-Stock Commercial Bank "Dnipro-Service Bank":** Simferopol St., 17; tel. 46-05-41; 47-28-54. • **Commercial Bank "Heobank":** Bilostotsky St., 59.

BOOKSTORES

Budynok Knyhy: Dzerzhynsky St., 43. • **Budynok Naukovo-Tekhnichnoyi Knyhy:** prospekt Marksa, 55. • **Akademknyha:** prospekt Gagarina, 24. • **Bukinist:** Artem St., 2. • **Suchasnyk:** prospekt Marksa, 94-a.

TOURISM

Dniprointur: prospekt Marksa, 125, tel: 50-28-31.
Suputnyk Youth Travel Agency: prospekt Marksa, 60; tel. 44-15-77; 44-13-67.
Dniproturyst Association: Fuchyk St., 30; tel. 47-06-65; 47-04-04; 47-15-60.
Organizes tours through the Dnipro riverlands. The most popular tours are: "The
Third Century of Struggle and Achievements," "The Grain-Growing Region,"
"Churches and Cathedrals of Dnipropetrovsk," "Dnipro River Cruise," "Kozak
Glory" (excursion to one of the Zaporozhian Sich outposts), "Kozak Battlegrounds"
(excursion to Zhovti Vody), and "Woodlands" (excursions to Kryvy Rih, Pavlohrad,
Dniprodzerzhynsk, and Poltava).
Intouryst-Dnipro: Lenin St., 8; tel. 45-41-32; 45-30-54.

POST OFFICE, TELEPHONE

Main post office: prospekt Marksa, 62; tel. 45-43-22; 065; 069.
Telegraph: prospekt Marksa, 62; tel. 45-31-52; phone-in service: tel. 066; to
order telephone calls: tel. 073; international calls: tel. 079.
Central calling point: prospekt Marksa, 60; tel. 09.

MEDICAL SERVICES

Emergency: tel. 03.
Municipal Pharmaceutical Information Center: tel. 067.
Pharmacies: No. 1: prospekt Marksa, 40; tel. 44-85-88. • No. 3: Komsomolska
St., 25; tel. 45-15-63. • No. 5: Artem St., 3-a; tel. 44-13-41.

TRANSPORTATION

Dnipropetrovsk railway station: prospekt Marksa, 108; Reservations: tel. 50-39-
53, 004. Information: tel. 50-41-11, 42-28-70, 009. Station master: tel. 50-25-86. •
Dnipropetrovsk-South railway station: tel. 50-74-00, 50-74-2-05. • **Airport:** Dni-
propetrovsk-42; tel. 39-00-21, 99-55-77. • **Dnipro-Avia:** Lenin Naberezhna St., 37,
tel. 42-55-30. • **Pidhorodne Airport** (local connections): village of Pidhorodne, tel.
29-05-29, 29-05-21. • **River port:** Gorky St., 19; tel. 42-26-69. • **Ticket office:** tel.
42-67-56, 49-82-09. • **Bus station:** Kurchatov St., 1; tel. 42-66-18; 001. • **Bus terminus No. 2:** Richkovy Port; tel. 44-27-03, 001. • **Bus terminus No. 3:** Baykalska
St.; tel. 27-00-21; 001. • **Taxi reservations** (24-hour): tel. 002. • **Police:** tel. 02. •
Lost and found: tel. 41-54-51. • **Time:** tel. 061. • **Weather:** tel. 45-90-83.
Autoservice: Karun St., 9; tel. 23-25-94.

TOURING HISTORIC CITIES AND VILLAGES

DNIPRODZERZHYNSK (until 1936 — Kamyanske)

Port city on the right bank of the Dnipro River, 35 km from Dnipropetrovsk.

First mentioned in documents for the year 1750, this city was originally a village founded by the Zaporozhian Kozaks. When the New Sich was established it was part of the Kodak palanka. The city owes its development to the metallurgical plant that was built there in 1887.

MYKOLAYIVSKY (ST. NICHOLAS') CATHEDRAL, 1894. Its exterior is embellished with ornamentation in the old-Ukrainian style. Today it houses the Dniprodzerzhynsk Historical Museum.

KAPULIVKA

Village in the Nikopol district.

Ivan Sirko (d. 1680), a Kozak chieftain of the Zaporozhian army, is buried in the village.

KYTAYHOROD

Village in the Tsarychany district, 53 km from the Kobelyaky railway station.

First mentioned in written sources for the year 1667. During the Tatar invasions a fortification surrounded by a palisade and ramparts was constructed on the banks of the Opil river. Inside was a small settlement of people, who would take down the "kytayka" (red flag) in times of danger.

VARVARIVSKA (ST. BARBARA'S) CHURCH, 1756. Restored in the 1980s.

MYKOLAYIVSKA (ST. NICHOLAS') CHURCH, 1757. A brick church constructed in the Baroque style. Paintings from the 18th cent. have been preserved.

USPENSKA (DORMITION) CHURCH, 1754. A brick church constructed in the Baroque style. Restored in 1969-1973.

Kapulivka. Grave of Ivan Sirko.

Novomoskovsk. Troyitsky (Holy Trinity) Cathedral, 1775-80.

NIKOPOL

River port city on the right bank of the Kakhovka Water Reservoir, 121 km from Dnipropetrovsk.

On the site of the present city there was a Kozak crossing over the Dnipro-Mykytyn Rih. In 1648 Bohdan Khmelnytsky was elected Hetman of Ukraine here. The defeat of the Polish garrison by the Hetman's insurrectionists launched the national-liberation war against Poland. The founding of a cast-iron foundry in the second half of the 19th cent. accelerated the development of the city.

RIZDVO (NATIVITY) CHURCH, 1812-20. Built in the Classical style. Paintings from the 19th-20th cent. have been preserved.

NOVOMOSKOVSK

City on the right bank of the Samara River, 27 km from Dnipropetrovsk.

Here in the 17th cent. the Zaporozhian Kozaks established their winter settlements; in 1688 they built the fortress Novo-Bohorodsk. In the early 17th cent. the lands between the monastery and the fortress were settled by Zaporozhian Kozaks. The poor of the city took part in the Koliyivshchyna movement.

MYKOLAYIVSKA (ST. NICHOLAS') CHURCH OF THE SAMARSKY MONASTERY, 1782-87. Built of stone in the Baroque style by K. Tarnovsky. The monks' cells (1816-20) are linked by a corridor system on one floor. The church and cells in the Samarsky-Pustynno-Mykolayivsky Monastery (built in 1602 at the site of the Samar fortress) were built by the Zaporozhian Kozaks. In the 17th cent. the monastery suffered extensive damage and was later razed to the ground. It was rebuilt in 1670.

TROYITSKY (HOLY TRINITY) CATHEDRAL, 1775-80. This wood structure was built in the Baroque style by the folk craftsman A. Pohribnyak. In 1888 it was restored by architect H. Kharmansky. It is the only wood church in Ukraine with nine cupolas.

BELL TOWER, 19th cent. A wood structure built on the west side of the cathedral; restored in the 1980s.

PETRYKIVKA

Village on the Chaplynka River, 22 km from the Bahliy railway station.

The first home in the settlement belonged to the Kozak Petryk. The village was first mentioned in documents dating to the 18th cent. In the 18th cent. the village was renowned for its decorative chests, rugs, and dresses.

A Museum of Applied Art featuring craftsmen producing the famous Petrykivka crafts is located in the village.

CHURCH OF RIZDVO (NATIVITY), 19th cent. A brick structure.

SEMENIVKA

Village in the Pyatykhatky district, 7 km from the Pyatykhatky railway station.

VOZNESENSKA (ASCENSION) CHURCH, 1823. This brick church built in the Classical style is one of the finest in the Dnipropetrovsk region.

STARI KODAKY

Village in the Dnipropetrovsk district, 12 km from the Sursko-Lytovsk railway station.

KOZAK FORTRESS, 1635. Built on the right bank of the Dnipro River by the French engineer, G. le Vasseur de Beauplan. In August 1635 it was captured and destroyed by the Ukrainian Kozaks led by I. Sulyma. It was rebuilt in 1638 and recaptured in 1648 during the national-liberation war. Tsar Peter I ordered it demolished in 1709. The fortress had been built in the old-Dutch style, and was surrounded by a rampart and a ditch. Today only a section of the ramparts remains.

Donetsk Region

Located in southeastern Ukraine in the steppe belt, reaching the Sea of Azov. The region consists of an undulating plain. The principal river is the Siversky Donets. The climate is temperate-continental. Established in 1932. Area: 26,500 sq. km. Population: 5,377,000.

History

The region was first settled during the early Paleolithic era. Twenty-five monuments from the Neolithic Age (8th cent. B.C.) notably burial grounds near Maryupol have been uncovered. In the 7th cent. B.C. the territory of the region was inhabited by Scythian tribes; in the 2nd cent. B.C. — by the Sarmatians. The Huns appeared in the region in the 4th cent., and in the 6th-7th cent., the Avars and Bulgarians. In the 8th-10th cent. the area was inhabited by the tribes of the Saltiv culture. In the late 9th cent. the Pechenegs invaded the area, and in the 11th cent., the Polovtsians. In the 11th-13th cent. some territories of Donets region were part of the Polovtsian lands. In 1185 a battle was fought between the Prince of Novhorod-Siversky Ihor Svyatoslavych's armies and the Polovtsians, which was masterfully described in the epic "The Tale of Ihor's Host." In 1223 the princes of Kyiv fought the Tatars at the river Kalka (now Kalchyk River). In the 16th-18th cent. the southern lands were controlled by the Crimean Khans and the right bank was ruled by the Zaporozhian Kozaks. The northern territories of the region formed part of Slobidska Ukraine. In 1707-08 the town of Bakhmut (now Artemivsk) was one of the centers of a popular uprising led by K. Bulavin. The uprising was crushed and the Kozak towns and settlements were burned by order of Tsar Peter I. With the establishment of the Ukrainian defense line against the Turks in 1731, the Donets lands began to be settled by foreign colonists, especially the Germans. The development of coal mines, metallurgical plants and railroads brought an influx of Russian businessmen and workers to the Donets region. Thus began the gradual Russification of the region and

Monument to T. Shevchenko in Donetsk.

the Ukrainian language eventually disappeared from educational institutions, businesses, and factories.

PROMINENT INDIVIDUALS

BORN IN THE REGION:

I. Dzyuba (1931), literary critic, political and social leader; in Mykolayivka, Volnovakhsk district. • **H. Kostoprav** (1908-38), Greek poet; in Yanisol (now Kuybysheve), Volodarsky district. • **S. Prokofiev** (1891-1953), Russian composer; in Sontsivka (now Krasne), Chervonoarmiysk district. • **M. Skrypnyk** (1872-1933), political figure. • **V. Sosyura** (1898-1965), poet; in Debaltseve. • **B. Teneta-Huriy** (1903-35), writer; in Donbas, died in a Soviet prison. • **O. Tykhy** (1927-84), educator, human rights activist; in Yuzivka, Konstantyniv district, died in a Soviet prison.

DONETSK (until 1924 — Yuzivka)

City and regional center on the Kalmiyus River, 871 km from Kyiv.

In 1869 Yuzivka, a workers' settlement, was established to provide manpower for a metallurgical plant belonging to an Englishman named D. Yuz (probably Hughes). In 1924-61 the city name was Stalino. Population: 1,073,000. Telephone code: 0622.

MONUMENTS

T. Shevchenko, 1955. Sculptors: M. Vronsky and A. Oliynyk. Architect: V. Sharapenko. (Shevchenko Blvd.).

I. Franko Bust, 1957. Renovated in 1970. (Kirov St., 36).

O. Pushkin Bust, 1969. Sculptor: N. Ginzburg. Architect: Y. Tomylo. (Pushkin Blvd.).

MUSEUMS

Regional Museum: Cheluskintsi St., 189-a; tel. 55-34-74. • **Museum of Art:** Pushkin Blvd., 35; tel. 93-37-27. • **Hall of Exhibitions:** Pushkin Blvd., 31; tel. 93-57-12.

THEATERS, PHILHARMONIC

Opera and Ballet Theater: Artem St., 82; tel. 92-23-48. • **Ukrainian Music and Drama Theater:** Artem St., 74-a; tel. 93-28-62. • **Puppet Theater:** prospekt Illicha, 18; tel. 95-77-77. • **Philharmonic:** Postyshev St., 117; tel. 93-12-89.

HIGHER EDUCATIONAL INSTITUTIONS

Donetsk University: Universitetska St., 24; tel. 91-92-74; 93-30-28. • **Medical Institute:** prospekt Illicha, 16; tel. 9597-41; 95-53-41. • **Music-Pedagogical Institute:** Artem St., 44. • **Polytechnical Institute:** Artem St., 58; tel. 91-07-09; 92-20-04. • **Institute of Commerce:** Shchors St., 31; tel. 9318-14. • **Branch of Kharkiv Institute of Railroad Transportation Engineers:** Hirnycha St., 6. • **Scientific Center of the Academy of Sciences of Ukraine:** Luxemburg St., 54. • **Institute of Applied Mathematics and Mechanics:** Universytetska St., 17. • **In-**

Donetsk.

DONETSK

B   Excursion office

   Hotels:
     1 Shakhtar
     2 Druzhba
     3 Ukraïna
     4 Turyst
     5 Donbas
     6 Kyïv
     7 Zhovten

   Restaurants:
     1 Kosmos
     2 Iuvileinyi
     3 Troianda
     4 Zolota rybka
     5 Vuhlyk
     6 Moskva
     Note. Restaurants Donbas, Druzh-
     ba, Turist, Ukraïna and Shakh-
     tar are attached to the hotels
     of the same names

   Railway Station

   Bus Station

   Monuments:
     1 Taras Shevchenko
     2 A. S. Pushkin
     3 At the grave of Russian
     economist V. V. Bervi (N. Fle-
     rovsky)

   Monument to heroic stratonauts

   Museums:
     1 Local Lore
     2 Art

   Theaters:
     1 Opera and Ballet
     2 Music and Drama

   Philharmonic Society

   Circus

stitute of Physical-Organic Chemistry: Luxemburg St., 70. • Physical-Technical Institute: Luxemburg St., 72. • Institute of Industrial Economy: Universytetska St., 77. • Ukrainian-language secondary school: Kyivsky Prospekt, 7.

LIBRARIES, ARCHIVES

Central Municipal Library: Cheluskintsiv St., 123. • Central Scientific-Technical Library: Syerov St., 56. • N. Krupska Library: Artem St., 84. • Regional Children's Library: Artem St., 84. • State Archive of the Donetsk Region: prospekt Luhatenka, 12.

PARKS, BOTANICAL GARDENS, PLANETARIUM

Park of Culture and Recreation: Universytetska St. • Botanical Gardens (280 ha, greenhouse — 5,000 sq. m): prospekt Illicha, 110; tel. 94-12-80. • Planetarium: Artem St., 65; tel. 55-52-48.

SPORTS COMPLEXES

Lokomotyv Sport Palace: Artem St., 147; tel. 91-36-46. • Shakhtar Central Stadium: Stadionna St.; tel. 66-03-32; 66-20-61. • Dynamo Sports Complex: Donetska St., 60-a; tel. 93-05-65. • Lokomotyv Stadium: Cheluskintsiv St. • Metalurh Stadium: Kuybyshev St. • Swimming Pool of the Polytechnical Institute: Cheluskintsiv St., 196-a.

HOTELS

Polyot: City Airport; tel. 51-56-02. • Donbas: Artem St., 80; tel. 93-13-66. • Olympia: Pavlo Popovych St., 35; tel. 58-65-86. • Druzhba: Universytetska St., 48; tel. 91-1968. • Kyiv: Pushkin Blvd., 11; tel. 92-05-04. • Motel: prospekt Illicha, 95a; tel. 94-32-70. • Turyst: Shevchenko Blvd., 20; tel. 93-91-16. • Ukrayina: Artem St., 88; tel. 9119-50. • Shakhtar: prospekt Titova, 15; tel. 55-66-14.

RESTAURANTS, CAFES

Ukrayina: Artem St., 88; tel. 55-84-32. • Donbas: Artem St., 80; tel. 93-19-08. • Druzhba: Universytetska St., 48; tel. 91-19-87. • Kosmos: Artem St., 275; tel. 55-83-99. • Neptun: Shevchenko Blvd., 98; tel. 94-71-09. • Troyanda: Artem St., 145; tel. 55-50-61. • Shakhtar: prospekt Titova, 15; tel. 55-65-66. • Vilnius: Kyivsky Prospekt, 7; tel. 58-50-39. • Moskva: Artem St., 71; tel. 9300-35. • Yuvileyny: Luxemburg, 61; tel. 93-03-04. • Zolota Rybka: Universytetska St., 27; tel. 93-62-91. • Turyst: Shevchenko Blvd., 20; tel. 93-91-15. • Kyiv: Pushkin Blvd., 4; tel. 93-07-64. • Chervona Kalyna: Shevchenko Blvd., 88; tel. 94-41-09. • Shakhtobudivnyk: prospekt Illicha, 85; tel. 95-42-03. • **Baku:** prospekt Panfilova, 67; tel. 53-20-43. • **Izyumynka:** prospekt Lenina, 4; tel. 66-06-50. • **Teatralny:** Artem St., 121; tel. 93-65-84. • **Pyvny Bar:** Konsomolsky Prospekt, 33; tel. 93-60-74. • **Nektar:** Artem St., 119; tel. 93-01-51. • **Natalka:** prospekt Hurova, 15.

STORES

Central Univermah (Department Store): Artem St., 34; tel. 9345-15. • **Bily Lebid:** Artem St., 143; tel. 55-15-99. • **Raduha:** Aksakov St., 21; tel. 66-74-61. • **Mayak:** Artem St., 160; tel. 55-51-54. • **Ukrayinsky Suvenir:** Universytetska St., 30; tel. 93-36-62. • **Donchanka:** Artem St., 148; tel. 5850-55. • **Druzhba:** Konsomolsky Prospekt, 28. • **Budynok Knyhy (books):** Artem St., 147-a. • **Rubin:** prospekt Illicha, 1; tel. 93-37-61. • **Izumrud:** Universytetska St., 56-a; tel. 55-54-11. • **Samotsvity:** Kyivsky Prospekt, 7; tel. 58-50-00.

BANKS

National Bank of Ukraine (Regional Branch): Artem St., 387; tel. 92-80-40; Fax: 93-51-96. • **Donetsk Commercial Bank "Ikar-Bank":** Pyatdesyatoyi Hvardiyskoyi Dyviziyi St., 17; tel. 94-90-92, 94-21-43. • **Donetsk Commercial Bank for Economic and Social Development of VO Donetsk Coal Enterprise "Donvuhlekombank":** Artem St., 63; tel. 99-80-43, 99-80-44. • **First Ukrainian International Bank:** Chelyuskintsiv St., 107; tel. 99-10-36, 93-33-82. • **Commercial Bank "Donkombank":** Postyshev St., 117; tel. 91-68-26, 91-69-60. • **Donetsk Commercial Bank "Donbirzhbank":** Kirov St., 145; tel. 94-95-41. • **Commercial Bank "Aktseptbank":** Pushkin St., 20; tel. 3524-04, 35-13-08. • **Commercial Bank "Kapital":** Universytetska St., 89; tel. 58-69-94, 58-96-96. • **Investment Credit Commercial Bank "Donbas":** Kharytonov St., 10; tel. 99-65-95.

TOURISM

Tourist Office: prospekt Konstytutsiyi, 3; tel. 92-15-76.
Suputnyk: Artem St., 125; tel. 92-65-94.

POST OFFICE, TELEPHONE

Main post office: Artem St., 72; tel. 93-58-48, 93-07-23.
Telegraph: Artem St., 72; tel. 92-14-95.
Calling points: Artem St., 80. • Kyivsky Prospekt, 1. • Pryvokzalna Ploshcha. Railroad Station.
Fax: prospekt Khmelnytskoho, 102.

MEDICAL SERVICES

Emergency: tel. 03.
Emergency Hospital: Shchors St., 47; tel. 95-69-06, 93-35-72.
Pharmacies: Artem St., 69; tel. 93-22-70. • Artem St., 282; tel. 51-23-41. • Artem St., 110; tel. 58-02-23. • Postyshev St., 129; tel. 93-57-22. • Gorky St., 154; tel. 93-18-32.

TRANSPORTATION

Railway station: Pryvokzalna Ploshcha; Information and tickets: tel. 005. Ticket Agencies: prospekt Illicha, 52; tel. 95-96-39. • Universytetska St., 35; tel. 93-40-59. • Shchetynin St; tel. 22-1232.
Airport: tel. 006; 55-53-09, 51-57-22; International sector: tel. 51-15-85.
Ukraine Airlines: Artem St., 167; tel. 58-81-80.
Bus Terminal North: Kyivsky Prospekt, 1; tel. 55-22-10.
Bus Terminal South: Misksad; tel. 66-51-19.

AUTO SERVICING

Road Service Complex: Artemivsk, 711 km autoroute E-40 Kyiv-Kharkiv-Rostov; tel. 6-34-53.

TOURING HISTORIC CITIES AND VILLAGES

ARTEMIVSK (until 1924 — Bakhmut)

City on the Bakhmutka River, 82 km from Donetsk.
Established over 400 years ago. Center of the salt industry.

MYKOLAYIVSKA (ST. NICHOLAS') CHURCH, 1789. On the Bakhmutka river. Wood.

VSIKH SVYATYKH (ALL SAINTS) CHURCH, Early 20th cent. Located near the railway station.

DRUZHKIVKA

City near the Kryvy Torets and Kazenny Torets Rivers, 86 km from the Donetsk railway station.

IVANIVSKA (ST. JOHN'S) CHURCH, 1898-1900. Built with white brick in the ancient Ukrainian and Byzantine architectural style.

HORLIVKA

City, 47 km from Donetsk.
Founded in the early 18th cent. on the site of the Zaporozhian Kozaks' winter quarters and homesteads. The settlement was named after the engineer P. Horlov.

SVYATOPOKROVSKA (PROTECTION) CHURCH, 19th cent. In the village of Zaytseve. (Take a bus from the Zaytseve railway station).

MYKOLAYIVSKY (ST. NICHOLAS') CATHEDRAL, 1905. In the village of Kocheharka. (Streetcar No. 7).

Pedagogical Institute of Foreign Languages: Rudakov St.

KHOMUTIVSKY STEP

Novoazovsky district, 32 km from Mariupol. A branch of the Ukrainian Steppe Preserve, 1028 ha. It contains more than 500 varieties of steppe plants. The best time to see the steppe is from mid-May to early June.

MAKIYIVKA

City, 15 km from Donetsk.
Established on the site of a former Zaporozhian advanced post, by the Kryvyi Torets River.

Makiyivka Commercial Bank "Shakhtekonombank:" Radyanska St., 2; tel. 90-25-39.

CHURCH OF ODYHITRIYSKA BOHORODYTSYA (MOTHER OF GOD), 19TH-20TH cent. Built in the Byzantine style. According to legend, the miraculous icon of the Mother of God was painted by Luke the Evangelist. The Byzantine Emperor Constantine IX Monomakh (1042-54) blessed his daughter with this icon when she married Prince Vsevolod, son of the Ukrainian Prince Yaroslav Mudry (the Wise). In the early 12th cent. the son of Vsevolod, Volodymyr Monomakh, transferred the icon to Smolensk.

Makiyivka Engineering-Construction Institute: Derzhavin St, 1; tel. 90-29-38.

MARYUPOL

City near the mouth of the Kalmius River, 121 km south of Donetsk. Founded as Pavlivsk in 1778 at the site of the Domakha Zaporozhian winter settlement of the 16th cent.; in 1611 it became the center of the large Kalmius district in the Zaporozhian free lands. In 1779 Greek settlers renamed it Maryupol; from 1948-90 it was known as Zhdanov. Population: 600,000. Telephone code: 0629.

Cooperative Bank "Azovbank": tel. 33-41-07; 33-33-65.

Base Port of the Azov Sea Maritime Navigation: tel. 5-83-73; 59-22-18; 5-82-63. Ships to the Mediterranean Sea Basin, East and West Africa, and the European continent.

Svyatohirsky (Holy Hills) Uspensky (Dormition) Monastery, 17th-19th cent.

Regional Museum: Pershoho Travnya St., 30.

A. Kuyindzhi Art Museum: prospekt Metalurhiv, 25.

Russian Drama Theater (built on the site of St. Maria Mahdalyna Church): Teatralna Ploshcha.; tel. 33-33-67.

Metallurgical Institute: Respubliky St., 7; tel. 33-21-10.

SLOVYANOHIRSK

City, Slovyansk district, on the Siversky Donets River, 6 km from the railway station of the same name. Population: approx. 600,000.

SVYATOHIRSKY (HOLY HILLS) USPENSKY (DORMITION) MONASTERY, 17th-19th cent. Located on the right bank of the Siversky Donets river. In the 15th cent. the monks dug passages through a chalky, rock-filled mountain and built a church on its peak. Documents dating to 1526, 1538-39, 1541, 1555, and 1571, mention Svyati Hory as one of the Donets outposts. The monastery was first mentioned in documents dating to 1624. It was surrounded by walls which protected the monastery from aggressors. In 1679 the monastery was plundered by the Crimean Tatars. It was closed in 1783 and reopened in 1844 under the name Svyatohirska Uspenska Pustyn (Hermitage). The monastic complex includes: the Mykolayivska (St. Nicholas') Church (17th cent.), Uspensky (Dormition) Cathedral (1859-60), cells (1887), an underground passage (17th cent.), Pilgrims' pavilion (19th cent.), towers (19th cent.), refectory-type church, Pokrovska (Protection) Church and bell tower (1847-51). Since 1922 the monastery has been used as a rest-home and sanatorium. Restoration and conservation work was begun by the architect M. Hovdenko in 1963-73.

SLOVYANSK (until 1784 — Tor)

City on the Kazenny Torets River, 110 km from the Donetsk railway station. Population: approx. 300,000. First mentioned in documents dating to 1646 as the Kozak fortress Tor. In the mid-17th cent. it was the center of the salt-mining and salt industry. In the years 1685-1764 it became a military city of the Izyumsky regiment. In 1784 renamed Slovyansk. In 1969 a monument to T. Shevchenko was erected in the city.

Ivano-Frankivsk Region
(until 1962 — Stanyslaviv)

Lies in the northeastern part of the Ukrainian Carpathian Mountains, the Transcarpathians and part of Opillya. The terrain is mountainous and hilly; part of the region's territory consists of flatlands. The highest ranges are the Gorgony (with a maximum elevation of 1836 m) and Chornohora (reaching 2061 m). The principal rivers are the Dnister, Prut, and Cheremosh. The climate is temperate-continental. The rich mineral resources of the region include natural gas, oil, gold, manganese, potassium salts, brown coal, common salts, ozokerite, and mineral water springs. Established in 1939. Area: 13,900 sq. km. Population: 1,458,000.

History

Human settlements appeared in the Paleolithic era, approximately 100,000 years ago. Dwellings from this period were unearthed in the village of Bykivnya near the Dnister River. Jewelry, weapons, and work tools (8th-7th cent. B.C.) were excavated near the village of Hrushky and Nyzhniv in the Tlumach district. Over 20 settlements of the Trypillian culture have been uncovered in the south-eastern part of the region.

Yaremcha. View of the Carpathian Mountains.

In the second half of the 1st cent. the Slavic tribe of the White Croatians settled in the foothills; the Tyvertsian tribe inhabited the territory between the Dnister and Prut Rivers. In 981 the region was part of Kyivan Rus'-Ukraine. From the mid-12th cent. the region was successively part of the Galician, Volodymyr-Volynsky, and Galician-Volynian Principalities. The Galician-Volynian Principality became a mighty state during the rule of King Danylo of Halych. In the 12th-13th cent. art, education, and literature flourished in the region. The Galician-Volynian Chronicle, depicting historical events during the years 1201-09, was compiled here. In the 14th cent. the territories of the region came under Lithuanian and then Polish rule. The region was embroiled in the Ukrainian national-liberation war of 1648-54. In the fall of 1648, the Zaporozhian Kozaks arrived in Rohatyn, Dolyna, and Nadvirna. During the 1630s-40s the Opryshky (Freedom Fighters) movement with a popular social base arose in the region. The most renowned Opryshky leader was O. Dovbush. The region was acquired by Austria in the 18th cent. During the 19th cent. industry began to be developed in the area.

During the First World War fierce battles were fought here between the armies of the German-Austrian alliance and Tsarist Russia. In 1918 thousands of Ukrainian patriots fought in the Polish-Ukrainian War for an independent Western Ukraine. In 1919 the act unifying the Western Ukrainian National Republic (ZUNR) and the Ukrainian National Republic (UNR), with its capital in Kyiv, was signed in Stanyslaviv (now Ivano-Frankivsk). In the summer of 1919 the territory was occupied by Poland. After 17 September 1939 the region became part of the Ukrainian SSR. During the Second World War, the population took an active part in establishing the Ukrainian Insurgent Army (UPA) which fought against the German armies, Soviet troops, and, in the early 1950s, against NKVD units.

PROMINENT INDIVIDUALS

BORN IN THE REGION:

S. **Bandera** (1909-59), head of the Organization of Ukrainian Nationalists, OUN (b), political figure; in Stary Uhryniv, Kalush district, assassinated by a KGB agent, buried in Germany. • M. **Hayvoronsky** (1892-1949), composer; in Zalishchyky, died in Canada. • S. **Hordynsky** (1906), artist, poet, art expert; in Kolomyya, lives in the U.S. • R. **Ivanychuk** (1929), writer; in Trach, Kosiv district. • V. **Kasiyan** (1896-1976), graphic artist; in Mykulyntsi, Snyatyn district. • N. **Kobrynska-Ozarkevych** (1855-1920), writer; in Beleluya, Snyatyn district. • A. **Kos-Anatolsky** (1909-83), composer; in Kolomyya. • B. **Kravtsiv** (1904-75), poet; in Lopyanka, died in the USA. • H. **Kruk** (1911-88), sculptor; in Bratyshiv, died in Germany. • D. **Pavlychko** (1929), poet, civic and political figure; in Stopchativ, Kosiv district. • M. **Plavyuk** (1926), president of Ukrainian National Republic in Exile (UNR), head of the Organization of Ukrainian Nationalists, OUN(m), political leader; in Rusiv, Snyatyn district. • N. **Roksolana-Lisovska** (1505-61), wife of the Turkish Sultan, Turkish political figure; in Rohatyn, buried in Istambul. • V. **Stefanyk** (1871-1936), writer, social and political figure; in Rusiv, Snyatyn district. • **I. Vahylevych** (1811-66), writer; in Yasen, Rozhnyativ district.

BURIED IN THE REGION:

A. Chaykovsky (1857-1935), writer; in Kolomyya. • **M. Cheremshyna** (1874-1927), writer; in Snyatyn. • **N. Kobrynska** (1855-1920), writer; in Bolekhiv. • **M. Mohylnytsky** (1811-73), poet; in Yablunka, Bohorodchany district. • **D. Sichynsky** (1865-1909), composer; in Ivano-Frankivsk. • **V. Stefanyk** (1871-1936), writer, civic figure; in Rusiv, Snyatyn district.

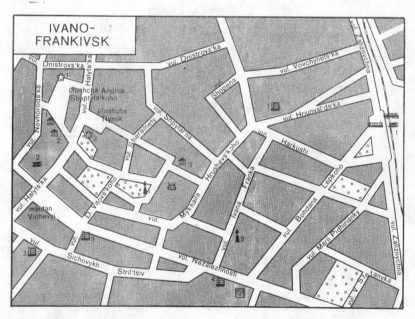

Hotels:
1 Roksolana
2 Dnister
3 Kyïv
4 Ukraïna

Restaurants:
1 At the Railway Station
2 Karpaty
Note. Restaurants Kyïv, Dnister and Ukraïna are attached to the hotels of the same names

Railway Station

Bus Station

Monuments:
1 Adam Mickiewicz
2 Ivan Franko

Architectural monuments:
1 Jesuit Collegium, 1742
2 Jesuit Church, 1763
3 Greek-Catholic Cathedral, 1743

Museums:
1 Art
2 Local Lore

Ivan Franko Ukrainian Theater of Music and Drama

Philharmonic Society

IVANO-FRANKIVSK (until 1962 — Stanyslaviv)

Regional center located in the estuary of the Bystrytsya-Nadvirnyanska and Bystrytsya-Solotvynska rivers. Population: 246,000. Telephone code: 0340.

Flint objects from the Neolithic Age and stone axes from the Bronze Age have been uncovered in the city. In the mid-17th cent. the village of Zabolottya, named Stanyslaviv in 1662, was on the main trading route between Lviv and the Danube River mouth. In 1772 the city came under Austrian rule (from 1867 — Austro-Hungary). In 1690 Trinitarian monks from Warsaw arrived in Stanyslaviv, followed by the Jesuits in 1716. Many Armenian merchants lived here. In 1866 the city became an important railway junction. In 1906 a Ukrainian gymnasium was founded here.

CHURCHES, HISTORICAL AND ARCHITECTURAL MONUMENTS

PARAFIYALNY KOSTEL (PARISH ROMAN CATHOLIC CHURCH), 1672-1703. Architects: F. Corassini and K. Banoye. In the second half of the 19th cent. the interior was painted by E. Fabiansky. Now an Art Museum containing 10,000 paintings. (Maydan Mytropolyta A. Sheptytskoho).

VIRMENSKA TSERKVA (ARMENIAN CHURCH), 1742. An example of Baroque style. Formerly a Museum of Religion History, this church was reverted to the Ukrainian Autocephalous Orthodox Church. (Virmenska St.).

KAFEDRALNY SOBOR SVYATOHO VOSKRESINNYA (HOLY RESURRECTION CATHEDRAL), 1753-63. Built in the Baroque style by the architect S. Potocki. Renovated in 1885 and 1955. Today the church belongs to the Ukrainian Catholic Church. (Maydan Mytropolyta A. Sheptytskoho, 19).

FORMER CITY HALL, 1695. After renovations made in 1929-32 it acquired a cruciform shape. The basement was used as a jail for opryshky (brigands). On 15 April 1990 the red Soviet flag was removed from the tower and replaced with the Ukrainian national blue-and-yellow flag.

MONUMENTS

T. Shevchenko, 1952. Sculptor: Y. Nykolyshyn. (Park of Culture and Recreation).

A. Mickiewicz, 1898. Sculptor: T. Blotnicki. (Ploshcha Mitskevycha).

Kafedralny Sobor Svyatohovoskresinnya (Holy Resurrection Cathedral), 1753-63.

Hrushevsky St.

D. **Sichynsky,** 1943. Sculptor: M. Zoriy.
E. **Zhelekhivsky,** 1886. (Skorbota Sq.).

MUSEUMS

Museum of Regional Ethnography: Halytska St., 4; tel. 2-21-22. • **Art Museum:** maydan Sheptytskoho, 8; tel. 4-21-52. • **Literary Museum:** B. Lepky St., 27; tel. 2-50-47. • **Geological Museum:** Karpatska St., 15; tel. 4-22-31. • **Osvity Prykarpattya Museum:** Shevchenko St., 57; tel. 2-40-69.

THEATERS, PHILHARMONIC

Music and Drama Theater: Nezalezhnosti St., 42. • **Puppet Theater:** Nezalezhnosti St., 10-a. • **Philharmonic:** Kurbas St., 3. • **Hutsul Song and Dance Ensemble:** Kurbas St., 3.

HIGHER EDUCATIONAL INSTITUTIONS

Carpathian University: Shevchenko St., 57. • **Oil and Gas Institute:** Karpatska St., 15. • **Medical Institute:** Halytska St., 2. • **Theological Institute:** Sirko St., 3. • **Economics Lyceum, Business Center:** Dnistrovska St., 28.

LIBRARIES, ARCHIVES

General-Scientific Library: Vasylyanok St., 17. • **Scientific-Medical Library:** Mazepa St., 101. • **Municipal Library:** Korol Danylo St., 16. • **Youth Library:** Nezalezhnosti St., 12. • **Regional State Archive:** Hrundvaldska St., 3. • **Municipal State Archive:** Hrundvaldska St., 11.

NEWSPAPERS

Halychyna: Hrushevsky St., 21 (8th floor); tel. 2-50-90. • **Zakhidny Kuryer:** Hrundvaldska St., 8; tel. 2-50-88. • **Ridna Zemlya:** Hrushevsky St., 31; tel. 2-52-47. • **Ukrinform correspondent:** Kyivska St., 6-a; tel. 3-11-94.

SPORTS COMPLEXES

Olimp Sports Complex: Sakharov St., 38. • **Zaroslyak Mountain Sports Training Base:** Hoverlyanska St., 31; tel. 4-15-91. • **Ukrayina Sports Training Base:** tel. 4-12-70. • **Avanhard Sports Training Base:** Danylo Halytsky St., 3; tel. 4-11-40.

HOTELS

Ukrayina: Nezalezhnist St., 52; tel. 4-31-35; 4-32-69. • **Kyiv:** Nezalezhnist St., 4; tel. 2-50-31. • **Dnister:** Sichovi Striltsi St., 12; tel. 2-79-07. • **Druzhba:** Dymytrov St., 3; tel. 9-65-86. • **Roksolana:** Hrundvaldska St., 7-9; tel. 2-52-21.

RESTAURANTS, CAFES

Yuvileyny: Halytska St., 7; Tel. 3-21-20. • **Bystrytsya:** Halytska St., 111; tel. 4-44-38. • The **Ukrayina, Kyiv,** and **Dnister** restaurants are located in the hotels listed under the same names. • **Molochne:** Komarov St., 6. • **Kazka:** Dnistrovsk St., 23. • **Sadko:** Mazepa St., 238. • **Atlant:** Mazepa St., 9. • **Vatra:** Nyzova St., 3. • **Domashnya Kukhnya:** Halytska St., 85.

STORES

Prykarpattya Univermah (Department Store): Dnistrovsk St., 3. • **Universam:** Dnistrovsk St., 26. • **Rubin:** Nezalezhnosti St., 36. • **Minolta:** Nezalezhnist St., 16. • **Bukinist:** Nezalezhnist St., 19. • **Khudozhniy Salon (Art):** Nezalezhnist St., 53. • **Budynok Mebliv (Furniture):** Halytska St., 57.

BANKS

Ukrainian National Bank (Regional Branch): Nezalezhnist St., 19; tel. 2-50-65. • **"Prykarpatlisbank" Commercial Forestry Development Bank of the Carpathian Region:** Vasylyanky St., 48; tel. 4-43-90, 4-01-71. • **"Zakhidbudhazbank" Commercial Development Bank for the Building Industry, Gas, Highway, and Social Development of the Western Ukrainian Regions:** Hrushevsky St., 21; tel. 2-32-93, 3-76-20. • **"Zakhidkoopbank" Cooperative Bank of the Ivano-Frankivsk Region:** Bandera St., 1; tel. 2-50-02, 2-52-06. • **"Prykarpattorhbank" Commercial Development Bank of Food Preparation Industries in the Carpathian Region:** Hrushevsky St., 11; tel. 3-05-24.

Kryvorivnya. The Summer home of Ivan Franko.

TOURISM

Inturyst-Ivano-Frankivsk: Hrushevsky St., 21; tel. 2-57-07.
Ivano-Frankivsk-turyst: Mazepa St., 135; tel. 2-57-10.
Tours: "Through the Hutsul Land," "Winter in the Carpathians," "Carpathian Circle," "Health Resorts in the Carpathians," "Three Hundred Years of History in Ivano-Frankivsk."

POST OFFICE, TELEPHONE

Post Office: Sichovi Striltsi St., 13-a; tel. 2-26-60; 066.
Telephones: Vichevy Maydan, 2; tel. 2-41-25; 2-20-99.

MEDICAL SERVICES

Emergency: tel. 03.
Pharmacies: Dovha St., 26; tel. 4-25-81. Pharmacy reserved for former political prisoners and veterans: Nezalezhnist St., 12; tel. 2-41-56.
Pharmaceutical information: tel. 067.

TRANSPORTATION

Railway station: Pryvokzalna Ploshcha; tel. 005; Railroad Station master: tel. 3-14-65.
Inter-Urban Bus Station: Dymytrov St., 14; tel. 4-44-40. • Tychyna St., 1; tel. 4-42-27.
Airport: Daduhin St., 264-a; tel. 3-00-37.
Ukraine Airlines International booking office: Sichovykh Striltsiv St., 15; tel. 3-10-68.
Taxi reservations: tel. 058; 2-30-23; 2-34-57.

TOURING HISTORIC CITIES AND VILLAGES

DELYATYN

Village in the Nadvirna district on the Prut River. Population: 8,000.

CHURCH OF RIZDVO BOHORODYTSI (NATIVITY OF THE MOTHER OF GOD), 1620; **BELL TOWER,** 1785. Relocated in 1785 from Luhy to its present site in Posych. Rebuilt in 1894-1902. This wood structure is one of the finer examples of the Hutsul school of folk wood architecture. (Kovpak St., 1-a).

Halych. Church of Rizdvo Khrystove (Nativity of Christ), 13th-15th cent.

HALYCH

City on the right bank of the Dnister River, 26 km by car from Ivano-Frankivsk. Population: 7,000.

The village of Krylos, the original seat of ancient Halych (1113), is located 6 km from the city. In 1937 a sarcophagus containing the remains of Prince Yaroslav Osmomysl was excavated beneath the mosaic pavement of the 12th cent. Dormition Cathedral. This stone sarcophagus is now located in the Ivano-Frankivsk Ethnographic Museum.

The 13th cent. Galician-Volynian Chronicle was compiled in Halych, as was the Halych Gospel, one of the earliest literary monuments of Ukrainian writing in Kyivan Rus'-Ukraine. Many works of religious art were created here, including icon of the Protection of the Mother of God and the 14th cent. miniatures of the Halych Gospel.

ZAMOK (CASTLE), 14th-17th cent. Ruins, located on a mountain overlooking the right bank of the Dnister River. Construction of the castle began in 1367. In 1590-1633 the Tatars launched 29 attacks on the castle, which was finally destroyed in 1621. It was restored in 1658 and destroyed again in 1676 by Turkish-Tatar forces.

CHURCH OF RIZDVO KHRYSTOVE (NATIVITY OF CHRIST), 13th-14th cent. First mentioned in historical documents dating to 1550. Suffered extensive damage due to numerous raids. Restored in 1825. Acquired its present appearance after restorations in 1904-06. (Architect: L. Levynsky). A monumental painting of the 20th cent. has been preserved.

Halych. Zamok (Castle) ruins, 14th-17th cent.

KOLOMYYA

Kolomyya.

City on the left bank of the Prut River, 65 km from Ivano-Frankivsk. Population: 70,000.

First mentioned in the Halych-Volynian Chronicle for the year 1240. The name comes from the Myya creek, which empties into the Prut River. The city suffered devastation from Tatar and Turkish invasions and fires. In the 17th-18th cent. the local population participated in the Opryshky (Freedom Fighters) movement. The city is famous for its master-ceramicists and woodcarvers.

CHURCH OF BLAHOVISHCHENNYA (ANNUNCIATION), 1587. This wood structure is the finest example of the Hutsul school of folk architecture.

Y. Kobrynsky Museum of Folk Art of the Hutsul Region and Pokuttya, 1902. Built by the architects L. Bekker and N. Krychkovsky. Contains twenty exhibition halls.

KOSIV

City on the Rybnytsya River, 113 km from Ivano-Frankivsk. Population: 9,000.

Founded in the 15th cent. A center of Hutsul crafts and mountainous health resort, located in the pine woods of the Carpathian Mountains. Known for its folk art fairs featuring woodcarvings, embroideries, rugs, and works produced by local folk art technical colleges.

VASYLIVSKA (ST. BASIL'S) CHURCH, BELL TOWER, 1825. An example of the Hutsul folk architectural style. Wood.

KOSMACH

Village in the Kosiv district, 37 km from the Kolomyya railway station.

Founded in the 14th cent., the center of Ukrainian Easter egg painting. Oleksa Dovbush, a famous Ukrainian brigand, died tragically here. The village features a unique private museum, established by the ethnographer M. Yusypchuk.

PETROPAVLIVSKA (SS. PETER AND PAUL'S) CHURCH; BELL TOWER, 1904-05. Built by the craftsmen of Sokolivka village. This magnificent tall structure embodies the typical features of early 20th cent. Hutsul architecture.

KRYLOS

Village in the Halych district on the Lukva River, 6 km from the Halych railway station. Population: Over 2,000.

VASYLIVSKA KAPLYTSYA (ST. BASIL'S CHAPEL), 1500. Constructed on the site of the Uspensky (Dormition) Cathedral (1157). Was partly destroyed by the Mongolian Tatars in 1676 and rebuilt in 1600-1702. Restored in 1825, 1926 (Architects: L. Levynsky and I. Starosolsky); 1972-76. A white stone relief depicting a dragon was uncovered in the ruins of the Dormition Cathedral.

Berkut Restaurant.

KRYVORIVNYA

Village in the Verkhovyna district on the Chorny Cheremosh River, 14 km from Verkhovyna, 42 km from the Vorokhta railway station.

The summer home of the writers I. Franko and H. Khotkevych from 1900-14. I. Franko established a Hutsul theater here in 1910. The village was visited by the writers M. Kotsyubynsky, O. Oles, Yu. Fedkovych, V. Stefanyk, I. Trush, and I. Severyn. The first president of Ukraine, M. Hrushevsky, owned a house in the village.

CHURCH OF RIZDVO BOHORODYTSI (NATIVITY OF THE MOTHER OF GOD), BELL TOWER, 1818. The interior of this wood church has tempera paintings dating to the 19th cent. A superlative example of the Hutsul school of folk architecture.

I. Franko Literary-Memorial Museum, founded in 1953, is located in the village.

Krylos. Uspensky (Dormition) Church, 16th cent.

MANYAVA

Village in the Bohorodchany district, 25 km from the Nadvirna railway station. Population: 3,000.

MANYAVSKY SKYT (1611); MONASTERY. The first wood church was built in 1612; in 1619 the Vozdvyzhenska (Elevation) Church was built. In 1676 the monastery was destroyed by

Manyavsky Skyt, 1611.

the Turks. The monastery was closed in the 18th cent. and has since deteriorated. Stone and wood structures surrounded by a stone wall with towers have been preserved. In 1972-80, the Skyt was restored by the architect L. Dmytrovych. Many frescos have been preserved.

PNIV

Village in the Nadvirna district on the Bystrytsya-Nadvirnyanska River. Population: over 4,000.

ZAMOK (CASTLE), 16th cent. Ruins located 3 km from the Nadvirna railway station. In 1648 rebels led by S. Vysochan captured the castle, causing partial destruction. This castle was considered the best fortified structure in Ukraine.

ROHATYN

City located 61 km from Ivano-Frankivsk. Population: 9,000.

Founded in the 12th cent. In 1520 invading Tatars abducted a girl named Nastya Lisovska, who was sold into the harem of the Turkish Sultan Suleyman II (the Magnificent). Later, known as Roksolana, she became his wife and played an influential role in Turkish politics during the 1520s-50s.

RIZDVO BOHORODYTSI (NATIVITY OF THE MOTHER OF GOD) CHURCH, 14th-15th cent. Surrounded by defensive walls. In 1869 the interior was painted by Y. Pankevych. A unique structure of 14th-15th cent. Ukrainian architecture.

SVYATODUKHIVSKA (HOLY SPIRIT) CHURCH, 1598. Restored in 1895, this church is one of the most outstanding examples of Galician folk architecture.

MYKOLAYIVSKA (ST. NICHOLAS') CHURCH, 1729. This wood church was renovated in 1977-78 and housed a Historical-Ethnographic Museum. A rare example of Galician folk architecture.

MYKOLAYIVSKY KOSTEL (ST. NICHOLAS' ROMAN CATHOLIC CHURCH), 15th cent. Built in the Gothic style combining elements of the late Renaissance period. The church suffered extensive damage due to Turkish and Tatar raids. Restored in 1969-1973 in the Renaissance and Baroque styles.

Pniv. Zamok (Castle) ruins, 16th cent.

SHEVCHENKOVE

Village under the jurisdiction of the village of Zalukva, Halych district.

ST. PANTELEYMON'S CHURCH, 12th cent. The only 12th-13th cent structure that has been preserved in Western Ukraine. Was rebuilt as a monastic church of the Roman Catholic Franciscan Fathers; destroyed during Tatar raids in 1575 and 1676, and in 1915. Rebuilt in 1926; renovated in 1965-69. Fragments of Cyrillic script dating to 1212 have been preserved. Combines features of ancient Ukrainian and Romanesque styles.

Rohatyn. Svyatodukhivska (Holy Spirit) Church, 1598.

SNYATYN

City located 107 km from Ivano-Frankivsk. Population: 11,000.

Founded as a fortress in the 12th cent. Was an important trading center. A large cache of Roman coins and other treasures of the 2nd-4th cent. have been unearthed in the city. The original name of the city was Ksnyatyn (1158), derived from Kostyantyn Stroslavych, one of Prince Yaroslav Osmomysl's army commanders. In 1387 it was captured by the Poles who established a Roman Catholic bishopric in the city. In 1448 the city acquired the Magdeburg Law. In the second half of the 15th cent. Snyatyn was an important strategic border point. The city was frequently raided by the Tatars, Turks, and Moldovians. During the liberation war of 1648-54 the residents of Snyatyn joined the ranks of Hetman Khmelnytsky's Kozak army.

The city was visited by V. Stefanyk, I. Franko, M. Lysenko, L. Martovych, and M. Pavlyk.

CITY HALL, 1861. This 50-m high stone building was completed in 1909 and was the tallest of its kind in Western Ukraine.

Museums dedicated to the writer M. Cheremshyna and the artist V. Kasiyan are located in the city.

Snyatyn. City Hall, 1909.

TYSMENYTSYA

City located on the banks of the Vorona and

Yaremcha. Dovbush Cliffs.

Strymba Rivers, 10 km from the Ivano-Frankivsk railway station.

CHURCH OF RIZDVO BOHORODYT-SI (NATIVITY OF THE MOTHER OF GOD), 1736. This wood structure combines the artistic traditions of Carpathian folk architecture. Paintings from the 19th cent. have been preserved.

BELL TOWER, 18th cent. This rectangular wood structure is a unique example of Hutsul wood architecture.

YAREMCHA

City located 65 km from Ivano-Frankivsk, and 23 km from the district center of Nadvirna. Population: 10,000.

Many places in the vicinity of this city are associated with the brigand chieftain O. Dovbush. Yaremcha is one of the major tourist centers in the Hutsul region. The Hutsulshchyna Tourist Complex is located in the city.

MYKHAYLIVSKA CHURCH (ST. MICHAEL'S), 17th cent. A wood structure, located on a hill near the village of Dora. Twentieth cent. paintings adorn the walls. Built in the Hutsul folk style. (Halan St., 32).

CHURCH OF ST. IOAN MYLOSTYVY (ST. JOHN THE MERCIFUL), BELL TOWER, 18th cent. These wood structures are some of the finest examples of the Hutsul folk architecture. (Kovpak St., 2).

AUTO SERVICING

Complex of the Highway Service: Horodenka, 241 km, Mohyliv-Podilsky-Kolomyya-Delyatyn; tel. 2-16-42.

Yaremcha. Hutsulshchyna Restaurant.

Kharkiv Region

Most of the region is located in the Dnipro Lowland near the Dnipro River. In the north and northeast it abuts the ridges of the Central-Russian Upland, and in the southeast, the ridges of the Donets mountain range. The climate is temperate-continental. The principal river is the Siversky Donets. Established in 1932. Area: 31,400 sq. km. Population: 3,184,000.

History

The earliest traces of human habitation date to the early Paleolithic Age. Remains of settlements of the Scythian and Alan tribes of the late Paleolithic era have also been uncovered. Slavic tribes began to settle these territories at the beginning of the new era. In the 10th cent. the region was part of Kyivan Rus'-Ukraine. After the Tatar invasion of the 13th cent. the region was de-populated. Ukrainians began re-settling the territories only in the 16th cent., coinciding with frequent attacks by the Crimean Tatars. To fortify the borders the following towns were built: Voronizh, Bilhorod, Tsareborysiv (now Chervony Oskil), Tor, and others. The first major wave of Ukrainian settlement commenced in 1651, when the Kozaks created the Slobody settlements (A large village on a highroad), known today as the cities of Sumy, Lebedyn, Kharkiv, and Okhtyrka. These lands acquired the name of Slobidska Ukraine or Slobozhanshchyna. In the 17th cent. the land was divided by regiment, administrative divisions which were typical of the Hetman era. In 1765 this form of autonomy was liquidated by Catherine II. The most important cultural centers were monasteries which were founded immediately after the region was settled. In the 19th cent. Kharkiv University was an important cultural force in Ukraine.

Sharivka. Palace, 19th cent.

PROMINENT INDIVIDUALS

BORN IN THE REGION:

O. Dosvitniy-Skrypal (1891-1934), writer; in Vovchansk, executed. • H. Khotkevych (1877-1938), writer, composer; in Kharkiv, executed. • H. Kvitka-Osnovyanenko (1778-1843), writer;

in Osnova, Kharkiv region. • **P. Panch** (1891-1978), writer; in Valky. • **I. Ryepin** (1844-1930), artist; in Chuhuyiv. • **O. Slisarenko** (1891-1937), writer; in Kakhivtseve, Velykoburlytsk region, executed. • **S. Vasylkivsky** (1854-1917), painter; in Izyum. • **U. Vukhnal-Kovtun** (1906-37), writer; in Chornobayivka, Izyum region, executed. • **M. Yalovy-Shpol** (1895-1934), writer; in Dar-Nadyezhda, Sakhnovshchansk region, executed. • **D.Yavornytsky** (1877-1940), historian, archeologist, writer, ethnographer, folklorist; in Sobtsivka. • **M. Yohansen** (1895-1937), writer; in Kharkiv, executed. • **O. Zalyvakha** (1925), artist; in Husynka, persecuted.

BURIED IN THE REGION:

Ch. O. Alchevska (1882-1931), poet; in Kharkiv. • **D. Bahaliy** (1857-1932) historian, academician; in Kharkiv. • **P. Hulak-Artemovsky** (1790-1865), poet; in Kharkiv. • **M. Khvylovy** (1893-1933), writer; in Kharkiv. • **M. Kropyvnytsky** (1840-1910), actor, dramatist; in Kharkiv. • **O. Potebnya** (1835-91), academician; in Kharkiv. • **H. Skovoroda** (1722-94), poet, philosopher; in Skovorodynivka. • **M. Skrypnyk** (1872-1933), politician, statesman; in Kharkiv. • **M. Sumtsov** (1854-1922), academician, ethnographer, literary specialist; in Kharkiv. • **S. Vasylkivsky,** (1854-1917), artist; in Kharkiv.

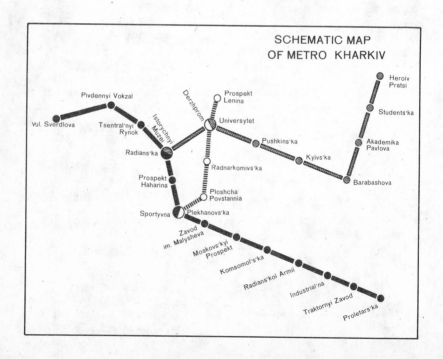

SCHEMATIC MAP
OF METRO KHARKIV

KHARKIV

City located at the confluence of the Kharkiv, Lopan, and Uda Rivers. Population: over 1.5 million. Telephone code: 0572.

The city was first mentioned in historical documents in 1655, when 500 Kozaks and their families settled in the area. In the late 17th cent. Kharkiv was one of the largest commercial centers in Ukraine. From December 1919 to June 1934 it was the capital of Soviet Ukraine. The Ukrainian cultural renaissance commenced here in the years 1920-30. M. Khvylovy and L. Kurbas lived and worked in Kharkiv, and established the VAPLITE writers' organization, and the Berezil Theater. The first wave of repressions of the Ukrainian intelligentsia began in Kharkiv.

CHURCHES, HISTORICAL AND ARCHITECTURAL MONUMENTS

POKROVSKA (PROTECTION) CATHEDRAL, 1689. The oldest building in the city, dating to the founding of the Kharkiv fortress. A brilliant reflection of the Ukrainian Baroque era of the 17th cent. During the Second World War it sustained extensive damage and was renovated in 1960-65 by the architects V. Petechynsky and V. Kornyeyeva. The bell tower resembles a defense tower. The cathedral was part of the fortification system of the Kharkiv fortress. (Universytetska St., 8).

ARKHIYEREYSKY BUDYNOK (BISHOPS' BUILDING), 1820-26. Built in the Classical style; belonged to the Protection Monastery.

OLD CORPUS OF THE UNIVERSITY, (1766-77). Built by the architect M. Tykhmenyev; was the residence of the General-Governor. From 1805 to 1958 it housed the University of Kharkiv. The oldest building in Kharkiv built in the Classical style.

USPENSKY (DORMITION) CATHEDRAL, 1771-77. Built in the Baroque style, the church resembles a palace and is used as a recital hall for organ music.

BELL TOWER OF THE USPENSKY (DORMITION) CATHEDRAL, 1821-48. Built in the Classical style (Architects: E. Vasylyev and A. Thon). 88,9 m high. Renovated in 1972-75.

Uspensky (Dormition) Cathedral, 1771-77.

KHARKIV

📖 Hotels:
  1 Inturyst
  2 Kharkiv
  3 Pivdennyi
  4 Pershotravnevyi
  5 Chervona Moskva
  6 Start

🍴 Restaurants:
  1 Kryshtal'
  2 Liuks
  3 Hirka
  4 Kharkiv-Pasazhyrs'kyi
  5 Stare misto
  6 Tsentral'nyi
  7 Levada
  Note. Restaurants Inturyst, Kharkiv and Pivdennyi are attached to the hotels of the same names

🚃 Railway Stations:
  1 Kharkiv-Pasazhyrskyi
  2 Kharkiv-Levada

🚌 Bus Stations

🛡 Monuments:
  1 Vasil Karazin, Ukrainian scientist and inventor
  2 Taras Shevchenko
  3 Mykhailo Kotsiubynskyi
  4 Nikolai Gogol
  5 Hryhoriy Skovoroda

🏛 Architectural monuments:
  1 Intercession Cathedral, 1689
  2 Dormition Cathedral, 1771—1777; bell tower, 1821—1848
  3 Complex of old University buildings, 1766—1777

🎭 Theaters:
  1 A. S. Pushkin Russian Theater of Drama
  2 M. Lysenko Theater of Opera and Ballet
  3 T. Shevchenko Ukrainian Theater of Drama
  4 Musical Comedy

🎵 Philharmonic Society

MONUMENTS

T. Shevchenko, 1936. Sculptor: M. Manizer. Architect: Y. Langbard. (In Shevchenko Park).
M. Hohol. (Ploshcha Poeziyi).
V. Karazin, 1905. Sculptor: I. Andrioti. Architect: O. Beketov. (In Shevchenko Park).
O. Pushkin. (Ploshcha Poeziyi).

Kharkiv Hotel

MUSEUMS

Historical Museum: Universytetska St., 10; tel. 22-46-66. • **Art Museum:** Radnarkomivska (Sovnarkomivska) St., 11; tel. 43-35-85. • **Natural Science Museum:** Trynkler St., 8; tel. 43-38-86. • **Planetarium:** provulok Kravtsova., 15; tel. 43-41-90. • **Aerokosmichny:** Myronosnytska St., 54-b; tel. 45-24-86. • **Literary Museum:** Frunze St., 6; tel. 47-01-09.

THEATERS

T. Shevchenko Ukrainian Drama Theater: Sumska St., 9. • **O. Pushkin Russian Drama Theater:** Skrypnyk St., 7. • **Lysenko Theater of Opera and Ballet:** Sumska St., 31. • **Puppet Theater:** ploshcha Radyanskoyi Ukrayiny, 24.

HIGHER EDUCATIONAL INSTITUTIONS

Kharkiv University: ploshcha Svobody, 4; tel. 43-61-96. • **Aviation Institute:** Chkalov St., 17; tel. 44-98-56. • **Automobile and Road Institute:** Petrovsky St., 25; tel. 43-30-66. • **Institute of Railway-Transport Engineers:** Feyerbakh St., 7; tel. 21-20-67. • **Institute of Communal-Construction Engineering:** Revolutsiyi St., 2; tel. 43-21-62. • **Civil Engineering Institute:** Sumska St., 40; tel. 43-38-12. • **Industrial Engineering Institute:** Lenin St., 9-a; tel. 30-23-04. • **Institute of Arts:** ploshcha Radyanskoyi Ukrayiny, 11/13; tel. 22-56-28. • **Institute of Culture:** Bursatsky Spusk, 4; tel. 22-24-14. • **Medical Institute:** Lenin St., 14; tel. 43-30-53. • **Physical Fitness Institute:** Pushkinska St., 49; tel. 43-0223. • **Nutrition Insti-**

Kharkiv University.

tute: Klochkivska St., 333; tel. 3223-29. • **Polytechnical Institute:** Frunze St., 21; tel. 47-0551. • **Radioelectronics Institute:** Lenin St., 14; tel. 43-3053. • **Industrial Art Institute:** Chervonoznamenna St., 8; tel. 43-10-56. • **Institute of Agriculture:** village of Rohan, tel. 99-7332. • **Pedagogical Institute:** Artem St., 29; tel. 43-08-25. • **Pharmaceutical Institute:** Pushkinska St., 53; tel. 47-01-25. • **Juridical Institute:** Pushkinska St., 77; tel. 43-01-06.

LIBRARIES, ARCHIVES

Stanislavsky Music and Theater Library: provulok Inzhenerny, 1-a. • **Korolenko Scientific Library:** provulok Korolenka, 18. • **Central University Science Library:** ploshcha Svobody, 4. • **Regional Archive:** prospekt Moskovsky, 7. • **Municipal Archive:** Universytetska St., 13. • **Central Archive of Scientific-Technical Documentation of Ukraine:** Universytetska St.

NEWSPAPERS, JOURNALS

"Vechirny Kharkiv": Moskovsky Prospekt, 247; tel. 92-02-05. • **"Panorama":** Hosprom, 6, 8th Fl.; tel. 43-11-70. • **"Berezil":** Chernyshevsky St., 59; tel. 47-61-62. • **"Inzhener":** prospekt Lenina, 19-b, kv. 42; tel. 43-80-22.

PUBLISHERS

"Osvita": Hosprom, 4 pod.; tel. 47-80-82. • **"Osnova":** ploshcha ovstannya, 17: tel. 21-93-39. • **"Parytet" Ltd.:** Rymarska, 18; tel. 43-27-22. • **"Prapor":** Chubar St., 11; tel. 47-72-52. • **"Kharkiv":** Moskovsky Prosperkt, 247; tel. 92-22-46.

PARKS

Central Park of Culture and Recreation: Sumska St., 81. • **Park of Culture and Recreation:** Plekhanov St., 134; Myr St., 3. • **Peremoha Park of Culture and Recreation:** Traktorobudivnyky St., 100-B. • **Shevchenko Park:** Sumska St., 35. • **Zoological Garden:** Sumska St., 35. • **University Botanical Garden:** Otakar Yarosh St.

SPORTS COMPLEXES

Metalist Stadium: Plekhanivska St., 65. • **Sports Palace:** prospekt Marshala Zhukova, 2. • **Aquarena Olympic Sports Training Center:** Klachkovska St., 43/47.

HOTELS

Airport Hotel: Aeroflotska St.; tel. 50-52-20. • **Druzhba:** prospekt Gagarina,

185; tel. 52-20-91. • **Intouryst:** prospekt Lenina, 21; tel. 32-05-08. • **Myr:** prospekt Lenina, 27-A; tel. 30-55-43. • **Turyst:** Moskovsky Prospekt, 144; tel. 92-01-74. • **Kharkiv:** ploshcha Svobody., 7; tel. 45-63-67.

RESTAURANTS, CAFES

Airport: Aeroflotska St., 16. • **Hirka:** provulok Teatralny, 11/13. • **Budynok Lisnyka:** Bilhorodske shosse. • **Luks:** Sumska St., 3. • **Myr:** prospekt Lenina, 27-A. • **Teatralny:** Sumska St., 27. • **Turyst:** prospekt Moskovsky, 144. • **Kharkiv:** ploshcha Svobody., 8. • **Centralny:** ploshcha Rozy Luxemburg, 20. • **Stare Misto:** Kvitka-Osnovyanenko St., 12.

STORES

Central: ploshcha Rozy Luxemburg, 1/3. • **Kharkiv:** prospekt Moskovsky, 147. • **Dytyachy svit:** ploshcha Radyanskoyi Ukrainy, 9. • **Ukrayina:** prospekt Traktorobudivnykiv, 59. • **House of Commerce:** Suzdalski Ryady. • **Podarunky:** ploshcha Svobody, 6. • **Knyzhkovy Svit (books):** ploshcha Radyanskoyi Ukrayiny, 2/2. • **Universam:** prospekt Traktorobudivnykiv, 57. • **Universam:** Heroyi Pratsi St., 35. • **Universam:** prospekt Moskovsky, 256. • **Akademknyha:** Chernyshevsky St., 85/87. • **Kobzar Bookstore:** prospekt Lenina, 36. • **Ukrayinsky Suvenir:** prospekt Moskovsky, 1. • **Charivnytsya:** ploshcha Radyanskoyi Ukrainy, 16.

BANKS

National Bank of Ukraine (Regional Branch): ploshcha Poeziyi, 1; tel. 23-00-03. • **Kharkiv Commercial Bank for the Development of Light Industry "Kharkivlehbank:"** Shevchenko St., 24; tel. 43-26-03, 40-66-07. • **Kharkiv Commercial Bank "Promin:"** Korolenko St., 25; tel. 27-75-74, 27-09-59. • **Commercial Innovation Bank "Kharkivinkombank:"** ploshcha Radyanskoyi Ukrayiny, 1; tel. 2258-22, 20-67-79. • **Kharkiv Commercial Bank "Dobrodiy:"** Hohol St., l; tel. 22-50-62, 43-51-92. • **Regional Commercial Bank "Rehionbank:"** Darvine St., 4; tel. 43-23-65. • **Innovation Commercial NPK Bank "Nauka (Science), Promyslovist (Industry), Kultura (Culture):"** prospect Lenina, 60; tel. 33-27-14. • **Joint-Stock Bank "Diskont (Discount):"** Rymarska St., 32; tel. 43-38-47.

TOURISM

Inturyst-Kharkiv: prospekt Lenina, 21; tel. 32-00-90.
Suputnyk: Myronosytska St., 1; tel. 47-11-59.
Regional Tourism and Excursions Council: ploshcha Radyanskoyi Ukrainy., 1; tel. 22-30-11.
EXCURSIONS: "Touring the historical sites of the city;" "Kharkiv — an indus-

trial, scientific, and cultural center of Ukraine;" "Drobytsky Yar — the site of mass executions of Kharkiv Jewry by the Nazis;" "Cultural buildings of Kharkiv (cathedrals, churches, synagogue, Roman Catholic Church);" "Chuhuyiv — homeland of the artist Repin"; "Museum and Grave of the Ukrainian philosopher H. Skovoroda" (in the village of Skovorodynivka).

POST OFFICE, TELEPHONE

Post office: Kirov St., 6; tel. 21-15-55.
Post Office: ploshcha Vokzalna, 7; tel. 22-57-56.
Telegraph: Chervonozhovtneva St., 18; tel. 20-61-91; 40-4141.
Calling points: ploshcha Svobody.; tel. 43-00-15. • Prospekt Lenina, 39; tel. 32-20-26. • Luxemburg St., 10; tel. 22-06-15.

MEDICAL SERVICES

Emergency: tel. 03.
Information office of Emergency Service: tel. 22-89-24.
Pharmacies: Sumska St., 60; tel. 47-02-33. • Ploshcha Radyanskoyi Ukrayiny; tel. 22-73-50.

TRANSPORTATION

Railway station: ploshcha Pryvokzalna; tel. 005; Tickets: tel. 20-37-61.
Bus Terminus: prospekt Gagarina, 22; tel. 21-65-02.
Bus Stations: Suzdalski Ryady, 12; tel. 23-00-06. • Ploshcha Povstannya; tel. 27-57-55. • Lisopark; tel. 44-01-76. • Provulok Donetsky; tel. 50-53-47; 50-54-08.
Airport: prospekt Gagarina; tel. 50-53-47; 50-54-08.
Taxi reservations: tel. 058.

AUTO SERVICING

Ukrinteravtoservis: Biolohichna St., 4-b; tel. 23-31-32. Auto servicing: provulok Botanichny, 22; tel. 43-17-39.

TOURING HISTORIC CITIES AND VILLAGES

CHERVONY OSKIL (until 1919 — Tsareborysiv)

Village, Izyum district, on the Oskil River, 5 km from the Bukyne railway station, 150 km from Kharkiv. Population: approx. 4,000. Established in 1600 as a fortress; frequently attacked by the Tatars. Settled by Kozaks in 1637.

SVYATOHIRSKY (HOLY HILL) MONASTERY, 1624. First mentioned in documents dating to 1624, the monastery was surrounded by mighty walls and equipped with cannons. Frequently raided and restored.

CHUHUYIV

City on the Siversky Donets and Chuhivka Rivers, 56 km from the Kharkiv railway station. Population: 25,000. First mentioned in 16th cent. documents. Part of the Pereyaslav and Chernihiv principalities. Near the town remains of an ancient fortification dating to the Kyivan Realm period have been uncovered. The city was settled by Ukrainians in 1651 after several Tatar invasions. The Chuhuyiv fortress was an important defensive structure.

POKROVSKY (PROTECTION OF THE BLESSED VIRGIN MARY) CATHEDRAL, 1824-34. Built in the Classical style; restored in 1972.

HEADQUARTERS OF THE MILITARY SETTLEMENTS, 1830. A majestic building in the Classical style.

Monument to I. Repin, (1844-1930). Erected in 1956 in honor of the creator of the famous painting "Zaporozhians writing a letter to the Turkish Sultan." Sculptor: M. Manizer.

I. Repin Commemorative Plaque. On the exterior of the artist's parental home. (Horna St.).

The I. Repin Museum and Repin Park are also located in the city (1944).

IZYUM

City and railway station on the Siversky Donets River, 138 km from Kharkiv. Population: 65,000. Was part of Kyivan Rus'-Ukraine. In the 12th cent. it was frequently attacked by nomads. In 1185 Prince Ihor camped here. In the 17th cent. the Izyum Fortress was built; demolished

Chuhuyiv. Pokrovsky (Protection) Cathedral, 1824-34.

Izyum. Voznesenska (Ascension) Church, 1819-26.

in 1680 and rebuilt in 1681. In 1865 the Kozak regiment of Izyum was based here. **SPASO-PREOBRAZHENSKY (TRANS-FIGURATION OF THE REDEEMER) CATHEDRAL,** 1686. One of the first structures of the Izyum fortress (1681). Renovated in 1751 and rebuilt in 1902-03 in the Ukrainian Baroque style. In 1953-55 the cathedral was restored to its original appearance.

MYKOLAYIVSKA (ST. NICHO-LAS') CHURCH, 1809-23. Built in the Classical style. The walls are covered with thematic ornamental paintings of the 19th-20th cent.

VOZNESENSKA (ASCENSION) CHURCH, 1819-26. Built in the Classical style, renovated in 1903. The bell tower is noted for its ornamentation.

LYUBOTYN

City, Kharkiv district. Population: approx. 30,000.

ESTATE, 19th cent. Surrounded by a magnificent park. All the structures were built in the transitional Classical-Eclectic style. Among the buildings which have been preserved are the palace (19th cent.), built in the Romantic style featuring elements of the Classical and Gothic styles; renovated in 1929-39 and rebuilt in 1946; Mykolayivska (St. Nicholas') Church (1843), built in the Classical style, and servants' quarters (19th cent.).

PARKHOMIVKA

Village, Krasnokutsky district, on the river Kotelva, 32 km from the Huta railway station. Population: approx. 8,000.

POKROVSKA (PROTECTION OF THE BLESSED VIRGIN MARY) CHURCH, 1808. Part of the local estate. Built in the Classical style by the architect P. Yaroslavsky.

ROKYTNE

Village, Novovodolazk district, on the river Mozh, 3 km from the Ordivka railway station. Population: approx. 2,000.

Lyubotyn. Estate, 19th cent.

MYKOLAYIVSKA (ST. NICHOLAS') CHURCH, 1805. Part of the estate, built in the monumental Classical style. One of the finer churches in the Kharkiv region.

PALACE, 19th cent. Built in the classical style. One of the finer examples of country home architecture of the 19th cent.

SHARIVKA

Village, Bohodukhiv district, on the Merchyk River, 13 km from the Vodyana railway station. Population: approx. 5,000.

ESTATE, 19th cent. Established as a park in the early 19th cent. Includes a palace (19th cent.) in the pseudo-Gothic style with Renaissance features; guard-house (19th cent.) with an ornate entrance gate; the main building and a forester's house. ·

PARK, 19th cent. On the slopes of a large ravine, 70 ha, surrounds the palace. Known for its 250-300 year-old oak trees. The Sharivka health resort, one of the finest medical establishments in Ukraine, is located on the grounds of the estate.

STARY MERCHYK

Village, Valkiv district, a railway station. Population: approx. 5,000.

ESTATE, 18th cent. A stone gate decorated with Scythian sculptures leads to the complex, which includes a palace (1776-78), a masterpiece of estate architecture; servants' quarters (18th cent.); two wing buildings (18th cent.); a barn (18th cent.), and a 50 ha park on the Merchyk River. The complex reflects the transitional Baroque-Classical period in Ukrainian architecture.

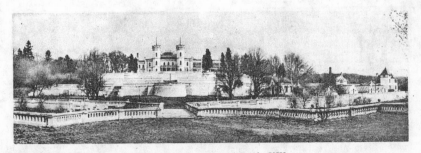

Sharivka. Estate and Park, XIX.

Kherson Region

In southern Ukraine, in the steppe belt of the Black Sea Lowland on both banks of the Dnipro River, directly north of the Black Sea and the Sea of Azov. The land is flat; the principal river is the Dnipro, on which the Kakhovka Reservoir is located. The climate is temperate-continental, with mild winters and minimal snowfall, and dry, hot summers. Established in 1944. Area: 28,500 sq. km. Population: 1,283,000.

History

The region was settled during the late Paleolithic era. Settlements of the Mezolithic, Copper, and Bronze Ages have been excavated. In the 8th-7th cent. B.C. the steppes of Kherson were part of the Scythian state, with its center in the Kamyanske Horodyshche. In the 2nd cent. B.C. the Black Sea lands were settled by the early Slavic tribes of Zarubyntsi culture. In the 2nd-6th cent. A.D. Slavic settlements of Chernyakhiv culture appeared. In the 10th-13th cent. the territory was part of Kyivan Rus'-Ukraine. From the 13th cent. the Dnipro Lowland was occupied by the Tatars; during the 15th cent. it was under Turkish rule.

After the establishment of the Zaporozhian Sich in the 16th cent., the lands were settled by the Kozaks, who organized numerous campaigns against the Turks and Tatars. The Kozaks who fought against various invaders during the 17th cent. were led by the chieftains I. Sirko, M. Khanenko, and Colonel S. Paliy.

After the destruction of the Chortomlyk Sich in 1709 the Zaporozhians established the Kamyanska Sich and later, the Oleshkiv Sich. The Kozaks participated in the peasant movement of 1768 (Koliyivshchyna). In 1775 the Russian Empress Cath-

Kherson Region. Askaniya Nova Preserve.

erine II ordered the destruction of the Sich. In the 19th cent. Kherson region was settled by Ukrainians and Germans.

PROMINENT INDIVIDUALS

BORN IN THE REGION:

O. Berdnyk (1927), writer, former political prisoner; in Vavylove. • **D. Buzko** (1891-1943), writer; in Kherson, died in prison. • **I. Dniprovsky-Shevchenko** (1895-1934), writer; in Kalanchak. • **M. Kulish** (1892-1937), playwright; in Chaplynka, executed. • **M. Skladovsky** (1846-92), painter; in Bilozirtsi, Kherson district. • **M. Zhuk** (1883-1964), painter; in Kakhovka.

BURIED IN THE REGION:

K. Hordienko (?-1733), Chieftain of the last Zaporozhian Sich (Oleshky), Hetman I. Mazepa's deputy; in Respublikanets, Beryslav district. • **V. Hoshkevych** (1860-1928), archaeologist; in Kherson.

Kherson. M. Kulish Music and Drama Theater.

KHERSON

City, regional center, river and sea port, on the Dnipro river, 25 km from the Dnipro River estuary. Population: 360,000. Telephone code: 0552.

Founded in 1778 on the site of fortifications built by Oleksander Shants in 1737. Named in honor of Khersones Tavriysky, a city on the southwestern bank of the Crimea. Originally a city-fortress and shipyard; the first ship of the Black Sea Fleet set sail from here in 1783. In the early 20th cent. it became an important export port.

CHURCHES, HISTORICAL AND ARCHITECTURAL MONUMENTS

ARSENAL, 1784. A stone structure designed to store various armament, including gun powder. Two three-storied structures with a six-column portico have been preserved. (Perekopska St., 10).

LIBRARY, 1896. Architect: M. Tolvynsky. Built in the Eclectic style with Classical elements. Presently houses the Regional Library. (Dvadtsyat Pershe Sichnya St., 24).

HREKO-SOPHIYSKA (ST. SOPHIA'S GREEK) CHURCH, 1780. A wall painting, wood carvings and sculptures have been preserved. (Chervonoflotska St., 13).

KATERYNSKY (ST. CATHARINE'S) CATHEDRAL, 1782-87; **BELL TOWER,** 1806. Built in the Classical style by the architect I. Starov. Presently used as an exhibition and lecture hall. (Perekopska St., 13).

MYKOLAYIVSKA (ST. NICHOLAS') CHURCH, 1819. Built in the Classical style. (Dobrokhotov St., 31).

OCHAKIV GATE, late 18th cent. A rectangular stone structure. Located in the western part of the fortress. Only a section of a defense rampart has been preserved. (Perekopska St., 13).

SVYATODUKHIVSKY (HOLY GHOST) CATHEDRAL, 1804-36. A stone structure built in the Classical style. (Dekabrysty St., 36).

MONUMENTS

T. Shevchenko, 1971. Sculptor: I. Bilokur. Architect: Y. Tarasov.

First Ship Memorial, 1972. Sculptors: I. Bilokur, and V. Potrebenko. Architect: Y. Tarasov.

D. Howard Memorial, 1828. Erected in honor of the English physician who came to Kherson to fight an epidemic and died there. Architect: V. Stasov. Built in the Classical style; granite.

Bell Tower, 19th cent.

KHERSON

B   Excursion office

🏨   Hotels:
1 Kyïv
2 Dynamo
3 Pershe Travnia
4 Fregat

🍴   Restaurants:
1 Orbita
2 Kyïv
3 Kherson
4 Dnipro

🚂   Railway Station

⚓   Sea and River Stations

🐚   Central market

📍   Monuments:
1 George Howard, English doctor-humanitarian

2 Generalissimo Alexander Suvorov, Russian military leader

🏛   Architectural monuments:
1 Remnants of the 18th—19th century fortress. Here, in the territory of the former St. Catherine's Cathedral, Field-Marshal General Grigory Potemkin is buried
2 Holy Ghost Cathedral, 1836
3 Greek-Sophia's Church, 1780

✿   Museums:
1 The Shovkunenko Art Museum
2 Museum of Local Lore

🎭   Theaters:
1 Puppet
2 Ukrainian Theater of Music and Drama

🎼   Philharmonic Society

MUSEUMS

Regional Museum: Lenin St., 9; tel. 4-10-83.
• **O. Shovkunenko Art Museum:** Lenin St., 34; tel. 4-01-24. • **Literary Museum:** Gorky St., 1; tel. 6-30-66. • **Exhibition Hall of the Union of Artists of Ukraine:** ploshcha Svobody, 1; tel. 6-46-96.

THEATERS

M. Kulish Music and Drama Theater: Gorky St., 7. • **Puppet Theater:** Sorok Rokiv Zhovtnya St., 8.

HIGHER EDUCATIONAL INSTITUIONS

O. Shovkunenko Art Museum.

Industrial Institute: Boryslavske shosse, 24. • **Pedagogical Institute:** Sorok Rokiv Zhovtnya St., 27. • **Agricultural Institute:** Luxemburg St., 23. • **Branch of the Mykolayiv Shipbuilding Institute:** prospekt Ushakova, 44.

LIBRARIES, ARCHIVES

General Scientific Library: Dnipropetrovsk St., 2. • **Youth Library:** Dekabrysty St., 14-a. • **Children's Library:** Chervonostudentska St., 21. • **Regional Archive:** Radyanska St., 3.

Kherson Childrens Music School.

SPORTS COMPLEXES

Sports Base of Kherson VSM: Fortus St., 38; tel. 7-10-62, 7-06-58. • **Krystal Stadium:** Kirov St., 3; tel. 4-32-23; 2-55-26.

HOTELS

Frehat: prospekt Ushakova, 2; tel. 4-11-17. • **Kyiv:** prospekt Ushakova, 43; tel. 6-26-04. • **Bryhantyna:** Paton St., 4; tel. 7-37-31.

RESTAURANTS, CAFES, BARS

Frehat: prospekt Ushakova, 2; tel. 4-05-22. • **Kyiv:** Myrny Blvd., 3; tel. 2-26-31. • **Kher-**

son: Lenin St., 26; tel. 2-45-30. • **Ekspres:** prospekt Ushakova, 2; tel. 49-62-51. •
Lunny: prospekt Ushakova, 2; tel. 49-64-42. • **Disco:** prospekt Ushakova, 2; tel.
49-65-65. • **Valyutny Bar:** prospekt Ushakova, 2. • **Perlyna:** Heroyi Stalinhrada St.;
tel. 6-32-06. • **Okean:** Suvorov St., 15; tel. 2-45-50. • **Teatralne:** Gorky St., 20; tel.
2-53-28.

STORES

Tsentralny Univermah (Department store): prospekt Ushakova, 49. • **Budynok
Knyhy (Books):** ploshcha Svobody, 1. • **Tekhnichna Knyha:** Suvorov St., 19. •
Bukinistychna Knyha: Suvorov St., 7/9. • **Mystetstvo (Art):** Radyanska St., 29. •
Suveniry: Suvorov St., 27. • **Khudozhniy Salon-Mahazyn:** prospekt Ushakova, 51.

BANKS

Ukrainian National Bank (Regional Branch): Komsomolska St., 21; tel. 2-33-
56. • **Commercial Bank "Kherson:"** Svobody St., 1; tel. 4-51-70.

TOURISM

Inturyst-Kherson: prospekt Ushakova, 2 (Hotel Frehat): tel. 2-26-19.
Foreign Tourists' Agency: tel. 49-63-43.
Inturyst-Kherson suggests excursions to museums, historical sites, especially
Scythian burial grounds, Askaniya Nova — the Black Sea Biospheric Preserve (May
to November), as well as cruises on the Dnipro river, and to the Black Sea beaches.

Theater.

POST OFFICE, TELEPHONE

Post office: prospekt Ushakova, 41; tel. 2-34-42.
Post Office in Hotel Frehat: prospekt Ushakova, 2; tel. 4-14-77.
Central calling point: prospekt Ushakova, 41;
tel. 2-41-25.
Fax: Post Office, tel. 2-33-29; Hotel Frehat, tel.
49-63-43.

MEDICAL SERVICES

Emergency: tel. 03.
Pharmacies: ploshcha Svobody, 2; tel. 6-50-34.

TRANSPORTATION

Railway station: tel. 005, 4-84-15.

Ticket office: Petrenko St., 28; tel. 4-94-08.

Bus station: Mykolayivske Shosse, 2; tel. 4-94-11.

Bus station (suburban routes): tel. 4-94-11.

Maritime port: prospekt Ushakova, 4; tel. 29-12-99.

River port: Odeska Ploshcha; tel. 28-23-39.

Airport: tel. 4-94-36 (Bus No. 48 from the Central Marketplace — Rynok).

Ukraine Airlines: Mayakovsky St., 6; tel. 4-94-17; Foreign Tourists' Sector (reservations and tickets): tel. 4-94-17.

Taxi reservation: tel. 058.

Cars and drivers are available at Inturyst-Kherson: tel. 49-63-43.

Park. "Marichka.

AUTO SERVICING

Avtoservis: Mykolayivske shosse, 5 km; tel. 4-83-85.

TOURING HISTORIC CITIES AND VILLAGES

ASKANIYA-NOVA (until 1841 — Chapli)

Askaniya-Nova.

Village, Chaplynsky district, 21 km from the Kalanchak railway station. Population: 4,500.

ASKANIYA NOVA PRESERVE, 1828. A German Duke named Anhalt-Ketenski, established a settlement and named it in honor of his estate in Germany. Later the land was taken over by German settlers named Falz-Fein. In 1874 a zoo and in 1887, a Botanical Garden were added. The preserve contains a zoo, botanical park, and a virgin steppe preserve, the only one of its kind in Europe. In 1984 it was included in the International Network of Nature Preserves. It is located on 33,000 ha, and is visited by 200,000 visitors yearly.

BERYSLAV

City and port on the right bank of the Kakhovka Reservoir, 12 km from the Kozatske railway station.

In the 15th cent. it was a Lithuanian customs-house; in the 16th cent., — the Kyzykermen (Maiden's Fortress) Turkish fortress; in 1695 — captured by Ukrainian Kozak regiments.

VVEDENSKA (PRESENTATION AT THE TEMPLE) CHURCH, 1776. Was named Voskresenska. In 1784 this wood church was transported on the Dnipro River from the Zaporozhian Perevolochna Fortress. An ancient wooden cross and Gospel (1697) have been preserved.

CHERVONY MAYAK

Village, Beryslav district, on the banks of the Kakhovka Reservoir, 66 km from the Kakhovka railway station.

A burial ground dating to the Neolithic period and the Bronze age, and an ancient Scythian-Sarmatian settlement have been excavated here. In 1781 the Sofroniv Hermitage was established and in 1803 a Monastery was transferred from Bizyuky, Smolensk gubernia. The monastery consisted of 70 stone structures.

HRYHORIYE-BIZYUKIV (or PROPASNY [lost]) MONASTERY, 1781. Parts of the stone walls, three towers, the Pokrovska (Protection of the Blessed Virgin

Mary) Church, gate (1898), some of the service buildings (mid-19th cent.), sections of a rampart, and caves opening on the Dnipro River have been preserved.

HOLA PRYSTAN

City on the Kokhka River, 18 km from Kherson. Population: 13,000.

CHORNOMORSKY (BLACK SEA) NATURE RESERVE, 1927. 57,000 ha, extends from the Dnipro-Buzk estuary in the west to Karkinytsky Bay in the east. The shallow bays of the rivers, estuaries and islets in the Black Sea and Sea of Azov are the home of many seasonal migrating birds.

Excursions to the bird islands: May-November, tel. 2-64-71.

NOVA KAKHOVKA

City on the left bank of the Dnipro River, 78 km from Kherson.

KORSUN MONASTERY, 18th cent. Sections of the limestone walls (3,5 m high) have been preserved, as well as the northeastern stone tower (8.8 m high, diameter 3.6 m); the central and western gate, sections of Dmytrivska (St. Demetrius') Church (1797-1802), refectory-type church (1804), and some of the service buildings.

RESPUBLIKANETS

Village, Beryslav district.

KAMENSKA SICH. Remains of the last Zaporozhian Sich have been preserved in the village, where Kost Hordiyenko, a deputy to Hetman I. Mazepa and the head of the Oleshkivska Sich until 1728 is buried.

TYAHYNKA

Village, Beryslav district, 30 km from the Kozatske railway station.

KOZATSKA SLAVA (Kozak Glory), 1992. A monument erected on the island of Tyahyn to commemorate the 500th anniversary of the first battle between the Zaporozhian Kozaks and the Turks.

Khmelnytsky Region

In the western part of Ukraine, in the forest-steppe zone of the Volynia-Podillya Upland. The climate is temperate-continental. There are more than 90 rivers in the region which are part of the Dnister, Southern Buh and Prypyat Basins. Established in 1937. Area: 20,600 sq. km. Population: 1,524,000.

History

The territory began to be settled in the Paleolithic Age. Among the dozens of archaeological sites excavated in Ukraine, one of the oldest, dating back 300,000 years, was found near the village of Luky-Vrublevetsky. Over 150 monuments of the Trypillian culture have also been uncovered. In the first half of the 1st cent. A.D. the southwest group of eastern Slavs inhabited the region.

In 1199 these territories were part of the Galician-Volynian Principality. In the 12th-13th cent. the region was economically well-developed. The fortress towns with their garrisons of Kyivan armies protected the southwestern Rus'-Ukraine from the Pecheneg and Polovtsian tribes. In 1241 the Podillya region was invaded and destroyed by the Tatars. In the second half of the 14th cent. the territory came under Lithuanian rule. Fortresses and fortifications were constructed and trade and commerce flourished.

The Lithuanians and Poles fought among themselves for control of the rich, fertile lands. After capturing western Podillya in 1434, Polish magnates created a voyevodeship with its center in Kamyanets-Podilsky. The fight against foreign oppres-

Along the historic roads of the Khmelntysky Region.

sion continued. The anti-feudal uprising of peasants (1431), and the Kozak-peasant uprising were led by S. Nalyvayko (1594-96). Finally in 1653 and in 1655 the Ukrainian armies were able to rout the Polish armies. The population took an active part in the liberation war waged by Hetman B. Khmelnytsky and the peasant-Haydamaky uprisings of the 17th cent.

In the city of Kamyanets-Podilsky alone there are over one hundred important monuments dating to the 12th-19th cent. and ranks third in historical importance. After the Second World War there were over 500 churches and monasteries in the region, which were later used for non-religious purposes or partially destroyed.

PROMINENT INDIVIDUALS

BORN IN THE REGION:

O. Burkhardt-Klen (1891-1947), poet; in Serbynivka, Starokonstyantyniv district, died in Germany. • **H. Kostiuk** (1902), writer, civic and political figure; in Boryshkivtsi, Kamyanets-Podilsky district, lives in the USA. • **V. Manyak** (1934-92), writer, co-director of the Memorial Society, head of the Association of Researchers of the Famine-Genocide of 1932-33; in Kryshtopivka, Volochyska district. • **M. Smotrytsky** (1572-1633), writer, cultural and educational figure; in Smotrych, Dunayivtsi district.

BURIED IN THE REGION:

Baal-Shem-Tov Israel (1690-1760), founder of the Chassidim sect in Judaism; Medzhybizh in the Letychiv district. • **U. Karmalyuk** (1787-1835), national hero; in Letychiv.

KHMELNYTSKY (until 1954 — Proskuriv)

Regional center on the Southern Buh and Ploska Rivers. Telephone code: 0380.

First mentioned in documents dating to 1493 as a guard signal point, designed to warn residents about enemy approaches. The town suffered great devastation from invasions of the Crimean Tatars and was leveled in 1512 and 1593. During the 16th-18th cent. the city residents participated in battles against the Poles. In 1653 the population joined the armies of Hetman Khmelnytsky. Later it was under Turkish occupation for 27 years. After its liberation the city was rebuilt, and in the 18th cent. it became a privately owned city and from 1663 was the property of the Zamojski family. In 1822 it was destroyed by fire. The urban population grew as a result of the development of trade and commerce. In the early 19th cent. the city was one of the largest grain-trading centers.

MONUMENTS

B. Khmelnytsky, 1967. Sculptor: M. Vronsky. Architect: A. Sydorenko.

T. Shevchenko, 1992. Sculptors: I. Znoba and V. Znoba. Architect: V. Hromykhin.

MUSEUMS

Regional Ethnography Museum: Podilska St., 12; tel. 6-50-65; 6-61-73. • **Art Museum:** Proskurivska St., 47; tel. 6-47-61; 6-61-15. • **H. Vereysky Art-Memorial Museum:** Chervonoarmiyska St., 5; tel. 6-85-59.

THEATERS, PHILHARMONIC

Music and Drama Theater: Soborna St., 60. • **Puppet Theater:** Hrushevsky St., 103. • **Philharmonic:** Gagarin St., 7.

HIGHER EDUCATIONAL INSTITUTIONS

Technological Institute: Instytutska St., 11.

LIBRARIES, ARCHIVES

M. Ostrovsky State General Research Library: Teatralna St., 28. • **Youth Library:** Soborna St., 33. • **T.**

Smotrych river.

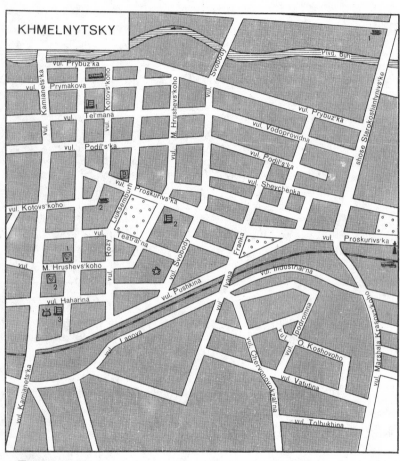

KHMELNYTSKY

B   Excursion office

📖   Hotels:
    1 Kolos
    2 Zhovtnevyi
    3 Podillia

🍴   Restaurants:
    1 Turyst
    2 Ukraïna
    Note. Restaurants Zhovtnevyi
    and Podillia are attached to
    the hotels of the same names

🚃   Railway Station

🚌   Bus Station

♟   Monument to Bohdan Khmelnytskyi

☆   G. S. Vereisky Art-Memorial Museum

🎭   Theaters:
    1 Ukrainian Theater of Music and
    Drama
    2 Puppet

🎵   Philharmonic Society

Shevchenko Children's Library: Svobody St., 51. • Regional Archive: Hrushevsky St., 99.

PARKS, BOTANICAL GARDENS

M. Kotsyubynsky Park: Luxemburg St. • I. Franko Park: Proskurivska St. • Park of Culture and Recreation: Parkova St., 1. • Arboretum: prospekt Myru.

SPORTS COMPLEXES

Podillya Stadium: Proskurivska St., 67; tel. 6-51-01.

HOTELS

Eneyida: Teatralna St., 8; tel. 9-12-42; 9-12-25. • Zhovtnevy: Proskurivska St., 44; tel. 6-46-69; 6-04-33. • Podillya: Shevchenko St., 34; tel. 6-10-83; 6-77-18. • Tsentralny: Gagarin St., 5; tel. 6-47-23; 6-77-04.

RESTAURANTS, CAFES, BARS

Veselka: Kamyanetska St., 155. • Dorozhniy: Proskurivska St., 92. • Zhovtnevy: Proskurivska St., 44. • Podillya: Shevchenko St., 34. • Silistra: ploshcha Svobody, 1-b. • Turyst: Starokonstyantynivske shosse, 10. • Ukrayina: Kotovsky St., 73. • Tsentralny: Gagarin St., 7. • Krystal: Proskurivska St., 15. • Malvina: prospekt Myru, 57/2. • Mriya: Gagarin St., 9. • Teatralne: Soborna St., 58. • Alkor: Prybuzka St., 2. • Sekay: Instytutska St., 8/1. • Fok: Industriyalna St., 88. • Hryl: Proskurivska St., 25. • Neptun: Proskurivska St., 25. • Ukrayinska Smazhenyna: Soborna St., 16.

STORES

Dytyachy Svit: Proskurivska St., 4/3. • Elektronika: Zarichanska St., 40. • Komertsiyny: Proskurivska St., 22. • Universam Kooperator: Kamyanetska St., 170. • Malvina (souvenirs): Soborna St., 69. • Podarunky: Proskurivska St., 21. • Promtovary: Zarichanska St., 2. • Prana: Kamyanetska St., 67. • Tsentralny: Proskurivska St., 50. • Yunist: Kamyanetska St., 5. • Druzhba: Soborna St., 16. • Dumka: Zarichanska St., 16. • Znannya: Kamyanetska St., 71. • Knyzhkovy Svit (books): Podilska St., 25. • Suchasnyk: Proskurivska St., 17.

BANKS

National Bank of Ukraine (Regional Branch): Volodymyrska St., 91; tel. 6-50-

03. • **Joint-Stock Commercial Bank "Fiatbank:"** Proskurivska St., 12; tel. 6-90-47; 6-47-18.

TOURISM, RESORTS

Inturyst-Khmelnytsky: Shevchenko St., 34; tel. 6-93-67; 6-76-56; 6-77-47.
Medobory Tourist Club: Shevchenko St., 8; tel. 9-77-93.
Travel and Excursion Agency: Proskurivska St., 15; tel. 6-63-62; 6-72-97; 6-90-65. Tours of: Khmelnytsky-Kamyanets-Podilsky; Khmelnytsky-Kamyanets-Podilsky (including stop-over in Kryvche, Ternopil region); Khmelnytsky-Medzhybizh; Khmelnytsky-Polonne-Poninka; Khmelnytsky-Samchyky.
Sataniv Health Resort: in Slobidka Ivanovetska, Horodotsky district. Renowned for its Naftusya mineral water; tel. 9-12-23; 9-82-08.
Health Resorts: Tovtry, Zbruch, Berizka.

POST OFFICE, TELEPHONE

Main post office: Proskurivska St., 90; tel. 6-42-42; 6-63-91; 6-84-64.
Calling points: Proskurivska St., 73; tel. 6-46-23; 6-54-53; 6-64-82.
Fax: Proskurivska St., 13; tel. 6-46-23.
Postal Services Bureau: tel. 069

MEDICAL SERVICES

Emergency: tel. 03
Pharmacies: No. 1: Kamyanetska St., 38; tel. 6-12-63; 6-50-33; 6-56-23. • No. 170: Pilotska St., 2; tel. 6-62-72; 9-12-33. • No 176: Chervonokozacha St., 54; tel. 9-47-47.

TRANSPORTATION

Railway station: Shevchenko St., 85; tel. 6-51-11.
Hrechany Station: Vokzalna St., 135; tel. 5-96-35.
Inter-urban bus terminus: Vinnytske shosse, 23; tel. 3-80-50.
Suburban Bus Terminus (east): Shevchenko St., 66; tel. 6-64-95.
Suburban Bus Terminus (west): Prymakov St., 29; tel. 6-52-09.
Airport: tel. 6-46-35; 2-50-02; 6-51-70. Bus No. 17.

AUTO SERVICING

Avtoservis: provulok Myru, 102; tel. 3-04-05.

TOURING HISTORIC CITIES AND VILLAGES

ADAMIVKA

Village, Vinkivtsi district, 25 km from the Dunayivtsi railway station. Renowned decorative pottery center.

POKROVSKA (PROTECTION OF THE BLESSED VIRGIN MARY) CHURCH, 1773. In 1884 a bell tower was added to its western facade. A rare example of a three-steepled church of the 18th cent.

BAKOTA

Village in the Kamyanets-Podilsky region, on the Dnister tributary, 35 km from the Kamyanets-Podilsky railway station.

First mentioned in the chronicles for the year 1024. In the 13th cent. it was a political-administration center of the Dnister Lowlands, beginning with the 14th cent. - Podillya and part of the Galician-Volynian Principality.

Remains of settlements of the late Paleolithic and Neolithic Age, the Chernyakhiv culture (2nd-6th cent.) and the ruins of an ancient city and Cave Monastery (12th-13th cent.) have been unearthed in the village.

MYKHAYLIVSKA (ST. MICHAEL'S) CHURCH. Ruins.

HOVORY

Village in the Vinkivtsi district on the Ushytsi River, 30 km from the Bar railway station. Founded in the 16th cent.

PALACE. This 16th cent. landowner's manor consists of several buildings.

IZYASLAV

City and railway station on the Horyn River, 146 km from Khmelnytsky.

In the 13th cent. it was part of the Galician-Volynian Principality. In 1466 the Princes Zaslavsky began building a castle on the banks of the Horyn River. In the 15th-16th cent. it became an important trading and commercial center in southern Volynia.

Bakota. Caves Monastery, 12th-13th cent.

ST. BERNARD'S MONASTERY, early 17th cent. The monastery complex includes: a Roman Catholic Church, cells, 6 m-wide walls, with towers and gates. The buildings are constructed in the 17th cent. Baroque style.

ST. BERNARD'S ROMAN CATHOLIC CHURCH, 1606-10. Built by the architect Ya. Madlena in the Baroque style.

CASTLE (ruins), 1539. The local princes and feudal lords kept their most valuable property here. The foundations and lower floor were built out of natural stone.

KOSTEL SVYATOHO IOANA KHRESTYTELYA (ROMAN CATHOLIC CHURCH OF ST. JOHN THE BAPTIST), 1599. Built by the architect Y. Madlena. The church was destroyed in 1648 and rebuilt in 1756. It was a defensive structure until the 18th cent. An example of the successful union of Gothic and Renaissance elements.

KOSTEL SVYATOHO YOSYFA, (ROMAN CATHOLIC CHURCH OF ST. JOSEPH), 1750-60. Architect: P. Fontana. Served as a monastery and mission.

PALACE (ruins), 18th cent.

KAMYANETS-PODILSKY

One of the oldest cities in Ukraine, in the central part of the Volynian-Podillian Upland on the Smotrych River, the left tributary of the Dnister River, 102 km from Khmelnytsky.

Kamyanets was first mentioned in the Armenian Chronicles of 1060-1062. The Hypatian Chronicle states: "In 1240-41 the Tatar Hordes of Khan Baty destroyed the city." In the 12th-13th cent. it was an important commercial center, situated on the route from Kyiv to the Balkans. Until the mid-14th cent. Kamyanets was part of the Galician-Volynian Principality. In 1362 it fell under the rule of the Lithuanian Koriatovych princes and in 1393 the population of Kamyanets took part in an uprising against the Lithuanian feudal lords.

In 1430 Poland gained control of the city and in 1432 it was granted the rights

Kamyanets-Podilsky.

of Magdeburg Law. In 1463 it became the capital of Podillya voivodeship and was proclaimed a royal city. Under Polish rule the city grew into a center of international trade and artisanry. The city was well-fortified and protected the southeastern frontier of the Polish Commonwealth. The Ukrainian, Armenian, and Lithuanian-Polish burghers had their own municipal self-government, but the rights of Ukrainian citizens gradually diminished. The population opposed the foreign occupation and took part in the anti-Polish national-liberation war of 1648-54 led by B.

Defense fortress,
XVI-XVIIth cent.

Khmelnytsky. In 1672 the city was plundered by the Turks and remained in Turkish hands until 1699. In the 18th cent. the people of Kamyanets joined the Haydamaky Movement to fight the Polish oppressors. In 1793 Kamyanets came under Russian rule. It was a gubernia capital from 1797, when growth of the city began to accelerate. A printing house was founded, as well as a gymnasium, the first bookstore, and a public library. The Kamyanets-Podilsky Ukrainian State University was founded on 1 July 1918 by Ivan Ohiyenko, the future Metropolitan of the Ukrainian Orthodox Church in Canada. The city was the capital of the Ukrainian National Republic for almost eight months in 1919.

During the Second World War the city suffered extensive damages and great loss of life (85,000). In 1941 Kamyanets became the regional center.

CHURCHES, HISTORICAL AND ARCHITECTURAL MONUMENTS

FORTRESS, 11th-16th cent. A monument of military architecture of the feudal era. The first fortifications were built in the 11th-12th cent. In the early 16th cent. the fortress was re-designed by the Italian military engineer Camilius, and seven towers were built. In the 17th cent. bastion structures were built (New Fortress). The Old Fortress occupies almost 5 ha. Part of an underground passage has been uncovered.

TOWERS: New East Tower (Black). Built by the architect Yov Pretvych in 1544. There is a deep well dug through a 40-m thick cliff; Karmalyuk Tower (1503-17) is the tallest; here the national hero Ustym Karmalyuk was imprisoned three times. White Tower (1510-31); Rozhanka Tower (1505); Denna Tower and Mala Tower, were used to store gunpowder; Vodyana Tower (Water Tower) was located on the banks of the Smotrych River and was used to supply water to the castle. Today these structures are part of the Historical Museum and Preserve.

CASTLE BRIDGE (Turkish). A stone structure connecting the fortress with the old town. Built during the ancient Rus' era. During the Turkish occupation of the 17th cent. it was renovated; hence the name.

MEDIEVAL FORTIFICATION STRUCTURES, 15th-16th cent. Two rows of fortified crenelated stone walls connected by mighty bastions. (Skelyasta St.).

Arcade of former Armenian Church.

CITY GATE, 16th-17th cent. Part of the mighty fortifications that sealed off the entrance to the old town. (Starobulvarny Spusk).

ARMENIAN BASTION, 16th-17th cent. The remains of a citadel and Kazematna Bashta (tower), attesting to Armenian participation in the defense of the city, have been preserved. (Starobulvarny Spusk).

RUSKA BRAMA (GATE), 16th-17th cent. This complex defensive and hydrotechnical structure is, in fact, a fortress. The gate was used as the main entrance to the city. By means of dams the water-level of the river was raised, and the gate thus served as a defensive structure.

POLISH GATE, 16th-17th cent. Together with the Ruska Gate, this gate is an example of the hydrotechnical-defensive system in Eastern Europe. Features local architectural elements: beams and wood ligatures embedded in the walls.

KUSHNIRSKA (FURRIER'S - Stefan Batory) TOWER, 16th-18th cent. A seven-storied crenelated structure, built with funds provided by furriers (kushnir) defending the city. An outstanding monument of defense architecture. (Staroposhtovy Spusk).

MYKOLAYIVSKA (St. NICHOLAS') CHURCH, 14th cent. Its original appearance has been preserved. Built by Armenian settlers in 1392 and their leader Sinan Kotlubey. The church is a pillar-less structure, with the altar located in the apses and crenelated windows. Built in the late Romantic style.

ARMENIAN MYKOLAYIVSKY (ST. NICHOLAS') CATHEDRAL, 15th-17th cent. The church was destroyed in 1672 by the Turks and was restored during the following century. Only a fragment of the gallery has been preserved. A five-storied belfry was built as a defense structure (stone crenelated tower). Fragments of a fresco painting have been preserved.

PETROPAVLIVSKA (SS. PETER AND PAUL'S) CHURCH, 1580. A stone, tripartite structure with fragments of 16th cent. frescoes. After capturing the city, the Turks gave this church to the Polish Catholics. During the 18th cent. male and female brotherhoods existed at the church. This monument is one of only a few three-storied churches which reflect the evolution of Ukrainian architecture and its ties with Moldova.

PETROPAVLIVSKY (SS. PETER AND PAUL'S) CATHEDRAL ENSEM-

Khrystovozdvyzhenska (Elevation of the Holy Cross) Church, 17th-18th cent.

BLE, 15th-19th cent. Consists of four outstanding monuments in which the Gothic, Renaissance, Baroque, and neo-Gothic styles are skillfully combined.

KOSTEL (ROMAN CATHOLIC CHURCH). Built by local master craftsmen, it has retained the features of an ancient Ukrainian church. Today it houses a Museum-Preserve and a concert hall for organ music.

TURKISH MINARET, 1672-99. A Catholic church converted to a Muslim mosque. A 36.5 m high minaret was added later. In 1756 the city residents erected a bronze statue of the Madonna in gratitude for their liberation from the Turks.

TRIUMPHAL ARCH, 1871. Built in the late Baroque style, the arch has been preserved with few changes. The structure is decorated with stone carvings with plant motifs.

BELL TOWER. A three-tiered structure built out of stone blocks.

FRANCISCAN CHURCH, 14th-18th cent. Originally a monastery, with a Baroque-style bell tower.

TRINITARIAN (HOLY TRINITY) ROMAN CATHOLIC CHURCH, 18th cent. Noted for its highly-evolved technique of sculptural composition.

DOMINICAN MONASTERY, 15th-18th

Tower of Armenian Church, XV-XVIth cent.

cent. Combines several structures built at different times, representing different periods of Ukrainian architecture and civil engineering. Until 1866 the monastery housed a Catholic seminary.

KOSTEL (CATHOLIC CHURCH). Built by the Dominican Fathers who arrived in Kamyanets in the 14th cent. Has features of the Gothic, Renaissance, and Baroque styles. The interior decor, paintings, ornaments, and gold leaf gilding attests to the skills of the master-masons, sculptors, and carvers. During the Turkish occupation the church was used as a mosque and housing for the military. A beautiful example of the Oriental craft of stone carving.

KHRYSTOVOZDVYZHENSKA (ELEVATION OF THE HOLY CROSS) CHURCH, 17th-18th cent. A unique monument of the Podillian school of wood architecture. Built on a stone foundation to protect the church from flood-waters. Located in the city outskirts called Karvasary, derived from the word "caravansarai," an inn in eastern countries where caravans rested for the night.

CITY HALL, 17th-18th cent. The former building of the Polish magistracy. One of the original structures in the medieval city situated on the "Tatar Route," traversed by merchants' caravans on their way to the Crimea, Kafa, and the Middle East. The city hall was the seat of political life. The Ukrainian national hero Ustym Karmalyuk was tortured on the square in front of it. (Tsentralna Ploshcha).

BUILDING OF THE RUS' MAGISTRACY, 16th cent. In 1658 the Polish King Jan Casimir gave his approval for the use of this building by the Ukrainian community. It was used for meetings of the Podillya nobility and later as a theater.

ARMENIAN WAREHOUSES, 16th-18th cent. Armenians settled in the old town in the 11th cent. and played a major role in the development of trade and commerce. Defense structures, residential buildings, churches, and seminaries, attesting to the highly-evolved culture of Armenia, have been preserved. Armenian residential buildings of the 14th-19th cent. are located on Tsentralna Ploshcha.

ARMENIAN WELL, 17th cent. This building, designated a republican historic site, was destroyed during the German occupation and restored in 1958.

TURKISH BUILDINGS, 17th cent. Ruins of Turkish houses, the residence of the Turkish deputy Halil-Pasha, a harem, and Turkish bastions.

FORTRESS BARRACKS, 18th cent. Built for the military garrison.

BUILDING OF CHARTORYISKY FAMILY, 16th cent. Belonged to the Polish magnates. A fine example of residential architecture of the Renaissance style incorporating ancient Ukrainian architectural traditions. Stone carvings predominate in the interior. An outstanding monument erected by local master builders.

MUSEUMS

State Historical-Cultural Preserve: Yoan Predtecha St., 2; tel. 2-25-21; 2-37-84. The Preserve contains close to 100 architectural monuments and other artifacts.

PARKS

Park of Culture and Recreation: Shevchenko St., 22. • **Botanical Garden:** Ukrayinka St., 64.

KYTAYHOROD

Village, Kamyanets-Podilsky district, 35 km from the Kamyanets-Podilsky railway station. First mentioned in documents dating to 1607.

KOSTEL DIVY MARIYI (ST. MARY'S ROMAN CATHOLIC CHURCH), 1772-76. Combines the late Renaissance style with Baroque principles of designing facades.

Medzhybizh. Castle, 14th-16th cent.

LETYCHIV

District center, 51 km from Khmelnytsky. The Lithuanians took over these lands in 1362 and built a fortress in Letychiv. In the 15th-16th cent. it was plundered by the Crimean Tatars and the Turks. In 1648-54 the population actively participated in the anti-Polish uprisings and in 1734 in the peasant-Haydamaky revolts. In the 1830s Letychiv was the center of the struggle against serfdom.

MYKHAYLIVSKA (ST. MICHAEL'S) CHURCH, 17th cent. An example of a church doubling as a fortress.
CASTLE WALLS AND TOWER WITH THE USPENSKY (DORMITION) ROMAN CATHOLIC CHURCH, 16th-17th cent. This church, which defended the town from the Tatars, is a monument of early defensive architecture.
KOSTEL (ROMAN CATHOLIC CHURCH) OF THE DOMINICAN MONASTERY, 1606-38.
Monument to U. Karmalyuk, 1974. Sculptor: V. Znoba. Architect: I. Shmulson.

MEDZHYBIZH

Letychiv. Castle Walls and Tower, 16th-17th cent.

Village, Letychiv district, 25 km from the Derazhnya railway station.

First mentioned in the Hypatian Chronicle for the year 1146. Parts of an ancient settlement from the 11th-13th cent. have been preserved, indicating that Medzhybizh was a well-fortified border point. From the late 12th cent. it belonged to the Galician-Volynian Principality. In 1241 the Golden Horde captured the village.

CASTLE, 14th-16th, 19th cent. Built on the

site of 12th cent. fortifications. An important monument of military engineering. Has several crenelated towers. From the high fortress walls the adjacent roads leading to the fortress could be seen.

PALACE, 16th cent. In the northeastern part of the fortress; a church was built here in 1586. Its austere lines are softened by refined Baroque-style pediments and high roof.

TROYITSKY (HOLY TRINITY) CHURCH (ruins), 1632. In the Baroque style.

BRANCH OF THE REGIONAL ETHNOGRAPHY MUSEUM: Zhovtneva St., 1; tel. 9-71-30; 9-71-23.

PYLYAVA (until the 18th cent. — Pylyavtsi)

Village, Starosynyavsky district, on the banks of the Ikva River, 35 km from the railway station.

The castle in Pylyava already existed in 1501. The village is closely connected with the name of Hetman Khmelnytsky and the Zaporozhian Kozaks, who won a decisive victory in 1648 in Korsun over the Polish armies. To commemorate this historic battle a monument was erected in the village.

SATANIV

Village, Horodotsky district, on the left bank of the Zbruch River, 18 km from the Zakupne railway station.

For almost 300 years the village was ruled by the Polish nobility.

TOWN GATES, 15th-16th cent. Built to replace the ancient entrance to the city; rebuilt in the 16th cent. and joined with the castle; part of the defensive ramparts of the city. Built in the Renaissance and Baroque style.

CASTLE, 14th-16th cent. Three pentahedron-shaped towers and one ancient round tower built of wood dating to the 16th cent. have been preserved.

TROYITSKY (HOLY TRINITY) MONASTERY, 16th-18th cent. Includes the Holy Trinity Church (17th cent.), bell tower with monks' cells, the gates, and walls. Participants of the peasant-Kozak uprisings, brutally suppressed by the Polish armies, were tortured and buried alive in the monastery.

SYNAGOGUE, 1532. A stone structure built in the Renaissance style.

Sataniv. Synagogue, 1532.

STAROKOSTYÁNTYNIV

City, at the confluence of the Ikopot and Sluch Rivers, 48 km from Khmelnytsky.

Established in the 16th cent., this city was well-fortified and conveniently situated on important trading routes.

Starokostyantyniv. Defense Tower (ruins), 16th-17th cent.

CASTLE, 1516-71. Established by Prince K. Ostrozky for the defense of the region against Tatar invasions. It remained standing following the most devastating invasion of the Tatars in 1618, when the neighboring villages were completely destroyed. The castle complex includes: the palace with its defense tower, remains of a church, the bell tower, and entrance gate. Beneath the palace are wells-cells that lead to the river. They served as warehouses for ammunition and arms.

KOSTEL OF IOANA KHRESTYTELYA (ROMAN CATHOLIC CHURCH OF ST. JOHN THE BAPTIST), 1754. An example of late Baroque architecture.

KOSTEL (ROMAN CATHOLIC CHURCH), ruins, 1612. Part of the Dominican Monastery structures.

STARY KRYVYN

Village, Slavuta district, 12 km from Slavuta, on the Shepetivka-Zdolbuniv railway line.

VOSKRESENSKA (RESURRECTION) CHURCH, 1763. A wood structure built in the Ukrainian Baroque style. The shape of the church resembles a ship. Built by local master builders. The remains of a Neolithic settlement have been unearthed.

STARY OSTROPIL

Village, Starokostyantynivsky district, 15 km from the Pasichna railway station.

Sutkivtsi. Pokrovska (Protection) Church-Fortress, 14th-16th cent.

PREOBRAZHENSKA (TRANSFIGURATION OF OUR SAVIOUR) CHURCH, 1840. This monument is one of a handful of rotundas built in the Classical style.

SUTKIVTSI

Village, Yarmolyntsi district, 15 km from the Yarmolyntsi railway station.

CASTLE, 14th-17th cent. One of the strong points located on the route traversed by the Tatar hordes.

POKROVSKA (PROTECTION OF THE BLESSED VIRGIN MARY) CHURCH-FORTRESS, 14th-15th cent. In the 18th cent. this structure was rebuilt as a defense structure. The church walls have crenelated windows.

VELYKA RADOHOSHCH

Village, Izyaslav district, 27 km from the Izyaslav railway station.

MYKHAYLIVSKA (ST. MICHAEL'S) CHURCH AND BELL TOWER, 1799. A wood church with three domes and numerous interior woodcarvings. A monument of the folk architectural style.

POKROVSKA (PROTECTION OF THE BLESSED VIRGIN MARY) CHURCH AND BELL TOWER, 1800. In the village of Mala Radohoshch.

YAMPIL

Village, Bilohirya district, on the Horyn River, 2 km from the Lepesivka railway station.

TYKHOMLSKE HORODYSHCHE (SETTLEMENT), 12th cent. Ruins of a 16th cent. fortress have been preserved. First mentioned in the Chronicle for the year 1152. A city of the Ukrainian appanage princes established when Volyn was united with Kyivan Rus'-Ukraine in 981.

ZAPADYNTSI

Village in the Letychiv district, 30 km from the Derazhnya railway station.

MYKHAYLIVSKA (ST. MICHAEL'S) CHURCH AND BELL TOWER, 1733. A wood church. Wood carvings of the 18th cent. have been preserved. One of the finer examples of the Volynian school of monumental folk architecture.

ZHVANETS

Village in the Kamyanets-Podilsky region on the left bank of Dnister River, 24 km from the Kamyanets-Podilsky railway station.

First mentioned in the chronicles for the year 1431. Converted to a fortress in the 16th cent. In 1621 the Kozak army, headed by Hetman P. Sahaydachny, was stationed in the village, and later fought in the Battle of Khotyn against the Turks and Tatars. In 1653 a major battle was fought near the village between Hetman Khmelnytsky's forces and the Polish army.

In the village are the ruins of the fortress.

VIRMENSKY KOSTEL (ARMENIAN CHURCH), 1782-86. An example of the late Baroque style.

The remains of ramparts are located on the site of a battle fought by Khmelnytsky's armies.

ZINKIV

Village in the Vinkivtsi district, 35 km from the Dunayivtsi railway station.

First mentioned in documents dating to 1404. One of the largest cities in Ukraine in the 16th cent. A center of folk ceramics.

MYKHAYLIVSKA (ST. MICHAEL'S) CHURCH, 1769. This wood church is an outstanding example of the Podillian school of folk architecture

TROYITSKY KOSTEL (TRINITY ROMAN CATHOLIC CHURCH), 1750. Ruins.

ESTATE, 19th cent. A brick building constructed in the Classical style.

Kirovohrad Region

Located in the steppe and forest-steppe of the southern Dnipro Upland between the Dnipro and Buh Rivers. The region is a fertile elevated plain. The climate is temperate-continental; the winters are mild and the summers hot. Established in 1939. Area: 24,600 sq. km. Population: 1,250,000.

History

The region was first settled in the Paleolithic Age. Remains of settlements of the Trypilian culture and approximately 20 settlements of Chornolis culture (10th to 7th cent. B.C.) have been unearthed. In the 7th cent. B.C. the region was settled by the nomadic Scythian tribes. More than 50 settlements containing early-Slavic monuments of Chernyakhiv culture have been excavated. In the 9th cent. the northern part of the region was part of Kyivan Rus'-Ukraïne. In the mid-13th cent. these lands came under Lithuanian rule and were occupied by Poland after the Union of Lublin in 1569.

In the second half of the 16th cent. part of the territory was conquered by the Ukrainian Kozaks who, throughout the 17th cent., defended the local population from attacks by the Crimean Tatars.

After the Russo-Turkish War of 1735-39, it became part of Russia. During the 17th cent. peasant-Haydamaky detachments fought in this region.

In 1764 the Yelysaveta province of the Novorosiysk gubernia was created. In the early 19th cent. the territories of the present Kirovohrad region were part of the Podillya and Kyivan gubernias.

PROMINENT INDIVIDUALS

BORN IN THE REGION:

I. Karpenko-Kary-Tobilevych (1845-1907), playwright, actor, theater director; in Arsenivka, Novomyrhorod district. • **A. Konoshchenko-Hrabenko** (1857-1932), folklorist; in Oboznivka, Kirovohrad district. • **M. Kropyvnytsky** (1840-1910), playwright, theater director; in Bezhbayraky (now Kropyvnytske), Novoukrayinsky district. • **H. Lohvyn** (1910), art expert, writer; in Kosivka, Oleksandriysky district. • **Ye. Malaniuk** (1897-1968), poet, publicist; in Novoarkhanhelsk, died in the USA. • **Yu. Meytus** (1903), composer; in Yelysavethrad (now Kirovohrad). • **S. Plachynda** (1928), writer; in Shevchenkovy Khutir. • **V. Vynnychenko** (1880-1951), writer, political figure; in Yelysavethrad (now Kirovohrad), died in France. • **Yu. Yanovsky** (1902-54), writer; in Mayerovy Khutir (now Nechayivka), Kompaniyivka district.

BURIED IN THE REGION:

I. Karpenko-Kary (1845-1907), playwright, theater director; in Korlyuhivky (near Nadiya Khutir), Kirovohrad district. • **V. Sukhomlynsky** (1918-70), educator; in Pavlysh, Onufriyiv district.

Kirovohrad. City center.

KIROVOHRAD

**(until 1924 — Yelysavethrad,
1924-34 — Zinovyevsk)**

Regional center on the Inhul River, 392 km from Kyiv. Population: 246,000. Telephone code: 0522.

Its founding in the mid-18th cent. is connected to the construction of St. Elizabeth's Fortress in 1754 on the former lands of the Zaporozhian Sich, and was designed to be a defensive structure to ward off attacks by the Turks and Crimean Tatars. The settlement around the fortification, owing to its location on a trading route, developed into a city. It was named Yelysavethrad in 1775.

In 1934 the city was renamed Kirovo, and in 1939, Kirovohrad.

*Pokrovska (Protection)
Church, 1850.*

CHURCHES, HISTORICAL AND ARCHITECTURAL MONUMENTS

POKROVSKA (PROTECTION OF THE BLESSED VIRGIN MARY) CHURCH, 1850. A brick structure built in 1850 west of the military town. It is an example of Eclectic architecture, with some 17th-cent architectural features. In the interior are fragments of a painting from the second half of the 19th century.

HRETSKA (GREEK) CHURCH, 1812. A stone structure, enlarged in 1898; paintings restored in 1905. Near the church is a stone belltower.

ST. ELIZABETH'S FORTRESS, 1754. Only sections of the fortress walls have been preserved.

MONUMENTS

M. Kropyvnytsky, 1969. Sculptor: E. Kuntsevych.

T. Shevchenko, 1982. Sculptors: M. Vronsky and I. Honchar. Architect: A. Hubenko.

V. Vynnychenko Memorial Plaque, 1992. On the Building of the Men's Gymnasium, where the writer was a student. (Shevchenko St., 3).

Hretska (Greek) Church, 1812.

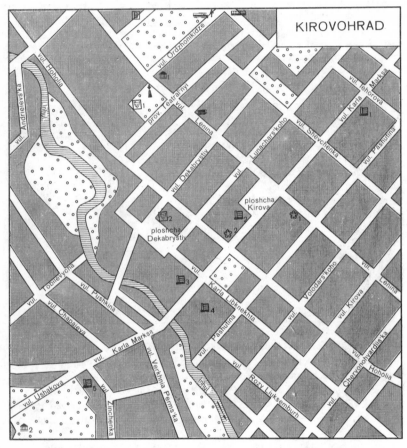

KIROVOHRAD

B   Excursion office

Hotels:
1 Ievropa
2 Ukraïna
3 Kyïv
4 Inhul
5 Turyst

Restaurant Vesna
Note. Restaurants Ievropa, Ukraïna and Kyïv are attached to
the hotels of the same names

Railway Station

Bus Station No. 2

Monument M. L. Kropyvnytskyi,
playwright, founder of Ukrainian professional realistic theater

Architectural monuments:
1 Complex of 19th-century buildings (the palace, ensemble
of the former military school
and manège)
2 Yelyzavetynska Fortress, 18th c.

Museums:
1 Local Lore
2 Picture Gallery

Theaters:

1 Kropyvnytskyi Theater of Music
and Drama
2 Puppet

MUSEUMS

Museum of Regional Ethnography: Lenin St., 40; tel. 2-58-34. • M. Kropyvnytsky Museum: Proletarska St., 40; tel. 22-14-79. • I. Karpenko-Kary Memorial
Museum-Building. The residence of the renowned theater director. (Tobilevych St.,
16). • Art Gallery: Marx St., 63; tel. 24-42-73. • I. Karpenko-Kary-Tobilevych
Memorial Museum and Preserve: Khutir Nadiya (near the village of Korlyuhivky,
30 km from Kirovohrad; tel. 22-15-39.

THEATERS, PHILHARMONIC

M. Kropyvnytsky Music and Drama Theater: Lenin St., 4. • Puppet Theater:
Liebknecht St., 9-a. • Philharmonic: Ordzhonikidze St., 8.

HIGHER EDUCATIONAL INSTITUTIONS

Agricultural Machine-Building Institute: prospekt Pravdy, 70-a. • Pedagogical
Institute: Shevchenko St., 1.

LIBRARIES, ARCHIVES

D. Chyzhevsky Scientific Library: Marx St., 24. • Children's Library: Shevchenko St., 5/22. • O. Boychenko Youth Library: Dekabrystiv St., 6/15. • Regional Archive: Korolyov St., 3. • City Archive: Korolyov St., 3. • Regional Archive (Births & Deaths Registration): Lenin St., 12.

SPORTS COMPLEXES

Sports Complex: Yan Tompa St., 1; tel. 3-30-81. • Zirka Stadium: Gagarin St.,
1-a; tel. 2-47-20; 2-45-45.

HOTELS

Dobrudzha: prospekt Pravdy, 68-a; tel. 55-54-04. • Turyst: Ushakov St., 1; tel.
24-46-80, 24-47-75. • Kyiv: Marx St., 50; tel. 24-42-90, 24-42-77. • Ukrayina:
Dzerzhynsky St., 82/40; tel. 22-66-41, 22-25-45. • Yevropa: Marx St., 22; tel. 24-
68-09, 24-96-54. • Inhul: Marx St., 53; tel. 24-39-71.

RESTAURANTS, CAFES, BARS

Airport: Korolenko St., 2. • Vesna: Lenin St., 13. • Dobrudzha: prospekt Pravdy, 68-a. • Yevropa: Marx St., 15. • Turyst: Ushakov St., 1. • Kyiv: Marx St., 50.
• Kirovohrad: Marx St., 53. • Ukrayina: Dzerzhynsky St., 60. • Verbychenka:

Robitnycha St., 19. • **Vechirniy:** Poltavska St.,
4. • **Chervona Ruta:** Velykovyskivske shosse,
7. • **Kozatska Zastava:** Kiltseva Doroha. • **Varenychna:** Lenin St., 28. • **Ukrayinski Stravy:**
Pyatdesyat Rokiv Zhovtnya, 18. • **Yatran:** Marx
St., 42. • **Berizka:** Marx St., 6/3. • **Dytyache:**
Marx St., 55. • **Inhul:** Naberezhna St., 1. • **Do-
rozhne:** prospekt Pravdy, 1. • **Zodiak:** Korolen-
ko St., 28-a. • **Kulishna:** Chervonohvardiyska
St., 44. • **Kryzhynka:** Shevchenko St., 17/7. •
Teatralne: Pyatdesyat Rokiv Zhovtnya St., 2. •
Mriya: Marx St., 23/13. • **Kosmos:** Shatylo St.,
13. • **Hrechanyky:** Marx St., 30. • **Pyvny Bar:**
Dekabrystiv St., 2.

O. Boychenko Youth Library.

STORES

Yuvileyny: 50 rokiv Zhovtnya, 17. • **Univermah (Department Store):** prospekt
Pravdy, 66. • **Harnizonny:** Shevchenko St., 3-a. • **Univermah:** Stepnyak-Kravchyn-
sky St., 33. • **Tovary Kirovohradshchyny:** Naberezhna St., 1. • **Oksana:** Shev-
chenko St., 26. • **Dytyachy Svit:** Marx St., 48. • **Zroby Sam:** Kropyvnytsky St., 80.
• **Tovary Dlya Molodi:** 50 rokiv Zhovtnya St., 20. • **Moda:** Frunze St., 10. • **Khu-
dozhny Salon (Art):** Hohol St., 91. • **Rubin:** Shevchenko St., 26. • **Knyzhkovy
Svit (Books):** Naberezhna St., 1. • **U Sviti Knyh (Books):** Zhovtnevoyi Revolutsiyi
St., 31. • **Suchasnyk:** Marx St., 46. • **Kobzar:** Shevchenko St., 34/25.

BANKS

Ukrainian National Bank (Regional Branch): Marx St., 33; tel. 2-25-52. • **Svitlovodsk Commercial Bank "Dniprobank":** in Svitlovodsk, Zhovtneva St., 4; tel.
2-99-39; 4-31-73. • **"Kolos" Commercial Bank:** Tymiryazev St., 84; tel. 24-95-61;
24-27-92.

TOURISM

Inturyst-Kirovohrad: Ushakov St., 1-a; (Hotel Turyst; tel. 24-65-03; 22-16-71.
Suputnyk: Frunze St., 10; tel. 27-35-77.
Ukrprofintur: Frunze St., 8; tel. 27-40-33.
Kirovohrad Tourism and Excursion Agency: Frunze St., 8; tel. 27-22-60; 27-
31-51.
**Local excursions to the I. Karpenko-Kary (Tobilevych) Memorial Museum
and Preserve:** Khutir Nadiya (30 km from Kirovohrad); St. Elizabeth's Fortress.

POST OFFICE, TELEPHONE

Post office: Hohol St., 72; tel. 24-25-96; 22-85-66; 22-27-76.
Telegraph: Hohol St., 74; tel. 066.
Calling points: Marx St., 93; tel. 22-57-31; 22-49-87. • Marx St., 91; tel. 22-87-70.
Inter-urban calling points: Pyatdesyat Rokiv Zhovtnya St., 1; tel. 23-40-61. •
Korolenko St., 34; tel. 27-30-38. • Volkov St., 13; tel. 55-25-25.
Fax: Marx St., 93; tel. 22-87-70.

MEDICAL SERVICES

Emergency: tel. 03.
Farmatsiya Association Information Service: tel. 067.
Pharmacies: Naberezhna St., 1; tel. 24-97-03. • Lenin St., 10; tel. 22-66-12. •
Prospekt Komunistychny, 4-a; tel. 22-68-42.

TRANSPORTATION

Railway Station: Popovych St., 1; tel. 005; 29-22-53.
Bus terminus for intercity connections: Korolenko St.; tel. 004; 24-79-86.
Suburban bus terminus: prospekt Pravdy, 1; tel. 23-20-39.
Airport: Korolenko St.; tel. 22-56-71.
Ukraine Airlines (Advance tickets): Marx St.; tel. 006; 24-96-25. International
Sector: Marx St.; tel. 24-96-25.
Taxi reservations: tel. 058.

TOURING HISTORIC CITIES AND VILLAGES

MYKOLAYIVKA

Village in the Kirovohrad district, 25 km from Kirovohrad, and 5 km from the Shostakivka railway station.

THE KHUTIR NADIYA MUSEUM-PRESERVE. The residence in which I. Tobilevych (Karpenko-Kary) lived and where he wrote 11 plays. At various times the major figures of the Ukrainian theater lived here (M. Sadovsky, P. Saksahansky, M. Sadovska-Barilotti)

NOVOMYRHOROD

City located 80 km from Kirovohrad on the Velyka Vis River.

ILLINSKA (ST. ELIAS') CHURCH, 1786. A brick structure built in the transitional Baroque-Classical style.

PAVLYSH

Village in the Onufriyivka district in the Omelnychka River valley, 7 km from the district center.

Founded in the early 17th cent. by the Kozak Chieftain But; originally called Butivka. The V. Sukhomlynsky Memorial-Pedagogical Museum is located in the village.

Novomyrhorod. Illinska (St. Elias') Church, 1786.

ROZUMIVKA

Village in the Oleksandrivsky district on the Bovtyshi River, 25 km from the Fundukliyivka railway station.

KHRESTOVOZDVYZHENSKA (ELEVATION OF THE HOLY CROSS) CHURCH, 19th cent. Built in the Classical style, this brick structure was rebuilt in 1883-1885. Presently used as a Historical-Ethnographic Museum.

VESELIVKA

Village in the Novomyrhorod district, 27 km from the Novomyrhorod railway station.

KURHAN. A burial mound dating to the Bronze Age (2nd cent. B.C.).

Luhansk Region
(formerly Voroshylovhrad region)

Located in southeastern Ukraine. Most of the terrain is hilly and interwoven with deep ravines. In the south it extends to the Donets Ridge (up to 367 m — Mehetna Grave). Part of the Donetsk coal basin is located in Luhansk region. The climate is temperate-continental. The rivers of the Luhansk region flow into the Siversky Donets basin. There are 60 lakes in the region; the principal river is the Vovche. Established in 1938. Area: 26,700. sq. km. Population: 2,887,000.

History

The first settlements appeared during the early Paleolithic Age. During the Copper and Bronze Ages, the land was settled by cattle-breeding and agricultural tribes. There have been numerous excavations of remains of the Scythian-Sarmatian era (7th-3rd cent. B.C.), and of burial grounds of Saltivsky culture (8th-10th cent.). Most of the territory was part of the Pereyaslav Principality. In the 10th-14th cent. the area was invaded by nomadic tribes and in 1223-24 by the Tatars. In order to protect the southern borders a number of fortresses were built in the 17th cent. Most of the inhabitants of the Luhansk lands were fugitives from Ukraine and Russia who were later joined by Kozaks from the Zaporozhian Sich. The population of Luhansk supported Stenka Razin's rebellion in 1670-71 and K. Bulavin's rebellion in 1707-08. The population of Luhansk helped to deter attacks of the Turkic nations. Serbs, Croats and Montenegrans were invited to help in the construction of fortresses; thus, a new territory called "Slav-Serbia" was created. In the early 18th cent. coal-beds were discovered in Luhansk region; in the second half of the 18th cent. the region became an important industrial center.

PROMINENT INDIVIDUALS

BORN IN THE REGION:

V. **Dal** (1801-72), Russian writer, scientist, dialectologist; in Luhansk. • **I. Lukyanenko-Savych,** (1914), poet. • **M. Rudenko** (1920), writer, former head of the Ukrainian Helsinki Monitoring Group; in Yuryivka; in Lutuhyne district, was persecuted. • **I. Svitlychny** (1929-92), poet, political prisoner, Polovynkyne, Starobilsk district.

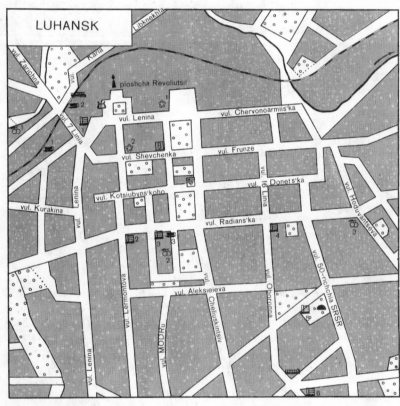

LUHANSK

ploshcha Revoliutsii

vul. Lenina

vul. Chervonoarmiis'ka

vul. Shevchenka

vul. Frunze

vul. Kotsiubyns'koho

vul. 16 Donets'ka

vul. Kurakina

vul. Radians'ka

vul. Aleksieieva

vul. Zarichna

Karla Libknekhta

vul. 7 Linia

vul. Lenina

vul. Lermontova

vul. MODRu

vul. Cheliuskintsiv

vul. Lenina

vul. 16 Linia

vul. Oborona

vul. Hoduvanseva

vul. 50-richcha SRSR

Excursion office

Hotels:
1 Zhovten
2 Dynamo
3 Radians'kyi
4 Pernyk
5 Arena
6 Turyst

Restaurants:
1 Ukraïna
2 At the Railway Station
3 Iuvileinyi
Note. Restaurants Pernyk and Turist are attached to the hotels of the same names

Railway Station

Bus Station

Markets:
1 At the Railway Station
2 Covered
3 Central

Monument to V. I. Dal

Museums:
1 Art
2 History and Local Lore

Theater of Music and Drama

Philharmonic Society

Circus

LUHANSK (formerly Voroshylovhrad)

City and regional center on the Olkhovka and Luhan Rivers, railway and highway junction. Population: 504,000. Telephone code: 0642. In 1795 on the site of present-day Luhansk there was a cannon foundry which supplied the demands of the Black Sea Fleet. In 1882 Selyshche, Kamyany Brid and neighboring settlements, joined to create the city of Luhansk. Its name changed several times: 1935-58 it was Voroshylovhrad; in 1958-70 — Luhansk; in 1970-90 — Voroshylovhrad; in 1990 it reverted to its former historical name.

MONUMENTS

V. Dal, 1981. Sculptors: V. Orlov and N. Ovcharenko. Architect: H. Holovchenko. (Dal St.).

MUSEUMS

Regional Museum: Shevchenko St., 2; tel. 55-12-52. • **V. Dal Building-Museum:** Dal St., 12; tel. 52-41-55. • **Regional Art Museum:** Poshtova St., 3; tel. 55-39-77. • **Museum of History and Culture of Luhansk City:** Marx St., 30; tel. 52-22-14.

THEATERS, PHILHARMONIC

Ukrainian Music and Drama Theater: Oboronna St., 11; tel. 54-60-31. • **Russian Music and Drama Theater:** Kotsyubynsky St., 3; tel. 53-40-31. • **Regional Philharmonic:** Lenin St.; tel. 52-31-21.

HIGHER EDUCATIONAL INSTITUTIONS

Mechanical-Construction Institute: Molodizhny Kvartal, 20-a; tel. 46-23-90. • **Agricultural Institute:** Pyatdesyat Rokiv Oborony Luhanska, 1. • **Shevchenko Pedagogical Institute:** Oboronna St., 2.

LIBRARIES, ARCHIVES

Regional Universal Library: Radyanska St., 78. • **Main Municipal Library:** kvartal Volkova, 1. • **Regional Children's Library:** Radyanska St., 78. • **Medical Library:** Odynatsyata Liniya, 3. • **Trade Union Library:** ploshcha Rozy Luxemburg, 2. • **Culture Building of the Railway Workers:** Pushkin St., 2. • **State Regional Archive:** Radyanska St., 85; tel. 52-05-96. • **Regional Archive:** ploshcha Heroyiv Velykoyi Vitchyznyanoyi Viyny, 3; tel. 52-25-71.

PARKS

Park Pershoho Travnya: Liebknecht St., 64. • Arboretum: Linyov St., 85.

SPORTS COMPLEXES

Avanhard Stadium: Oboronna St., 4-a; tel. 54-73-72. • Kolos Equestrian Base: Hostra Mohyla; tel. 54-86-47. • Swimming Pools: Yunist: Oboronna St., 4-a; tel. 54-46-22. • Delfin: kvartal Volkova. • Dynamo: Radyanska St., 50. • Spartak: Pyatdesyatrichchya SRSR, 33-a. • Sports Stadium: Liebknecht St., 2. • Sports complex: Lermontov St., 2-h.

HOTELS

Arena: Khersonska St., 5; tel. 53-35-09. • Luhansk: Radyanska St., 78-a; tel. 52-61-36. • Oktyabr (Zhovten): Pushkin St., 3; tel. 52-30-41. • Sovyetskaya (Radyansky): Radyanska St., 54; tel. 53-63-85. • Turyst: Oboronna St., 112; tel. 54-45-89. • Zaliznychoho Vokzalu (at the railway station): Pyatyorkin St., 6; tel. 52-15-03.

RESTAURANTS, CAFES

Druzhba: Persha Donetska St., 16; tel. 53-32-29. • Luhan: Oboronna St., 4; tel. 54-52-66. • Pernyk: Oboronna St., 4; tel. 53-31-25. • Ukrayina: Pushkin St., 3; tel. 52-04-72. • Yuvileyny: Radyanska St., 56; tel. 53-44-45. • Turyst: Oboronna St., 112; tel. 54-45-59. • Cardiff: Perhsa Donetska St., 15; tel. 53-11-39. • Airport restaurant: tel. 53-60-43. • Railway station restaurant: Pyatorkin St., 6; tel. 53-13-09. • Arktyka: Radyanska St., 59-a; tel. 53-83-03. • Brygantyna: Radyanska St., 5; tel. 95-32-40. • Disco: kvartal Pyatdesyatrichchya Zhovtnya, 4-a; tel. 46-23-36. • Yevropa: Marx St., 22; tel. 52-30-73. • Snizhynka: ploshcha Heroyiv Velykoyi Vitchyznyanoyi Viyny, 4; tel. 53-23-96. • Sportyvne: Radyanska St., 52; tel. 53-3590. • Teatralne: Kotsyubynsky St., 3; tel. 53-60-27. • Feniks: Radyanska St., 65; tel. 53-00-83.

STORES

Tsentralny: Radyanska St., 54. • Univermah Rosiya (Department store): Oboronna St., 2. • Dytyachy svit (Children's store): Cheluskintsiv St., 1-a. • Kokhana: ploshcha Heroyiv Velykoyi Vitchyznyanoyi Viyny, 7. • Men's Wear: ploshcha Heroyiv Velykoyi Vitchyznyanoyi Viyny, 7. • "Lutri" Knitwear: Kotsyubynsky St., 23. • Suveniry: Radyanska St., 67. • Items for Youth: Vatutin St., 36. • Bohatyr: Radyanska St., 66. • Luhan: Marx St., 1. • Izumrud: (Smarahd, with currency exchange bureau) Titov St., 17. • Daleva Lavka (second-hand bookstore): Shevchenko St., 4. • Budynok Odyahu (Clothing): Radyanska St., 77. • Sporttovary: Oboronna St., 109. • Music Store: Marx St., 5. • Sheet Music: ploshcha Heroyiv Velykoyi Vitchyznyanoyi Viyny, 7. • **Za Rulem (Behind the wheel):** Oboronna St., 109. • **Raketa:** Radyanska St., 61.

BANKS

National Bank of Ukraine (Regional Branch): Radyanska St., 83; t. 53-30-47. • **Luhansk Commercial Bank for Coal Industry Development "Vuhleprohresbank:"** Radyanska St., 83; tel. 57-36-62; 53-24-40; 53-21-30.

TOURISM

Regional Tourist Agency: Oboronna St., 112; tel. 54-33-51; 54-45-56.
City of Luhansk Travel and Excursion Agency: Marx St., 26; tel. 52-73-95; 52-73-96; 52-87-14.
Suputnyk International Youth Tourism Agency: Persha Donetska St., 16; tel. 53-12-62; 53-00-76.
Intouryst-Luhansk: Dyomkin St., 18; tel. 53-05-96; 53-44-53.

POST OFFICE, TELEPHONE

Main Post Office: Poshtova St., 22; tel. 52-50-12; 52-34-70.
Central Telegraph: ploshcha Heroyiv Velykoyi Vitchyznyanoyi Viyny, 10; tel. 53-31-90.
Central calling point, fax: ploshcha Heroyiv Velykoyi Vitchyznyanoyi Viyny, 10; tel. 53-31-90.
Telegraph bureaus and telephone booths are located in hotels.

MEDICAL SERVICES

Emergency: tel. 03.
Pharmacies: Pushkin St., 6; tel. 52-23-35. • Ploshcha Heroyiv Velykoyi Vitchyznyanoyi Viyny, 6; tel. 53-20-96. • Shevchenko St., 4; tel. 55-15-02.

TRANSPORTATION

Railway station: Pyatyorkin St., 6; tel. 52-10-87; 009; 52-22-43.
Bus station: Oboronna St., 28; tel. 54-22-30; 009; 54-60-62.
Airport (out of town, bus No. 236 from the Tekhniky Building); tel. 57-52-25; 53-01-03.
Ukraine Airlines: 16 Liniya, 4; tel. 55-16-42; 53-72-05.
Intourist International Booking Office: Dyomkin St., 18; tel. 53-44-53. **Taxi reservations:** tel. 058.
Aist Information Agency: (information on stores, theaters, cinemas, wake-up service): tel. 009.

TOURING HISTORIC CITIES AND VILLAGES

MYKHAYLIVKA

Village, Pereval district, 12 km from the Komunarsk railway station. In 1878 teacher Chrystyna D. Alchevska built a school here at her own expense. In the years 1889-94 the noted Ukrainian writer and lexicologist Borys Hrinchenko taught there.

CHURCH OF ARKHANHEL MYKHAYIL (ST. MICHAEL THE ARCHAN-GEL), 1787. Renovated in 1824 and 1932. Paintings from the 19th-20th cent. have been preserved.

OSYNOVE

Village, Novopskovsk district.

USPENSKA (DORMITION) CHURCH, 1802. The architecture reflects the transitional period from the Baroque to the Classical style. Paintings from the 19th cent. have been preserved.

STARY AYDAR

Village, Stanychno-Luhansky district, 7 km from the Krasnozerivka railway station.

MYKHAYLIVSKA (ST. MICHAEL'S) CHURCH, 1787. Built in the Classical style with Baroque features.

PRESERVES

STANYCHNO-LUHANSKY RESERVE. 494 ha. On the left bank of the Siversky Donets River, 25 km from Luhansk.

STRILTSIVSKY STEPPE, 1931. 25 ha, 12 km from the village of Milove and the Chertkove railway station. The central part of the steppe is flatland, with valleys and ravines on the outskirts. Approximately 235 varieties of steppe plants and 175 varieties of meadow and forest plants grow here.

Lviv Region

It is situated in the western part of Ukraine. Several physiographic regions meet here, resulting in a variety of landforms and relief. The highest point in the region is Mount Pikuy (1405 m). The climate is moderate-continental. The principle rivers are the Dnister (250 km within the regional boundaries), the Western Buh, Stryi, and Vereshytsya. Area: 21,800 sq. km. Population: 2,777,000. Ukrainians: 90%.

Created in 1939.

History

The Lviv region was first settled in the Paleolithic Age. A hunters' settlement which existed 20,000 years ago was discovered near the village of Hlynyany (Zolochiv district); traces of a large settlement dating to 3th-4th cent. B.C. have been uncovered near the village of Mali Hrybovychi (Zhovkva district). Near the village of Vysotske (Brody district) 200 burial sites were uncovered, together with numerous other remains, which now comprise Vysotsky culture of 6th-9th cent. B.C. The ancient Ukrainian settlement of Plisnesk dating to the 9th-12th cent. was uncovered near the village of Pidhirtsi (Brody district). This was an important crafts and trading center in Rus'-Ukraine, mentioned twice in "The Tale of Ihor's Host". At the beginning of 1241 the Mongol warriors of Khan Baty razed Plisnesk to the ground.

In the 9th cent. the territory of the Lviv region was part of Kyivan Rus'-Ukraine and in the 12th cent. it formed part of the Galician Principality. In 1199 the Volynian Prince Roman Mstyslavovych (1160-1205) united the lands of Galicia and Volyn; his son Danylo, an able ruler who founded many cities, later inherited the throne of the Galician-Volynian State.

Lviv Region. Castle at Olesko, 13th-18th cent.

After the decline of the Galician-Volynian Principality in 1349, the region was occupied by Poland and remained under its rule for several centuries. The population suffered under Polish and German colonial rule, which became more oppressive following the Treaty of Lublin in 1569. After the first Partition of Poland, Galicia came under Austrian rule.

The revolutionary events of 1848 gave rise to a number of political reforms: serfdom was abolished, a Parliament was created, and Galicia became a province of the Austro-Hungarian Empire. During World War I many battles took place on the territory of the Lviv region. Among the participants of these military campaigns was the legion of Ukrainian Sichovi Striltsi (Riflemen of the Sich), formed from the ranks of patriotic Galician youth. After the fall of the Austro-Hungarian Empire the Western Ukrainian National Republic (ZUNR) was proclaimed in Eastern Galicia on 1 November 1918. Shortly after, the region was occupied by Poland and after 17 September 1939 — by the Soviet Union.

After World War II the population of the Lviv region was subjected to brutal repressions by the Soviet authorities. Members of the intellectual elite became a bulwark of the dissident movement, whose members helped to further the Ukrainian national cause, particularly in the late 1980s, leading to the rebirth of Ukrainian statehood.

Approximately 2,000 historical, architectural, and cultural monuments have been preserved on the territory of the Lviv region. Regional museums display thousands of examples of the material culture of the Ukrainian people, works of art, and ancient manuscripts.

PROMINENT INDIVIDUALS

BORN IN THE REGION:

P. Andrusiv (1906-81), artist; village of Kamyanobrid; died in the US. • **A. Chaykovsky** (1857-1935), writer; Sambir. • **T. Chuprynka-Shukhevych** (1907-50), political activist, commander of the Ukrainian Insurgent Army (UPA), head of the Ukrainian Supreme Liberation Council (UHVR); Krakovets in the Yavoriv district. • **I. Franko** (1856-1916) writer, scholar, civic activist; village of Nahuyevychi in the Drohobych district. • **Ya. Holovatsky** (1814-88), poet, ethnographer, historian, pedagogue; village of Chepeli in the Brody district. • **D. Hrytsay** (1907-43), political activist, commander of the Ukrainian Insurgent Army (UPA); village of Dorozhiv in the Drohobych district. • **I. Kalynets** (1939), poet, former political prisoner; Khodoriv. • **I. Kalynets-Stasiv** (1940), poetess, political activist, former political prisoner; Lviv. • **F. Kolessa** (1871-1947), composer, musicologist; village of Tatarske, now Pishchany. • **P. Konashevych-Sahaydachny** (?-1622), Hetman, educational activist; village of Kulchytsi in the Sambir district. • **Ye. Konovalets** (1891-1938), political activist, head of the Organization of Ukrainian Nationalists; village of Zashkiv in the Zhovkva district; assassinated in Rotterdam. • **U. Kravchenko-Schneider** (1860-1947), writer, educational activist; Mykolayiv. • **I. Krypyakevych** (1886-1967), historian, academician; Lviv. • **Yu. Kulchytsky** (1863), hero of Vienna; village of Kulchytsi in the Sambir district. • **L. Kurbas** (1887-1937), actor, director of the Berezil Theater; Sambir; executed. • **A. Melnyk** (1890-1964), leader of OUN, Yakubova Volya. • **O. Myshuha** (1853-1940), singer; village of Novy Vytkiv in the Radekhiv district. • **O. Nyzhankivsky** (1862-1919), composer; Stryi. • **Ya. Pasternak** (1892-1962), archaeologist; village of Khyriv in the Stary Sambir district. • **Ye. Petrushevych** (1863-1940), political activist, president of the Western Ukrainian National Republic; Bus'k. • **O. Pritsak** (1919) historian, academician; village of Luka in the Lviv district. L. von Sacher-Masoch (1836-95), writer, founder of Masochism. **M. Shashkevych** (1811-43), writer, educational and religious activist; village of Pidlyssya in the Zolochiv district. • **V. Shchurat** (1871-1948), literary scholar, poet, academician; village of Vysloboky in the Kamyanko-Buh district. • **A. Sheptytsky** (1865-1944), Metropolitan of the Ukrainian Greek-Catholic Church, civic activist; village of Prylbychi in the Yavoriv district. • **M. Skoryk** (1938) composer; Sambir. • **L. & S. Syzaniy** (16th-17th cent.), writers, educational activists; village of Potelychi in the Zhovkva district. • **M. Tarnavsky** (1869-1938), General, commander-in-chief of the Ukrainian Galician Army; village of Baryliv in the Radekhiv district. • **O. Tarnavsky** (1917-92), poet; Lviv; died in the US. • **I. Trush** (1869-1941), artist; village of Vysotske in the Brody district. • **M. Voznyak** (1881-1954), literary scholar, academician; village of Vilky-Mazovietski (now Volytsya) in the Zhovkva district. • **I. Vyshensky** (mid-16th cent. ca. 1621-33), writer, polemicist-satirist; village of Sudova Vyshnya in the Zhovkva district. • **M. Yavorsky** (1885-1937), academician, historian, political activist; village of Korchmyn in the Sokal district. • **S. Yavorsky** (1658-1722), church leader, Metropolitan, philosopher; Yavoriv.

BURIED IN THE REGION:

O. Myshuha (1853-1922), singer; village of Novy Vytviv. • **O. Nyzhankivsky** (1863-1913), composer; Stryi.

(See, also Lychakiv and Yanivsky cemeteries.)

Museum of Folk Architecture and Folkways.

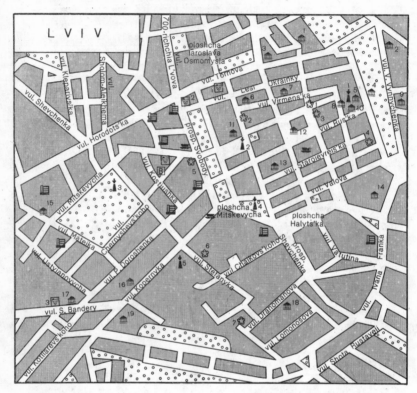

	Excursion office
	Hotels
	Restaurants

Monuments:
1 Ivan Fedorov, first printer. 2 Ivan Pidkova, one of the leaders of Ukrainian and Moldavian people's struggle against Turkish yoke. 3 Ivan Franko. 4 Adam Mickiewicz. 5 Vasyl Stefanyk

Architectural monuments:
1 Benedictine Church with cells, 1595. 2 Presentation Church (barefooted Carmelites), 17th c. 3 St. Mary-Snizhna's Roman Catholic Church, 13th—19th cc. 4 Powder Tower, 1554—1556. 5 Royal Arsenal, 17th c. 6 Transfiguration Church, 18th—19th cc. 7 Ensemble of Armenian community buildings, 14th—20th cc. 8 Dominican Monastery Ensemble, 18th—19th cc. 9 Carmelite Church, 17th—20th cc. 10 Ensemble of Lviv

Brotherhood buildings, 1572—1578. 11 Jesuit Church, 1610—1636. 12 Ensemble of dwelling and public buildings in Rynok Square, 14th—19th cc. 13 Latin Cathedral, 1360—1481. 14 Ensemble of Bernardine Monastery buildings, 17th—18th cc. 15 Ensemble of St. Yura's Cathedral buildings, 1744—1770. 16 Palace with gates, 19th c. 17 St. Magdalene's Roman Catholic Church, 1615—1630. 18 St. Nicholas Roman Catholic Church, 1745. 19 St. Lazarus Roman Catholic Church, 1670

Museums:
1 Drugstore-Museum. 2 Natural Sciences. 3 History. 4 Old Munitions. 5 Ethnography and Handicrafts. 6 Picture Gallery. 7 Ukrainian Fine Arts.

Theaters:
1 Zankovetska Ukrainian Drama. 2 Ivan Franko Opera and Ballet. 3 Organ music Concert Hall.

LVIV

City and regional center on the Poltva and Zubrya Rivers, a railway junction and airport. Population: over 800,000. Telephone code: 0322.

The city was founded in the mid-13th cent. by the Galician-Volynian King Danylo Halytsky and named in honor of his son Lev. The first documented reference to the city appeared in the chronicle for the year 1256. In the 1270s Prince Lev designated Lviv as the capital of his state. In April 1340 the Polish King Casimir attacked Lviv, captured the castle, looted the state treasury of valuables, and ordered the city to be burned to the ground. The residents of Lviv, led by the nobleman Dmytro Detko, who was in power from 1340 to 1349, successfully repulsed the invaders. From 1387 Lviv was ruled by Polish kings and was the center of the voivodeship.

In the spring of 1648 the Kozak armies of Hetman B. Khmelnytsky laid siege to Lviv. On October 14-15 of that year M. Kryvonis' forces, aided by the city residents, stormed the fortress of Vysoky Zamok.

After the first Partition of Poland in 1772 Lviv became part of Austria and the administrative center of a newly-created province.

In 1784 a university was founded in Lviv. After 1848, lectures were conducted partially in the Ukrainian language, in addition to Latin, German, and Polish.

During the 1830s a civic-literary group known as the "Rus'ka Triytsya" (Ruthenian Trinity) was formed in Lviv, whose members published the Ukrainian-language anthology "*Rusalka Dnistrovaya*" (1837). The first Ukrainian newspaper "*Zorya Halytska*", the organ of the Supreme Ruthenian Rada, was founded in Lviv.

In 1868 the "Prosvita" Society, a civic, cultural, and educational organization was created and branches of this society quickly spread to other parts of Ukraine. In 1873, on the initiative of O. Konysky and M. Drahomanov, a literary society was established; in 1892 it was re-organized as the Shevchenko Scientific Society. Although its activities ceased with the Bolshevik occupation of Western Ukraine, the Society was renewed in 1989.

The first train arrived at the newly-built Lviv Railway Station on 4 November

View of historic Lviv.

1861. In October of 1884 a municipal telephone communications system was installed and the first electric streetcars began running in 1894.

The Ukrainian Sich Union (USS), headed by K. Trylyovsky, was created in 1912 and in March 1914 the Society of Sichovi Striltsi (Riflemen of the Sich), headed by V. Starosolsky, was established in Lviv.

The Ukrainian National Rada (UNR) was founded on 18 October 1918 and the following month, on 1 November the Military Committee occupied key government posts in the city. The Ukrainian National Rada then proclaimed the Western Ukrainian National Republic (ZUNR).

Polish troops occupied Lviv in 1918. In 1921 the underground University of Lviv was founded. Members of the Regional Executive of the Organization of Ukrainian Nationalists (OUN) were tried in 1936. On 22 September 1939 Lviv was occupied by the Red Army and Ukrainian cultural and political activities ceased. Mass arrests of Ukrainian activists were carried out. In the latter days of June 1941, on the eve of the German occupation of Western Ukraine, Soviet secret police forces of the NKVD executed hundreds of Ukrainian patriots detained in Lviv prisons on Lontsky and Zamarstynivsky Streets, in Brygidky Prison, and other detention centers. On 30 June 1941 the Ukrainian State Administration, headed by Ya. Stetsko, was founded in Lviv.

In the final days of July 1944 the Germans retreated from Lviv, which was then occupied by Soviet forces. In the following years the Soviet regime unleashed a campaign of mass repressions against the nationally-conscious Ukrainian population and liquidated the Ukrainian Greek-Catholic Church. On 11 April 1945 Metropolitan Yosyf Slipyj, together with other hierarchs of this Church, was imprisoned.

During the 1960s Ukrainian opposition to Soviet totalitarianism began growing in strength, coinciding with the emergence on the political scene of a group of intellectuals known as the "Sixtyers." The following two decades saw the rise of a vocal dissident movement.

In 1987 the Lev Society, a cultural and civic organization promoting the rebirth of Ukrainian culture, was established in Lviv. In June and July 1988 mass meetings were held in Lviv in support of democracy and Ukrainian independence.

CHURCHES, HISTORICAL AND ARCHITECTURAL MONUMENTS

SVYATOHO MYKOLAYA (ST. NICHOLAS') CHURCH, 13th cent. The earliest example of monumental architecture in the city. The first references to the church appeared in 1292. In the princely era the church also served as a civic and political center. The St. Nicholas Brotherhood was active in the church in the mid-16th cent. The original appearance of the church was altered as a result of substantial reconstruction undertaken in the 17th-18th cent. Today the church is under jurisdiction of the Ukrainian Autocephalous Orthodox Church. (Khmelnytsky Blvd., 28).

SVYATOHO ONUFRIYA (ST. ONUPHRIUS') CHURCH, 16th-19th cent. The church dates to the princely era. It was restored in 1463; around 1530 Prince K.

Ostrozky provided funds to build a brick church, which became the nucleus of the present structure. Its present appearance is the result of reconstruction undertaken in 1680, 1776, and the 19th cent. In 1991 the church was transferred to the Basilian Order. (Khmelnytsky Blvd., 36).

ST. PARASKEVA-PYATNYTSYA CHURCH. One of the most interesting architectural monuments of ancient Lviv, first mentioned in documents dating to the 15th cent. The church was built with funds provided by the Moldavian Prince Vasyl Lupul. An ancient Ukrainian iconostasis, comprising 70 icons painted by the 17th cent. Lviv artists, is preserved in the

St. Bernardine Convent Complex, 17th cent.

church. Today it is under the jurisdiction of the Ukrainian Autocephalous Orthodox Church. (Khmelnytsky Blvd., 63).

SVYATOHO MARTYNA (ST. MARTIN'S) ROMAN CATHOLIC CHURCH. Founded in 1630 for use by the Carmelite Order. Its present Baroque appearance dates to 1736. A hospital for war veterans once existed in the monastery. Today it belongs to the Evangelical Christian-Baptists. (Dekabrystiv St., 8).

SVYATOHO IVANA KHRESTYTELYA (ST. JOHN THE BAPTIST'S) ROMAN CATHOLIC CHURCH, 13th cent. The favorite place of worship of Prince Lev's wife, the Hungarian Princess Konstantsiya. Construction of the church began in the late 14th cent. when it was under the jurisdiction of Armenian Uniates of the Basilian Order. In 1887 the architect Yu. Zakharevych completed substantial restorations in the neo-Romantic style. (Ploshcha Stary Rynok).

MATERI BOZHOYI NEUSTANNOYI POMOCHI (formerly MARIYI SNIZHNOYI ROMAN CATHOLIC CHURCH), 14th-19th cent. Founded by German colonists who settled in Lviv during the rule of Prince Lev. Rebuilding due to fires in the 17th cent. and reconstruction in 1888-92 completely altered the church's original appearance. Eighteenth cent. Baroque carvings have been preserved. Presently Ukrainian Greek-Catholic church (Ploshcha Volodymyra Velykoho).

SISTERS STUDITE CONVENT (formerly BENEDICTINE CONVENT), 1597-1616. The complex includes a church (1597-1616), convent building (1611-67), Baroque-style entry gate (18th cent.). Presently Ukrainian Greek-Catholic Convent. (Ploshcha Vicheva, 2).

PREOBRAZHENSKA (TRANSFIGURATION) CHURCH. A former Trinitarian Roman Catholic church, it was rebuilt in 1898 by the architect S. Havryshkevych. It was the first church in Lviv to revert to the Ukrainian Greek-Catholic Church in 1990. (Krakivska St., 2).

VIRMENSKY (ARMENIAN) CATHEDRAL, 1363-70. Over the centuries the

Boyim Chapel, 1609-15.

cathedral was restored and enlarged several times. The oldest section of the church is the eastern wing (14th cent.) The first addition was the arcade (1437) on the south side of the church. Reconstruction in 1723 gave the church a Baroque appearance. Final restorations were undertaken in 1908. Of particular value are the 15th cent. sculptural groupings depicting St. Thomas and St. Sophia with her daughters.

ROMAN CATHOLIC CATHEDRAL, 1360-1479. Erected by the master builder Nychko. After restorations in 1760-78 Gothic elements were replaced by Baroque architectural features. Sculptures by M. Poleyovsky, F. Olendzky, I. Obrotsky and paintings by the artist S. Stroyinsky embellish the cathedral. Until the late 18th cent. there was a cemetery next to the church, containing numerous chapels, most of which were dismantled. Only the most valuable ones were preserved. (Ploshcha Katedralna).

BOYIM CHAPEL, 1609-15. Built at the request of H. Boyim. Sculptors: J. Pfister and H. Scholz. The interior is noted for the richness of its relief and sculptural decorations. Of particular note is the "Pieta" sculptural grouping by J. Pfister, a famous work of 17th cent. art in Lviv. (Ploshcha Katedralna).

KAMPIANY CHAPEL, 1619. Built into the north side of the Roman Catholic church by P. Rymlyanyn and V. Kapinos. The exterior is noted for its original architectural-structural decor. In the center are reliefs depicting episodes from the New Testament, sculpted by J. Pfister and H. Horst. (Ploshcha Katedralna).

PLOSHCHA RYNOK (MARKET SQUARE). This architectural ensemble occupies a special place in the civil architecture of Lviv. In the center of the square (142 x 129 m) is the city hall. References to the square first appeared in the municipal acts of 1381, when the original wood structure was destroyed by fire. A new city hall was constructed in the 15th cent. In 1826 this structure collapsed; the present structure was built in 1827-35 by the architects A. Vondrashko, Y. Markl, F. Treter, and Yu. Hlohovsky. Its present appearance is the result of reconstruction un-

Kornyakt's Tower. In the center Dominicans Cathedral, 16th cent.

dertaken following a fire in 1848. Many historical events have taken place on the Market Square. In Medieval times an execution pillar stood opposite the city hall. Here in 1564 the Moldovian Prince Tomsha was executed, followed by Ivan Pidkova in 1578. On 1 November 1918 the Ukrainian blue-and-yellow flag was raised at City Hall. The state flag of Ukraine was raised permanently on 3 April 1990. A total of 44 buildings, featuring a variety of architectural styles (Renaissance, Baroque, Empire) surround the square on all four sides. At one time or another each structure was rebuilt, restored, and enlarged. Elements of 15th-16th cent. Gothic architecture have been preserved on the facades of basements and first floors.

Uspenska (Dormition) Church, 16th-17th cent.

CHORNA KAMYANYTSYA (BLACK BUILDING), 1588-89. This structure is the finest example of residential architecture of the Renaissance period and was probably built by the architects P. Barbon and P. Rymlyanyn. In 1596 it became the property of Ya. Lorentsovych who opened one of the first pharmacies in Lviv. A third story was added, and a fourth in 1884 (Ploshcha Rynok, 4).

KORNYAKT'S PALACE, 1580. The most imposing building in Lviv, built for a wealthy Greek merchant by the architects P. Barbon and P. Rymlyanyn. It was restored after 1640 when it became the property of King Jan Sobieski of Poland. In 1678 the facade was embellished with figures of knights, and the portal with masks and garlands. Substantial rebuilding and restorations undertaken during the 17th-19th cent. obliterated the original stylistic features. In the courtyard of the building stood a three-tiered Renaissance arcade-loggia ("Italian doors"), which was restored in the 1930s. (Ploshcha Rynok, 6).

"PROSVITA" BUILDING, 1763. Architect: Jan de Witte. Built on the site of four 16th-17th cent. buildings. One of the finest examples of Baroque residential architecture. In the mid-19th cent. it was purchased by the "Prosvita" Society and a number of cultural and educational institutions were located there: the administration of the "Prosvita" Society, the bookstore of the Shevchenko Scientific Society (NTSh), the editorial board and press of the *"Dilo"* newspaper and the magazine *"Hromadsky Holos"*. On 30 June 1941 the Act restoring the independence of Ukraine was proclaimed in this building. (Ploshcha Rynok, 10).

USPENSKA (DORMITION) CHURCH COMPLEX, 16th-17th cent. A distinguished monument of Renaissance architecture. This church was the focal point of the Orthodox community in Lviv. In the mid-16th cent. the Dormition Brotherhood, which had its own school and imprimery, was founded here. The leading figures in

Tryokh Svyatyteliv (Three Saints') Chapel, 1578-91.

the Brotherhood were the brothers Yuriy and Ivan Rohatynets. Many cultural and educational activists worked in the Brotherhood school, among them Stefan and Lavrentiy Zyzaniy, Kyrylo Stavrovetsky (Trankvilion), Pamva Berynda, Iov Boretsky, and others. The complex includes: the Uspenska (Dormition) Church (1591-1629) built by the architects P. Rymlyanyn, V. Kapynis, and A. Prykhylny; the interior of the church features 17th-18th cent. wall paintings, and an iconostasis built in 1773 by the sculptors M. Filevych and F. Olendzky. The stained-glass windows were created by the artist P. Kholodny in the 1920s-30s; Tryokh Svyatyteliv (Three Saints') Chapel (1578-91), was constructed by the Lviv master builder A. Pidlisny and integrated in the mid-19th cent. with the Dormition Church; in 1671 the chapel was rebuilt by O. Balaban; in 1697 an iconostasis was built by the artist O. Lyanytsky; a 65 meter-high bell tower (1572-78) built by the architect P. Barbon with funds provided by the Greek merchant K. Kornyakt. Today the complex is under the jurisdiction of the Ukrainian Autocephalous Orthodox Church. (Pidvalna St., 9).

BERNARDYNSKY KOSTEL (ST. BERNARD'S ROMAN CATHOLIC CHURCH), 1600-30. Architects: B. Avelides, P. Rymlyanyn, and A. Prykhylny. This church, in the shape of a basilica, is surrounded by the monastic walls and an immense defensive wall extending from Mytna St. to Vynnychenko St. The interior of the church contains numerous wood altars carved by the 18th cent. Lviv master craftsmen. A decorative column standing opposite the facade was erected in 1736 in honor of St. Jan of Duklya, the patron saint of the Bernadines. Today the church is under the jurisdiction of the Ukrainian Greek-Catholic Church. (Ploshcha Soborna, 4).

MUNICIPAL ARSENAL, 1554-56. A fortifications structure built by the architect I. Lys and reconstructed in 1574-1575 by the architect Mochyhemba. The arsenal was destroyed during an attack by Swedish forces in 1704, but was rebuilt within two years. The building was renovated in 1979-81. In 1981 it was designated the Arsenal Weapons' Museum. (Pidvalna St., 5).

GUNPOWDER TOWER, 1554-56. Was part of the municipal fortifications system

Fortifications Complex, 16th cent.

guarding the southern approach to the city. Restored in 1954. In 1959 it was designated the Architects' Building. (Pidvalna St., 47).

ROYAL ARSENAL, 1639-43. Built in the Baroque style by the architect P. Grodzicki with funds provided by the Polish King Wladislaw IV. Since 1939 it has housed the Lviv Regional State Archive. (Pidvalna St., 13).

DOMINICAN ROMAN CATHOLIC CHURCH, 1745-64. One of the most magnificent Baroque structures in Lviv; architect: J. de Witte. The facade was completed by K. Fessinger in 1792-98 following a fire. Sculptor: S. Fessinger. The interior contains many priceless works of art: 16th cent. alabaster tombstones, a marble monument to A. Hrother. (Stavropihiyivska St., 1).

KOSTEL YEZUYITIV (JESUIT ROMAN CATHOLIC CHURCH), 1610-30. Built in the Italian Baroque

Sobor Svyatoho Yura (St. George's Cathedral), 1744-70.

style by G. Briano. One of the largest churches in Lviv: 41 m long, 22.5 m wide, and 26 m high. (Teatralna St., 11).

JESUIT COLLEGE. This three-story structure was originally a Jesuit monastery. Hetman B. Khmelnytsky studied at the Jesuit monastery school in the early 17th cent. In the 18th cent. the school was designated an academy. High school No. 62 is located here. (Teatralna St. and prospekt Svobody).

FORMER BUILDINGS OF THE SHEVCHENKO SCIENTIFIC SOCIETY, 19th cent. Eclectic in style. The first building once housed a large library and museum, in which many distinguished Ukrainian writers and scholars worked: I. Franko, M. Hrushevsky, V. Hnatyuk, M. Pavlyk, F. Kolessa, M. Voznyak, I. Trush; Lesya Ukrayinka, B. Hrinchenko, V. Stefanyk, L. Martovych, M. Cheremshyna and many other writers, scholars, civic and political figures visited the library. A publishing house and the editorial boards of the "Literaturno-Naukovy Visnyk" (*Literary-Scientific Herald*) (1898-1906) and the "Zapysky Naukovoho Tovarystva Shevchenka" (*Notes of the Shevchenko Scientific Society*) were located in the second building. The Social Studies Institute has been located in building No. 24 since 1951. (Vynnychenko St., 24 & 26).

SVYATOHO PETRA I PAVLA (SS. PETER AND PAUL'S) CHURCH, 1786. The vestibule and bell tower were built in 1798 by the architect K. Fessinger, the

View of Lviv.

iconostasis in 1862. The church is under the jurisdiction of the Ukrainian Autocephalous Orthodox Church. (Lychakivska St., 82).

SOBOR SVYATOHO YURA (ST. GEORGE'S CATHEDRAL), 1744-70. A classic example of Ukrainian Baroque architecture and the main church of the Ukrainian Greek-Catholic Church. Construction was begun in 1774; after the death of the original architect B. Meretyn, construction work was supervised by S. Fessinger (until 1764). Decorative work was completed in 1772. The cathedral contains sculptures by Pinzel, S. Fessinger, and M. Filevych and paintings by the artists L. Dolynsky and Yu. Radyvylivsky. Located opposite the cathedral are the Metropolitan's Palace (1772; architect: K. Fessinger), encircled by several 19th cent. buildings and a barrier with two gates (1765). In the courtyard is a bell tower built in 1865. In 1946 the church was transferred to the jurisdiction of the Russian Orthodox Church and in 1990 it reverted to the Ukrainian Catholic faithful. Here, in April 1991, the Ukrainian Catholics welcomed Cardinal Myroslav Lyubachivsky, the head of the Church. In August and September 1992 special commemorative Masses were celebrated in honor of Patriarch Yosyf Slipyj (1892-1984). His remains were re-buried alongside Metropolitans Andrey Sheptytsky (1805-1944) and Sylvestr Sembratovych (1836-98). (Ploshcha Svyatoyurska, 5).

MAIN BUILDING OF THE UNIVERSITY, 1877-81. Architect: J. Hochberger. The Galician Seym (Parliament) was originally located here. The imposing facade features stately porticos with columns and a loggia, and allegorical sculptural groupings depicting "Work" and "Education" at the entrance; the Attic depicts "Galicia, and the Vistula and Dnister Rivers" (sculpted by T. Riher). The building was transferred to the university in 1920. (Universytetska St., 1).

LYCHAKIV CEMETERY. Established in 1786. The area of the cemetery is 40 ha, divided into 86 tracts containing approximately 3,500 monuments and sculptures executed by eminent sculptors and architects. Of particular note are the works of memorial sculpture by such artists as H. Witwer, A. and J. Schimser, H. Baronch, K. Hodebsky, Yu. Markovsky, H. Kuznevych, and others.

Monument at the grave of V. Ivasyuk.

Many distinguished Ukrainians are buried in Lychakiv Cemetery. It is the final resting place of writes: **I. Franko** (1856-1916). S. Goszczynski (1801-76), Polish poet. • **V. Hzhytsky** (1895-1973). • **A. Lototsky** (1881-1949). • **D. Lukiyanovych** (1873-1965). • **M. Pavlyk** (1853-1915). • **M. Shashkevych** (1811-43). • **V. Shashkevych** (1839-85). • **O. Turyansky** (1880-1933). • **H. Tyutyunnyk** (1920-61). H Zapolska (Korvin-Piotrowska, 1857-1921), Polish writer. • ARTISTS: **P. Kovzhun** (1896-1939). • **O. Kulchytska** (1877-1967). • **O. Kurylas** (1870-1951). • **A. Manastyrsky** (1878-1969). • **O. Novakivsky** (1872-

Ploshcha Mitskevycha.
Monument to the author (center).

1935). • **I. Trush** (1869-1941). • COMPOSERS AND MUSICOLOGISTS: **V. Barvinsky** (1888-1963). • **V. Ivasyuk** (1949-79). • **A. Kos-Anatolsky** (1909-83). • **S. Lyudkevych** (1879-1979). • **A. Vakhnyanyn** (1841-1908). • FOLKLORISTS-ETHNOGRAPHERS: **V. Hnatyuk** (1871-1924). • **F. Kolessa** (1871-1947). • **V. Shukhevych** (1849-85). • HISTORIAN: **I. Krypyakevych** (1886-1967). • ARTIST: **S. Krushelnytska** (1895-1976). • DISTINGUISHED SCHOLARS, PUBLICISTS, AND CIVIC ACTIVISTS: **V. Barvinsky** (1851-83). S. Banach (1892-1945), Polish mathematician. • **O. Ohonovsky** (1833-94). • **O. Terletsky** (1850-1902). • THE FOREMOST UKRAINIAN NATURAL SCIENTIST: **I. Verkhratsky** (1846-1919). • ACADEMICIANS AND LITERARY SCHOLARS: **V. Shchurat** (1871-1948). • **M. Voznyak** (1881-1954).

In 1991 Lychakiv Cemetery was designated a Historical-Memorial Museum and Cultural Preserve. (Mechnykov St.; Streetcar No. 7).

YANIVSKY CEMETERY. Established in the 1870s. The area of the cemetery is 25 ha divided into 44 tracts. The Ukrainian artist **M. Sosenko** (1875-1920) and the poet **Bohdan-Ihor Antonych** (1909-37) are buried in tract No. 31; tract No. 38 contains the graves of the **Ukrainian Sichovi Striltsi** (Riflemen of the Sich) who died in November 1918 during the battles of Lviv. **Gen. M. Tarnavsky** (1859-1938), the commander-in-chief of the Ukrainian Galician Army (UHA) is also buried here.

The graves of the Ukrainian Sichovi Striltsi (Riflemen of the Sich) which were desecrated in the Soviet period are being restored today by the Memorial Society. (Shevchenko St.; Streetcar No. 7).

MONUMENTS

T. Shevchenko, 1992. Sculptors: V. and A. Sukhorsky. Architects: Yu. Dyba and Yu. Khoromey. (Prospekt Svobody)

Monument to I. Fedorov, 1977.

I. **Franko**, 1964. Sculptors: V. Borysenko, D. Krvavych, E. Mysko, V. Odrekhivsky, and Ya. Chayka. Architect: A. Shulyar. (I. Franko Park, Universtytetska St.)

M. Shashkevych, 1990. Sculptor: D. Krvavych Architect: M. Fedyk.

A. Mickiewicz, 1905. Sculptors: M. Parashchuk and A. Popel. (Ploshcha Mitskevycha).

I. **Pidkova**, 1981. Sculptor: P. Kulyk.

I. **Fedorov**, 1977. Sculptors: V. Borysenko and V. Podolsky. Architect: O. Konsulov. (Pidvalna St.)

Victims of the Lviv Ghetto, 1992. Sculptors: L. Shterenshteyn and Yu. Shmukler. Architect: V. Plykhivsky.

V. Stefanyk. (Stefanyk St.)

MUSEUMS

Historical Museum: ploshcha Rynok, 4, 6, and 24; tel. 72-06-71. • **Arsenal Museum:** Pidvalna St., 5; tel. 72-19-01. • **Literary Lviv Museum:** Hvardiyska St., 18; tel. 35-10-33. • **National Museum** (two locations): Drahomanov St., 42; tel. 72-80-63; prospekt Svobody, 20; tel. 74-22-80. • **O. Novakivsky Memorial Art Museum:** Mickiewicz St., 11; tel. 72-94-08. • **O. Kulchytska Memorial Art Museum:** Mickiewicz St., 7; tel. 72-57-67. • **I. Trush Memorial Art Museum:** Trush St., 28; tel. 35-34-13. • **L. Levytsky Museum:** Ustyanovych St., 10; tel. 72-48-78. • **Art Gallery:** Stefanyk St., 3; tel. 74-40-47. • **Rusalka Dnistrova Museum:** Kopernyk St., 42; tel. 72-47-96. • **Religious History Museum:** ploshcha Stavropihiyska, 1; tel. 72-00-32. • **Museum of Regional Ethnography and Artistic Crafts:** prospekt Svobody, 15; tel. 72-70-12. • **Open Funds:** ploshcha Rynok, 10; tel. 74-33-88. • **Museum of Folk Architecture and Folkways:** Chernecha Hora, 1; tel. 71-80-17. • **Pharmacy Museum:** Drukarska St., 2; tel. 72-00-41. • **I. Franko Literary-Memorial Museum:** Franko St., 152; tel. 76-44-17. • **S. Krushelnytska Literary-Memorial Museum:** Chernyshevsky St., 23; tel. 72-92-96.

Ploshcha Rynok. Diana Fountain, 1793.

PUBLISHING HOUSES, NEWSPAPERS, MAGAZINES

I. Franko Theater of Ballet and Opera.

Svit: Universytetska St., 1; tel. 72-68-90, 74-31-45. (Trolleybus 9, 10, 12). • **Kamenyar:** Pidvalna St., 3; tel. 72-19-49, 72-27-74, 72-27-74. (Streetcar 1, 2, 9). • **Television and Radio Union, Television Studio:** Vysoky Zamok; tel. 72-46-13, 72-26-10. • **Regional Radio:** Knyaz Roman St., 6; tel. 72-36-61. (Streetcar 3). • **Za Vilnu Ukrayinu:** M. Vorony St., 3; tel. 72-89-04, 72-17-50. (Streetcar 3, 2). • **Vysoky zamok:** Volodymyr Velyky St., 2; tel. 34-32-63, 34-32-88. (Trolleybus 3). • **Moloda Halychyna:** Volodymyr Velyky St., 2; tel. 63-35-70, 35-13-41. • **Ratusha:** Vynnychenko St., 8; tel. 76-76-94; 76-55-60. (Streetcar 1, 2, 7, 9). • **Zemlya i Volya:** Volodymyr Velyky St., 2; tel. 35-32-88. • **Zhyttya i Pratsya:** Volodymyr Velyky St., 50; tel. 64-86-61, 64-86-64. • **Post-Postup:** prospekt Shevchenka, 23; tel. 74-31-56, 74-42-88. (Streetcar 2, 3). • **Militseysky Kuryer:** Sichovykh Striltsiv St., 9; tel. 78-27-98, 78-27-97.(Trolleybus 9, 10). • **Shlyakh Peremohy:** Pryrodna St., 12; tel. 34-20-04. (Streetcar 2). • **Armiya Ukrayiny:** Ternopilska St., 34; tel. 42-04-30, 42-04-33. • **Ploshcha Rynok:** Chernyshevsky St., 5; tel. 72-55-44. • **Dzvin:** Knyaz Roman St., 6; tel. 72-36-20, 72-59-44. (Streetcar 3). • **Svitlo i Tin:** Pushkin St., ›, tel. 34-22-62, 35-42-43. (Streetcar 2, 9). • **Respublikanets:** V. Stefanyk St., 10; tel. 72-00-33, 72-30-94. (Streetcar 2). • **Lvivska Reklama:** V. Velyky St., 2; tel. 63-40-69. (Trolleybus 3).

THEATERS, PHILHARMONIC, CIRCUS

I. Franko Theater of Ballet and Opera: prospekt Svobody; tel. 72-88-60. • **M. Zankovetska Ukrainian Academic Drama Theater:** Lesya Ukrayinka St., 1; tel. 72-07-62. • **First Ukrainian Children's and Youth Theater:** Hnatyuk St., 11; tel. 74-12-66. • **L. Kurbas Youth Theater:** Kurbas St.; tel. 74-20-68. • **Voskresinnya Theater-Studio:** ploshcha Peremohy, 5. • **Theater of Ukrainian Army:** Horodotska St., 38; tel. 33-31-88. • **Puppet Theater:** ploshcha Danyla Halytskoho, 1; tel. 74-42-56. • **Philharmonic:** Chaykovsky St., 7; tel. 72-67-24; 72-10-42. • **Circus:** Horodotska St., 83; tel. 72-29-46.

Lviv University.

HIGHER EDUCATIONAL INSTITUTIONS

University: Universytetska St., 1; tel. 79-41-11. (Trolleybus 9, 10, 12) • **Uni-**

versity "Lviv Politechnika": Bandera St., 12; tel. 72-47-33. (Streetcar 1, 2, 9; Trolleybus 9, 10, 12). • **Medical Institute:** Pekarska St., 69; tel. 72-26-60. (Streetcar 2, 7). • **Forestry Technology University:** Pushkin St., 103; tel. 35-24-41. (Streetcar 2). • **M. Lysenko Higher Music Institute (Conservatory):** Nyzhankivsky St., 5; tel. 74-31-06. (Streetcar 3). • **Academy of Veterinary Medicine:** Pekarska St., 50; tel. 75-67-84. (Streetcar 2, 7). • **Institute of Trade and Economics:** Tuhan-Baranovsky St., 10; tel. 74-03-45. (Streetcar 2, 7). • **Institute of Applied and Decorative Arts:** Kubiyovych St., 38; tel. 42-81-24. (Trolleybus 1).1 • **I. Fedorov Ukrainian Printing Institute:** Pid Holoskom, 19; tel. 59-94-32. (Trolleybus 13). • **Institute of Physical Education and Sport:** Kosciuszko St., 11; tel. 72-70-42. (Streetcar 1, 2, 9).

LIBRARIES, ARCHIVES

V. Stefanyk Research Library of the Academy of Sciences of Ukraine: Stefanyk St., 2; tel. 74-43-72. (Streetcar 1, 2, 9). • **Lviv University Research Library:** Drahomonov St., 5. (Streetcar 1, 2, 9). • **Regional Library:** ploshcha Halytska, 10; tel. 72-36-41. (Streetcar 1, 2, 9; MT 34). • **Regional Scientific-Medical Library:** Rus'ka St., 20; tel. 72-58-00. (Streetcar 1, 2, 9). • **Central Historical Archive:** ploshcha Soborna, 5; tel. 72-30-63. (Streetcar 1, 2, 3, 9). • **Regional Archive:** Pidvalna St., 13. (Streetcar 1, 2, 9).

DENOMINATIONS

Ukrainian Greek-Catholic Church: Svyatoho Yura (St. George's) Cathedral: ploshcha Svyatoho Yura, 5; tel. 72-00-07, 79-86-87, 79-86-93. (Trolleybus 9, 10, 12).

Ukrainian Autocephalous Orthodox Church: Lychakivska St., 91; tel. 75-59-93; Svyatykh Apostoliv Petra i Pavla (SS. Peter and Paul's) Church. (Streetcar 2, 7).

Ukrainian Orthodox Church (Kyiv Patriarchate), Svyatopokrovska (Holy Protection) Church: M. Hrushevsky St., 2; tel. 72-48-25. (Streetcar 3).

Roman Catholic Church: Cathedral at ploshcha Katedralna, 1; tel. 72-56-82. (Streetcar 2, 9).

Evangelical Christians (Prayer Hall): Dekabrystiv St., 8; tel. 52-74-70, 59-23-24.

Evangelical Christian Baptists (Prayer Hall): Bahryany St., 30; tel. 76-34-25, 76-34-66.

Seventh Day Adventists (Prayer Hall): Bahryany St., 30; tel. 72-54-26.

Judaism: Synagogue at Brativ Mikhnovskykh St., 4.

Polytechnical Institute.

PARKS

Stryi. A monument of landscape art. Area: 58 ha Established between 1879 and 1894. Completed by A. Rering. • **I. Franko Park.** Located in the central part of Lviv. Formerly a Jesuit park. During the siege of 1648 by Hetman B. Khmelnytsky's armies, Kozak artillery was stationed here. Designated a municipal park in 1773. Area: 12 ha. • **B. Khmelnytsky Central Park of Culture and Recreation.** Established in the 1950s. Area: 26 ha. • **Vysoky Zamok Park.** An example of a highland park. Landscaping of the park began in 1835. Features 45 species of trees and shrubs planted in 1853. Highest point: 413 m above sea-level. Area: 35 ha. • **Zalizna Voda Park.** Established in 1905. Area: 19.5 ha. Features mineral springs containing iron. • **Botanical Gardens of Lviv University.** Established in 1911. Area: 18.5 ha. Contains more than 1,200 plant species. (Cheremshyna St., 44).

Dnister Hotel.

SPORTS COMPLEXES

Central Stadium "Ukrayina": Lypova Aleya, 5; tel. 42-15-27. (Trolleybus 11). • **Water Sports Complex:** Knyahynya Olha St., 114; tel. 64-84-78, 63-53-65. (Streetcar 3). • **SKA Sports Complex:** Kleparivska St., 39-a; tel. 33-25-46. (Trolleybus 4; Streetcar 7). • **Sports Palace:** Petrushevych St., 1; tel. 76-33-24. (Trolleybus 1, 5, 11). • **"Dynamo":** D. Vitovsky St., 51; tel. 34-00-89. (Streetcar 1, 9). • **"Spartak":** A. Melnyk St., 18; tel. 35-42-79. (Streetcar 2).

HOTELS

Inturyst: ploshcha Mitskevycha, 1; tel. 72-59-52. • **Dnister:** Mateyko St., 6; tel. 72-07-83. • **Grand Hotel:** prospekt Svobody, 13; tel. 76-90-60. • **Lviv:** Semysotrichchya Lvova St., 7; tel. 79-22-70. • **Turyst:** Konovalets St., 103; tel. 35-23-91; 35-10-65. • **Suputnyk:** Knyahynya Olha St., 116; tel. 65-24-21; 65-24-29.

RESTAURANTS, CAFES

Inturyst: ploshcha Mitskevycha, 1. • **Dnister:** Mateyko St., 6. • **Halych:** prospekt Svobody, 19. • **Pid Levom:** ploshcha Rynok, 20. • **Kozatski Stravy:** Hetman Mazepa St., 11. • **Chervona Shapochka:** prospekt Svobody, 6/8. • **Vechirniy Lviv:** ploshcha Torhova, 6. • **Teatralny:** Teatralna St., 23. • **Na Rynku:** ploshcha Rynku, 34.

STORES

Tsentralny Univermah (Department Store): Shpytalna St., 1; branch: ploshcha Rynok, 32. • Lviv Univermah (Department Store): Knyahynya Olha St., 106. • Suveniry: ploshcha Rynok, 28. • Ukrayinski Suveniry: Horodotska St., 35. • Khudozhnyk (Art Salon): ploshcha Mitskevycha, 5.

BOOKSTORES

Molodist: ploshcha Mitskevycha, 5. • Medychna Knyha: ploshcha Rynok, 15. • Tekhnichna Knyha (Technical Books): ploshcha Rynok, 10. • Poeziya: Teatralna St., 1. • Ukrayinska Knyharnya: prospekt Shevchenka, 12. • Druzhba: ploshcha Mitskevycha, 10.

BANKS

Natsionalny bank Ukrayiny (National Bank of Ukraine): Kopernyk St., 4; 74-12-29. • Aktsionerno-komertsiyny "Elektrobank" ("Elektrobank" Joint-Stock/Commercial Bank): Hrabovsky St., 11; 72-39-20; 72-69-35. • Aktsionerne tovarystvo Zakhidno-ukrainsky komertsiyny bank (AT ZUKB) (Joint-Stock Society of the Western Ukrainian Commercial Bank — AT ZUBK): Levytsky St., 67; tel. 75-05-41; 75-09-77. • Komertsiyny bank "Karpaty" ("Karpaty" Commercial Bank): Okunevsky St., 1. • Komertsiyny bank "Hals-Bank" ("Hals-Bank" Commercial Bank): Zelena St., 149-a; tel. 42-51-62; 42-26-68. • Aktsionerno-komertsiyny bank "Halytsky" ("Halytsky" Joint-Stock/Commercial Bank): Hnatyuk St., 11; tel. 72-70-71; 72-99-28. • Kooperatyvny bank "Dnister" ("Dnister" Cooperative Bank): Semysotrichchya Lvova St., 59; tel. 52-75-80; 52-91-61. • Komertsiyny bank "Verkhovyna" ("Verkhovyna" Commercial Bank): Kopernyk St., 4; tel. 72-25-48; 72-25-48. • Aktsionerno-komertsiyny bank "Lviv-Vest" ("Lviv-Vest" Joint-Stock/Commercial Bank): Airport a/s 1234; tel. 69-27-68; 69-22-57. • Komertsiyny bank "Lviv" ("Lviv" Commercial Bank): prospekt Shevchenka, 17; tel. 72-47-17; 72-26-32.

TOURISM

Lvivturyst Company: Stryiska St., 12; tel. 72-50-52. • Branches: "Pearl of the Sub-Carpathians" Tourist Complex: city of Drohobych, Truskavetska St., 83. • "Carpathian Springs" Tourist Base: village of Rozluch in the Turka district. • Arnica Tourist Complex: village of Dubyna in the Skole district.

Truskavets Travel and Excursion Agency: Truskavets, Shevchenko St., 2; tel. 5-13-84.

Morshyn Travel and Excursion Agency: village of Morshyn, Pryvokzalna St., 68; tel. 40-95.

Chervonohrad Travel and Excursion Agency: Chervonohrad, Shevchenko St., 16; tel. 2-14-58.

Mykolayiv Travel and Excursion Agency: Mykolayiv, ploshcha Rynok, 4; tel. 3-18-02.

Skole Travel and Excursion Agency: Skole, Danylo Halytsky St., 3; tel. 2-14-80.

Lviv Travel and Excursion Agency: Kosciuszko St., 18; tel. 74-11-01.

Inturyst Service Agency: ploshcha Mitskevycha, 1; tel. 72-67-51; fax: 74-21-82.

Halintur Regional Company: ploshcha Dombrovskoho, 6; tel. 72-19-41.

Lviv Branch of the Suputnyk International Youth Tourism Company: Ohienko St., 18; tel. 72-95-03; 79-84-79. • Branches: Chervonohrad, Svyaty Volodymyr St., 113; tel. 2-32-80. • Morshyn: Litniy Teatr; tel. 36-09; 42-34. • Zhovkva: Lvivska St., 7; tel. 22-164; 21-474.

These travel agencies offer a variety of excursions to historical and architectural monuments, museums in Lviv and vicinities: castles in Olesko and Mukachiv, Zhovkva, Berestechko, Skeli Dovbusha (Dovbush's Cliffs) — Morshyn-Bolekhiv, mountainclimbing in the Carpathians (Mount Hoverla), visits to the Pochayiv Monastery.

POST OFFICES, TELEPHONE

Main post office: Slowacki St., 1; tel. 065.

Fax: Mateyko St., 6 (Dnister Hotel); tel. 79-70-06; 72-46-07; fax: 74-43-67.

MEDICAL SERVICES

Emergency: tel. 03.

Pharmacies: No. 24: Kopernyk St., 1; tel. 72-66-16. • No. 34: Semysotrichchya Lvova St., 1; tel. 72-18-64.

Pharmaceutical information (concerning availability of medications in Lviv pharmacies): tel. 067.

TRANSPORTATION

Train station: ploshcha Vokzalna; tel. 005, 748-20-68. (Streetcar 1, 6, 9; Bus 2, 18).

Bus station: Stryiska St., 271; tel. 63-24-73 (Trolleybus 5, 3; Bus 18).

Airport: tel. 69-21-12. (Trolleybus No. 9).

Ukrainian Airlines Offices: ploshcha Peremohy, 5; tel. 72-75-58; international office: tel. 72-78-18.

Public transport: There are 8 streetcars and 15 trolleybuses routes in Lviv.

Taxi reservations: tel. 79-90-71.

AUTO SERVICING

Ukrinavtoservis: 1 Travnya St., ATP 14662; tel. 62-62-50.

Autoroute Service Complex: village of Bartativ in the Horodok district, 19 km a/d E-40 Lviv-Mostysk autoroute; tel. 9-24-52.

TOURING HISTORIC CITIES AND VILLAGES

BELZ

City in the Sokal district on the Solokiya River, 12 km from Chervonohrad, 25 km from Sokal.

One of the most ancient cities in Ukraine and the historic capital of an independent principality, which was consolidated with the Galician-Volynian Principality in the 12th cent. In the 13th-14th cent. this city played an important role on the world scene and was the center of the Belz lands in the 15th-16th cent. Some sections of the defensive walls dating to the princely era have remained intact.

PYATNYTSKA CHURCH, 17th cent. A wood structure, restored in 1979.

DOMINICAN MONASTERY, 1653. The monastery complex includes: Mykolayivsky (St. Nicholas') Roman Catholic Church (17th cent.) and cells (1743). Built in the 17th-18th cent. Baroque style.

TOWER, 1606. Only the municipal archive has been preserved. Restored in 1969 and 1979.

MONUMENT TO THE 950TH ANNIVERSARY OF THE CITY, 1980. Sculptor: V. Savchuk. Architect: B. Cherkes.

BILOHORSHCHA

Village administrated by the village of Zymna Voda in the Pustomyt district, 10 km from Lviv.

This village is associated with **Gen. T. Chuprynka** (1907-50), the commander-in-chief of the Ukrainian Insurgent Army (UPA). On 5 March 1950 Gen. Taras Chuprynka (Roman Shukhevych) died in a bunker in the vicinity of this village, following a shoot-out with NKVD troops. The general's bodyguards died with him.

BRODY

City and railway station on the Sukhovylka River, 93 km from Lviv.

First mentioned in documents dating to 1084, this city recently celebrated its 900th anniversary.

THE BATTLE OF THE "HALYCHYNA" UKRAINIAN DIVISION. A battle took place here on 17-22 July 1944 between the Ukrainian division and the Red Army. The Ukrainian division was surrounded by the 13th army corps and more than 3000 Ukrainian troops breached the line near the villages of Knyazhe and Pochapy. Several thousand Ukrainian soldiers in both armies died in this battle.

YURIYIVSKA (ST. GEORGE'S) CHURCH, 17th cent. This stone structure was rebuilt in the 19th cent. and restored in 1867. A striking example of Galician folk architecture.

SYNAGOGUE, 1742. A stone structure built on the site of a wood building. Restored in 1777.

CASEMATES, 1630-35. Built by the architects A. del'Acqua and G. de Beauplan, the casemates comprised the central section of fortifications on the site of the former castle. An example of defensive architecture.

BUS'K

City on the Western Buh River, 53 km from Lviv, 5 km from the Krasne railway station.

First mentioned in the "Tale of Bygone Years" for the year 1097.

ONUFRIYIVSKA (ST. ONUPHRIUS') CHURCH, 1680, 1758; **BELL TOWER,** 18th cent. This wood structure is an example of the distinctive style of Galician folk architecture. Restored in 1970.

CHURCH OF ST. PARASKEVA, 1708. A wood structure. Interior paintings were executed by V. Leontovych (1889) and M. Sirsky (1890) A brilliant example of Galician folk architecture. Restored in 1983.

MONUMENT TO INDEPENDENCE, 1992. The first monument in Ukraine dedicated to the Act of Independence of Ukraine. Erected 1 December 1991. Sculptor: Ya. Motyka.

CHERVONOHRAD (until 1951 — Krystynopil)

City on the Western Buh River located 73 km from Lviv. Founded in 1692.

SVYATODUKHIVSKY (HOLY SPIRIT) ROMAN CATHOLIC CHURCH OF THE ST. BERNARD MONASTERY; CELLS, 18th cent. This Baroque-style church was built in 1642 and restored in 1927.

YURIYIVSKA (ST. GEORGE'S) CHURCH AND CELLS OF THE BASILIAN MONASTERY, 1771-76. Architect: I. Zelner. Has features of the late Baroque and Classical styles. Restorative work was undertaken in 1959 by the architect I. Starosolsky. During the 1970s-80s the church housed a museum; it was returned to the faithful in 1991.

DROHOBYCH

City at the foothills of the Carpathians, 102 km from Lviv.

The founding of the city dates to the late 11th cent., when a fortified settlement known as Bych existed here. This settlement was burned to the ground and in its place arose a "second Bych" — "druhy Bych". During the 14th cent. Drohobych was one of the largest saltworks in the Sub-Carpathian region. During the 17th-18th cent. Ukrainian-language brotherhood schools were founded in Drohobych. An important cultural and educational center in the city was the gymnasium, founded in 1858. In 1896 it was relocated to a three-story building, which is now the main building of the Pedagogical Institute. In 1880 there were 36 petroleum companies in the city. Drohobych was a major theater of war during World War I. In 1918, with the creation of the Western Ukrainian National Republic, a county branch of the national Rada was active here. Drohobych is associated with the renowned Western Ukrainian writer Ivan Franko who set-

Drohobych. Church of Vozdvyzhennya Chesnoho Khresta (Elevation of the Holy Cross), 16th cent.

tled here as an eight-year old boy. After completing his studies at the gymnasium, he left at the age of 19. Franko last visited Drohobych on 1 February 1912, for a public reading of his famous poem "Moses."

A Pedagogical Institute was founded here in 1952.

ST. BARTOLOMEY (ST. BARTHOLOMEW'S) ROMAN CATHOLIC CHURCH, 1392-1541. Built on the site of an ancient Ukrainian palace which belonged to a royal administrator. Restored at the end of the 1980s.

SVYATOHO YURA CHURCH (ST. GEORGE'S), 16th-17th cent.; **BELL TOWER,** 1670. One of the most distinguished examples of Galician folk architecture. In 1657 the church was relocated from the village of Nadiyevo (Ivano-Frankivsk region) and re-assembled in Drohobych. The interior contains an iconostasis from 1659 and 17th cent. wall paintings. Built in the style of the Ukrainian Renaissance. Restored in 1974-75. The church comprises part of the holdings of the Historical-Ethnographic Museum.

CHURCH OF VOZDVYZHENNYA CHESNOHO KHRESTA (ELEVATION OF THE HOLY CROSS), 16th cent. The original appearance of the church, which was rebuilt in 1661, has not been preserved. It is one of the finest structures in Western Ukraine to be built in the Galician folk architectural style. The church contains 17th cent. paintings and unique icons of the 15th-18th cent. Restored in 1970-71 by the architects I. Mohytych and I. Starosolsky.

VOZNESENSKY (ASSUMPTION) ROMAN CATHOLIC CHURCH, 15th cent.; **BELL TOWER,** 1551. Built on the site of a castle. Stained-glass windows designed by Ya. Mateyko, S. Vyspyansky, and Yu. Mehoffer have been preserved. Restorations in 1902 greatly altered the original appearance of the church.

Monument to the Abolition of Serfdom, 1848. Located opposite the church of Preobrazhennya Khrystovoho (Transfiguration of Christ).

Monument to I. Franko, 1967. Sculptors: E. Mysko, V. Odrekhivsky, and Ya. Mateyko. Architects: Ya. Novakivsky and O. Konsulov.

Monument to T. Shevchenko, 1991. Sculptor: V. Odrekhivsky.

Drohobych Ethnographic Museum: Hohol St., 42; tel. 2-20-64.

HORODOK (until 1939 — Horodok Yahaylonsky).

City on the Vereshchytsya River, 30 km from Lviv. Population: over 13,000.

This city was first mentioned in documents dating to 1213 as a settlement of the Galician-Volynian Principality. In 1235 the armies of King Danylo Halytsky were bivouacked here. The Kozak armies of Hetman B. Khmelnytsky, aided by the local peasantry, captured the city in 1648. During World War II several thousand men died at the hands of the German and Soviet armies.

ACTION OF THE UKRAINIAN MILITARY ORGANIZATION IN HORODOK. On 30 November 1932 eleven members of the Ukrainian Military Organization (UVO) launched an attack on the municipal treasury. Two students, Mykhaylo Berezynsky and Volodymyr Staryk, died during the attack. Two other members of the groups, Dmytro Danylyshyn (age 24) and Vasyl Bilas (age 21) were given the death sentence by the Polish court. Before his death one of the defendants said, "My only regret is that I can no longer work on behalf of our beloved Ukraine."

HRUSHIV

Village in the Yavoriv district.

MYKHAYLIVSKA (ST. MICHAEL'S) CHURCH; BELL TOWER, 1715. Both of these wood structures are a superb example of Galician folk architecture. The church gained renown during the 1970s and 1980s after parishioners reported seeing a vision of the Blessed Virgin Mary.

Hrushiv. Mykhaylivska (St. Michael's) Church, 1715.

KREKHIV

Village in the Zhovkva district, 12 km from Zhovkva.

First mentioned in historical sources dating to 1456.

BASILIAN MONASTERY, 17th-18th cent. Located at the foot of Pobiyna Mountain. The following structures have been preserved: Mykolayivska (St. Nicholas') Church (1721-37), built on the site of

*Krehkiv. Church of
St. Paraskeva, 1724.*

the former Troyitska (Holy Trinity) Church (1638); restored in 1779 and 1854; a bell tower (17th-18th cent.), cells (18th cent.), walls with gates and towers (17th-18th cent.). The monastery was restored in 1991.

CHURCH OF ST. PARASKEVA, 1724. This wood structure was erected by the local master builder I. Khomyak and restored by the architect I. Mohytych in 1971-72.

KULCHYTSI

Village located on the right bank of the Dnister River in the Sambir district, 10 km from Sambir. First mentioned in documents dating to 1377.

Three Hetmans of the Zaporozhyan Armies were born here: P. Konashevych-Sahaydachny, M. Zhmaylo, and I. Sulyma.

MONUMENT TO P. KONASHEVYCH-SAHAYDACHNY, 1992. Sculptors: D. Krvavych, M. Posikira, and L. Yaremchuk. Architect: M. Fedyk.

LAVRIV

Village in the Stary Sambir district, 12 km from Stary Sambir.

ONUFRIYIVSKA (ST. ONUPHRIUS') CHURCH, 15th-16th cent.; **CELLS,** early 20th cent. Belonged to a local monastery which burned down in 1549. Was rebuilt in the Ukrainian Baroque style in 1675-1705. Frescos dating to the 15th-16th cent. have been preserved on three walls.

MEZHYHIRYA

Village in the Peremyshlyany district, 6 km from Peremyshlyany, 30 km from the Bibrka railway station.

UNIV MONASTERY-FORTRESS, 15th-19th cent. Founded in 1400 by Prince Fedir Lyubartovych as a defensive structure. Until the early 19th cent. there was a high wall and deep moat surrounding the monastery. Restorations were undertaken in 1710-41. The monastery is a unique example of defensive architecture in Ukraine. The monastery complex includes: Uspenska (Dormition) Church (16th cent.) built in

*Lavriv. Onufriyivska
(St. Onuphrius') Church,
15th-16th cent.*

*Mezhyhirya. Univ
Monastery-Fortress, 15th-19th*

the Gothic-Renaissance transitional style; cells (17th-19th cent.), defensive walls with gates and towers (15th-18th cent.) Metropolitan's residence (19th cent.).

MORSHYN

Village in the Stryi district, 14 km from Stryi, 89 km from Lviv.

RESORT. A balneological-therapeutic health resort was established here in 1878. The local mineral springs and ozocerite are used in therapy together with other waters which have curative properties.

NAHUYEVYCHI

Village located in the Zbir River Valley in the Drohobych district, 12 km from Drohobych.

The birthplace of the distinguished Ukrainian writer I. Franko, who spent the early part of his life here. On the occasion of the 125th anniversary of his birth, "The Poet's Path" — a sculptural and artistic ensemble of works was established in the village. In 1981 the estate of Franko's parents was restored. Today it houses a memorial complex. A museum and branch of the Lviv Literary-Memorial Museum dedicated to Ivan Franko was founded here in 1946. In the center of the village is a monument to the writer, erected in 1986. Sculptors: E. Mysko and Y. Sadovsky.

NEMYRIV

Village on the Smerdyuk River in the Yavoriv district, 18 km from Yavoriv.

RESORT. Established in 1814. Many tourists come here to drink the mineral waters which are rich in hydrogen sulphide.

OLESKO

Village in the Busk district, 23 km from Bus'k and 6 km from the railway station.

CASTLE, 13th-18th cent. Built on a hill by one of the sons of the Galician-Volynian Prince Yuriy Lvovych. The castle was described as a mighty fortress in documents dating to 1327. During the 15th and 18th cent. the Tatars made frequent attacks on the castle. In the 16th cent. it was rebuilt in the Italian Renaissance style. Its 17th cent. appearance was restored in 1961-65 by the architects I. Mohytych, I.

Starosolsky, E. Plamenytska, and A. Shulyar. Today a museum and art gallery are located in the castle. Tel. 2-52-80.

KOSTEL SVYATOHO YOSYFA (ST. JOSEPH'S ROMAN CATHOLIC CHURCH); CELLS OF THE CAPUCHIN MONASTERY, 1739. The church was partially destroyed following an earthquake in 1838. Its original appearance was restored in 1844. Today it is the exhibition hall of "Olesky zamok" Museum and Cultural Preserve.

TROYITSKY (HOLY TRINITY) ROMAN CATHOLIC CHURCH, 16th cent. Was twice destroyed by fire (1803, 1841), restored in 1847. A section of the church is built in the Gothic and Renaissance styles. Restoration work undertaken in 1927 somewhat altered the original appearance of the church.

PIDHIRTSI

Village situated on the slopes of the Voronyaky Mountains in the Brody district, 24 km from Brody, 16 km from the Ozhydiv railway station.

The village was founded at the turn of the 14th-15th cent. and was located 3 km from the city of Plisnesk, which was razed to the ground by the Mongol Hordes of Khan Baty. Only the ruins of the city (160 ha) surrounded by 12-meter high walls have been preserved.

CASTLE, 1635-40. The castle complex includes: a palace surrounded by a system of ditches and walls, Svyatoho Yosyfa i Vozdvyzhennya (St. Joseph and the Elevation of the Holy Cross) Roman Catholic Church (1752-66), a Baroque-style gate (18th cent.), and a park with various buildings (17th-18th cent.). The castle was built by the architects A. del'Aqua and G. de Beauplan. According to legend, Hetman Khmelnytsky pitched his tent beneath a 400-year-old linden tree which is still standing in the park.

MYKHAYLIVSKA (ST. MICHAEL'S) CHURCH, 1720. This wood church was restored in 1920-23.

ONUFRIYIVSKA (ST. ONUPHRIUS') CHURCH OF THE BASILIAN MONASTERY AND CELLS, 18th cent. Renovated in 1953. The monastery complex is a distinguished example of Galician Baroque architecture.

PIDLYSSYA

Village in the Zolochiv district, 15 km from Zolovchiv and 6 km from the Ozhydiv railway station.

Markiyan Shashkevych, the writer who spearheaded the Romantic cultural revival of Western Ukraine and the leading figure in the "Ruthenian Trinity" literary group,

Stare Selo. Castle, 1635-40.

was born here in 1811. In 1986 his parental home was restored and the M. Shash-kevych Museum-Estate was founded; tel. 93-327.

POTELYCH

Village in the Zhovkva district, located 24 km from Zhovkva and 7 km from Rava Rus'ka railway station.

The village was first mentioned in the Hypatian Chronicle for the year 1262.

SVYATODUKHIVSKA (HOLY SPIRIT) CHURCH, 1502; BELL TOWER, 1593. A unique monument of Ukrainian wood architecture. The interior features ancient wall paintings of the 1520s-40s.

BELL TOWER OF THE TROYITSKA (HOLY TRINITY) CHURCH, 1593. This wood structure is one of the finest examples of Uкrainian folk architecture.

SAMBIR

City on the Dnister River, 76 km from Lviv.

In the first half of the 13th cent. fortifications known as Pohonych, destroyed by the Tatars in 1241, once stood on the site of present-day Sambir. In the 14th-15th cent. Sambir was an important guild center and a frequent target of Tatar raids. In 1604 a detachment of soldiers under "False Dmitriy," who was married to Maryna, the daughter of the Sambir headman, Mniszek, departed from Sambir to Moscow. In 1649 the Ukrainian residents of Sambir welcomed the Zaporozhyan Kozaks to their city.

In 1918 soldiers of the Ukrainian Galician Army born in Sambir fought courageously against the Polish armies.

During the first half of the 16th cent. education flourished in Sambir. The icon-painter Fedusko worked here in the 16th cent. Hetman P. Sahaydachny obtained his early education in Sambir. In the 1930s the Boykivshchyna Ethnographic Museum was established in Sambir.

CITY HALL, 16th cent. A new brick building with a 40-meter tower was built in 1638-68 following a fire. In 1844 it was reconstructed.

KOSTEL IOANA KHRESTYTELYA (ST. JOHN THE BAPTIST) ROMAN CATHOLIC CHURCH, 16th-17th cent. Combines features of the Gothic and Renaissance style. A tower was added in 1574. After a fire in 1637 reconstruction of the church was completed in 1642.

JESUIT COLLEGE, 1756-59. Architect: Yu. Karshnytsky. A rectangular, two-story structure.

KOSTEL SVYATOHO STANISLAVA (ST. STANISLAV'S ROMAN CATHOLIC CHURCH), 18th cent. After restorations were completed in 1981 the church was converted to a recital hall for organ music.

CHURCH OF RIZDVA PRESVYATOYI BOHORODYTSI (NATIVITY OF

THE BLESSED VIRGIN MARY), 19th cent. A memorial plaque in recognition of M. Shashkevych's contributions to education hangs on a side wall.

MEMORIAL PLAQUE, 1914. Installed on the 100th anniversary of Taras Shevchenko's birth.

SHKLO

Village in the Yavoriv district, 12 km from Yavoriv.

SANATORIUM. Treatment is based on natural hydrogen sulphide springs and mudbaths.

AUTO SERVICING: Village of Duliby; tel. 5-32-55.

SKOLE

City in the foothills of the Carpathian Mountains on the Opir River, 106 km from Lviv.

Although the city was founded earlier, it was first mentioned in documents dating to 1397. According to a folk legend about the battle between Svyatopolk and Svyatoslav, the sons of Grand Prince Volodymyr Svyatoslavovych, Svyatopolk shouted: "Gore them all!" The entire army of Svyatoslav was destroyed and since then the valley between the mountains has been called "Skole" — "Gored."

CHURCH OF ST. PARASKEVA, 17th cent.; **BELL TOWER,** 1760. These wood structures were erected by master builders of the Boyko school. Restored in 1967, the church housed an ethnographic museum until 1991, when it was transferred to the church.

SOKAL

City on the right bank of the Western Buh, located 90 km from Lviv.
First mentioned in documents dating to 1411.

AUTO SERVICING: Village of Zhvyrka; tel. 2-29-90.

MYKOLAYIVSKA (ST. NICHOLAS') CHURCH, 16th cent. It was rebuilt after the fires of 1613 and 1671, and restored in 1694. Damaged during World War II, it was rebuilt again in 1971-75 and converted to a municipal Historical-Ethnographic Museum. This church is a monument of Ukrainian Renaissance architecture.

KOSTEL BOHORODYTSI (BLESSED VIRGIN MARY) ROMAN CATHOLIC CHURCH OF THE ST. BERNARD MONASTERY, 17th cent. Built in the Baroque style. It was rebuilt and restored several times after being damaged in fires.

SPRYNYA

Village in the Sambir district located 10 km from Sambir.

Near the village is the historic "Lisnychivka", where the Ukrainian Supreme Liberation Council (UHVR) was founded on 11-15 July 1944.

STARE SELO

Village in the Pustomyty district, 37 km from the district center and 18 km from Lviv.

CASTLE, 16th-17th cent. This wood castle built in 1448 stands near the historic village of Zvenyhorod on the Volosky route to Lviv. Rebuilt several times (1584, 1589, 1642), the castle is an example of Ukrainian defensive architecture.

IVANIVSKA (ST. JOHN'S) CHURCH, 17th cent. This wood church once stood near the castle; in 1742 it was relocated to this village.

TRUSKAVETS

City in the foothills of the Carpathian Mountains, 9 km from Drohobych and 112 km from Lviv.

HEALTH RESORT. Known for its medicinal waters. The chief feature of the health resort is therapy based on "Naftusya," a type of mild mineral water containing hydrocarbons, calcium, and magnesium. Ozocerite and other mineral waters are also utilized for therapeutic purposes.

VELYKY LYUBIN

Village and health resort in the Stryi district, 14 km from Stryi and 89 km from Lviv.

The curative properties of the hydrogen sulphide waters in this village were first described in documents dating to 1578. More than 13,000 visitors visit this resort every year.

VOLYA VYSOTSKA

Pidhirtsi. Castle, 16th-17th cent.

Village on the Balanda River in the Zhovkva district, 5 km from Zhovkva and 38 km from Lviv.

First mentioned in documents dating to 1530.

MYKOLAYIVSKA (ST. NICHOLAS') CHURCH, 1598; **BELL TOWER,** 18th cent. These wood structures are an example of Galician folk architecture. In the church is an iconostasis built in 1655. The icons were painted by I. Rutkovych in 1688-89.

ZHOVKVA
(in 1951-1991 — Nesterov)

Zhovkva. Church of Rizdvo Bohorodytsi (Nativity of the Blessed Virgin Mary), 1705.

A historic city situated on the slopes of the Roztochchya Mountains, 32 km from Lviv. Mount Haray is 368 m above sea-level.

In the princely era the village of Vynnyky, first mentioned in the chronicles for the year 1368, was founded on the site of present-day Zhovkva. In 1588 the city became part of the land holdings of S. Zholkevsky, the provincial administrator of Belz. In 1603 this magnate obtained royal permission to rename the city Zhovkva. A Renaissance-style castle was built in the city in 1594-1606. In 1676 it was partially rebuilt by the architects P. Beber and P. Shchaslyvy and served as the residence of King Jan Sobieski.

In the late 17th cent. more than 30 painters and craftsmen lived in Zhovkva. Their work laid the foundations of realism in Western Ukrainian art.

The Zhóvkva imprimery. Founded by the Basilian Fathers, became an important cultural and educational center. Its history is depicted in a memorial room, opened in 1985.

CHURCH OF RIZDVO BOHORODYTSI (NATIVITY OF THE BLESSED VIRGIN MARY), 1705. This wood church contains an iconostasis built in 1708 by the carpenter Kunash and a painter related to I. Rutkovych. It was restored in 1968.

SVYATOYI TRIYTSI (HOLY TRINITY) CHURCH, 1720. This wood church is an example of Galician architecture. It was restored in 1976-81 by the architects B. Kindzelsky and I. Mohytych.

TROYITSKA (HOLY TRINITY) CHURCH OF THE BASILIAN MONASTERY, 1612-1905. Built on the site of a church belonging to the Basilian Order, whose monastery once stood next to the church. The first abbot of this monastery was Metropolitan Dosifey (1691-93) who is buried in the crypt beneath the church. The iconostasis, built by I. Rutkovych, is now displayed in the National Museum in Lviv. In 1901 reconstruction of the church in the Baroque style by the architect E. Kovach completely altered its original appearance. A 17 cent. southern portal sculpted in white stone in the Renaissance style has been preserved. Interior paintings were executed in 1911-13 by the artist Yu. Butsmanyuk.

ROMAN CATHOLIC PARISH CHURCH, 1606-23. Built in the Renaissance style by the architects P. Shchaslyvy and A. Prykhylny. The tombstones of the Zholkevsky family (sculpted in 1623-36 by V. Zychlyvy) and the Sobieski family (sculpted in 1693 by A. Schlutter) are located in the church. Several priceless paintings were relocated from the church to the Olesko Zamok Museum.

SYNAGOGUE, 1692-1700. Located in the Jewish quarter, this monument has features of the Renaissance and Baroque styles. During World War II the synagogue was destroyed by fire and restored in 1955-56.

CASTLE, 1594. Situated in the city center, the castle was part of a system of fortifications. In 1606 a zoological garden was created near the castle. It was restored in 1935 by the architect A. Lobos; restorations were also undertaken in 1972-76. It is a distinguished example of the Ukrainian Renaissance.

ZOLOCHIV

City and railway station located 70 km from Lviv. The first documented references to the city appeared in 1442.

MYKOLAYIVSKA (ST. NICHOLAS') CHURCH, 16th cent.; **BELL TOWER, 1886. Restoration work undertaken in 1765 altered the original appearance of the church.**

VOSKRESENSKA (RESURRECTION) CHURCH, 1624-27; **BELL TOWER,** 19th cent. Destroyed by fire in 1691, the church was rebuilt in 1693. It is an example of Galician Renaissance architecture.

CASTLE, 16th-17th cent. Situated on Kupyna Hill. Its architecture is reminiscent of Italian Renaissance palaces. Restored in 1979.

VOZNESENSKY (ASSUMPTION) ROMAN CATHOLIC CHURCH, 1731-63. Restored in 1878 and 1907.

ZVENYHOROD

Village on the Bilka River in the Pustomyty district, 25 km from Lviv.

This village was the historic capital of the independent Zvenyhorod Principality. The first references to the village appeared in the chronicles for the years 1086 and 1087. It was one of the wealthier cities of Kyivan Rus'-Ukraine and many princes struggled to gain control over it. In the early 12th cent. Zvenyhorod was ruled by Volodar, the Prince of Peremyshl. Control of the city passed to his son Volodymyrko, who established the capital of his principality here in 1124. Later he annexed the Peremyshl Principality, and the lands of Terebovlya and Galicia to Zvenyhorod. In 1144 Volodymyrko relocated the capital to Halych. After his death Yaroslav Osmomysl inherited the Galician Principality in 1152 and later bequeathed Zvenyhorod to his son Volodymyr. In 1206-08 the city

Zhovkva. St. Lawrence Roman Catholic Church, 1604-18.

was ruled by Roman, son of Ihor Svyatoslavo-vych, the Prince of Novhorod-Siversky, who led a campaign against the Polovtsians in 1185. When Mstyslav Udaly, Prince of Novhorod occupied the Galician throne, in 1221 he transferred the administration of the city to the nobleman Sudoslav. In 1227 Udaly routed the armies of the Hungarian king, thereby liberating the Galician-Volynian Principality from foreign occupation. References to Zvenyhorod last appeared in the chronicle for the year 1235, when King Danylo Halytsky's armies laid siege to the city in an unsuccessful attempt to gain control of it. In 1241 the hordes of Batu Khan destroyed Zvenyhorod.

Zhovkva. Synagogue, 1692-1700.

Archaeological excavations of the village commenced in 1953. The Museum of the History of Zvenyhorod was established in 1990.

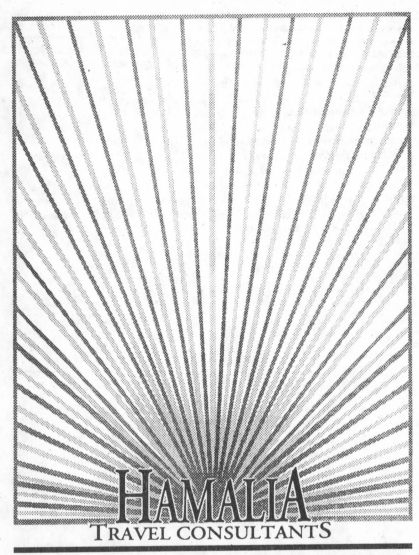

Mykolayiv Region

Located in the southernmost part of Ukraine in the Black Sea Lowland, exiting on the Black Sea. The northern part of the region lies within the Dnipro Upland. The climate is temperate-continental, and partly maritime. The principal rivers are the Southern Buh, Inhul, Inhulets, and Vysunnya. The estuaries of the Southern Buh and Dnipro rivers converge in the south. Established in 1937. Area: 24,600 sq. km. Population: 1,360,000.

History

The territory was first settled in the Paleolithic Age nearly 250,000 years ago. Remains of settlements from the Mezolithic period have been excavated. Buh-Dnister culture, one of the most ancient agrarian cultures in Europe, emerged in the Neolithic Age. The tribes of the Trypilian culture living in the southern part of the region engaged in farming during the Copper Age and the early Bronze Age (4th-3rd cent. B.C.). The northern part of the region was settled by the tribes of cattle herders. In the 2nd and 1st cent. B.C. tribes with highly-developed farming and cattle-herding traditions emerged. At the end of the Bronze Age the region was inhabited by the Cimmerians, first mentioned by the ancient Greek poet Homer. In the 7th cent. B.C. the territory was settled by Scythians and Greek settlers from the Mediterranean region, who established the first state on Ukrainian territory. Borysthen, the oldest Greek city, was established in 647 B.C. on the island of Berezan. In 545 B.C. the city of Olvia was founded at the mouth of the Hipanis (Southern Buh River) and Borysthen (Dnipro River). In 450 B.C. it was visited by Herodotus, who provided the first description of the history, geography, and customs of the people living on Ukrainian territory. In 331 B.C. Zopirion, Alexander the Great's army commander, tried unsuccessfully to capture Olvia. In the 2nd cent. B.C., Olvia was ruled by the Scythian King Skilura and later was annexed to the Pontus Kingdom of Mithridates.

The Mykolayiv Region.
Southern Buh River.

In the 1st cent. A.D. the city of Olvia was restored and became part of the Roman Empire. In the late 4th cent. Olvia was sacked by the Huns. In the 5th-6th cent., farming settlements of Chernyakhiv culture expanded in the region; these were later integrated with the tribe of Anty, as described in Byzantine sources. During the 6th-9th cent., the number of agricultural settlements diminished significantly as a result of incursions made by the nomadic tribes of Avars, Bulgarians, Khazars, and Hungarians.

In the early 9th cent. the rulers of Kyivan Rus'-Ukraine built foreposts leading to the open sea. From the mid-10th cent., the Pechenegs appeared in the area, followed by the Polovtsians. In the mid-13th cent. the territory came under the rule of the Golden Horde. In the years 1362-1569 the region was ruled by Lithuania; after the Union of Lublin it became part of the Polish-Lithuanian state. The southern part of the region was controlled by the Crimean Khan and the Ottoman Porto. From the 17th cent. some of the Mykolayiv territory belonged to the Zaporozhian Sich and to the Buh-Hardivsk, Inhulets, and Pohnoyska Kozak districts. From the end of the 17th cent. urbanization and economic development began in the region. In the 19th and early 20th cent. the Mykolayiv region became one of the main suppliers of animal grain feed on the world market. Forced collectivization and the genocidal famine of 1932-33 destroyed the rural economy of the region. Industrialization helped to integrate the region into the military-industrial complex of the former USSR.

PROMINENT INDIVIDUALS

BORN IN THE REGION:

A. Antoniuk (1943), artist; Pervomaysk. • **M. Arkas** (1853-1909), historian, composer, archeologist; Mykolayiv. • **Dniprova Chayka-Antlevska** (1861-1917), writer; Zeleny Yar, Domaniv district. • **B. Mozolevsky** (1936), poet, archeologist; Mykolayivka, Veselynske district. • **M. Sadovsky-Tobilevych** (1856-1933), actor, theater director, writer; Kostuvate, Bratske district. • **P. Saksahansky-Tobilevych** (1859-1940), actor, theater director; Kostuvate, Bratske district. • **M. Vinhranovsky** (1936), writer, poet; Pervomaysk. • **O. Yanata** (1888-1938), political figure; Mykolayiv, died in a Soviet prison.

BURIED IN THE REGION:

M. Arkas (1853-1909), historian; Mykolayiv.

MYKOLAYIV

City and regional center located on the banks of the Buzk River estuary, 602 km from Kyiv. Population: over 500,000. Telephone code: 0512.

The territory of the city was settled in ancient times. The remains of settlements from the Neolithic Age, ancient cemeteries of the early Bronze Age, settlements of the late Bronze Age, the Graeco-Roman period, and the early Slavonic period (the 5th-4th cent.) have been excavated.

Mykolayiv was founded in 1789 and named after St. Nicholas (Mykola) in honor of the Kozak capture of the Turkish fortress Ochakiv on this saint's day. Life in the city was intimately tied to the sea fleet. The headquarters of the Black Sea Fleet and the shipbuilding industry were located here. During the Soviet period Mykolayiv was the largest shipbuilding center in the Soviet Union.

Although the specific conditions under which the city developed were not conducive to cultural development, the first astronomical observatory in Ukraine was founded here in 1827.

CHURCHES, HISTORICAL AND ARCHITECTURAL MONUMENTS

ASTRONOMICAL OBSERVATORY, 19TH cent. Its meridian is recorded in international astronomical atlases. (Observatorna St., 1; Streetcar No. 1).

BUILDING OF THE BLACK SEA FLEET HEADQUARTERS, 19th cent. Now the Shipbuilding Museum. (Admiralska St., 4; Streetcar No. 1).

SVYATO-MYKOLAYIVSKA (ST. NICHOLAS') CHURCH, 1813-17. Built in the Classical style. Its ornamentations and paintings have been preserved. (Faleyivska St., 4; Streetcar No. 1).

CHURCH OF PRESVYATA BOHORO-DYTSYA (MOTHER OF GOD), 19th cent. (Lyahin St., 12; Streetcar No. 1).

KATOLYTSKY KOSTEL (ROMAN CATH-OLIC CHURCH), 19th cent. (Dekabrystiv St., 32; Streetcar No. 1, 3).

VODOHINNA VEZHA (WATER TOWER), 19th cent. (Ryumin St.; Streetcar No. 2, 4, 5).

MONUMENTS

T. Shevchenko, 1984. Architect: V. Shchedrov. Sculptor: H. Kovalchuk. (Shevchenko Sq.).

M. Arkas Memorial Plaque, 1992. Architect: O. Bondarenko. Sculptor: V. Fedorchuk. (Admiralska St., 34).

Svyato-Mykolayivska (St. Nicholas') Church, 1813-17.

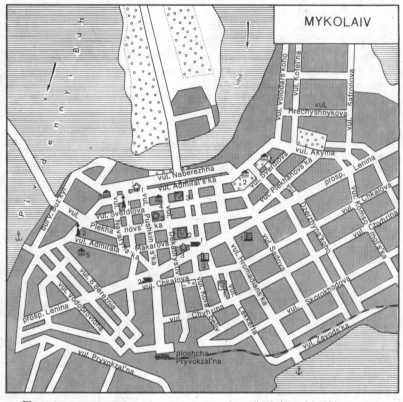

Hotels:
1 Mykolaïv
2 Ukraïna

Restaurants:
1 Karavela
2 Neptun
Note. Restaurants Mykolaïv and Ukraïna are attached to the hotels of the same names

Railway Station

Sea passenger terminal

River Station

Monuments:
1 N. A. Rimsky-Korsakov
2 Taras Shevchenko

Architectural monuments:
1. Building of the former old

sailors' barracks, 19th c.
2 Building of the former boys' gymnasium, 1850
3 Building of the former officers' club
4 St. Nicholas' Church, 1813—1817
5 Observatory, 1821—1827

Museums:
1 History of Shipbuilding and Fleet (former building of the naval headquarters, architectural monument, 1793)
2 V. Vereshchagin Museum of Art
3 Local Lore

Theaters:
1 Ukrainian Music-and-Drama
2 Puppet
3 V. Chkalov Russian Theater of Drama

Kazka Children's City.

MUSEUMS

Museum of Regional Ethnography: Dekabrystiv St., 32; tel. 37-74-59. • **Ship-building Museum:** Admiralska St., 4; tel. 35-13-49. • **Vereshchahin Art Museum:** Velyka Morska St., 47; tel. 35-23-67.

THEATERS, PHILHARMONIC

Music and Drama Theater: Dunayev St., 59. • **Drama Theater:** Admiralska St., 27. • **Puppet Theater:** Potyomkin St., 53.

HIGHER EDUCATIONAL INSTITUTIONS

Shipbuilding Institute: Skorokhodov St., 5. • **Pedagogical Institute:** Luxem-burg St., 24. • **Agricultural Institute:** Karpenko St., 23. • **Cultural-Educational Faculty of the Kyiv Institute of Culture:** Dekabrystiv St., 17.

LIBRARIES, ARCHIVES

Scientific Library: Moskovska St., 9. • **Regional Archive:** Vaslyayev St., 43.

PARKS

Petrovsky Park: Potyomkin St. • **Peremoha Park:** Solyany. • **Kazka Children's City:** Dekabrystiv St., 38-a.

SPORTS COMPLEXES

Evis Stadium: Sportyvna St.; tel. 37-72-43.

HOTELS

Ukrayina: prospekt Lenina, 73; tel. 36-80-00. • **Turyst:** Karpenko St., 46; tel.

34-30-03. • **Mykolayiv:** prospekt Lenina, 107; tel. 37-50-00. • **Inhul:** Admiralska St., 34; tel. 35-65-49.

RESTAURANTS, CAFES

Turyst: Karpenko St., 46. • **Ukrayina:** prospekt Lenina, 73. • **Yuvileyny:** prospekt Zhovtnevy, 273. • **Mykolayiv:** prospekt Lenina, 107. • **Okean:** prospekt Myru, 40.

STORES

Pivdenny Buh: prospekt Lenina, 259. • **"Dytyachy Svit" Univermah (Children's Department Store):** Shevchenko St., 64. • **Khudozniy Salon (Art):** Radyanska St., 5. • **Moloda Hvardiya (Books):** Radyanska St., 3. • **Khudozhniy Kram:** Dekabrystiv St., 17.

BANKS

Natsionalny Bank Ukrayiny (National Bank of Ukraine — Regional Branch): Faleyivska St., 14; tel. 35-20-39. • **Komertsiyny bank "Spivdruzhnist" ("Spivdruzhnist" Commercial Bank):** Morekhidna St., 2-a. • **Mykolayivsky komertsiyny aktsionerny bank rozvytku promyslovosti i sotsiyalnoyi sfery Ukrayiny "Mykkombank" ("Mykkombank" — Mykolayiv Commercial-Joint Stock Industrial and Social Development Bank of Ukraine):** Luxemburg St., 52; tel. 35-54-40; 39-72-72. • **Komertsiyny aktsionerny bank "Yantar" ("Yantar" Commercial-Joint Stock Bank):** city of Ochakiv, Lenin St., 26; tel. 2-22-28. • **Komertsiyny bank "Lehprodbank" ("Lehprodbank" Commercial Bank):** Luxemburg St., 54.

TOURISM

Suputnyk: ploshcha Lenina, 1; tel. 35-99-48.

POST OFFICE, TELEPHONE

Main post office: Admiralska St., 27/1; tel. 35-25-40.
Telegraph: Admiralska St., 27/1; tel. 35-25-53.
Fax: Admiralska St., 27/1; tel. 35-25-56.
Central calling point: Radyanska St., 2; tel. 35-34-46.

MEDICAL SERVICES

Emergency: tel. 03.
Pharmacies: No. 1: Potyomkin St., 217; tel. 24-51-76. • No. 3: Faleyivska St., 5; tel. 35-54-22.

TRANSPORTATION

Railway station: Pryvokzalna St., 1; tel. 29-51-07.
Bus station: prospekt Zhovtnevy; tel. 24-31-15.
Airport: tel. 006.
Ticket office: prospekt Lenina, 74-a; tel. 37-35-50.
Taxi reservations: tel. 058.

TOURING HISTORIC CITIES AND VILLAGES

BOHDANIVKA (until 1801 — Hard)

Village in the Voznesensk district, 51 km from Voznesensk, on the right bank of the Southern Buh River.

This large village was founded in the late 16th cent. after Zaporozhian Kozaks built underwater enclosures for fishing ("hard" — hence the old name). Later this settlement became the center of the Buh-Hard fortification of the Zaporozhian Sich. A Zaporozhian ferry crossing was located here, and to the end of the 18th cent. was one of the most important crossings on the Southern Buh River.

KINBURN SPIT

Situated between Yahorlytsky Bay and the Dnipro River estuary in the Ochakiv district. The Black Sea Preserve and the remains of the center of the Prohnoyska palanka (fortification) and the Kinburn Fortress are located here.

KOZYRKA

Village in the Ochakiv district, 35 km from Ochakiv.

In the southern part of the village are remains of an ancient Greek settlement from the 1st cent.

MYHIYA

. Village in the Pervomaysk district, 23 km from Pervomaysk, on the left bank of the Southern Buh River.

In the early 18th cent., Kozak winter quarters were established here; they were named after the ten islands-rapids (the Great Myhiyiv Island and Small Myhiyiv Island). The camps of the Haydamaky were located on these islands. In 1768 during the Koliyivshchyna peasant uprisings Haydamaky units led by Y. Solon and F. Shvydky camped here.

OCHAKIV

Located on the right bank of the Dnipro-Buzk estuary, 58 km from Mykolayiv. Population: approx. 15,000

An ancient Greek settlement has been excavated here. In 1415 the Lithuanian Prince built the Dashiv Fortress, which was later captured by the Tatars. In 1492 the

*Ruins of the ancient
Greek city of Olvia.*

Tatar Khan Menhli-Ghirey built the Kara-Kermen fortress at this site, subsequently captured by the Turks and renamed Achi-Kale. During the 16th-17th cent. the Zaporozhian Kozaks made frequent raids on this fortress. In 1792 the city of Ochakiv was founded at the site of the fortress.

MYKOLAYIVSKA (ST. NICHOLAS') CHURCH, 15th-19th cent. Built in 1804 on the site of a mosque; rebuilt in 1842. Since 1972 it has housed a military history museum.

An **Ethnographic Museum** (ploshcha Suvorova) and the **Sudkovsky Art Museum** (Lenin St., 1) are located in the city.

OSTRIV BEREZAN

Located 12 km west of Ochakiv.

On the island are remains of the ancient Greek city of Borysthen and the strongpoint of the Rus' warriors who stopped here before setting sail on the open seas.

PARUTYNE

Village in the Ochakiv district, 33 km from Ochakiv.

In the southern part of the village are ruins of the ancient Greek city of Olvia, which lasted for a millennium — from the 6th cent. B.C. to the 4th cent. A.D.

PERVOMAYSK

City located at the confluence of the Synyukha River and Southern Buh River, 180 km from Mykolayiv. Population: over 60,000.

Here in 1676 the Kozaks built the Orlyk fortification as a defense against the Tatars and

*Pervomaysk. Pokrovska
(Protection) Church, 1805.*

Turks. In 1743 the Myrhorod Colonel V. Kapnist and the French engineer de Bosquet built a trench with six bastions on the site of the Kozak fortifications. In 1769 the Tatars set fire to the Orlyk and destroyed the fortifications. Here in 1918-19 the armies of the Ukrainian National Republic fought the Bolshevik forces.

Near the town remains of Neolithic and Bronze Age settlements have been excavated, as well as Cimmerian burial grounds, a Scythian settlement, and settlements of Chernyakhiv culture.

POKROVSKA (PROTECTION OF THE BLESSED VIRGIN MARY) CHURCH, 1805; **BELL TOWER,** 1839. Built in the Classical style typical of southern Ukraine. It is a one-domed church, crucifiction in plan. The bell tower is a three-tiered structure.

Odesa Region

Situated in southwestern Ukraine, within the boundaries of the forest-steppe and steppe zone. Its southernmost tip borders on the Black Sea. The main part of the territory consists of the Black Sea Lowlands. Its major rivers are the Danube, Dnister, and the Southern Buh. Their tributaries are the Dnister, Khadzhibey, Kuyalnytsky, and Tylihulsky. The Odesa region is home to the "Danube Bullrushes" nature preserve. The climate is moderate-continental, characterized by mild winters with litte snow, and hot, dry summers. Created in 1932. Area: 33,3 thousand sq. km. Population: 2,635,000 inhabitants.

History

The first settlements on the territory of the present region date to the Early Paleolithic Age. They consisted of ancient settlements and ruins of cities belonging to the Cimmerian, Scythian, Sarmatian, Greek, and Slavonic cultures. During the period of Kievan Rus'-Ukraine the region was populated by the Ulychi and Tyvertsi tribes. In 1239-1240 the Mongol-Tatar hordes annexed the Black Sea lands to the Golden Horde. At the beginning of the 15th century these lands were seized by Lithuania and by Turkey in the 1480s. With the signing of the Yassy Peace Treaty of 1791, concluding the Russo-Turkish war of 1787-1791, the lands of the Odesa region came under Russian rule.

Bilhorod-Dnistrovsky fortress. XII-XV cent.

At the beginning of the 19th century the peasants' struggle against serfdom intensified in the Odesa region. Serfs began fleeing in great numbers to Kozak units in the Danube region.

TYPICAL SOUVENIRS FROM THE BLACK SEA LANDS:

Sea turtles, coral, mounted fish and other sea animals, decorative and applied art pictures, Ukrainian embroidery, childrens' toys.

PROMINENT INDIVIDUALS

BORN IN THE REGION:

K. Dankevych (1905-84), composer, Odesa. • **S. Karavansky** (1920), writer, former political prisoner. • **Yu. Lypa** (1900-44), publicist, Odesa. • **N. Strokata** (1926), human rights defender, Odesa.

BURRIED IN THE REGION:

V. Filatov (1875-1956), ophthalmologist, Odesa.

ODESA

The regional center and sea port located on the southwestern shore of the Black Sea, 490 km. south of Kiev. It is one of the largest cities in Ukraine and serves as the southern gateway of the state. It is an important industrial, scientific, cultural, and resort center, with a population of 1,132,000. Telephone code: 0482.

Odesa is associated with many talented writers, among them M. Kulish, V. Sosyura, Yu. Yanovsky, O. Dovzhenko. It was the destination of various foreign writers, such as A. Mickiewicz, G. Oldridge, G. Simenon, W. Saroyan.

Few cities have such a rich literary biography as Odesa and, naturally, the city is host to a literary museum.

Odesa has a flourishing theatre life: there are seven theatres, a philharmonic orchestra, circus, and opera and ballet hall.

The history of Odesa is replete with numerous historic events which are captured in the names of the city's 1400 streets, squares, prospects, boulevards, and historical and cultural monuments.

Within a short period of time the city, with its beautiful harbor on the Black Sea, has become "Ukraine's southern window to Europe", and an important cultural center. The city has Richelieu Lyceums, a university, an Opera and Ballet Theatre, a public library, and an astronomical observatory. It has been a center for publishing literary works and a Ukrainian anthology and is the site of a film studio.

Odesa is a member of the World Federation of Twinned Cities. Of all Ukrainian cities, it has been twinned with the greatest number of cities around the world (17): Oulu (Finland), Alexandria (Egypt), Tripoli (Libya), Genoa (Italy), Yokohama (Japan), Vancouver (Canada), Marseilles (France), Liverpool (Great Britain), Baltimore (U.S.A.), Haifa (Israel), Valencia (Spain), Calcutta (India) and others.

*Odesa Opera
and Ballet Theatre.*

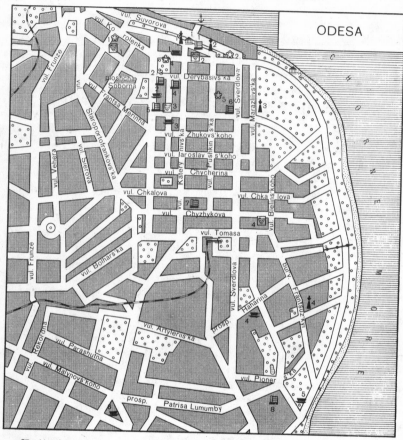

ODESA

📖 Hotels:
   1 Londons'kyi
   2 Pasazh
   3 Velykyi Moskovs'kyi
   4 Spartak
   5 Tsentral'nyi
   6 Chervonyi
   7 Chorne More
   8 Arkadiia

🍴 Restaurants:
   1 Ukraïna
   2 Teatral'nyi
   3 Kyïv
   4 More
   5 Perlyna
   6 Varna

🚂 Railway Station

⚓ Marine passenger terminal

🗿 Monuments:
   1 A. F. Richelieu

   2 A. S. Pushkin
   3 Taras Shevchenko
   4 V. P. Filatov, famous ophtal-
   mologist and surgeon

🏛 Architectural monuments:
   1 Potemkin Staircase, 1837—42
   2 Arcade (remnants of the quar-
   antine wall), 1803—1807

✿ Museums:
   1 Art
   2 Archaeology
   3 Literature
   4 Local Lore
   5 Western and Oriental Art

🎭 Theaters:
   1 Ukrainian Theater of Music and
   Drama
   2 Opera and Ballet
   3 Russian Drama
   4 Musical Comedy

Odesa is constantly hosting exhibits, symposia, and conferences. It is the site of consulates and trade commissions of many countries, and dozens of branches of friendship and cultural exchange societies are active in the city.

Many roads lead to Odesa, for this city is hospitable, cheerful, and picturesque. Every year approximately 100,000 tourists visit Odesa, attracted by its boulevards and Prymorsky Stairs, the marine railway and beautiful beaches, numerous new structures and the unusual architecture of old Odesa.

The Tatar settlement of Khadzhibei, first mentioned in 1415, was located on the present site of Odesa. During the Russo-Turkish War of 1787-1791, the Ukrainian Black Sea Kozaks, led by the chieftains A. Holovaty and Z. Chepyha, were the first to conquer the Turkish fortresses of Eni-Dunai and the settlement of Khadzhibei. In 1794 construction was begun on the military port and a city was founded. In 1795 Khadzibei was renamed Odesa.

Prymorsky Stairs.

In the period from 1797 to 1802 Odesa was part of the Novorossiysk Guberniya (province); from 1803 to 1917 it was part of the Odesa city administration (Kherson Guberniya).

CHURCHES, HISTORICAL AND ARCHITECTURAL MONUMENTS

TROYITSKA CHURCH, (Holy Trinity), 1808. Built in the Classical style. A southern altar was added in 1839 and a northern one in 1875. A section of its marble floors has been preserved.

ST. PAUL'S CHURCH, 1897. Built according to the design of the architect, H. Schevrembrandt. A brilliant example of the eclectic style prevalent at the end of the 19th century. Its plan and decor of the façades resemble Romanesque architecture.

BELVEDERE, 1826-1828. Stone. Has ten pairs of columns. Its construction is unique in the architectural heritage of Ukraine.

PRYMORSKY SKHODY (Maritime Stairs), 1837-1842. Architectural design by F. Boffo. Built in the Classical style. Consisting of 192 steps, they are 27 m. high and 136.5 m. long. (Prymorsky Boulevard).

OLD STOCK EXCHANGE, 1829-1837. The building was constructed in the Classical style by the architect, F. Boffo, for the Odesa goods exchange. Rebuilt by the architect, F. Morandi, in 1871-73, re-constructed in 1946-49. The main façade is embellished with sculptures and 12 columns. (Komuna St., 1).

OPERA AND BALLET THEATRE, 1884-1887. Designed by the Viennese architects H. Helmer and F. Felner who constructed theatres in Vienna, Budapest, Dresden, Zagreb. Built in the Renaissance style with elements of Baroque, decorated with sculptural groups and masks. The interior is designed in the Late Rococo style. Its five-tiered hall holds 1560 persons. Considered one of the finest in the world. (Tchaikovsky Lane, 3).

MARITIME MUSEUM BUILDING, 1841. Architect, H. Toricelli. Built in the Classical and Renaissance styles. (Lastochkin St., 6).

NEW STOCK EXCHANGE, 1894-1899. Architect, A. Bernardazzi. The façade is executed in forms of the Florentine Restoration. Decorated with ceramic plate, marble, stained glass windows. The interior is embellished with landscape panneaux, marble. The ceiling is of sculpted wood. Used as a symphony hall. (Rosa Luxemburg St., 15).

PALACE, 1805-1810. Built in the Classical style. Beneath the building are a basement, catacombs, and an artificial cave with grotto. The interior has an artistically decorated ceiling and parquet floors with encrustation. The Odesa Art Museum is located in the building. (Korolenko St., 5).

PALACE COMPLEX, 1826-1834. Constructed according to plans of the architect, F. Boffo, in the Classical style. The palace, belvedere, pavilion, and stables have been preserved. (Chervonoflotsky Provulok, 2).

MONUMENTS

A. Richelieu, 1828. Sculptor: I. Martos, architects: A. Melnikov, F. Boffo. (Prymorsky Boulevard).

T. Shevchenko, 1966. Sculptors: A. Bilostotsky, O. Suprun; architect: H. Topuz. (T. Shevchenko Park of Culture and Recreation).

A. Pushkin, 1889. Sculptor: Zh. Polonska; architect: Kh. Vasilyev. (Prymorsky Boulevard).

V. Filatov, 1967. Sculptor: A. Kovalev. (French Boulevard).

Odesa colonnade.

MUSEUMS

Archaeological Museum: Lastochkin St., 4; tel. 22-01-71. (Trolleybus 1,

2, 4, 10). • **Regional Museum of History and Ethnography**: Lastochkin St., 24-a; tel. 22-98-94, 22-84-90. (Trolleybus 1, 4, 5, 10). • **Art Museum**: Korolenko St., 5-a; tel. 23-82-72. (Streetcar 2, 3, 12; Trolleybus 2, 11). • **Museum of Western and Eastern Art**: Pushkin St., 9; tel. 24-67-47. (Trolleybus 1, 4, 5, 10). • **Personal collections**: Garibaldi St., 19; tel. 22-10-81. (Trolleybus 1, 4, 10).• **Literary Museum**: Lastochkin St., 2; tel. 22-00-02. (Trolleybus 1, 2, 4, 5, 10). • **Naval Museum**: Lastochkin St., 6; tel. 25-02-50. (Trolleybus 1, 4, 5, 10). • **A. Pushkin Literary-Memorial Museum**: Pushkin St., 13.

THEATRES, PHILHARMONIC

Opera and Ballet Theatre: Tchaikovsky St., 1; tel. 29-13-29, 25-24-08. (Trolleybus 1, 2). • **Ukrainian Musical-Drama Theatre**: Pasteur St., 15; tel. 25-52-67. (Trolleybus 2; Streetcar 2, 3, 12).• **Young Viewer's Theatre**: K. Liebknecht St., 48; tel. 22-48-51. (Streetcar 2, 3, 12; Trolleybus 1, 2, 5, 9). • **Regional Marionette Theatre**: Pasteur St., 62; tel. 23-20-58. • **Regional Philharmonic**: R. Luxemburg St., 15; tel. 25-91-02. (Trolleybus 1, 2, 5, 9, 10). • **Russian Drama Theatre**: K. Liebknecht St., 48; tel. 22-45-04. (Streetcar 2, 5, 9).

Central Theatre Box Office: Preobrazhenska St., 28; tel. 25-23-49.

HIGHER EDUCATIONAL INSTITUTIONS

University (1865): Peter I St., 2; tel. 23-82-95. • **Conservatory (1913)**: Ostrovydov St., 63; tel. 23-69-68. • **Medical Institute (1900)**: Narymanov Provulok, 2; tel. 23-33-24. • **Economics Institute (1921)**: Preobrazhenska St., 8; tel. 23-61-58. • **Institute of Low-Temperature Technology**: Peter I St., 1/3; tel. 23-22-20. • **Naval Engineers' Institute (1930)**: Mechnykov St., 34; tel. 22-19-92. • **Engineering-Building Institute (1930)**: Didrikson St., 4; tel. 23-33-42. • **Naval Academy**: Didrikhson St., 8; tel. 23-40-88; 23-41-78. • **Electro-Technical Communications Institute (1930)**: Chelyuskintsiv St., 1/3; tel. 23-22-44. • **Pedagogical Institute (1920)**: Staroportofrankivska St., 26; tel. 32-08-11. • **Hydro-Meteorological Institute (1932)**: Lviv St., 15; tel. 63-62-09. • **Agricultural Institute (1918)**: Sverdlov St., 99; tel. 22-37-23. • **Polytechnical Institute (1918)**: Shevchenko Prospekt, 1; tel. 22-19-92. • **Technological Food Industry Institute (1922)**: Sverdlov St., 112; tel. 25-32-84.

Information: tel. 22-73-94; fax: 22-14-65.

LIBRARIES, ARCHIVES

University Research Library: Preobrazhenska St., 24; tel. 21-26-66. (Streetcar 2, 3, 12). • **M. Gorky Research Library**: Pasteur St., 13; tel. 23-02-52. (Trolleybus 2; Streetcar 2, 3, 12).• **Regional General Research Library**: Troitska St., 49/51; tel. 25-50-69. (Streetcar 2, 3, 10, 12; Trolleybus 11).• **Regional Childrens' Library**:

Preobrazhenska St., 64; tel. 25-58-82. • **Regional Archive**: Zhukovsky St., 18; tel. 22-80-25. • **City Archive**: K. Liebknecht St., 35; tel. 22-18-94. • **Births and Deaths Registry, Odesa Regional Archive**: Derybasivska St., 12; tel. 22-60-98.

NEWSPAPERS, JOURNALS

"Chornomorski Visti": ploshcha Pyatdesyatrichchya SRSR, 1; tel. 65-10-23. • **"Zemlya i Lyudy"**: prospekt Lyumumby, 33-a; tel. 61-02-02. • **"Akh, Odesa"**: ploshcha Pyatdesyatrichchya SRSR, 1; tel. 69-93-79.

CIVIC ORGANIZATIONS

RUKH: Osypov St.,40; tel. 22-50-83. • **Social-Democratic Party**: tel. 26-13-80, 66-55-66. • **PDVU**: tel. 23-41-36. • **Christian-Democratic Party**: tel. 25-79-49. • **"Pivdenna Hromada"**: Pasteur St., 62; tel. 23-63-13. • **"Leleka"**: Engels St., 30. • **"Ukrayina" Society**: Byelinsky St., 5; tel. 25-69-42. • **"Znannya"**: Pushkin St., 10; tel. 22-33-66.

PARKS

T. Shevchenko Central Park of Culture and Recreation: Engels St., 1; tel. 22-12-81. • **Peremoha Central Park of Culture and Recreation**: Nevsky St., 56; tel. 32-89-18. • **Parks of Culture and Recreation**: Moyseyenko St., 32-b; tel. 25-33-96; Kosmonavtiv St., 17-a; tel. 26-30-87; Estonska St., 27; tel. 22-09-66. • **Zoo**: Estonska St., 25; tel. 22-55-89.

SPORTS COMPLEXES

Sports Palace: Shevchenko Prospekt, 31; tel. 22-30-64. • **Chornomorets Central Stadium**: Shevchenko Park; tel. 22-42-86; 25-92-50. • **SKA Swimming Pool**: Silskohospodarsky Lane, 2; tel. 29-80-34.

HOTELS

Chervony: Pushkin St., 15; tel. 22-72-20. • **Londonsky**: Prymorsky Boulevard, 11; tel. 22-50-19. • **Chorne More**: Rishelevska St., 52; tel. 24-20-28. • **Turyst**: Henuezka St., 24-a; tel. 61-89-03. • **Arkadiya**: Henuezka St., 24; tel. 60-82-00; 60-80-01. • **Velyky Moskovsky**: Derybasivska St., 29; tel. 24-40-16. • **Pasazh**: Preobrazhenska St., 34; tel. 22-48-49. • **Spartak**: Derybasivska St., 25; tel. 22-01-89. • **Tsentralny**: Preobrazhenska St., 40; tel. 22-48-61. • **Zhovtnevy**: Sverdlov St., 33; tel. 28-06-60. • **Yunist**: Pionerska St., 32; tel. 63-67-08. • **Delfin Camping ground**: Kotovsky Rd., 307; tel. 55-00-66. • **Viktoriya**: Henuezka St., 24-a; tel. 61-90-35; 61-89-03. • **Ekran** (Odesa Film production management): Frantsuzky Blvd., 33-a;

tel. 28-65-38. • **Sailors' hostel**: Shevchenko Prospekt, 29; tel. 60-86-91. • **Odesa Tourist Complex**: Haharin Plateau, 5; tel. 63-94-34. • **Dynamo**: Frantsuzky Blvd., 27; tel. 29-26-31.

RESTAURANTS, CASINOS, BARS

Pivdenna Palmira: Arkadiya Park; tel. 68-44-77. • **Svitlana**: Varnenska St., 2; tel. 61-86-02. • **Chorne More**: Rishelevska St., 52; tel. 24-10-29. • **Pecheskaho (and Terek Bar)**: Khalturin St., 12; tel. 25-03-95; 26-09-79. • **Ukrayina**: Katerynynska St., 12; tel. 25-13-38; 22-74-79. • **Chervony**: Pushkin St., 15; tel. 25-43-05. • **Zhanetta**: K. Liebknecht St., 23; tel. 22-23-47. • **Oulu**: Hohol St., 12; tel. 23-74-6. • **Prymorye**: Shevchenko Prospekt, 8-

Hotel "Chorne More" ("Black Sea").

a; tel. 60-71-68. • **Eldorado Casino**: Katerynynska St., 19; tel. 22-14-32. • **Richelieu Casino**: R. Luxemburg St., 15. • **Royal Flush Casino** (in the Zoryany cinema): Dobrovolsky Prospekt, 72; tel. 55-31-21. • **Night Currency Bar** (in the Londonsky Hotel): Prymorsky Blvd., 11; tel. 25-53-58. • **Nebezbechna Zona Discoteque and the Zirochka Cafe**: Gen. Petrov St., 25.

STORES

Central Odesa Department Store (univermah): Pushkin St., 72; tel. 25-09-95. **Merkator-Chorne More Supermarket**: Nevsky St., 57; tel. 45-85-43; 45-85-49. **Merkator Black Sea Supermarket**: Station 5 on the Chornomorska Road.

BANKS

National Bank of Ukraine (Regional Branch): Lenin St., 8; tel. 25-29-64.
Commercial Bank "Odesa:" Lumumba St., 33-a; tel. 65-40-87.
Commercial Bank "Porto-Franko:" Pushkinska St., 10; tel. 22-48-89, 21-70-13.
Commercial Stock Holding Bank "Nord Bank:" Babel St., 4/4; tel. 22-61-22; 22-29-88.
Odesa Commercial Bank "Investbank:" Lenin St., 59; tel. 24-01-29.
Commercial Bank "Enerhiya" (Energy): Illichevsk City, Oleksandriyska St., 6; tel. 6-80-90; 3-14-21.
Commercial Bank "Tarutino:" Tarutino village, prosp. Myru, 28; tel. 3-10-69; 3-21-02.

Resort "Moldova."

TOURISM, HEALTH RESORTS

Numerous tourist centers, camping grounds, rest-homes, health resorts, boarding houses, and beautiful beaches are spread out over a 100 km range — from the Chornomorsky Delfin camping ground near the village of Fontan to the north of Odesa, to Karalino-Buhaz and Lebedivka to the south.

The Intourist-Odesa General Agency for Foreign Tourism: R. Luxemburg St., 14; tel. 25-01-15, 22-30-03; fax: 23-24-76 "GID".

Odesaturyst, the Odesa Regional Tourist Excursion Association: Pl. Zhovtnevoyi revolyutsiyi, 1; tel. 25-02-87; 22-66-83.

Suputnyk, the Odesa Regional Bureau for International Youth Tourism: Pionerska St., 32; tel. 22-53-55, 25-92-53.

Zvyazkivets, the Center of Culture and Recreation: Ostrovydiv St., 100; tel. 21-60-36; 22-18-74.

Odesa Travel and Escursion Bureau: B. Khmelnytsky St., 62; tel. 33-68-30; teletype: 23-24-64.

Turyst. This bureau arranges approximately 100 different excursion: "Historic sites of the city of Odesa," "Opera Theatre," "Old Odesa," "Literary Odesa," "Theatrical Odesa," "Ukrainian Writers in Odesa," "Churches of Odesa," "Gifts of the Sun" (viticulture and wine-making); "Satirists and humourists of Odesa," "Architecture of Old Odesa," "Odesa — Port on the Black Sea," "Mykolayiv — City of Ships," and others.

There are 12 health resorts located in and around Odesa, equipped with all the facilities necessary for a complete cure: a mild sea climate, medicinal mud, beautiful beaches on the sea. A network of medical facilities insures the complex recuperation of patients suffering from various illnesses (sea baths, mud baths, carbonic baths, oxygen baths, hydrogen sulphide baths, radon and nitrogen baths, physiotherapy, therapeutic diets, electric light therapy, et al.)

The best known health resorts are the Kuyalnytsky, Malodolynsky, Lermontov, Arkadiya, Velyky Fontan, Chornomorka, Luzanivka, Prymorsky, Zatoka, Lebedivka, and Serhiyivka resorts.

Every year approximately 500,000 visitors seek a rest cure in these resorts.

ODESA BEACHES

"Arkadiya": Streetcar, 5; Trolleybus 5, 7, 13. • **"Delfin":** Streetcar 5. • **"Zoloty Bereh":** 16th Station B. Fontana; Streetcar 18. • **"Kurortny":** Streetcar 17, 18. • **"Luzanivka":** Streetcar 7; Bus 155. • **"Vidrada" ("Otrada"):** Streetcar 5. •

"Chayka": 10th Station B. Fontana; Streetcar 17, 18. • "Chornomorsky": Chornomorka Village; Streetcar 29.

POST OFFICES, TELEPHONE, FAX

Main post office and telegraph office: Sadova St., 10; tel. 26-67-89.

Central Calling Point: Sadova St., 10; tel. 26-67-65.

Municipal Technical Production Communications Network (Inter-city telephone and telegraph station — MTTS): Frunze St., 100; tel. 26-55-54; 22-87-12.

Provides the following services: telex, telefax, receiving and sending confidential telegrams, delivering correspondence to indicated addresses within a specified period of time, transmitting confidential information and conducting direct telegraph communication from the MTTS office, providing a direct, confidential channel of communication, inter-city and international telephone communication.

Odesinform LTD (provides operative communications services to all countries): tel. 24-19-42.

Communications point at the marine train station (sends telexes, faxes, letters, postcards, electronic mail: Suvorov St., 1; counter Ho. 24; tel. 22-39-45.

Militia: tel. 02. • **Fire:** tel. 01; 29-00-50. • **Information:** tel. 09. • **International calls:** tel. 079. • **Information on city/ country telephone codes:** tel. 069. • **Odesa Main Post Office Information:** tel. 065. • **Information on Long Distance Calls:** tel. 25-15-24. • **Telegram Pick-Up:** tel. 066. • **Time Information:** tel. 081. • **Weather Bureau:** tel. 63-43-26.

MEDICAL SERVICES

Emergency: tel. 03.

Pharmaceutical Administration Information: tel. 067.

Pharmacies: No. 1: Sadova St., 21; 22-24-08. • Ho. 2: Pasteur St., 22; tel. 23-54-78. • Ho. 3: Krasnoslobodska St. 42; tel. 32-06-11. • Ho. 4: Moskovska St. 7; tel. 23-32-18. • Ho. 5: 1905 St., 13; tel. 22-31-00. • Ho. 6: Katerynynska St., 8; tel. 24-96-93. • Ho. 7: Mizykevych St., 52; tel. 33-63-11.

TRANSPORTATION

Ukraine Airlines: tel. 21-35-76.

Central Airport: Ovidiopilska Road; tel. 006; 22-23-00; ticket reservation: tel. 66-70-51; 22-34-56.

Main Odesa Railway Station: Pryvokzalna Ploshcha, 2; tel. 005; 27-42-53; 27-42-54; 27-41-31; baggage information: tel. 27-42-55; 27-48-77; ticket reservation: tel. 083.

Bus station: Dzerzhynsky St., 58; tel. 004.

Marine train station: Suvorov St., 1; tel. 22-32-11.

Bus ticket reservations: tel. 084.
Lost and found: 22-42-10.
Taxi: tel. 080.
Black sea navigation port: Lastochkina St. 1; tel. 22-45-89; 22-20-42.

AUTO SERVICING

Road service: 1612 km. autoroad E-93 St. Petersburg-Kyiv-Odesa; tel. 24-90-32.
• Lyubashivka Village, 1517 km. a/d E-93 St. Petersburg-Kyiv-Odesa; tel. 9-16-35.
Autoservice: Leningrad Shose, 27; tel. 33-95-54. • Promyslova St., 20; tel. 32-13-73.

GOVERNMENT INSTITUTIONS

Ministry of Foreign Affairs of Ukraine: Vidradna St., 3, tel. 22-20-41; 22-08-50; 22-44-03.
Department of External Economic Relations and Trade, Regional State Administration: Shevchenko Prospekt, 4; tel. 28-05-33.
Department of Services for Foreign Consulates and Embassies, Regional State Administration: Sverdlov St., 83; tel. 22-67-84.
Department of External Economic Relations, Odesa Municipal Council of Peoples' Deputies: Pl. Komuny, 1; tel. 24-70-09.

CONSULATES

Republic of India: Kirov St., 31; tel. 22-43-33; 22-34-75.
Republic of Cuba: Tomas St., 7/9; tel. 25-14-69; 22-45-55.
Republic of Bulgaria: Posmitny St., 9, tel. 66-60-92.
Republic of Vietnam: Tolstoy St., 30; tel. 26-47-17.

*Troyitska Church
(Holy Trinity Church), 1808.*

DENOMINATIONS

CHURCHES AND PRAYER HALLS OFFERING RELIGIOUS SERVICES:

Cathedral of the Assumption: Preobrazhenska St., 70: tel. 25-82-63.
St. Elias Cathedral: Pushkin St., 79; tel. 22-31-95.
St. Demetrius Church (cemetery): 25-85-79.
Slobidska Church: Molodizhna St., 19; tel. 32-05-94.

Greek Church: Katerynynska St., 55; tel. 25-59-90.

Roman Catholic Church: Khalturin St., 5; tel. 23-89-20.

Synagogue: Odariy St., 5; tel. 23-03-70.

Evangelical-Baptist Prayer Hall: Serov St., 34; tel. 33-58-54.

Pentacostalist Prayer Hall: Kunytsi, 4.

Seventh Day Adventist Prayer Hall: Pivdenna St., 42.

German Evangelical-Lutheran Church: St. Paul's Church: Ostrovydova St., 68; Perekopska Dyviziya, 1, tel. 33-55-59.

TOURING HISTORIC CITIES AND VILLAGES

BILHOROD-DNISTROVSKY (until 1944 — Akerman)

A port city, 100 km from Odesa, on the Dnister tributary, 18 km from the Black Sea.

At the beginning of the new era the site was first occupied by a Greek colony; later, a Roman colony called Tira. In the 9th cent. the Ulychi and Tyvertsi tribes established the economic, political, and trading center of Bilhorod. From the 13th cent. Bilhorod was part of the Galician-Volynian Principality. Captured by Turkey in 1484 and renamed Akerman. During the 16th-18th cent. it was the capital of the Bilhorod Horde. With the signing of the Bucharest Peace Treaty of 1812 the city came under Russian rule. From 1918 to 1940 it was part of Rumania.

BILHOROD-DNISTROVSKY (AKERMAN) FORTRESS, 13th-15th cent. Was built by the master builder, Fedorko, on the ruins of the ancient Greek city of Tira. It had 35 towers, of which 20 have been preserved, two outside Gates — the Main Gate and the Ovidio-Polish Gate — and three internal gates. The walls were approximately 2 km long, 7 m high and 5 m thick. The fortress was surrounded by a deep moat, up to 23 m, bordered on both sides by the tributary. Its buildings comprised a small citadel (Genoa Castle, 12-13th c.), fortified by thick walls with four turrets. A unique monument of medieval defence architecture, the largest and sturdiest structure of its kind in Ukraine. Today it houses a branch of the Bilhorod-Dnistrovsky Museum.

ARMENIAN CHURCH OF THE THEOTOKOS (BOHORODYTSI, MOTHER OF GOD), 15-19th cent. A rare example of church construction in Ukraine.

GREEK CHURCH, 15-16th cent. Its architectural construction is extremely archaic. A rare type of church structure in Ukraine.

CRYPT CHURCH OF ST. JOHN OF SUCHAVA, 14-19th cent. Erected over a well, where, in 1330, according to popular lore, the Tatars murdered the Moldavian merchant, Ioan, who refused to convert to the Muslim faith. Has a stone well. Unique in the architectural heritage of Ukraine. (Shabska St., 116).

Bolhrad.
St. Nicholas' Church, 1871.

BOLHRAD

City, on a lake surrounded by bullrushes, 7 km from the Bolhrad railway station.

Founded in 1821 by Bulgarians fleeing Turkish oppression.

INZOV'S MAUSOLEUM, 1833. Built in the Classical style as a cemetery church, where I. Inzov was buried in 1846.

ST. NICHOLAS CHURCH, 1871. Built in the Classical style. Embellished with stucco ornamentation.

PREOBRAZNENSKY CATHEDRAL (of the Transfiguration), 1833-1838. Built in the Classical style. During 1912-1914 the interior of the cathedral was painted in the art nouveau style by the artist, I. Pyskarev.

IZMAYIL

A port city, on the left bank of the Danube, 286 km from Odesa, 80 km from the Black Sea. Population: 95,000.

Izmayil was conquered by Turkey in the 16th cent. and was converted to a fortress. The Zaporozhyan Kozaks waged campaigns on Izmayil in 1609 and 1621; until 1917, the city was part of the gubernia (province) of Besarabia.

Izmayil is a city with the largest number of preserved churches and important historical monuments in the region.

SVYATO-MYKOLAYIVSKA (St. Nicholas') **CHURCH,** 1852. Located on the territory of the fortress. One of the earliest constructions with elements of the Byzantine style. (Matrosova St., 23).

Izmayil. St. Nicholas' Church, 1852.

POKROVSKY CATHEDRAL (of the Protection of the Blessed Virgin Mary) and **BELLTOWER,** 1822-1836. Built in the Classical style. A colonnade was built onto the cathedral in later years. (Suvorov Prospect).

SVYATO-MYKOLAYIVSKA (St. Nicholas) **CHURCH,** 1833, 1899. Built in the Classical style.

RIZDVA CHURCH (of the Nativity), 1823. Archaic architecture, with no embellishments. (Kutuzov St., 24).

USPENSKA (Dormition) **CHURCH,** 1841. Located on the territory of the fortress. (Matroska St., 24).

MALA MECHET (Minor Mosque), 16th cent. The only remaining structure of the Turkish fortress; considered to be one of the best in Europe. In 1810 it was subordinated to the garrison Church of the Elevation of the Holy Cross.

10*

KILIYA

A port city, on the shore of the Kiliysky mouth of the Danube, 40 km from the Black Sea, 26 km from the Dzynilor railway station. Population: 26,000.

Originally the ancient Greek city-colony of Likostom, first mentioned at the end of 7 A.D. From the 10th cent. formed part of Kievan Rus'-Ukraine. Ukrainian Kozaks, under the leadership of various chieftains — S. Nalyvayko (1595), I. Sulyma (1635) and S. Paliy (1690s), waged campaigns against this city. Under Russian rule from 1812.

MYKOLAYIVSKA (St. Nicholas) **CHURCH,** 15th-17th centuries, **BELLTOWER,** 1891. According to popular lore, the church was founded in 1485 in memory of the city's liberation from the Turks. Was rebuilt numerous times. A rare example in Ukraine of a semi-underground church construction. (Dunayska St., 4).

KYRNYCHKY

Village, Izmayil district, 48 km from Izmayil.

USPENSKA (Dormition) **CHURCH,** 1841. Built in the Classical style. Its smooth walls are neither decorated nor painted.

LYPETSKE

Village, Kotovsk district, 12 km from the Kotovsk railway station.

MYKOLAYIVSKA (St. Nicholas) **CHURCH** and **BELLTOWER,** 1807. The oldest church structure in the Classical style in the Odesa region.

NERUBAYSKE

Village, Bilyayivsky district, 5 km from the Usatove railway station.

VOZNESENSKA CHURCH (of the Ascension), 1826. Built in the Classical style.

NOVA NEKRASIVKA

Village, Izmayil district, 12 km from the Izmayil railway station.

VVEDENSKA (the Presentation of the Holy Virgin) **CHURCH,** 19th cent. Erected by folk builders, it is archaic and unique in terms of its size and architecture.

STARA NEKRASIVKA

Village, Izmayil district, 7 km from the Izmayil railway station.

BELLTOWER OF THE CHURCH OF ST. JOHN THE DIVINE, 1823. Built in the Classical style.

PETRIVKA

Village, Kominternivsky district, 20 km from the Serbka railway station.

SADYBA. Village, 1820, 1892. In this village are preserved the palace, part of the park, and work buildings. The palace resembles a medieval castle. Elements of Gothic and Moorish architecture are evident in the structure. One of the oldest examples of architectural Romanticism in Ukraine.

USATOVE

Village, Bilayivsky district.

RIZDVA CHURCH (of the Nativity), 1822. Built in the Classical style.

Poltava Region

It is situated on the left bank of the Dnipro River in the Dnipro Lowland zone. The principal rivers in the region are the Vorskla, Psel (Pslo), and Sula. The climate is moderate-continental. There are many mineral springs in the region; the largest of them are located in Myrhorod and Hoholeve. Created in 1937. Area: 28,800 sq. km. Population: 1,771,000.

History

The territory of Poltava was settled in the Paleolithic Age and habitations from this period have been unearthed near the village of Hintsi in the Lubny district. Scythian agricultural settlements have been unearthed in the Poltava and Kotelva districts and the city of Poltava. Gold and silver articles belonging to ancient Slavic tribes were excavated in 1912 near the village of Mala Pereshchepyna in the Novosanzhary district. In the Kyivan Rus'-Ukraine period the territory of the region was part of the Pereyaslav Principality. Numerous city-fortresses were built above rivers for protection against the Polovtsian tribe: in Khorol (1084), Pisochen (1092), Holtov (1095), Lubno (1107), Pyryatyn (1154), Ltava (1174), Lkoml (1179) and in other locations. After the Tatar-Mongol invasions of the 14th cent. the Poltava region came

Poltava. Museum of Regional Ethnography.

under Lithuanian rule (1362) and under Polish rule in the late 16th cent. During this period several peasant-Kozak uprisings against the forces of occupation took place in the region. The leaders of the uprising were T. Tryasylo (1630), I. Sulyma (1635), P. Pavlyuk and D. Hunya (1637) and others. Residents of the Poltava region took part in the national-liberation war led by Hetman B. Khmelnytsky. After his death Hetman I. Vyhovsky attempted to liberate Ukraine from Muscovite oppression. In 1658 he signed the Treaty of Hadyach with Poland. During the Northern War of 1700-21 this region was the theater of war between Sweden and Russia. In 1708 Hetman I. Mazepa, with the help of King Charles XII of Sweden, attempted to liberate Ukraine from Muscovite rule, but both allies were defeated in the summer of 1709 in the Battle of Poltava. Serfdom was introduced in Ukraine after the defeat of the Ukrainian forces. Over the centuries the Russian Tsars gave away large tracts of Ukrainian land to their court favorites. In the late 18th cent. the Poltava region became part of the Chernihiv viceregency and the province of Poltava was created in 1802.

After the Bolshevik Revolution Ukrainian political and cultural-educational life was galvanized. After declaring war on the Ukrainian National Republic, in January 1918 Bolshevik forces gained control of the Poltava region and launched a campaign of terror against the civilian population. During 1918-22 anti-Bolshevik peasant uprisings took place in the counties of Zinkiv and Hadyach. The writer V. Korolenko, a resident of Poltava, criticized Bolshevik actions in the region. During the period of enforced collectivization many people were deported from the region or died of hunger as a result of the genocidal famine of 1932-33. In 1991 a burial mound was created near Lubny in memory of the famine victims. As a result of Stalin's campaign of terror during the 1930s many Ukrainian intellectuals were liquidated. The region suffered great damage during World War II. Hundreds of villages and homesteads disappeared from the map during the 1960s-80s.

The material and spiritual monuments of the past, including folklore, attest to the high level of the regional culture. The 18th cent. Poltava songwriter and singer Marusya Churay helped to spread the fame of Ukrainian songs. The Hustynya Chronicle appeared in the 17th cent., followed by the Chronicles of S. Velychko and H. Hrabyanka in the early 18th cent. During the 18th and 19th centuries Ukraine's colonial status contributed to a "brain drain" of intellectuals who left Poltava and settled in Russia. The writer I. Kotlyarevsky launched the national and cultural renaissance of Ukraine. The poet T. Shevchenko, who lived in the Poltava region from 1843 to 1846, greatly influenced the development of the local culture.

PROMINENT INDIVIDUALS

BORN IN THE REGION:

O. Afanasyev-Chuzhbynsky (1816-75), writer, ethnographer; village of Iskivtsi in the Lubny district. • **V. Barka-Ocheret** (1908), writer; village of Solonytsya in the Lubny district, lives in the US. • **M. Bashkyrtseva** (1860-84), artist, writer;

village of Havronka in the Dykanka district, died in Paris. • **O. Bilash** (1931), composer, poet; village of Hradyzk in the Hlobyne district. • **Marusya Churay** (first half of the 18th cent.), song-writer; Poltava. • **M. Drahomanov** (1841-95), historian, folklorist, civic activist; Hadyach; died in Bulgaria. • **M. Filyansky** (1873-1938), poet, artist; village of Popivka in the Myrhorod district; executed. • **L. Hlibov** (1827-93), poet-fabulist; village of Vesely Podil in the Semeniv district. • **M. Hohol (Gogol)** (1809-52), writer; village of Velyki Sorochyntsi in the Myrhorod district. • **O. Honchar** (1918), writer; village of Sukhe in the Kobelyaky district. • **Ye. Hrebinka** (1812-48), writer, poet; the Ubizhyshche homestead (today the village of Maryanivka) in the Hrebinka district. • **V. Kapnist** (1758-1823), poet, dramatist; village of Velyka Obukhivka in the Myrhorod district. • **I. Kotlyarevsky** (1769-1838), writer; Poltava. • **M. Lysenko** (1842-1912), composer; village of Hrynky in the Hlobyne district. • **H. Mayboroda** (1913-92), and **P. Mayboroda** (1918-1989), composers; Pelekhivshchyna homestead in the Hlobyne district. • **O. Meshko** (1905-91), publicist, political activist; village of Stari Sanzhary, was persecuted. • **Mstyslav (Stepan Skrypnyk)** (1898), His Holiness, the Patriarch of Kyiv and Ukraine; Poltava. • **S. Petlyura** (1879-1926), military and political leader, head of the Directory government of the Ukrainian National Republic; Poltava; assassinated in Paris. • **V. Samiylenko** (1864-1925), poet; village of Velyki Sorochyntsi in the Myrhorod district. • **M. Semenko** (1892-1938), Futurist poet; village of Kybyntsi in the Myrhorod district, executed. • **H. Skovoroda** (1722-94), writer, philosopher; Chornukhy. • **V. Symonenko** (1935-63), poet; village of Biyivtsi in the Lubny district. • **A. Teslenko** (1882-1911), writer; village of Kharkivtsi in the Lokhvytsya district. • **S. Velychko** (1670-1728), chronicler. • **F. Vovk** (1847-1918), ethnographer, anthropologist; village of Kryachkivka in the Pyryatyn district. • **V. Yaroshenko** (1898-1937), writer; village of Yakhnyky in the Lokhvytsya district; executed. • **M. Zerov** (1890-1937), literary scholar, poet, translator; Zinkiv; executed.

BURIED IN THE REGION:

D. Apostol (1654-1734), Hetman of Left-Bank Ukraine; village of Velyki Sorochyntsi in the Myrhorod district. • **P. Bodyansky** (1809-69), historian, ethnographer; Poltava. • **L. Borovykovsky** (1806-89), poet; village of Melyushky in the Khorol district. • **Ye. Hrebinka** (1812-48), writer; village of Maryanivka in the Hrebinka district. • **D. Huramishvili** (1705-92), Georgian poet; Myrhorod. • **V. Kapnist** (1758-1823), writer; village of Velyka Obukhivka in the Myrhorod district. • **V. Korolenko** (1853-1921), writer, civic activist; Poltava. • **I. Kotlyarevsky** (1769-1838), writer; Poltava. • **P. Myrny** (1849-1920), writer; Poltava. • **O. Slastion** (1855-1933), artist; Myrhorod. • **A. Teslenko** (1872-1911), writer; village of Kharkivtsi in the Lokhvytsya district. • **S. Velychko** (1670-1728), chronicler; village of Zhuky in the Poltava district.

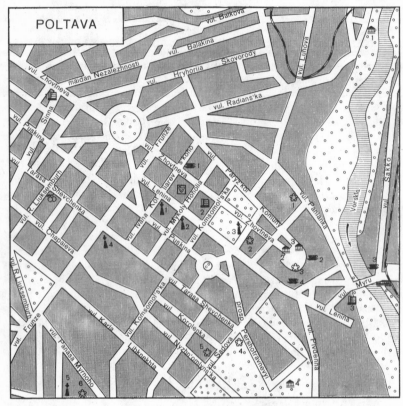

POLTAVA

🏛 ·Hotels:
  1 Kyïv
  2 Teatral´nyi
  3 Turyst ·

🍴 Restaurants:
  1 Teatral´nyi
  2 Lileia
  3 Lito
  4 Enei
  Note. Restaurants Kyïv and Turist are attached to the hotels of the same names

🚂 Railway Station Poltava-Pivdenna

🗿 Monuments:
  1 Ivan Kotliarevskyi
  2 Nikolai Gogol
  3 Taras Shevchenko
  4 M. V. Sklifosovsky
  5 Panas Myrnyi

🏛 Architectural monuments:
  1 Cathedral and bell-tower, 1689—
  1811
  2 Church of Our Savior, 1705
  3 Bell-tower of the Dormition
  Cathedral, 1774—1801
  4 Building of the former Institute
  for Daughters of the Nobility,
  1832

✿ Museums:
  1 Art
  2 Local Lore
  3 Museum-estate of Ivan Kotliarevskyi
  4 Ivan Kotliarevskyi Literary-Memorial
  5 Vladimir Korolenko Literary-Memorial
  6 Panas Myrnyi Literary-Memorial

🎭 Gogol   Theater   of   Music   and
Drama

POLTAVA

City, regional center, railway and autoroute junction located on the right bank of the Vorskla River, the left tributary of the Dnipro River, 333 km from Kyiv. Population: approx. 350,000. Telephone code: 0532.

Poltava is one of the most illustrious centers of Ukrainian national culture. Its precise date of founding is unknown. An ancient dwelling from the Paleolithic Age was unearthed in Bila Hora, one of the city districts. Remains of the Scythian and ancient Slavic cultures have been uncovered beneath Soborny Maydan.

A settlement known as Ltava was first described in the Hypatian Chronicle. The current name of the city was first mentioned in the 15th cent. In the 16th-17th cent. Poltava belonged to the Pereyaslav county seat. In 1646 Poltava was captured by Ya. Vyshnevetsky. During the liberation war of 1648 it was the base of the Poltava regiment. The Tatars raided the city several times, the final raid occurring in 1695. In the summer of 1709 a tragic battle was fought near Poltava between the armies of the Ukrainian Hetman I. Mazepa and Sweden's King Charles XII against the armies of the Russian Tsar Peter I. After being designated a provincial city in 1802, Poltava was subjected to Russian cultural expansion: the Russian style dominated architecture and the Russian language quickly replaced the Ukrainian language in schools and cultural institutions.

Out of a total of more than 30 high schools and gymnasiums, there are only 17 Ukrainian schools in Poltava. Only 44% of students study in the Ukrainian language.

CHURCHES, HISTORICAL AND ARCHITECTURAL MONUMENTS

SPASKA (REDEEMER'S) CHURCH, 1705-06. This wood church was built on the site of the Church of the Transfiguration of the Redeemer, which was destroyed

T. Shevchenko Monument, 1926.

by fire. It is the only example of 18th cent. wood architecture in the Poltava region. (Spaska St.).

KHRESTOVOZDVYZHENSKY (ELEVATION OF THE HOLY CROSS) CATHEDRAL, 1699-1709; **BELL TOWER,** 1786. Built with the aid of Kalistrat, the abbot of Lubny of the Mhar Monastery with funds provided by Kozak officers headed by Colonel M. Pushkar.

The 45-m. high four-story bell tower is built in the late Baroque style. T. Shevchenko painted the "Elevation" Monastery in 1845. The cathedral is the only seven-domed Ukrainian Ba-

Khrestovozdvyzhensky
(Elevation of the Holy Cross)
Cathedral, 1699-1709.

roque structure in Ukraine which has been preserved to the present time. It was transferred back to the church in 1992. (Suburb of Poltava, near the village of Chervony Shlyakh).

BELL TOWER OF THE USPENSKY (DORMITION) CATHEDRAL, 1774-1801. The Dormition Cathedral was the first stone structure to be built in Poltava. It was built in 1748-70 and destroyed in the 1930s. Only the bell tower remains intact. The height of the tower, including the spire, is approximately 44 m. The "Kyzykermen" bell, melted down from Turkish cannons in the late 18th cent., used to hang in the belfry. Today it is housed in the Ethnographic Museum. In 1992 the cathedral was transferred to the Ukrainian Autocephalous Orthodox Church. (Soborny Maydan, near the I. Kotlyarevsky Estate).

BUILDING OF THE THEOLOGICAL SEMINARY, 1875-76. S. Petlyura (1879-1925), the writers M. Nuayme (born in Lebanon, 1889-1988), P. Kapelhorodsky (1882-1937) and others studied here. Today it houses the Agricultural Institute. (Skovoroda St., 1).

THEOLOGICAL SCHOOL ("Bursa"), 1876. S. Petlyura graduated from the school a top student. Today it houses the Fruit Culture Technical School.

BUILDING OF THE PROVINCIAL ZEMSTVO (County council), 1903-08. Built in the Art Nouveau style by the architects V. Krychevsky and O. Shyrshov. The interior was painted by the artists S. Vasylkivsky and M. Samokysh. The facade is embellished with the coats of arms of the county cities of the province and decorated with ceramics and majolica made in Myrhorod and Opishnya. Today it houses an Ethnographic Museum. (Lenin St., 2).

BUILDING OF THE INSTITUTE FOR YOUNG NOBLEWOMEN. Built in 1828-32 by the architect L. Charlemagne. A third floor was added in 1866. During the 19th cent. P. Hulak-Artemovsky, L. Borovykovsky, P. Bodyansky, and other writers worked in the institute.

KRUHLA PLOSHCHA (ROUND SQUARE). In 1804-11 administrative buildings, including a meeting place for noblemen, the offices of the governor-general, and the main post office were built around the square.

KOTLYAREVSKY ESTATE. Reconstructed in 1969 by the architect V. Tertyshny and the builder A. Malynovska. The memorial complex includes a house, storehouse, pantry, and well with crane. T. Shevchenko's 1845 drawing of the estate was utilized by the builders. (Soborny Maydan or Ivanova Hora).

MONUMENTS

T. Shevchenko, 1926. Sculptor: I. Kavaleridze. In the form of a grave-mound sur-
mounted by the figure of T. Shevchenko. (Opposite the Ethnographic Museum).

I. Kotlyarevsky, 1903. Sculptor: L. Pozen.
Architect: O. Shyrshov. A tall pedestal sur-
mounted by a bronze bust of the poet; at the
base of the pedestal is a high relief depicting
scenes from the writer's works. (Kotlyarevsky
St., 7).

M. Hohol Music and
Drama Theater.

Grave of I. Kotlyarevsky. A tombstone erected in 1898 on the occasion of the
centenary of the publication of *Eneyida* (The Aeneid). Sculptor: L. Pozen. Artist: V.
Volkov. (I. Kotlyarevsky Park).

M. Hohol (Gogol), 1934. Sculptor: L. Pozen. (Intersection of Hohol and Lenin
Streets).

Shevchenko's Oak. Planted by the Poltava "Hromada" in May 1861 in com-
memoration of the relocation of the poet's body to Ukraine. A memorial plaque
hangs on the metal gate. (The tree is growing in an oak grove in the suburb of
Pavlenky).

MUSEUMS

Ethnographic Museum: ploshcha Lenina, 2; tel. 7-42-34. • **Art Museum:** Spaska St., 11; tel. 2-27-11; 7-27-46. • **Battle of Poltava History Museum:** Shvedska
Mohyla, 32; tel. 2-27-48. • **I. Kotlyarevsky Literary-Memorial Museum:** Pershotravnevy Prospekt, 18; tel. 7-41-60. • **I. Kotlyarevsky Estate:** Chervona Ploshcha,
3; tel. 7-20-73. • **V. Korolenko Literary-Memorial Museum:** Korolenko St., 1; tel.
7-22-00. • **Panas Myrny Building-Museum:** Myrny St., 56; tel. 3-12-27.

THEATERS, PHILHARMONIC

M. Hohol Music and Drama Theater: Zhovtneva St., 23. • **Puppet Theater:**
Pushkin St., 32. • **Philharmonic:** Hohol St., 10. • **Municipal Building of Culture:**
ploshcha Nezalezhnosti, 16.

HIGHER EDUCATIONAL INSTITUTIONS

Civil-Engineering Institute: provulok Pershotravnevy, 24. • **V. Korolenko Ped-
agogical Institute:** Ostrohradsky St., 2. • **Cooperative Institute:** Koval St., 3. •
Agricultural Institute: Skovoroda St., 1/3. • **Medical Stomatological Institute:**
Shevchenko St., 23.

LIBRARIES, ARCHIVES

I. Kotlyarevsky State Scientific Library: Shevchenko St., 3. • Youth Library: provulok Khorolsky, 3. • Regional Library: Gagarin St., 5. • Municipal Music and Theater Library: Lenin St., 4. • Regional State Archive: Pushkin St., 18/24.

PARKS

Peremoha Park of Culture and Recreation. • Zhovtnevy Park. • Petrovsky Park. • I. Kotlyarevsky Park. • Tree Park. • Youth Park.

SPORTS COMPLEXES

Kolos Stadium: ploshcha Dzerzhynskoho, 16; tel. 2-16-70, 2-14-86. • Swimming Pool: Frunze St., 9; tel. 7-06-04.

HOTELS

Ukrayina: Zhovtneva St., 41; tel. 2-43-43, 7-17-14. • Teatralny: Zhovtneva St., 19; tel. 2-43-21; 7-26-17. • Kyiv: Sinna St., 2/4; tel. 2-42-86, 2-42-81. • Turyst: Myru St., 12; tel. 2-09-21, 2-59-28. • Poltava Motel: Radnarkomivska St., 1; tel. 3-82-40, 3-00-24. • Zelena Dibrova: village of Kopyly in the Poltava district; tel. 2-25-63. • Lisny: village of Kopyly in the Poltava district; tel. 9-32-46, 9-32-44.

RESTAURANTS, CAFES, BARS

Velykotyrnovo: Proletarska St., 3; tel. 7-28-53. • Vechirni Zori: Kurchatov St., 14; tel. 4-29-94. • Dorozhniy: Kharkivske Shosse, 1; tel. 3-02-38. • Kyiv: Sinna St., 2; tel. 2-25-33. • Lileya: Chervona Ploshcha, 6; tel. 7-05-27. • Ltava: Hohol St., 33; tel. 7-05-17. • Poltava: Radnarkomivska St., 1; tel. 3-01-31. • Sady: 23 Veresnya St., 19; tel. 3-97-09. • Teatralny: Zhovtneva St., 26/14; tel. 2-56-27. Turyst: Myru St., 12; tel. 1-16-03. • Zirka: Zhovtneva St., 44; tel. 7-44-96. • Varenychna: Zinkivska St., 2. • Varenychna: Kalinin St., 11; tel. 3-66-04. • Dorozhna: Velykotyrnivska St., 3; tel. 6-58-98. • Iniy: Frunze St., 8. • Cafe: Airport; tel. 10-43-35. • Poltavski Halushky: Hohol St., 33; tel. 7-05-17. • Snizhynka: provulok Kosmichny, 16. • Ukrayinsky Borshch: Proletarska St., 20/20.; tel. 2-14-01. • Ukrayinsky Kulish: Marshall Biryuzov St., 40/1. • Cheburechna: Zinkivska St., 4; tel. 2-96-16.

STORES

Central Univermah (Department Store): Zhovtneva St., 28/13. • Avtotovary/ Sporttovary (Auto Accessories/Sports Equipment): Kyivske Shosse, 44. • Dytyachy Svit (Children's Department Store): Lenin St., 10/19. • Budynok Radio:

Zhovtneva St., 27. • **Mebli (Furniture):** Marshall Biryuzov St., 13. • **Moda:** Stepovoho Frontu St., 7. • **Molodizhny:** Velykotyrnivska St., 44. • **Narodni Promysly (Folk crafts):** Novy Bazar, 10. • **Poltavski Tovary:** Myru St., 9. • **Rubin:** Zhovtneva St., 27. • **Ukrayinsky Suvenir:** Zhovtneva St., 25. • **Cherevychky (Shoes):** Frunze St., 66. • **Yuvileyny:** Zhovtneva St., 74.

BANKS

Natsionalny bank Ukrayiny (National Bank of Ukraine, regional branch): Zhovtneva St., 17; tel. 2-16-01. • **Poltavsky komertsiyny bank (Poltava Commercial Bank):** Kotlyarevsky St., 2-a; tel. 2-78-63.

TOURISM

Regional Tourist and Excursion Council: Lenin St., 91; tel. 2-25-41, 1-17-07.
Travel and Excursion Agency: Lenin St., 91; tel. 1-14-70, 7-47-11.
Suputnyk International Youth Tourist Agency: Zyhin St., 1; tel. 2-49-26.
Inturyst: Radnarkomivska St., 1; tel. 3-57-47, 3-00-24.
Tourist Complex: Myru St., 12; tel. 2-59-28, 1-15-17.
Local Excursions: The Cities of Hohol (Poltava-Myrhorod-Sorochyntsi). • Hohol's Fatherland (Poltava-Dykanka-Hoholeve). • Dykanka's Old and New Glory (Poltava-Dykanka). • Visits with Folk Craftsmen (Poltava-Opishnya). • Landmark of Shumeykove (Poltava-Shumeykove). • The Poltava Battle-Field. • Ivanova Hora (I. Kotlyarevsky's Estate).

CULTURAL PRESERVES

Scythian Settlement: village of Bilsk in the Kotelva district.
Drahomanov and Kosach Estate: city of Hadyach.
Ancestral Home of the Philosopher and Poet H. Skovoroda Memorial Complex (estate, museum): village of Chornukhy.
Muravyov-Apostol Estate: village of Khomutets in the Myrhorod district.
Tree Park: village of Ustymivka in the Hlobyne district.
Mhar Monastery: Lubny district.
Kochubey Estate: village of Dykanka.
M. Hohol Museum and Cultural Preserve: village of Hoholeve in the Shyshaky district.
A. Makarenko Museum and Cultural Preserve: village of Kovalivka in the Poltava district.

SOUVENIRS OF POLTAVA

Typical souvenirs: Opishnya ceramics, embroideries from Poltava and Reshety-livka, Chornukhy willow crafts (baskets, shoes), wood carvings from Myrhorod and Kremenchuk, wool comforters and porcelain from Lubny.

POST OFFICES, TELEPHONE

Main post office: Zhovtneva St., 33; tel. 7-47-07, 7-20-29.
Telegraph-Telephone Station: Zhovtneva St., 33; tel. 7-20-01, 7-20-11.
Inter-urban calling points: Frunze St., 21; Proletarska St., 8; Khalturin St., 7.

MEDICAL SERVICES

Emergency: tel. 03.
Municipal Stomatological Polyclinic: Komsomolska St., 50; tel. 7-20-70; 7-22-39.
Private Polyclinic: Komsomolska St., 50; tel. 2-42-77.
Pharmacies: Chapayev St., 1; tel. 7-23-18. • Zhovtneva St., 32; tel. 7-31-14, 7-20-05. • Zhovtneva St., 73; tel. 7-50-18, 7-50-52. • Shevchenko St., 28; tel. 2-18-80.

TRANSPORTATION

Train stations: Poltava-Southern: ploshcha Slavy, 1; tel. 1-20-01. • Poltava-Kyiv: Kondratenko St., 12; tel. 10-72-53.
Bus terminus: Velykotyrnivska St., 1; tel. 6-57-93, 3-96-79.
Bus station No. 2: Shevchenko St., 65-a; tel. 7-44-10.
Airport: Ivashky Village; tel. 7-38-05.
Taxi reservations: tel. 058.

AUTO SERVICING

Autoservis: village of Kopyly in the Poltava district; tel. 7-29-58. • Komsomolsk: Portova St., 25; tel. 7-42-65. • Pyryatyn: Chervonoarmiyska St., 167; tel. 2-07-95.

TOURING HISTORIC CITIES AND VILLAGES

BILSK

Village in the Kotelevtsi district.

Nearby is the largest fortified settlement from Scythian times. Archaeologists believe that the ancient city of Helon, mentioned by Herodotus, was located here. Ancient barrows — the necropolis of the Helonians — have been preserved. The area of the settlement is 4,500 ha. The walls are 27.6 km long.

CHORNUKHY

Village located 2 km from the Kyiv-Sumy autoroute, 35 km from the Pyryatyn railway station, and 230 km from Poltava.

Was first mentioned in documents for the year 1261. Earthen ramparts (the so-called "forest settlement") have been preserved. Owned by the Vyshnevetsky magnates from the late 16th cent. In 1658 Hetman I. Vyhovsky was defeated in battle here. Was designated a district town in Lokhvytsya county in 1803. The philosopher and poet H. Skovoroda was born here in 1722. In 1972 the estate of H. Skovoroda's parents was reconstructed and today it houses the Historical-Ethnographic Museum.

DYKANKA

Village and center of the Dykanka district located 25 km from Poltava.

This village, first mentioned in documents dating to 1658, was the ancestral home of the Kochubey family. Only a few "Kochubey" trees remain of the ancient grove that once surrounded the palace. The palace, designed by the architect Cuarengi contained over 100 rooms, an art gallery, museum, and library, all of which were destroyed during the Bolshevik Revolution of 1917. In 1668 rebellious Kozaks killed Hetman Bryukhovetsky in Dykanka (he was buried in Hadyach). In 1709, on the eve of the Battle of Poltava, Hetman I. Mazepa was billeted here. The army staff of Sweden's King Charles XII was billeted in the nearby village of Velyki Budyshcha.

Dykanka. Mykolayivska (St. Nicholas') Church, 1794.

MYKOLAYIVSKA (ST. NICHOLAS') CHURCH, 1794; **BELL TOWER,** 1810. Built in the Classical style by the architect N. Lvov, this was the ancestral church and tomb of the Kochubey family. It once housed a museum of atheism and a branch of an ethnographic museum.

*Mhar. Mhar Monastery,
17th-18th cent.*

TROYITSKA (HOLY TRINITY) CHURCH, 1780. Built in the Baroque style by the architect M. Orlov. According to legend, Vakula, one of the characters in Hohol's story "Christmas Eve" painted the devil in this church.

Monuments to T. Shevchenko and M. Hohol, sculpted by L. Ilchenko and an Ethnographic Museum are located in the village.

HADYACH

City and railway station on the Psel River. Population: 24,000.

It was first mentioned in Polish documents dating to the first half of the 17th cent. and from 1648 was the base of the Hadyach Kozak regiment. In 1658 Hetman I. Vyhovsky signed the Treaty of Hadyach with the Poles. In 1782 the city became part of the viceregencies of Chernihiv and Kyiv. In 1802 it was designated a city in Poltava province. I. Bryukhovetsky, who was elected Hetman of Left-Bank Ukraine during the so-called "Black Council" of Kozaks in 1663, was buried here in 1668. Two km from the city is located the Zeleny Hay survey mark, where the Ukrainian poetess Lesya Ukrayinka lived and worked in an estate from 1899 to 1906. A memorial tablet is located on the site of the estate. The building in which the Ukrainian writer P. Myrny lived with his parents from 1858 to 1865 has been preserved.

VSIKHSVYATSKA (ALL SAINTS') CHURCH, 1836. Built in the Classical style.

HOHOLEVE (Vasylivka, Yanovshchyna)

Village in the Shyshaky district and the ancestral home of V. Hohol-Yanovsky (1777-1825). M. Hohol spent his childhood and adolescence here and returned in later years to visit his mother and sisters. In 1984 the M. Hohol's parents' estate (house, pavilion, and park) was reconstructed. Today it houses a museum and cultural preserve.

HRYNKY

Village in the Hlobyne district, located 17 km from the district center.

The ancestral home of the eminent Ukrainian composer M. Lysenko (1842-1912), who was born here and spent his youth. A monument to the composer is located in the village.

MHAR

Village on the Sula River, 6 km from Lubny.

MHAR MONASTERY, 17th-18th cent. Founded in 1619. The monastery complex includes: the Preobrazhensky (Transfiguration) Cathedral (1684-92), designed by the architects I. Baptyst, M. Tomashevsky, and A. Pyryatynsky. Its original appearance was altered after reconstruction. The interior contains a bas-relief. The cathedral is one of the finest Ukrainian Baroque structures combining the ancient Ukrainian architectural style of the 11th-12th cent. with Western European Baroque-Renaissance architecture; Bell Tower (1785, enlarged in 1837-44). Built in the Baroque style; Tepla Church (19th cent.) Built in the pseudo-Byzantine style. In 1654 the Patriarch of Constantinople Pattelariy (born 1580) was buried in a seated position in the monastery. Taras Shevchenko, who visited the monastery, mentions "the seated one" in his story *Blyznyata* (The Twins). In 1918 the Bolsheviks carried out a pogrom of the monastery and shot the abbot and 17 monks.

MYRHOROD

City on the Khorol River, 105 km from Poltava on the Kyiv-Poltava railway line. Founded in the 16th cent., the city was the base of the Myrhorod regiment from 1648. During the liberation war against the Poles, Hetman B. Khmelnytsky spent time here. It was designated a county city in 1802 and a district center in 1923.

SPASOPREOBRAZHENSKA (TRANSFIGURATION OF THE REDEEMER) CHURCH, 1732. The church features elements of the Ukrainian Baroque style. Seventeenth cent. canvasses and wall paintings have been preserved.

Monuments to T. Shevchenko and **M. Hohol,** an **ethnographic museum,** and a **balneological health resort** are located in the city.

OPISHNYA

Village in the Zinkiv district located 45 km from Poltava, on the Poltava-Hadyach autoroute.

This village is an ancient Ukrainian ceramics center. Opishnya ceramics are exhibited through-

Myrhorod. Myrhorod Resort.

Plishyvets. Pokrovska (Protection of the Blessed Virgin Mary) Church, 1906.

out the world and have been purchased by major museums.

A **National Museum** and **Cultural Preserve** devoted to Ukrainian pottery is located in the village.

PLISHYVETS

Village in the Hadyach district located on the right bank of the Psel River, 25 km from Hadyach.

POKROVSKA (PROTECTION OF THE BLESSED VIRGIN MARY) CHURCH, 1906. An example of Ukrainian national architecture, this church is a copy of a wood Kozak cathedral in Novomoskovsk, built in the 18th cent. It is almost 30 m high. The church was built between 1858 and the early 1920s with funds provided by Archbishop Parfeniy (born Pamfyl Levytsky) who was born in the village.

VELYKI SOROCHYNTSI

Village on the Psel River in the Myrhorod district.

Founded in the 17th cent., the village was the residence of Hetman D. Apostol in the 18th cent. The Sorochyntsi Fair is held yearly on the last Sunday of August.

PREOBRAZHENSKA (TRANSFIGURA- TION) CHURCH, 1732. Built in the Ukrainian Baroque style, the church was the burial place of the Ukrainian Kozak Hetmans. It contains a unique carved iconostasis (20 m long and 17 m high), one hundred 17 cent. paintings, and icons of the church's patrons — the Hetman and his wife Ulyana. M. Hohol was baptized in this church.

A **monument to M. Hohol** is located in the village.

Velyki Sorochyntsi. Preobrazhenska (Transfiguration) Church, 1732.

VYSHNYAKY

Village on the Khorol River in the Khorol district, 3 km from the district center.

TROYITSKY (HOLY TRINITY) CHURCH, 1794-99. Features elements from the transitional period from the Baroque to Classical styles.

ESTATE, 1805. Built in the Classical style by the architect N. Lvov.

T. Shevchenko, who visited here in 1845, refers to these buildings in his story *Blyznyata* (The Twins).

Rivne Region

It is situated on the Polissian plain and Volynian plateau and is densely intersected by many rivers. The largest of them is the Prypyat and its tributaries, the Horyn and Styr Rivers. This region has many lakes, especially in Polissia. The largest of them are Bile, Somyne, and Nobel. Forests occupy 38% of the territory. Seven northern districts in this region were exposed to radioactive fallout after the nuclear disaster at the Chernobyl power station. Created in 1939. Area: 20.1 thousand sq. km. Population: 1,186,400 inhabitants.

History

The first traces of human settlement date back to the Late Paleolithic Age. In 3rd-2nd cent. B.C. and the 2nd-3rd centuries the territory of the present region was settled by the early Slavic tribes of Zarubenets and Chernyakhiv cultures. In the 6th-7th centuries a state union of tribes headed by the Duliby-Volynians was established here. Approximately 100 remains of ancient settlements and graves have been excavated in the Rivne region. Settlements of Chernyakhiv culture near Varkovychi and Pidluzzhya in the Dubnivsky district and ruins of cities dating to the 10th century have been found. In the 10th century these lands were part of Kyivan Rus'-Ukraine. The towns of Dorohobuzh and Peresopnytsya (now — villages), which were centers of various independent principalities in the 11th-12th centuries, played a significant role in the history of this region. The "Dubnivske" (1539-1568), "Dorohobuzke" (1556-1561), and "Peresopnytske" Gospels (1556-1561) were written here. In 1991 L. Kravchuk, the President of Ukraine, swore an oath on the "Peresopnytske" Gospel. A monument has been erected in the village of Peresopnytsya in honor of this holy book.

Rivne Region. View of historic Ostroh.

The Rivne region of today once belonged to the Polician-Volynian Principality. After its decline in 1457 it came under Lithuanian rule. Polish expansionism in this region commenced with the signing of the Treaty of Lublin. In the 1570s Ostroh became an important political, economic, and cultural center and was known as the "Volynian Athens". Peasant rebellions took place in Derman, Ostroh, and Dubno in 1630-1636. A strong popular movement emerged during the liberation war of 1648-1654. During this time all of Rivne was affected by these rebellions. In the summer of 1651 B. Khmelnytsky's Kozak army fought a major battle against the Polish army in Berestechko, near the village of Plyasheva in the Radyvylivsky region.

Under the terms of the Treaty of Andrusiv (1667) this region remained under Polish control. In 1793 it came under Russian control. With the signing of the Treaty of Riga (1921) Rivne, as part of the voivodeship of Volyn, was annexed by Poland and in 1939 by the USSR.

PROMINENT INDIVIDUALS

BORN IN THE REGION:

L. Kravchuk (1934), President of Ukraine, village of Velyky Zhytyn in the Rivnensky district. • **V. Polishchuk** (1897-1937), poet, village of Bilche in the Mlynivsky district; died in prison. • **U. Samchuk** (1905-1987), writer, village of Derman, now Uspenske Druhe in the Zdolbunivsky district. • **M. Zhulynsky** (1940), critic, literary scholar, village of Novosilky in the Mlynivsky district.

BURIED IN THE REGION:

M. Smotrytsky (1572-1633), polemicist, religious-educational activist, Derman (now Uspenske Druhe).

RIVNE

City, an administrative center of the region. It is situated on the Ustya River, 321 km. from Kyiv. Population: approximately 300,000. Telephone code: 0362.

The city is first mentioned in 1282, the date of a battle fought between the Lithuanian and Polish armies. In the 16th century it became an important trading town. Despite frequent Tatar raids, the city quickly expanded and in the 15th century adopted the "Magdeburg law." During the liberation war of 1648-1654 Rivne was the site of a popular uprising. Russian armies entered the city in 1660, Polish armies in 1667, and Swedish forces in 1706.

Musical-Drama Theater.

In 1793 the city became a district center of the Volynian vice-regency under Russian rule. A gymnasium was established in 1839. Today the Regional Ethnographic Museum is located on its premises. During World War II the city was the capital of German-occupied Ukraine.

CHURCHES, HISTORICAL AND ARCHITECTURAL MONUMENTS

USPENSKA (DORMITION) CHURCH, 1756. According to legend, Ivan Gonta and the haydamaky prayed here before their battle with the Poles. The "chain of

Rivne park.

moral foundations" is preserved in the church vestibule. During the 18th century sinful parishioners were chained to it and forced to make public repentance. (Shevchenko St., 113).

VOSKRESENSKY (RESURRECTION) CATHEDRAL, 1895. A typical example of the Ukrainian style in late-19th century architecture. Until 1991 it housed a museum of atheism. (Soborna St., 39).

MUSEUMS

Museum of Regional Ethnography: Drahomanov St., 19; tel.2-33-67. • **National-cultural Youth Center:** Petlyura St., 31; tel. 2-69-01.

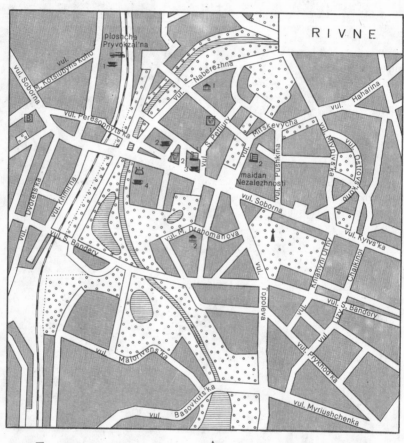

ploshcha Pryvokzal'na

RIVNE

vul. Soborna
vul. Kotsiubyns'koho
vul. Naberezhna
vul. Haharina
vul. Peresopnytska
vul. Mitskevycha
vul. S. Petliury
vul. Myrnva'ka
vul. Ostrovs'koho
vul. Pushkina
vul. Khmiura
maidan Nezalezhnosti
vul. Dvorets'ka
vul. Soborna
vul. Kyivs'ka
vul. Chaikhnoi
vul. S. Bandery
vul. M. Drahomanova
Kniazhni Olhy
vul. Topoleva
vul. S. Bandery
vul. Pryktnodka
vul. Malorivens'ka
vul. Myriushchenka
vul. Basovkuts'ka

B	Excursion office
	Hotels:
	1 Rivne
	2 Myr
	Restaurants:
	1 Vokzal'nyi
	2 Teatral'nyi
	3 Ukraïna
	4 Sport
	Railway Station

Monument to Taras Shevchenko

Architectural monuments:
1 Dormition Church, 18th c.
2 Building of the former gymnasium, 19th c.

Theaters:
1 Puppet
2 Music and Drama

Philharmonic Society

THEATERS, PHILHARMONIC

Musical-Drama Theater: ploshcha Teatralna, 1. • **Puppet Theater:** Petlyura St., 27. • **Philharmonic:** Drahomanov St., 4.

HIGHER EDUCATIONAL INSTITUTIONS

Institute of Electrical Engineering: Soborna St., 11. • **Pedagogical Institute:** Ostafov St., 37. • **Institute of Culture:** Bandera St., 12.

LIBRARIES, ARCHIVES

Science Library: Korolenko St., 6. • **Youth Library:** Kyivska St., 18. • **Childrens' Library:** Petlyura St., 43. • **Regional Archives:** Bandera St., 26

PARKS

Central Park of Culture and Recreation: Soborna St., 3-d. • **Hydropark.**

SPORTS COMPLEXES

Avanhard Stadium: Zamkova St., 34; tel. 2-32-27; 2-09-45. • **Avanhard Swimming Pool:** September 17th St., 82-a; tel. 3-52-27.

HOTELS

Myr: Mickiewicz St., 32; tel. 2-12-55. • **Rivne:** Soborna St., 112; tel. 2-50-26. • **Turyst:** Kyivska St., 36; tel. 6-18-96.

RESTAURANTS, CAFES

Myr: Mickiewicz St., 10; tel. 2-57-10. • **Horyn:** Kyivska St., 97; tel. 3-30-57. • **Lebid:** Naberezhna St., 1-a; tel. 6-94-13. • **Ukrayina:** Soborna St., 156; tel. 2-34-13. • **Turyst:** Kyivska St., 36; tel. 6-76-88. • **Druzhba:** Dvoretska St., 97; tel. 2-10-54. • **Teatralny:** Teatralna St., 1; tel. 2-21-13.

STORES

Central Department Store (Univermah): Soborna St., 17. • **Vidin Department Store:** Kurchatov St., 2. • **Slovo:** Soborna St., 57. • **Podarunky:** Myr St., 4.

BANKS

National Bank of Ukraine (Regional Branch): Petlyura St., 10; tel. 2-12-54. • **Stockholding Bank of Economic Developments "Ekonombank:"** Drahomaniv St., 32; tel. 2-04-95, 6-66-83. • **Cooperative Bank "Perspektyva:"** Orlov St., 39; tel. 4-32-99. • **Cooperative Bank "Izumrud:"** Soborna St., 195; tel. 6-38-00; 6-28-98. • **Commercial Bank "Zorya:"** Village Zorya; tel. 7-96-92, 7-93-85. • **Commercial Bank "Nyva:"** Drahomaniv St., 29.

TOURISM

Suputnyk: Pravda St., 1; tel. 2-22-85.

Excursion itineraries: Rivne — "Kozak Graves" Preserve. • Rivne-Pochayiv. • Rivne-Ostroh. • Rivne-Lutsk.

Rivneturyst: Kyivska St., 36; tel. 6-69-75.

Excursions to the ancient cities and villages in Rivne and other regions: "Rivne-Ostroh and vicinity"; Rivne-Korets; Rivne-Peresopnytsya; Rivne-Kremenets; "Route to Berestechko" excursion.

POST OFFICES

Main post office: Soborna St., 56; tel. 2-22-40.

Central calling point: Soborna St., 38.

Telegraph office: Soborna St., 56; tel. 2-42-25.

MEDICAL SERVICES

Emergency: tel. 03.

Pharmacies: No. 1: Nezalezhnist St., 3; tel. 2-20-65. • No. 48: Chernyak St., 8; tel. 4-11-93.

TRANSPORTATION

Train station: Pryvokzalna St., 1; tel. 9-12-58. **Cashier:** tel. 9-14-01. **Advance ticket office:** Kikvidze St., 16-a; tel. 9-14-02.

Bus terminus: Kyivska St., 34; tel. 004.

Tickets: Kyivska St., 70; tel. 2-45-31.

Airport: tel. 2-10-62.

Air Ukraine International: Myr St., 8; tel. 008, 2-67-11.

AUTO SERVICING

Ukrinteravtoservis: Gagarin St., 30; tel. 4-10-88.

TOURING HISTORIC CITIES AND VILLAGES

DERMAN

Village, Zdolbuniv district, 28 km. from the district center.

DERMANSKY MONASTERY, 1449. Written sources first mention this monastery in connection with the presentation by Prince K. Ostrozky of the manuscript book "Poucheniye" (Teachings) with autograph to the monastic church. The monastery had great land holdings. In 1575-1576 its director was the first printer, I. Fedorov. In 1602 a printing house and school of theology were founded in Derman. The monastery owned a valuable library of manuscripts and ancient printed books. From 1627 the prior of the monastery was the Ukrainian writer and polemicist, M. Smotrytsky. The Troyitska Church (Holy Trinity, 15th c.), a bell tower, and monks' cells have been preserved.

DUBNO

City, 45 km. from Rivne, on the Ikva River.

One of Ukraine's most ancient cities. First mentioned in the chronicle for the year 1100. Adopted the "Magdeburg law." Markets lasting four weeks were held here for twenty years (1774-1794).

CASTLE, 16th cent. Built near an ancient Ukrainian city. It was rebuilt in the 17th century according to the neo-Italian system of fortifications. In the 18th century it forfeited its strategic significance and was re-constructed. M. HoHol described the city in his work *Taras Bulba*. At various times it belonged to the Princes Ostrozky and Lyubomyrsky. Taras Shevchenko visited the city in 1846.

SPASO-PREOBRAZHENSKA (TRANSFIGURATION OF THE REDEEMER) CHURCH, 17th cent.

HEORHIYIVSKA (ST. GEORGE'S) CHURCH, 1709; **BELL TOWER,** 1869. Wooden structures.

CHURCH OF THE ST. BERNARD MONASTERY, 17th cent. Built in the Rococo style. Paintings dating to the 18th century have been preserved.

CARMELITE CONVENT COMPLEX, 1630-1686. Built in the early Rococo style.

LUTSKY GATES, 15th-16th cent. Located on the road from Dubno to Lutsk, the gates were the foundations of the city fortifications. Architecturally, the gates are a unique example of defense fortifications, not found anywhere else in Ukraine.

HOSHCHA

City, 30 km. from Rivne.

A unique park, established in the early 18th century, is located in the town. The park, an important national nature preserve, is modelled on an English maze garden. Among the trees growing in the park are the gingko and Japanese pagoda tree. The trunks of certain ash and chestnut trees are 2 m. in diameter.

MYKHAYLIVSKA (ST. NICHOLAS') CHURCH, 1639. It acquired its present appearance after reconstruction in 1888. Its architectural construction is unique.

KLEVAN

Village, Rivne district, 25 km. from Rivne.

CASTLE, 1475. Built as a defense structure on the site of an ancient Ukrainian city on the Stubla River. One of the oldest castles in Volyn. A brilliant example of Volynian defense architecture of the 15th-18th centuries.

RIZDVA (NATIVITY) CHURCH, 1777; **BELL TOWER,** 1844. Built in the early Classical style of Volyn.

BLAHOVISHCHENSKY (ANNUNCIATION) ROMAN CATHOLIC CHURCH, 1610-1630. Restored in 1747, 1830, 1901. Built in the early Rococo style of Volyn.

KORETS

City, 60 km. from Rivne. First mentioned in the Hypatian Chronicle for the year 1150.

TROYITSKY (HOLY TRINITY) CONVENT COMPLEX, 1620. Originally a Franciscan one, in 1863 it was transferred to the Orthodox. The convent complex

Korets. Troyitska Church, 1620.

includes the Troyitska (Holy Trinity) church (1620) with paintings of the 19th century, cells (1620), the church of Ivan Predtecha (St. John the Baptist) (1890), bell tower (1905). The architectural style of the convent reflects the particular features of Ukrainian art of the 17th-19th centuries.

MYKOLAYIVSKA (ST. NICHOLAS') CHURCH, 1834. Nineteenth-century paintings are located in the center of the church. Its architectural style combines Classical features with the style of Ukrainian wooden churches.

CASTLE, 15th-18th cent. Located on a hill, on the Korchyk River. Was a defense structure with a wall and moat. Was rebuilt as a castle in the Baroque style in 1780.

SV. ANTONIYA (ST. ANTHO-NY'S) ROMAN CATHOLIC CHURCH, 1533. In 1706 the interior of the church was decorated in the Baroque style. Was rebuilt in 1916. Eighteenth-century paintings have been preserved. The structure of the church combines architectural elements of the 16th-18th centuries and early 20th.

MEZHYRICH

Village, Ostroh district, 4 km. from Ostroh.

Mezhyrich. Troyitsky Monastery-Fortress, 15th-17th c.

In 1386 the Lithuanian Prince Vitaut issued a decree confirming Prince Ostrozky's right to the village, which adopted the "Magdeburg law" in 1605.

TROYITSKY (HOLY TRINITY) MONASTERY-FORTRESS, 15th-17th cent. One of the most renowned architectural complexes built in Ukraine in the 15th-17th centuries, whose construction reflects Volynian architecture with ancient Ukrainian elements and the Gothic-Renaissance style of the 15th-16th centuries. Several icons, among them the most valuable icon "Mother of God" from the 16th century, have been preserved.

OSTROH

City located on the Viliya River, 14 km. from the Ostroh railway stations, 46 km. from Rivne.

One of the oldest cities in Ukraine. First mentioned in the Hypatian Chronicle for the year 1100. At the end of the 16th century Ostroh became an important cultural and educational center. A Greek-Slavonic-Latin Collegium was founded here, as well as a printing center set up by I. Fedorov (in operation until 1612). The Ostrozka Bible was published here in 1581.

One of the most important monuments of Ukrainian historiography and literature of the 17th century is the "Ostrozky Chronicler" which describes events transpiring in Volyn and Galicia from 1500 to 1636.

PALACE, 14th-19th cent. Situated on a twenty-meter high hill, on the site of a former ancient Ukrainian city of the 11th-12th centuries. The "Zamkova Hora" complex includes a walled tower (1386) located on the slope of the hill. In the 16th century the palace was decorated in the Renaissance style and was rebuilt in the 19th century. In 1913-1915, after repairs and reconstruction, the palace was converted into a historical museum, library, and lecture hall (architect: V. Leontovych) and later, into a local ethnographic museum. It is a unique structure of the defense architecture of medieval Volyn. The palace complex includes the new tower, an important mon-

Ostroh. Lutsk Gate Tower, 15th c.

ument of Ukrainian architecture of the 16th century; the Bohoyavlennya (Epiphany) Church (15th-16th cent.), which combines elements of ancient Ukrainian church construction and Ukrainian architecture of the 16th-17th centuries.

Reconstruction of the church in the Gothic-Renaissance style in 1887-1891 changed its original appearance. The palace was the burial place of the Ostrozky princes and its silhouette was used as the city's coat-of-arms.

LUTSK GATE TOWER, 15th-16th cent. The tower protected the city from the side overlooking the road to Lutsk. Certain parts of the tower are built in the Renaissance style. An original example of the defense structures in Ukraine of the 16th century.

TATAR GATE TOWER, 15th-16th cent. Part of the complex of city fortifications, protected the city from side overlooking the road to Zvyahel (Novhorod-Volynsky).

USPENSKY (DORMITION) ROMAN CATHOLIC CHURCH, 15th-19th cent. Originally an Orthodox church, in 1442 it was rebuilt as a Roman Catholic Church of the Dominican Monastery. In 1887 it acquired pseudo-Gothic features and in 1897 the church was rebuilt in the Classical style.

MUSEUMS

Ethnographic Museum: Akademichna St., 5. • **History of Books and Printing Museum:** Papanin St., 3. • **Art Museum:** Akademichna St., 5. • **Ostrozky State Historical-Cultural Preserve:** Akademichna St., 5.

PLYASHEVA

Village, Radyvyliv district, 60 km. from the district center.

Near the village in June 1651 the Battle of Berestechko took place between the Ukrainian army of B. Khmelnytsky and the Polish army of King Jan Casimir. In the early stages of the battle the Ukrainian army was victorious, but at the height of fighting B. Khmelnytsky was betrayed

Ostroh. Round Tower, 15th c.

and captured by the retreating forces of the Crimean Khan Islam Ghirey III. The Poles immediately took advantage of this situation. An eyewitness, the Frenchman P. Chevalier, provided this description: "In one place, in a muddy patch of land, was a group of three hundred Kozaks valiantly defending themselves against a large number of attackers pressing on them from all directions. Finally, completely surrounded, the Kozaks perished. Only one remained and he fought for three hours alone against the entire Polish army." In 1846 Taras Shevchenko visited the battle site and dedicated his poem "The Field of Berestechko" to this tragic page in Ukrainian history.

HEORHIYIVSKA (ST. GEORGE'S) CHURCH-MAUSOLEUM, 1910-1914. Built by the architect V. Maksymov. The interior and exterior paintings were executed by the artist I. Yizhakevych. The church is a unique monument combining features of the Ukrainian Baroque with modern architecture. It was built in memory of the Kozaks who perished in the Battle of Berestechko. In 1967 it was converted into the "Kozak Graves" Historical-Cultural Preserve.

MYKHAYLIVSKA (ST. NICHOLAS') CHURCH, 1650. According to legend, on the eve of the Battle of Berestechko B. Khmelnytsky obtained a personal blessing from the Corinthian Metropolitan Ioasaph. The blessing of Kozak swords took place in this church, which is one of the oldest wooden churches in Volyn. Since 1967 it has housed the "Kozak Graves" Historical-Cultural Preserve.

MONUMENT IN HONOR OF THE 540TH ANNIVERSARY OF THE BATTLE OF BERESTECHKO, 1991. Every summer the memory of fallen Ukrainian Kozaks is honored.

Sumy Region

Located in northeastern Ukraine, in the Dnipro Lowland. It lies in the Polissya and forest-steppe zones. The climate is temperate-continental. It has 132 rivers that flow into the Dnipro Basin. In the north and east the region borders on three Russian regions. Are: 23.800 sq. km. Population: 1,431,000.

History

The settlement of the region began approximately 15,000 years ago. During the Bronze Age the area was inhabited by the ancient Slavic farming and cattle-breeding tribes. With the discovery of iron ore in the Dnipro River region (8th cent. B.C.), almost all the lands were settled by Scythian farmers. In the 7th-10th cent. the area was inhabited by the Slavic Siveriany tribe.

From the 9th cent. the Sumy lands were part of Kyivan Rus'-Ukraine, namely the Pereyaslav and the Chernihiv Principalities, and in the mid-12th cent., part of Novhorod-Siversky Principality. During this time many cities were built. Fierce battles among the various princes were fought, especially during the 1140s. The Polovtsian tribe took advantage of these destructive wars and launched attacks on the principalities. Their unsuccessful crusade against the Novhorod-Siversky Prince Ihor and other princes, is the subject of the oldest Ukrainian literary epic "The Tale of Ihor's Host." In 1239 the Tatars destroyed many ancient cities in the land. The Tatar Khans treated the population cruelly and much of the population perished at their hands.

In the 1350s-60s the Lithuanian Principality captured a major part of the present-day Sumy region. According to the peace treaty of 1503, which ended the war with Lithuania, almost all the Chernihiv and Siversk territories became part of the Muscovite State. The city of Putyvl became an important border point. In the early 17th cent. Polish incursions in the area intensified, accompanied by harsh colonial policies and violence which was directed at the population of the occupied Ukrainian lands. In 1652 the city of Romny was one of the

Sumy.

centers of anti-Polish peasant uprisings. In the 17th cent. the Tsarist administration donated these lands to the Russian nobility, as a result of which serfdom was introduced in the region. During the Second World War the region was devastated by numerous battles and approximately 111,000 people were killed.

PROMINENT INDIVIDUALS

BORN IN THE REGION:

B. Antonenko-Davydovych (1899-1984), writer; Romny. • **I. Bahryany** (1907-63), writer, political figure; in Kuzemyn, Okhtyrka district. • **M. Berezovsky** (1745-77), composer; in Hlukhiv. • **D. Bortnyansky** (1751-1825), composer; in Hlukhiv. • **P. Hrabovsky** (1864-1902), poet; in Pushkarne (now Hrabovske), Krasnopil district. • **O. Hryshchenko** (1883-1977), painter, art critic; in Korolevets, died in France. • **I. Kavaleridze** (1887-1978) sculptor, film director, playwright; in Ladansky Khutir (now Novopetrivka). • **M. Khvylovy-Fitilyov** (1893-1933), writer, publicist, political figure; in Trostyanets. • **L. Kovalenko** (1936-93) journalist, co-editor of memorial book *Famine — 33;* in Bochechky, Konotop district. • **F. Krychevsky** (1879-1947), painter; in Lebedyn. • **V. Krychevsky** (1873-1952), artist, architect; in Vorozhba, Lebedyn district, died in Venezuela. • **P. Kulish** (1819-97), writer, literary critic, political and cultural figure; in Voronizh, Shostka district. • **M. Lukash** (1919-1988), translator, linguist; in Krolevets. • **M. Markevych** (1804-60), historian, writer, ethnographer; in Dunaytsi, Hlukhiv district. • **O. Markovych** (1790-1865), historian, ethnographer; in Svarkove, Hlukhiv district. • **H. Narbut** (1886-1920), artist; in Narbutivka, Sumy district. • **O. Oles-Kandyba** (1878-1944), poet; in Bilopillya, died in Czechoslovakia. • **O. Vyshnya-Hubenko** (1889-1956), writer; in Hrun, Okhtyrka district.

BURIED IN THE REGION:

O. Lazarevsky (1834-1902), historian; in Pidlypne, Konotop district. • **A. Tereshchenko** (1800-73), patron of the arts, owner of sugar refineries; in Hlukhiv. • **H. Zatyrkevych-Karpynska** (1855-1921), actress; in Romny.

SUMY

City and regional center on the banks of the Pslo River and its tributaries Sumka and Strilky. Population: 200,000. Telephone code: 05422.

Established in 1655. Scholars have identified it as the city of Lypetsk as described in the chronicles. The population suffered greatly from various invaders. In 1656-58 one of the mightiest fortresses in Slobozhanshchyna was built here. In 1658 Sumy became the center of the Slobidsky Kozak Regiment, which distinguished itself in battles with the Turks in 1677-78.

During the 18th-19th cent. trades and industrial enterprises flourished here. After regimental rule was abolished, the Kozak regiment became a Hussars' regiment. The abolition of serfdom in 1861 helped to spur industrial development. Before the First World War there were nearly forty enterprises in the city.

Many distinguished individuals are connected with the city. The Ukrainian philosopher and poet H. Skovoroda visited Sumy many times in the 18th cent. T. Shevchenko visited Sumy in 1859. The writers B. Hrinchenko and V. Korolenko, as well as the composer Peter Tchaykovsky visited Sumy on numerous occasions.

CHURCHES, HISTORICAL AND ARCHITECTURAL MONUMENTS

VOSKRESENSKA (RESURRECTION) CHURCH, 1702. A two-tiered structure with a picturesque interior. One of the most outstanding monuments of the Slobozhanska school Ukrainian Baroque architecture, with three cupolas; stone. The church houses a Museum of Decorative and Applied Art.

BELL TOWER OF THE VOSKRESENSKA (RESURRECTION) CHURCH, 1906. Built in the Baroque style; a brick structure.

SPASO-PREOBRAZHENSKY (TRANSFIGURATION OF THE REDEEMER) CATHEDRAL, 1776-88. The 56 m bell tower forms part of the architectural composition. A single-domed four-column structure combining elements of the Renaissance, Baroque and Classical styles. The sculptured details of the cornices are masterfully executed; the walls are decorated in marble. The iconostasis is sculpted of white marble and malachite. The interior is decorated with beautiful paintings of biblical scenes by the artist V. Makovsky. Some of the paintings are exhibited in the Municipal Art Museum. (Soborna St., 31).

ILYINSKA (ST. ELIAS') CHURCH, 1851.

Voskresenska (Resurrection) Church, 1702.

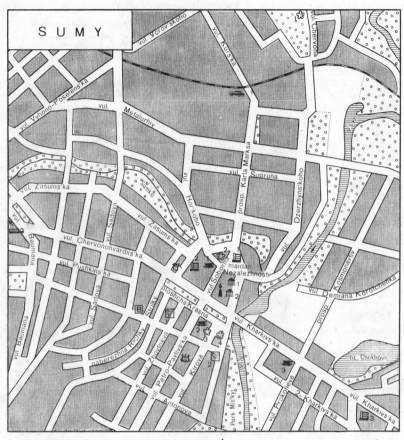

SUMY

B Excursion office

▤ Hotels:
    1 Sumy
    2 Ukraïna
    3 Khimik

▬ Restaurants:
    1 Iunist'
    2 Teatral'nyi
    3 Sumchanka

☋ Market

▰ Railway Station

▰ Bus Station

♟ Monument to Taras Shevchenko

▥ Architectural monuments:
    1 Resurrection Church, 18th c.
    2 Transfiguration of the Savior
    Cathedral, 18th c.

✿ Museums:
    1 Anton Chekhov House-Museum
    2 Applied Arts
    3 Local Lore
    4 Art

▨ Theaters:
    1 For children and youth
    2 Shchepkin Theater of Drama
    and Musical Comedy

Established in 1831. Built on an artificial elevation. Built in the Classical style with Eclectic elements.

TROYITSKY (HOLY TRINITY) CATHE-DRAL, 1901-14. Built in the Classical style with Baroque elements in its decor. Today it houses a concert hall for organ and chamber music of the Regional Philharmonic, as well as a Sculpture Museum. (Dzerzhynsky St., 32).

PANTELEYMONIVSKA (ST. PANTE-LEYMON'S) CHURCH, 1911. Designed by O. Shchusyev, this church is part of St. Panteleymon's Monastery. The two-storied cells and farming buildings have been preserved. West of the church is a bell tower.

PETROPAVLIVSKA (SS. PETER AND PAUL'S) CHURCH, 19th cent. A brick structure with cupolas, crucifiction in plan. The original interior ornamentation and several oil paint-

Spaso-Preobrazhensky (Transfiguration) Cathedral, 1776-88.

ings have been preserved. One of the finest examples of Classical architecture in eastern Ukraine.

MONUMENTS

T. Shevchenko, 1920. Sculptor: I. Kavaleridze. (T. Shevchenko Sq.).

Grave-site monuments. Erected on the grave-sites of the 19th cent. industrialists, cultural figures, educators, and patrons of art the Kharytonenko family. Marble sculptures on religious themes were executed by the French artist Aristide Croisie. (Central Cemetery).

MUSEUMS

Regional Museum: Kirov St., 2; tel. 22-17-74. • **Art Museum:** Chervona Ploshcha, 1; tel. 22-04-81. • **Museum of Decorative Art:** Maydan Nezalezhnosti, 19; tel. 22-01-55. • **A. Chekhov Building-Museum:** Chekhov St., 79; tel. 25-11-96.

THEATERS, PHILHARMONIC

M. Shchepkin Theater of Drama and Musical Comedy: Teatralna Ploshcha, 1. • **Children's and Youth Theater:** Zhovtneva St., 6. • **Philharmonic:** Soborna St., 63.

Hotel Sumy.

HIGHER EDUCATIONAL INSTITUTIONS

Physical-Technological Institute: Rymsky-Korsakov St., 2. • **Pedagogical Institute:** Romenska St., 87. • **Agricultural Institute:** Lenin St., 57.

LIBRARIES, ARCHIVES

Scientific Library: Stalinhrad St., 2. • **Children's and Youth Library:** Petropavlivska St., 53. • **T. Shevchenko Municipal Library:** Kooperatyvna St., 6. • **State Regional Archive:** Sadova St., 49.

PARKS

Druzhba Park: prospekt Marksa. • **Arboretum.** • **Botanical Park of the Pedagogical Institute.** • **Kazka Children's Park:** prospekt Marksa.

SPORTS COMPLEXES

Spartak Stadium. • **Dynamo:** urochyshche Tokari.

HOTELS

Sumy: ploshcha Nezalezhnosti, 1; tel. 27-00-7, 27-30-00. • **Ukrayina:** Frunze St., 1; tel. 22-25-20; 22-27-93. • **Zhovten:** Soborna St., 44; tel. 22-26-63. • **Khimik:** Kharkivska St., 30; tel. 33-77-07. • **Sport:** Gagarin St., 9; tel. 22-36-00. • **Zirka:** Kirov St., 157; tel. 22-45-70.

RESTAURANTS, CAFES, BARS

Sumy: ploshcha Nezalezhnosti, 1; tel. 27-31-01. • **Krystal:** Marx St., 28; tel. 22-04-57. • **Teatralny (with Casino):** Chervona Ploshcha, 5; tel. 27-20-23. • **Romantyka:** Heroyiv Stalinhrada St., 3; tel. 22-16-43. • **Dialoh:** Kharkivska St., 26; tel. 33-11-36. • **Slovyansky (Pyvny Bar):** Kharkivska St., 9; tel. 33-10-09. • **Berizka:** Kovpak St., 13; tel. 24-15-30.

STORES

Tsentralny Univermah (Department Store): Chervona Ploshcha, 3. • **Budynok Odyahu (Clothing):** Kooperatyvna St., 1. • **Dytyachy Svit (Children's Department Store):** Kirov St., 6. • **Radio:** Kharkivska St., 4. • **Olimpiyets:** Kharkivska St., 2. • **Tovary Sumshchyny:** Kharkivska St., 1. • **Elektrotovary:** Levanevsky St., 22. • **Frunzensky:** Gorky St., 25. • **Lypky:** Petropavlivska St., 123. • **Okean:** Petropavlivska St., 72. • **Dary laniv:** Soborna St., 35. • **Valyutny:** Kharkivska St., 3. • **Roza Hraf:** Soborna St., 34. • **Budynok Knyhy "Prometey" (Books):** Kirov St., 8. • **Ukrayinsky Suvenir:** Soborna St., 34. • **Khudozhniy Fond (Art):** Petropavlivska St., 1. • **Knyhy Ukrayiny (Books):** prospekt Marksa, 27. • **Romashka Flowershop:** Soborna St., 42.

BANKS

National Bank of Ukraine (Regional Branch): Kirov St., 21; tel. 2-27-28. • **Joint-Stock Commercial Bank "Biznesbank:"** Kirov St., 20; tel. 27-43-96. • **Commercial Bank:** Kirov St., 146/1.

TOURISM

Sumyturyst Tourist and Excursion Association: naberezhna Riky Strilky, 46; tel. 27-31-94.

Bureau of Transport Excursions in Ukraine and Abroad: tel. 27-30-43; 27-32-10.

To book excursions: tel. 27-41-24; 27-00-73.

Turyst Auto stop: tel. 27-51-67.

Suputnyk Youth Travel Agency: Pershotravneva St., 6; tel. 22-61-45.

Kyyanytsya Tourist Base: village of Kyyanytsya, Sumy district.

Yaroslavna Tourist Base: city of Putyvl.

Turservis Agency: ploshcha Nezalezhnosti, 1; tel. 27-50-73.

Intourist Agency: Kharkivska St., 9; tel. 32-04-02.

Mykhaylivska Tsilyna, 1961. A branch of Ukrainian Steppe Reserve. Under conservation since 1928. 202.4 ha. The only virgin steppe remaining in the forest-steppe zone. 503 species of plants, including 200 plants germane to the steppe.

POST OFFICE, TELEPHONE

Main post office: Pryvokzalna Ploshcha; tel. 25-10-84.

Telegraph-Telephone Station: Chervonohvardiyska St., 2; tel. 22-35-01.

Telephone calling stations: Petropavlivska St., 5; tel. 22-06-60. • Prospekt Marksa, 25; tel. 22-71-61.

MEDICAL SERVICES

Emergency: tel. 03; 22-11-98.
Pharmacies: Chervona Ploshcha, 8; tel. 22-16-13. • Gorky St., 34; tel. 25-76-27.
• Homeopathic Pharmacy: Gorky St., 23; tel. 27-11-47.

TRANSPORTATION

Railway station: Pryvokzalna Ploshcha; tel. 005, 284-21-17.
Bus Terminus: ploshcha Baumana, 40; tel. 004.
Airport: tel. 006.
Taxi reservations: tel. 002; 058.

TOURING HISTORIC CITIES AND VILLAGES

BAKYRIVKA

Village, Okhtyrka district, on the left bank of the Vorskla River, 11 km from the Kyrykivka railway station. Founded in 1685.

PYATNYTSKA CHURCH, 19th cent. A single-domed wood structure on a brick foundation. The bell tower is adjacent to the west side.

BOHDANKA

Village, Shostka district, 3 km from the Pyrohivka railway station.

In the 1850s-60s K. Ushynsky, a noted educator lived and worked in the village. A museum and monument dedicated to him are located here.

HAMALIYIVKA

Village, Shostka district.

HAMALIYIVSKY (KHARLAMPIYIV) MONASTERY, early 18th cent. Established in 1702 as a hermitage. The center of the complex is the rectangular, six-columned Rizdva Bohorodytsi (Nativity of the Mother of God) Cathedral. Its austere style is unique to Ukrainian architecture.

HLUKHIV

City on the Esman River, 146 km from Sumy.

Established in the 10th cent. First mentioned in the Hypatian Chronicle for the year 1152. In the 13th-14th cent. Hiukhiv was part of Chernihiv principality. After its liberation from Tatar bondage in 1350 it was ruled by Lithuania.

The city was constantly fortified, especially from the mid-17th cent. The Polish King Jan Casimir's armies retreated from the fortress built in 1663. Until the late-17th cent. Hlukhiv was the center of cannon and gunpowder production. During the 18th cent. it was the main administrative and business center of Left-Bank Ukraine. On 12 November 1713 the Hetman of Ukraine I. Mazepa was symbolically executed and anathemized opposite Mykolayivska (St. Nicholas') Church.

The Little Russian Collegium, the supreme ruling body of Ukraine, was established in 1722. In 1793 The Hlukhiv Singing School, first

Hamaliyivka. Hamaliyivsky (Kharlampiyiv) Monastery, 18th cent.

Hlukhiv. Mykolayivska (St. Nicholas') Church, 1686.

school of singing in Ukraine, was established to train singers and musicians for the royal court. Many famous Ukrainian singers and composers of the 18th cent. studied here, among them M. Berezovsky and D. Bortnyansky. Expansion of the city began in 1750 when K. Rozumovsky became Hetman of Ukraine. In the early 1780s cent. the city began to decline.

After 1861 Hlukhiv was a major grain-trading sugar-producing center in Left-Bank Ukraine.

MYKOLAYIVSKA (ST. NICHOLAS') CHURCH, 1686. The oldest architectural monument in the city and a brilliant example of the Ukrainian Baroque style. The interior is spacious, impetuous and majestic. Kozak Hetmans were elected on Narodna Ploshcha (Square) near the church. (Lenin St.).

SPASO-PREOBRAZHENSKA (TRANSFIGURATION) CHURCH, 1705. This pyramid-shaped church was built in the combined Baroque and Classical style. This structure has harmonious proportions and a distinct silhouette. (Ploshcha Rudenka).

ANASTASIYIVSKA (ST. ANASTASIA'S) CHURCH, 1896. The white marble iconostasis is masterfully executed. (Ploshcha Radchenka).

VOZNESENSKA (ASCENSION) CHURCH, 18th cent. (Voznesenske Cemetery).

TRIUMPHANT ARCH, 1766-85. Built by the architect A. Kvasov in the Classical style. During the Second World War the Arch was destroyed. Restored to its original appearance in the 1950s.

KHOTIN

Village, Sumy district, 20 km from Sumy.

Established in the 17th cent. Includes an estate founded in the late 18th cent. The only existing structure built by the architect G. Quarengi in the Classical style.

LEBEDYN

City, on the banks of the Vilshanka River, 47 km from Sumy.

Established in 1654; it was settled by fugitives from Polish rule in Right-Bank Ukraine. During the period of the national-liberation war of 1648-54 Lebedyn fortress, with 20 towers, was considered to be the best fortified in Ukraine. After the Northern War (1700-21), it began to deteriorate. The city coat of arms depicts a swan (lebid) on a gold background.

VOSKRESENSKA (RESURRECTION) CHURCH, 1789. A wood structure with vertical panelling. Today only the basic single-storied cruciform building has been preserved. Irreparable damage to the church was done during the Stalin era. (Kobyzhch St., 181).

VOZNESENSKA (ASCENSION) CHURCH, 1858. A square four-pillared structure with an arched wall near the altar. The bell tower is located over the entrance. The church reflects the masterful union of local architectural elements with the Classical and Baroque style. (Ploshcha Svobody, 37).

POKROVSKA (PROTECTION OF THE BLESSED VIRGIN MARY) CHURCH, 19th cent. A brick structure with a single dome and bell tower. (Luxemburg St., 44).

MYKOLAYIVSKA (ST. NICHOLAS') CHURCH, 1890s. The cornices, arches, and other decorations are made of brick. The Byzantine style is combined with Renaissance elements. (Shcherbakov St., 1).

TORHOVI RYADY (MARKET STALLS), 1847. Single-storied stores. The exterior is an open gallery with twin columns. (Internatsionalna Ploshcha, 37-39).

T. Shevchenko Monument, 1964. Height: 2.5 m. It has a multi-stepped pedestal. Sculptor: Y. Krasnozhon.

MEZHYRICH

Village, Lebedyn district, 15 km from the Lebedyn railway station.
Established in 1642 From 1658 it was a company city of the Sumy regiment.

USPENSKA (DORMITION) CHURCH, 1759-75. Built by L. Bilous, the archimandrite of the Kyivan Cave Monastery.

OKHTYRKA

City, 83 km from Sumy, on the Vorskla River.
Established in 1654. Until the mid-18th cent. it was an important strategic point on the southeastern border. Later, it was the center of the Kharkiv Gubernia. Today there are more than 20 industrial enterprises in the city. Cultural monuments, including an open-air museum, are located in the city center.

POKROVSKY (PROTECTION OF THE BLESSED VIRGIN MARY) CATHEDRAL, 1753-68. Designed by V. Rastrelli and built by the architect S. Dudynsky. Damaged during the Second World War. This unique Ukrainian Baroque church is noted for its spacious composition.

Okhtyrka. Mykhaylivska (St. Michael's) Church, 1884.

VVEDENSKA (PRESENTATION IN THE TEMPLE) CHURCH, 1774-84. Located at the main entrance to Pokrovsky (Protection) Cathedral.

KHRYSTOROZHDESTVENSKA (NATIVITY OF CHRIST) CHURCH, 1774. Built in the Classical style. Has precise proportions and austere interior decor. It is one of the finer examples of the architecture of Sumy region.

MYKHAYLIVSKA (ST. MICHAEL'S) CHURCH, 1884. A unique architectural structure on the outskirts of Okhtyrka. Constructed of red brick. Decorative elements are borrowed from Byzantine and Roman architecture.

HEORHIYIVSKA (ST. GEORGE'S) CHURCH, 1908. A massive and severe structure. Was used for storage purposes. (Kyivska St.).

TSVYNTARNA (CEMETERY) CHURCH, 19th cent. (Menzhynsky St.).

PUTYVL

District center located on the right bank of the Seym River, 100 km from Sumy, 22 km from the Putyvl railway station.

The area was settled in the 4th cent. B.C. In the 12th cent. it was the seat of the Olhovychi, the Novhorod-Siversky Princes. It was first mentioned in the Hypatian Chronicle for the year 1146. Putyvl is associated with "The Lament of Yaroslavna," the wife of the prince of Novhorod-Siversky who fought against the Polovtsian tribe. The "Lament" is one of the most moving moments in the renowned epic "The Tale of Ihor's Host." In the late 14th cent. Putyvl became the district center of the Lithuanian state; later, in 1500, the city became part of the Russian Empire. In the early 16th cent. the city was one of the main fortresses defending the state borders. In the mid-17th cent. it established trading relations with the Near East, the Balkans, and southeastern Europe.

Putyvl. Mykoly Kozatskoho (Mykola Kozatsky Church of St. Nicholas), 1735-37.

MOLCHANSKY MONASTERY, 16th-19th cent. Built on a hill near the Seym River. The complex of this stone fortress-monastery includes the Rozhdestva Bohorodytsi (Nativity of the Mother of God) Cathedral, bell tower, refectory with tower, and the Church of Rozhdestva Ioana Predtechi (Nativity of St. John the Baptist).

The main church, the Rozdestva Bohorodytsi Cathedral (Nativity of the Mother of God) (1575-85), was rebuilt in 1630, 1700, and the early 20th cent. The cellars of the cathedral were used as storehouses for food and gunpowder. (Shchors St., 18.)

SPASO-PREOBRAZHENSKA (TRANS-FIGURATION) CATHEDRAL, KHRESTO-VOZDVYZHENSKA (ELEVATION OF THE HOLY CROSS) CHURCH-BELL TOWER, 1617-93. Built as the main church of a convent founded in the 16th cent. The iconostasis and numerous paintings have been preserved. (Lunacharsky St.).

MYKOLY KOZATSKOHO (MYKOLA KOZATSKY CHURCH OF ST. NICHO-LAS), 1735-37. A monumental structure Built by the Ukrainian Kozaks of Putyvl. (Pershotravneva St.).

PYROHIVKA

Village, Shostka district, 3 km from the Pyrohivka railway station.

Nearby a Neolithic settlement has been excavated.

Romny. Svyatodukhivsky (Holy Ghost) Cathedral, 18th cent.

YOANA BOHOSLOVA (ST. JOHN THE DIVINE) CHURCH AND BELL TOWER, 18th cent. A wood structure, crucifiction in plan.

ROMNY

City and district center on the banks of the Sula River, 100 km from Sumy.

Mentioned by the name of Romen in the "Povchannya" ("Instruction") of Kyivan Prince Volodymyr Monomakh, as recorded in the Chronicle for the year 1096. In the 18th cent. it was a fortified city. In 1618 Romny was occupied by the Poles. The people of Romny actively participated in the liberation war of 1648-54. During the Northern War of 1700-08 the Swedish King, Charles XII, had his headquarters in Romny. In the 18th-19th cent. the city was an important commercial center.

SVYATODUKHIVSKY (HOLY GHOST) CATHEDRAL, 18th cent. Located on the highest peak of the city, the architecture of the church is in complete harmony with its natural surroundings. (Bazarna Ploshcha, 15).

VASYLIVSKA (ST. BASIL'S) CHURCH, 1751-80. (Bazarna Ploshcha, 15).

VOZNESENSKA (ASCENSION) CHURCH, 18th cent. A single-storied structure. The complex includes a bell tower.

T. Shevchenko Monument, 1918. Sculptor: I. Kavaleridze. (Shevchenko Blvd.).

A. Derevska Monument, 1982. Dedicated to a heroic mother, who rescued and raised 48 orphans during the World War II. Sculptor: A. Sypko. Architect: V. Minenko. (Shchuka St., 57).

Trostyanets. Voznesenska (Ascension) Church, 19th cent.

TROSTYANETS

City on the bank of the Boromlya River, 60 km from Sumy.

Established in the 1650s during the period of resettlement of Kozaks and peasants from Right-Bank Ukraine after the Battle of Berestechko. Named after the Trostyanka river. Urban development proceeded slowly. For many decades it was a village whose poverty contrasted sharply with the rich estates of the Golitsyn family (which included a circus, theater, two churches, stables).

The writer M. Khvylovy was born here.

BLAHOVISHCHENSKA (ANNUNCIATION) CHURCH, 1750. One of the oldest structures in the city. A single-domed church built in the early Classical style with Baroque elements.

VOZNESENSKA (ASCENSION) CHURCH, 19th cent. Distinguished by the richness of its relief facades. The 40 m bell tower is a masterpiece of folk masonry.

PALACE, 18th-19th cent. Residence of the Princes Golitsyns. Includes a forested park, arboretum with 300 year-old oak trees, and lakes. It has been designated a state nature reserve.

VELYKY BOBRYK

Village, Krasnopil region, on the bank of the Bobryk river, 7 km from the Zolotnytska railway station.

Established in 1676. An ancient settlement of the Siverian tribe of the 8th-10th cent. has been excavated nearby.

VOSKRESENSKA (RESURRECTION) CHURCH, 1808. Built in the square Classical style. The bell tower is a three-tiered structure and has an open arcade. A unique architectural monument.

VOLOKYTNE

Village, Putyvl district, on the bank of Kleven River, 10 km from the Banychi railway station.

First mentioned in 1684. Known for its porcelain since the 19th cent.

Voronizh. Mykhaylivska (St. Michael's) Church, 1776-81.

GOLDEN GATE, 19th cent. In a 25 ha park established in 1829-30. In the pseudo-Gothic style.

VORONIZH

Village, Shostka district, along the Osota River, 2 km from the Tereshchen railway station.

Established in 1177. In 1654 became the headquarters of the Nizhyn Kozak Regiment.

MYKHAYLIVSKA (ST. MICHAEL'S) CHURCH, 1776-81. Built in the Ukrainian Baroque style, with sculptured thematic relief.

Ternopil Region

It is situated in western Ukraine, on the Podilian Plateau which is between 300 to 432 m above sea level. The principle rivers in the region are the Dnister and its tributaries, the Zbruch, Nichlava, Seret, Strypa, and Zolota Lypa. The northern part of the region is intersected by the Viliya, Ikva, and Horyn Rivers which are part of the Prypyat Basin. Created in 1939. Population: 1,178,000. Area: 13,800 sq. km.

History

The territory of the Ternopil region began to be settled in the middle Paleolithic Age. In the Bronze Age (4-3 B.C.) it was settled by tribes of Trypillian culture. More than 50 of their settlements have been unearthed.

In the late 11th cent. several independent principalities were established which eventually united to form the Galician-Volynian Principality. The population fought off successive invasions of the Polovtsians, Lithuanians, Poles, and Hungarians.

In the 16th-17th cent. peasant serfs united in armed struggle against Polish rule. The uprisings of 1594-96 were led by a local resident named Severyn Nalyvayko. The peasant rebel movements continued during the national-liberation war of 1648-

Ternopil Region.
Pochayivska Lavra,
16th-17th cent.

54. In 1672 a large part of the territory was annexed by the Turkish Sultanate. Ten years later Poland regained control over Ternopil and in 1772 Austria claimed the larger part of the region. In November 1918 the region became part of the Western Ukrainian National Republic (ZUNR) and was reclaimed later by Poland. The Ternopil region became part of Soviet Ukraine in 1939.

The oldest remains of the material culture date back 50,000 years. Many settlements and dwellings from this period have been uncovered in the region. Tombs of the so-called Carpatho-Danubian Thracian mountain mass have been excavated in the Zalishchyky district near the villages of Lysychnyky, Kulakivtsi, and Kolodribka. The settlements of the Chernyakhiv culture have been intensively studied. Ten Roman coins were unearthed in the region and in 1848 a statue of an ancient Slavic pre-Christian god was found in the Zbruch River near the village of Lychkivtsi.

Although for centuries the Ukrainians in this region lived under harsh foreign oppression, the Ukrainian population of eastern Galicia was able to organize brotherhoods, schools, and gymnasiums. Publishing, art, and painting flourished here during the 16th-18th cent. The cities of Kremenets and Pochayiv had their own imprimeries. In Pochayiv in 1618 the printer K. Trankvilion (Stavrovetsky) published the famous theological book *Zertsalo Bohosloviya* (The Mirror of Theology). During its existence the Pochayiv imprimery published 187 books in Old Church Slavonic, Old Ukrainian, Polish, Ukrainian, and Latin.

Many castles were constructed in the Ternopil region, which is rich in monuments of folk wood architecture.

PROMINENT INDIVIDUALS

BORN IN THE REGION:

V. Barvinsky (1888-1963), composer; Ternopil, was persecuted. • **M. Boychuk** (1882-1937), painter; village Romanivka; executed. • **V. Hzhytsky** (1895-1973), writer; village Ostrivets; was persecuted. • **S. Krushelnytska** (1873-1952), opera singer; village of Bilyavyntsi. • **B. Lepky** (1872-1941), writer; village Kryvenky; died in Poland. • **Josyf Slipy** (1892-1984), Patriarch of Ukrainian Greek-Catholic Church; village Zazdrist in the Terebovlyansky district; was persecuted by the Soviets; died in Rome. • **Ya. Stecko** (1912-86), political leader, head of OUN(b) and ABN; village Kamyanka in the Terebovlya district; died in Germany.

BURIED IN THE REGION:

T. Bordulyak (1863-1936), writer; village of Velyky Khodachkiv. • **P. Duma** (1854-1918), poet; village of Drahomanivka. • **Ye. Kupchynsky** (1867-1938), composer, conductor; village of Sorotske.

TERNOPIL

City, regional center, railway junction, and airport. Situated on the Seret River. Population: 170,000. Telephone code: 0352.

The city was first mentioned in documents dating to 1540. Traces of the earliest settlers' dwellings have been unearthed in the suburban villages of Velyky Hlybochok, Petrykiv, and Stupky. Sopilche, the ancient Ukrainian fortification built on the site of present-day Ternopil, was destroyed during Khan Baty's military campaign against the Carpathian region. In 1349 Galicia was occupied by Poland.

Construction of a castle on the ruins of Sopilche — the nucleus of Ternopil — commenced in 1540. The castle suffered repeated damage from fires and devastation by war. In the early part of the 19th cent. Count F. Korytovsky rebuilt the castle into a palace and removed the fortifications, tower, and gate. An ordinary wall was built around the new structure.

Despite the ruinous effects of many wars, many important monuments of architecture, history, and culture have been preserved in the city. Many are eclectic in style.

The famous literary anthology *Rusalka Dnistrova*, was compiled in Ternopil by M. Shashkevych, I. Vahylevych, and Ya. Holovatsky. This book, published in Budapest in 1837, signalled the beginnings of modern Ukrainian literature in the Western Ukrainian lands.

CHURCHES, HISTORICAL AND ARCHITECTURAL MONUMENTS

CASTLE, 1540. Built on the site of the former settlement of Sopilche. It was rebuilt in the 19th century and all its defensive structures were dismantled. Substantial renovations were made in 1954. The "Old Castle" contains the nucleus of the 16th century defensive castle. It is the oldest city structure.

Ternopil. Old buildings on the lake.

VOZDVYZHENSKA (ELEVATION OF THE HOLY CROSS) CHURCH, 16th cent. A bell tower was built in 1627. Ancient Ukrainian building traditions are reflected in the style. Restored in 1959. Called the "Church on the Pond."

RIZDVA KHRYSTOVOHO (NATIVITY OF CHRIST) CHURCH, 1602-08. Erected by the master builder Leontiy. Reconstruction has altered the original appearance. A fine example of the 17th cent. school of Podilian architecture.

ROMAN CATHOLIC CHURCH OF THE DOMINICAN MONASTERY AND CELLS, 1749-79. Erected in the

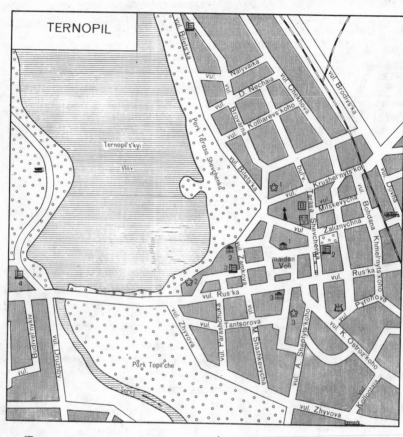

TERNOPIL

Ⓑ	Excursion office

📖	Hotels:
	  1 Chaika
	  2 Ukraïna
	  3 Ternopil'
	  4 Halychyna

🍴	Restaurant Khutir
	  Note. Restaurants Ukraïna, Ter-
	  nopil' and Halychyna are at-
	  tached to the hotels of the
	  same name

🚃	Railway Station
🚌	Bus Station

🕴	Monument to Taras Shevchenko

🏛	Architectural monuments:
	  1 Dominican Church, 1749
	  2 Castle, 16th c.
	  3 Church, 17th c.

✿	Museums:
	  1 Picture Gallery
	  2 Museum of Folk Dress
	  3 Museum of Local Lore

🎭	Taras Shevchenko Theater of Music and Drama
🎶	Philharmonic Society

historical core of the city by the architect A. Moshinsky, this church is a basilica built in the Baroque style. Restored in 1953, it has been used as a gallery of the Ternopil Ethnographic Museum.

MONUMENTS

T. Shevchenko, 1982. Sculptor: M. Nevesely. Architect: S. Kalashnyk. (Shevchenko Square).
A. Pushkin, 1959. Sculptors: M. Vronsky, O. Oliynyk, O. Skoblykov. Architect: Ye. Hronsky. (Zaliznychna St.).
V. Stus, 1992. Sculptor: D. Stetsko. (Stus St.).

MUSEUMS

Historical-Ethnographic Museum: Medova St., 3; tel. 2-44-77. • **Art Museum:** Krushelnytska St., 1-a; tel. 2-80-72.

Rizdva Khrystovoho (Nativity of Christ) Church, 1602-08.

THEATERS, PHILHARMONIC

T. Shevchenko Theater of Music and Drama: Shevchenko Blvd., 6. • **Puppet Theater:** Sichovykh Striltsiv St., 11-a. • **Philharmonic:** Knyaz Ostrozky St., 9.

HIGHER EDUCATIONAL INSTITUTIONS

Medical Institute: maydan Voli, 6. • **Pedagogical Institute:** Kryvonis St., 2. • **Institute of National Economy:** Hetman Mazepa St., 3. • **Tool-Building Institute:** Ruska St., 62.

LIBRARIES

Main Regional Scientific Library: Shevchenko Blvd., 19; tel. 2-41-89. • **Medical Scientific Library:** Ruska St., 41; tel. 5-07-69. • **Children's Library:** Kopernyk St., 17.

SPORTS COMPLEXES

Central Stadium: tel. 2-65-50. • **Sports Complex:** Ostrovsky St., 22.

HOTELS

Ternopil: Zamkova St., 12; tel. 3-30-20; 2-42-68. • **Halychyna:** Zaozerna St., 1-a; tel. 3-61-16. • **Ukrayina:** Shevchenko Blvd., 23; tel. 2-46-47; 2-15-25. • **Chayka:** Naberezhna St., 65-a; tel. 2-91-84.

RESTAURANTS, CAFES, BARS

Kalyna: Hetman Orlyk St., 4. • **Halychyna:** Zaozerna St., 1-a. • **Prolisok:** Velyka Berezovytsya. • **Podillya:** Bandera St., 154. • **Svitanok:** 15 Kvitnya St. • **Ternopil:** Zamkova St., 12. • **Ukrayina:** Shevchenko Blvd., 27. • **Khutir:** Zaozerna St. • **Yuvileyny:** prospekt Zluky, 33. • **Halaktyka:** Druzhby St., 9. • **Merydian:** Myru St., 3-a. • **Rayduha:** Bandera St., 164. • **Shokoladny:** Shevchenko Blvd., 27. • **Ukrayinska Nich:** Hetman Mazepa St., 2. • **Varenychna:** Hetman Sahaydachny St., 41. • **Zatyshok:** Ruska St., 2. • **Kashtan:** Krushelnytska St., 14. • **Kosmos:** Knyaz Ostrozky St., 1. • **Tyraspol:** Hetman Sahaydachny St., 1. • **Pizzeria:** Shashkevych St., 1.

STORES

Tsentralny Univermah (Department Store): Ruska St., 24. • **Novy Ternopil:** Myr St., 5. • **Almaz:** Zamkova St., 9. • **Dytyachy svit:** Ruska St., 52. • **Lileya:** Shevchenko Blvd., 39. • **Tovary Ternopolya:** Shevchenko Blvd.,' 43. • **Turyst:** Knyaz Ostrozky St., 5. • **Khudozhnyk (Salon):** Shevchenko Blvd., 43. • **Cheremshyna hastronom** (food): Danylo Halytsky Blvd., 5. • **Dnister Hastronom** (Food): Hrushevsky St., 1. • **Molochny:** maydan Voli, 1. • **Ovochi-Frukty** (Fruits & Vegetables): Myr St., 4. • **Podillya:** Hetman Mazepa St. • **Suputnyk:** Ruska St., 23. • **Kyiv:** Kyivska St., 10.

BANKS

Natsionalny bank Ukrayiny (Regional branch of the National Bank of Ukraine): Hrushevsky St., 6; tel. 2-10-42. • **Komertsiyny bank "Viktoriya" ("Viktoriya" Commercial Bank):** village of Volkovtsi in the Borshchiv district; tel. 3-67-17. • **Cooperative Bank "Ternopil Kredyt" ("Ternopil Kredyt" Cooperative Bank):** Slipy St., 8; tel. 2-30-93; 5-36-90. • **Komertsiyny Bank "Ekonomika" ("Ekonomika" Commercial Bank):** city of Chortkiv Shevchenko St., 13; tel. 2-39-48; 2-09-90.

TOURISM

Inturyst-Ternopil: Stary Rynok, 2; tel. 5-06-65; 5-16-16; 5-24-00; 7-04-19; 7-06-11.

Regional Tourism and Excursion Council: Medov St., 2; tel. 2-72-65; 2-55-72; 5-35-42.
Ternopil Travel and Excursion Agency: Teatralna St., 4; tel. 2-81-05; 5-07-65.

POST OFFICES, TELEPHONE

Central calling point: Zaliznychna St., 4; tel. 2-64-05; 2-23-70.
Automatic calling point: Lesya Ukrayinka St., 25; tel. 4-60-00.
Reservations for inter-urban/international calls: tel. 07; 071; 072.
Calling points are located at every hotel complex.

MEDICAL SERVICES

Emergency: tel. 03.
Central Pharmaceutical Information Service: tel. 067.
Pharmacies: Ruska St., 4. • Knyaz Ostrozky St., 41-a. • Opilsky St., 2. • Bandera St., 160. • Myr St., 13. • Zamkova St., 8. • Druzhby St., 9. • Klinichna St., 1.

TRANSPORTATION

Ukraine Airlines: tel. 2-36-47.
Airport: Pidvolochyske Shosse; tel. 006, 4-13-22, 4-32-63.
Bus Terminus: Obolonya St. 7; tel. 002; 2-23-03.
Advance Bus Tickets: tel. 2-53-56.
Train station /information/: tel. 005.
Ticket reservation /international travel/: tel. 2-10-63.
Taxi reservations: tel. 058; 4-41-72.
Filling Stations: Pyatnadtsyatoho Kvitnya St.; tel. 4-35-30. • Berezhanska St., tel. 3-20-17. • Village of Velyka Berezovytsya: tel. 2-63-24. • Village of Bila; tel. 2-33-32.

AUTO SERVICING

Autoservice: Brodivska St., 59; tel. 5-44-73. • Dovzhenko St., 2; 4-00-94. • Mykulynetska St., 40; tel. 2-97-03.

TOURING HISTORIC CITIES AND VILLAGES

BEREZHANY

City located on both sides of the Zolota Lypa River, 52 km from Ternopil. The first documented mention of this city appears in 1375.

CASTLE (ruins), 1554. Erected by Italian master builders following a system devised by Beauplan. In 1829 part of the castle was dismantled. The most important defensive structure of the Renaissance age in Ukraine.

MYKOLAYIVSKA (ST. NICHOLAS') CHURCH, 1691. This church is a brilliant example of the Galician school of wood architecture.

TROYITSKY (HOLY TRINITY) CATHEDRAL, 1768. Rebuilt in 1893-1903. One of the finest church structures in the region.

TROYITSKY (HOLY TRINITY) ROMAN CATHOLIC CHURCH, 1554. Built at the

Berezhany. Troyitsky (Holy Trinity) Cathedral, 1768.

same time as the castle, the church's original ornaments have been preserved. It formed part of the castle and was used as a mausoleum. An important monument of the Renaissance period.

MYKOLAYIVSKY (ST. NICHOLAS') ROMAN CATHOLIC CHURCH, 1630-83. Cells, 1716-42. Built for the St. Bernard Monastery, this church is an example of late Renaissance architecture.

RIZDVA BOHORODYTSI (NATIVITY OF THE BLESSED VIRGIN MARY) ROMAN CATHOLIC CHURCH, 1600; **BELL TOWER**, 1741. A defensive structure built in the Gothic-Renaissance style.

CITY HALL, 1811. Located in the center of Market Square. Built in the early Classical style. Today it houses the municipal Ethnographic Museum.

Berezhany. Castle (ruins), 1554.

BILCHE-ZOLOTE

Village in the Borshchiv district, 18 km from the district center.

In the neighboring vicinity the oldest settlements in the Ternopil region dating to the middle Paleolithic Age and two settlements of Trypillian and Chernyakhiv culture have been excavated. The remains of one of the largest ancient cities in Podillia have been unearthed on the banks of the Seret River, including a pagan sacrificial altar, one of the few that have been preserved in Ukraine.

PARK, 1800. Occupying an area of 11 ha, the park contains many rare species of trees, bushes, and flowers. In the center of the park is a lake with a lane of shade trees leading up to it. A monument of landscape architecture.

BORSHCHIV

City and railway station on the Nichlava River. Population: 13,000. First mentioned in documents dating to 1456.

ROMAN CATHOLIC CHURCH, 18th cent. The tower was rebuilt from a 17th cent. defensive tower.

Monuments to I. Franko (1983), A. Mickiewicz (1898) and an **ethnographic museum** are also located here.

BUCHACH

City and district center located on the banks of the Strypa River, 72 km from Ternopil. Population: 15,000. First mentioned in documents dating to 1397. In the 16th cent. the city was ruled by the magnates of the Potocki family who built a castle in the city. For a period of time the city was occupied by the Turks and Tatars.

CASTLE, 14th cent. Sections of the defensive walls have been preserved on a cliff overlooking the Strypa River. The castle was built in the Renaissance style and reflects Podilian defensive architecture of the 14th-16th cent. (Zamkova St.).

KHRYSTOVOZDVYZENSKA (ELEVATION OF THE HOLY CROSS) CHURCH, 1753-70. Designed by the architect I. Schilzer in the late Baroque style as part of the Basilian Monastery complex. The church contains 18th cent. wall paintings and monks' cells dating to the 17th cent. (Mickiewicz St.)

MYKOLAYIVSKA (ST. NICHOLAS') CHURCH, 1610; BELL TOWER, 19th cent. This defensive structure reflects the Byzantine style of architecture.

POKROVSKA (PROTECTION OF THE BLESSED VIRGIN MARY) CHURCH, 1764. Built by the architect I. Schilzer in the late Baroque style. Unique wood carvings have been preserved in the church.

Buchach. City Hall, 1750-51.

Chortkiv. Roman Catholic Church (1731).

CHURCH AT THE MONASTYRYOK SURVEY MARK, 16th cent. One of the rarest monuments of Ukraine. This church, which served as a fortress, is an example of Podilian stone architecture of the 16th cent.

USPENSKY (DORMITION) ROMAN CATHOLIC CHURCH, 1761-63. Built in the late Baroque style.

CITY HALL, 1750-51. Designed by the architect B. Meretyn and decorated with sculptures by Pinzel, this structure is 35 m high. It is noted for its sculptural compositions and is considered an important work of 18th cent. civil architecture.

CHORTKIV

City on the Seret River, 76 km from Ternopil. Population: approx. 100,000.

First mentioned in documents dating to 1522. During the uprisings of 1648 Chortkiv was one of the bases of the peasant rebels. From 1672 to 1683 the city was under Turkish rule, under Polish rule from 1699, and under Austrian rule from 1772. Until 1779 the Chortkiv castle was the residence of the Potocki magnates.

CASTLE, 1610. Situated on a mountain overlooking the river. Conservation measures for the preservation of its ruins were undertaken in the early 20th cent. One of the few private defensive structures in Podillya.

VOZNESENSKA (ASCENSION) CHURCH, 1738. This wood structure is an example of Podilian folk wood architecture. (Lomonosov St.).

USPENSKA (DORMITION) CHURCH, 1635. A unique monument of Podilian folk wood architecture. Enlarged in the 19th cent. (Kotovsky St., 12).

The **Carmelite monastic complex** (1635), **Roman Catholic church** (1731), **City Hall, old market** (19th cent.) and the **Ethnographic Museum** (Zelena St.; tel. 2-45-62) are also located in Chortkiv.

Suputnyk Hotel: Shevchenko St., 34; tel. 2-13-72; 2-12-64.

HUSYATYN

Village and railway station located on the banks of the Zbruch River. Population: 7,000. First mentioned in documents dating to 1159.

ONUFRIYIVSKA (ST. ONUPHRIUS') CHURCH, 16th cent. Designated as a defensive church. Its structure reflects a blend of Podilian and Moldavian architectural styles.

SYNAGOGUE, 16th-17th cent. Quadrangular in shape, this structure was built in the Renaissance style.

ST. BERNARD MONASTERY, 16th cent., 1610. The monastery buildings, Roman Catholic church, and cells were built in the Gothic-Renaissance style. During restorations made in the church in 1975 part of the inner walls was dismantled.

Zbruch Hotel: Pushkin St., 3; tel. 2-14-56; 2-12-09.

KREMENETS

City and railway station. Population: 25,000.

Husyatyn. Synagogue, 16th-17th cent.

One of the oldest cities of Ukraine, it ، ؟s first mentioned in the Hypatian Chronicle for the year 1226. The Tatars frequently raided the city, but in the year 1240 Khan Baty's armies were prevented from seizing the fortress on Zamkova Hora. In 1648 Kozak units led by M. Kryvonis captured the castle in Kremenets.

A lyceum was located in the city from 1805 to 1831.

A monument to T. Shevchenko and two monuments to the Polish poet J. Slowacki are located in Kremenets.

Ethnographic Museum: tel. 2-20-20; 2-27-38.

In the city and neighboring vicinities may be found the Kremenets Mountains, six nature preserves, and Kremenets Park.

Kyiv Hotel: Shevchenko St., 57; tel. 2-23-72; 2-27-56.

BOHOYAVLENSKY (EPIPHANY) MONASTERY, 1760. The monastery complex includes a Roman Catholic church, monks' cells, and a bell tower above the gate (early 20th cent.). Built in the late Baroque style.

CASTLE, 12th cent. During the 13th-14th cent. the wood fortifications were replaced by stone ones. Only the defensive walls and the gate tower have been preserved. An important defensive structure.

COLLEGIUM BUILDINGS, 1731-43. Built by the architect P. Hizhytsky in the late Baroque style, the collegium once included a Jesuit church and two academic buildings. Nearby is a park and botanical gardens created in 1809 by D. Miller. (Krupska St., 1).

MYKOLAYIVSKY (ST. NICHOLAS') CATHEDRAL AND CELLS, 1636. Built for the Franciscan Monastery in the Gothic-Renaissance style. In the 18th cent. the cathedral and gate tower were fashioned in the Baroque style.

MUSEUM-HOUSE OF J. SLOWACKI, 18th cent. Located in a building in which the Polish poet lived from 1814 to 1828. A marble bust of the poet was erected in the courtyard in 1969. Today the J. Slowacki Municipal Library is housed here.

PYATNYTSKE CEMETERY. Ukrainian Kozaks who died in battles to liberate Kremenets from Polish rule (1648 and 1651) are buried here.

KRYVCHE

Village on the Tsyhanka River, 15 km from Borshchiv. The towers and walls of a 17th cent. fortress have been preserved. One of the largest gypsum caves in the world is located here. **The Kryshtaleva Cave** is 18,785 m long and is open year-round. Mineral springs are located nearby.

MYKULYNTSI

Village in the Terebovlya district, on the banks of the Seret River, 13 km from Terebovlya.

The village was first mentioned in Prince Volodymyr Monomakhs' *Povchannya* (Instruction) in 1096. It was part of the independent Principality of Terebovlya in the 11th cent., the Galician Principality in the 12th cent., and from 1199 it belonged to the Galician-Volynian Principality.

PALACE, 18th cent. Built in the Classical style in the mid-19th cent. on the site of the former Potocki palace, today it is used as a hospital. (Chapayev St., 2).

CASTLE, 16th-17th cent. Located on a hill overlooking a river. Only the ruins of the defense tower and walls have been preserved. An example of the defensive architecture of the 16th-17th cent.

TROYITSKY (HOLY TRINITY) ROMAN CATHOLIC CHURCH, 1761-79. Built in the Baroque style by the architect A. Moshynsky.

A resort with therapeutic mineral springs is located in the village.

PIDHAYTSI

City located on the Koropets River in the Berezhany district, 24 km from the Potutory railway station.

USPENSKA (DORMITION) CHURCH, 1650-53. Built in the Renaissance style. The construction of its roof is unique in Ukraine. Contains 18th cent. Baroque paintings and sculptures.

SPASKA (ASSUMPTION) CHURCH, 1772; **BELL TOWER,** 19th cent. This wood structure was created by Galician folk master-builders.

SYNAGOGUE, 16th-17th cent. One of the oldest buildings in the city. Original foliate ornamentation has been preserved in the synagogue.

ROMAN CATHOLIC CHURCH,

Kremenets. View of the city.

the castle was erected on the site of an ancient 11th cent. city. The castle walls are
4-5 m thick.
CARMELITE MONASTERY, 1635-
39. A defensive structure built in the Re-
naissance-Baroque style.
**MYKOLAYIVSKA (ST. NICHO-
LAS') CHURCH**, 16th-17th cent. Rebuilt
in 1734. Used as a defensive structure.

*Terebovlya. Ruins of the Basilian
Monastery, 16th cent.*

VYSHNIVETS

Village in the Zbarazh district on the Horyn River, 16 km from the Kornachivka
railway station. Population: 5,000. First mentioned in documents dating to 1395, the
date of the construction of a castle. During the 15th-17th cent. the Tatars made frequent raids on Vyshnivets. A palace built in 1720 in an ancient park is located in the
village. The Ukrainian national poet T. Shevchenko visited the village in 1846, followed two years later by the French writer Honore de Balzac. The village is associated with the name of Prince Dmytro Vyshnevetsky-Bayda, the founder of the Kozak
military organization, who was executed in Constantinople in 1563.

ZALISHCHYKY

City, railway station, and harbor on the left bank of the Dnister River, 137 km
from Ternopil. Population: 13,000.
Archaeological treasures of the Bronze Age have been unearthed in this city,
which was located at the intersection of several important trading routes.
Today the city is an important resort area, known for its children's rheumatic
sanatorium and the Dnister tourist base. Seven nature preserves and parks are located
here, including Zalishchyky Park, a nineteenth-century monument of landscape architecture, an eighteenth-century palace, and Roman Catholic church.Also located here
are an ethnographic museum and the O. Makovey Literary-Memorial Museum (tel.
2-16-79).

ZBARAZH

City and railway station on the Hnizna River. Population: 14,000. First mentioned
in the chronicles for the year 1211. In 1648 the regiments of Hetman Khmelnytsky
laid siege to the city.

CASTLE, 1626-31. Situated on a mount and surrounded by swamps. Designed
by V. Scamozzi and built in the Renaissance style by the architect Van Peen, the

castle combines features of a palace and bastion fortifications, reflecting European defensive architectural traditions. (Morozenko St., 28).

ST. BERNARD'S MONASTERY, 1627. Consists of a Roman Catholic church, monks' cells, and gate tower. Eighteenth cent. paintings have been preserved in the church. The complex was built in the Baroque style.

A monument to B. Khmelnytsky (1954) and to A. Mickiewicz (1848), as well as a Historical-Ethnographic Museum (tel. 2-18-00) are located in the city.

ZBORIV

City on the Strypa River. Population: 8,000. Known as Verkhostav in the 12th cent. One of the most important battles between the armies of Hetman Khmelnytsky and the Polish King Jan Casimir II took place here in 1649.

A Monument to B. Khmelnytsky is located in the city.

Vinnytsya Region

Situated in the forest-steppe zone of Right-Bank Ukraine and occupies the Volynian-Podilsky and Dnipro Uplands. The climate is moderate continental, with mild winters and warm summers. The main rivers of the region are the Dnister and Southern Buh, with a dense network of tributaries. Area: 26.6 thousand sq. km. Population: 1,908,000.

History

The earliest settlements date to the Paleolithic Age. In the period of the feudal breakup of Kyivan Rus'-Ukraine the region was part of the Galician-Volynian Principality. Tatar-Mongol oppression commenced in 1259. From the middle of the 14th cent. the region was annexed by the Lithuanian state and after the Treaty of Lublin the territory came under Polish rule. The population of Podillya suffered greatly from the looting raids of the Turks and Crimean Tatars, particularly in the mid-14th cent. The inhabitants of the region took an active part in the liberation war of the Ukrainian nation in 1648-1654 led by the Hetman B. Khmelnytsky, and Kozak chieftains M. Kryvonis, D. Nechay, and I. Bohun.

In 1793 the viceregencies of Podillya and Bratslav were created. In 1797 they were liquidated as a result of the creation of the guberniya (province) of Podillya, with its center in Kamyanets-Podilsky.

Vinnytsya region. Palace at Voronovytsya, 18th cent.

PROMINENT INDIVIDUALS

BORN IN THE REGION:

V. Antonovych (1834-1908). Historian, archaeologist, ethnographer; Makhnivka, Kozyatyn district. • **M. Kotsyubynsky** (1864-1913). Writer; Vinnytsya. • **M. Leontovych** (1877-1921). Civic activist and composer, best known for his arrangement of a Ukrainian folk melody, known throughout the world as the immensely popular "Carol of the Bells"; Selevyntsi, now the village of Monastyrok. • **P. Nishchynsky** (1832-1896). Composer, poet, translator; Nemenka. • **O. Novakivsky** (1872-1935). Painter; Slobodo-Obodivka, now the village of Obodivka. • **S. Rudansky** (1833-1873). Writer; Khomutyntsi, Kalynivsk district. • **V. Stus** (1938-1985). Poet, civic activist; Haysyn, died in the Soviet Gulag. • **V. Yavorivsky** (1942). Writer, publicist, civic activist; Teklivka, Kryzhopilsky district.

BURIED IN THE REGION:

M. Leontovych (1877-1921). Composer; Markivka. • **P. Nishchynsky** (1832-1896). Composer; Voroshylivka. • **M. Pyrohov** (1810-1881). Surgeon; Vinnytsya.

VINNYTSYA

City, regional and district center, located on the shores of the Southern Buh, 260 km from Kyiv. Population: 379,000. Telephone code: 0432.

The city was first mentioned in documents dating to 1363 as a fortress built by the Lithuanian princes, the Karatovyches. In 1653-1667 the city was the base of the Vinnytsya regiment. City residents fought against Poland and participated in the popular uprisings led by S. Paliy in 1702-1704 and the Haydamaky uprisings which occurred in 1730-1760. In 1793 the city, together with all of Right-Bank Ukraine, fell under Russian rule.

Formerly a Kozak church, 17th cent.

In 1919-1925 the city was the center of the guberniya of Podillya; in 1925-1930 it was part of the Vinnytsya district. Since 1932 it has been the regional center of Vinnytsya.

CHURCHES, HISTORICAL AND ARCHITECTURAL MONUMENTS

DOMINICAN MONASTERY, 1624. This wooden structure, Mury (Walls), was part of the seventieth century defense fortification complex. In 1760 it was rebuilt into a brick Roman Catholic church. The monastery was closed in 1831. The church, caves, and defense tower have been preserved.

ROMAN CATHOLIC CHURCH, 1760. A rectangular brick structure. Its facade is constructed in the Baroque style. Fragments of the wall paintings dating to the 18th cent. have been preserved. Until 1991 the church was used as a hall for organ music.

JESUIT MONASTERY, 1610-1617. The monastery was part of the Mury Defense Complex, which included a Roman Catholic church (1610-1617), a collegium (1610-1617), cells (18th-19th cent.). Today it houses an ethnographic museum.

MYKOLAYIVSKA (ST. NICHOLAS') **CHURCH,** 1746, **BELL TOWER,** 19th cent. A wooden structure with three cupolas. During restoration work undertaken in 1970 the form, basic construction, and an arcade-gallery were restored. This structure is one of the better examples of folk architecture. Alongside it is a re-

Ukrainian Musical-Drama Theater.

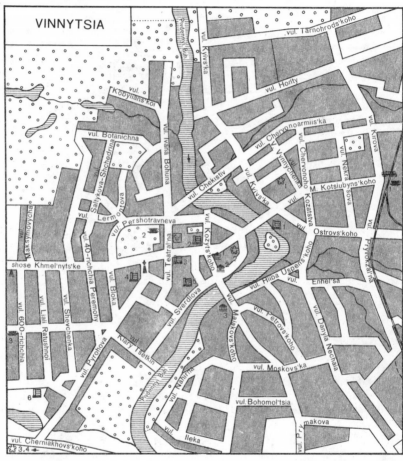

Hotels:
1 Pivdennyi Buh
2 Ukraïna
3 Vinnytsia
4 Zhovtnevyi
5 Podillia
6 Druzhba

Restaurants:
1 At the Railway Station
2 Pershotravnevyi
3 Kiel'tse
Note. Restaurants Zhovtnevyi, Ukraïna and Pivdennyi Buh are attached to the hotels of the same name

Railway Station

Monument to N. I. Pirogov

Monument commemorating the victory of Ivan Bohun's detachments over the Polish army in 1651

Architectural monuments:
1 Complex of 17th-century buildings
2 The Murs (Fortifications from the 1st half of the 17th c.)
3 Wooden Church of St. Nicholas, 1746

Museums:
1 M. Kotsiubynskyi Literary-Memorial
2 Local Lore
3 N. I. Pirogov Museum-Estate
4 N. I. Pirogov's burial vault

Music-and-Drama Theater

stored bell tower. Today it is a branch of the ethnographic museum. (Mayakovsky St., 6).

VILLA IN PYATNYCHANY, 18th cent. The villa complex includes various 18th cent. structures, e.g. a palace and pavilion, situated in a park occupying 32 ha. The landscaped park contains many coniferous trees and leafy plants. (Michurin St., 32).

MONUMENTS

M. **Kotsyubynsky,** 1964. Sculptor: I. Honchar.

Bust of T. Shevchenko, 1991.

MUSEUMS

Museum of Regional Ethnography: Lenin St., 19; tel. 2-26-71, 5-15-85. • M. **Kotsyubynsky Literary-Memorial Museum:** Bevz St., 17; tel. 5-26-87. • M. **Pyrohov Villa-Museum:** Pyrohov St., 157; tel. 6-69-37.

Monument of M. Kotsyubynsky.

THEATERS, PHILHARMONIC

Ukrainian Musical-Drama Theater: ploshcha Teatralna, 13; tel. 2-26-63. • **Summer Theater:** Central Park of Culture and Recreation; tel. 2-69-12. • **Regional Puppet Theater:** Tolstoy St., 6-a; tel. 2-39-66. • **Regional Philharmonic:** Lenin St., 62; tel. 2-20-98. • **Rayduha Cinema and Concert Hall:** Central Park of Culture and Recreation; tel. 2-07-11.

HIGHER EDUCATIONAL INSTITUTIONS

Medical Institute: Pyrohov St., 56. • **Pedagogical Institute:** Chervonopraporna St., 32. • **Agricultural Institute:** Sonyachna St., 3. • **Polytechnical Institute:** Khmelnytske shosse, 95. • **Vinnytsya Campus of the Kyiv Trade and Economics Institute:** Lenin St., 87.

Monument of M. Leontovych.

LIBRARIES, ARCHIVES

General Scientific Library: Lenin St., 73. • Central Municipal Library: Khmelnytske shosse, 4. • State Archives: Lenin St., 17.

SPORTS COMPLEXES

Avanhard Sports Complex: Lenin St., 1; tel. 2-70-45. • Lokomotyv Stadium: Chervone Kozatstvo St., 16; tel. 7-16-28.

HOTELS

Vinnytsya: Lenin St., 69; tel. 2-17-71. • Dubovy Hay: village of Stryzhavka; tel. 5-45-68. • Zhovtnevy: Pyrohov St., 2; tel. 2-65-40. • Podillya: Pushkin St., 4; tel. 2-75-96. • Ukrayina: Kozytsky St., 36; tel. 2-17-61. • Pivdenny Buh: ploshcha Zhovtneva; tel. 2-38-76. • Druzhba: Trydtsyatyrichcha Peremohy St., 21; tel. 6-83-93; 4-94-48.

RESTAURANTS, CAFES, BARS

Zhovtnevy: Pyrohov St., 2. • Pivdenny Buh: ploshcha Zhovtneva. • Keltse: Kosmonavtiv St., 35. • Druzhba: Trydtsyatyrichchya Peremohy. • Ukrayina: Kozytsky St., 36. • Dubovy Hay: village of Stryzhavka. • ESKO: Teatralna St., 24. • Pershotravnevy: Central Park of Culture and Recreation. • U Viktora: Kozytsky St., 36. • Viter Mandrivok: Pushkin St., 42. • Pizzeria: Keletsky St., 89. • Valentyna: Teatralna St., 20. • Levada: Obyizne shosse. • Hermes: Lenin St., 34. • Lisova storozhka: Nemyrivske shosse, 12th km. • Pikova Dama Cafe-Discoteque: Central Park of Culture and Recreation. • Casino: ploshcha Zhovtneva.

STORES

Central Department Store (Univermah): ploshcha Gagarina. • Ukrayinsky Suvenir: Lenin St., 39. • Syurpryz: Lenin St., 71. • Lyuks: Lenin St., 41. • Tovary Vinnychyny: prospekt Yunosti, 43-a. • Dytyachy Svit: prospekt Kotsyubynskoho, 102. • Budynok Odyahu: Kotsyubynsky St., 11. • Budynok Torhivli: Kyivska St., 104. • Turyst: Kyivska St., 55.

BANKS

National Bank of Ukraine (Regional Branch): Lenin St., 36; tel. 2-20-27. • Commercial Bank "Vinnytsya": Khmelnytske shosse, 7; tel. 5-22-90; 9-92-53. • Commercial Bank "Ahroprogres": 9th January St., 48; tel. 2-60-56.

TOURISM

Inturyst-Vinnytsya: Pyrohov St., 2; tel. 5-61-81.
Ukrproftur, Vinnytsyaturyst: Pushkin St., 4; tel. 2-59-59.
Suputnyk: Lenin St., 87; tel. 2-47-39.
Vininter: Pershotravneva St., 160; tel. 2-47-44.
Tourist-Sports Union: Pushkin St., 42; tel. 5-51-83.

POST OFFICES, TELEPHONES

Main post office: Lenin St., 10; tel. 2-06-17.
Telegraph office: Lenin St., 10; tel. 2-18-37.
Central calling points: Lenin St., 10. • Kotsyubynsky St., 28. • Kosmonavtiv St., 56-a.
Fax: Lenin St., 10; tel. 2-52-29.

MEDICAL SERVICES

Emergency: tel. 03.
Pharmacies: No. 2: Lenin St., 53; tel. 2-27-37. • No. 4: Pyrohov St., 17; tel. 2-78-37. • No. 6: Kotsyubynsky St., 78; tel. 2-35-80. • No. 214: Kyivska St., 54; tel. 2-55-67. • No. 274: prospekt Yunosti, 20/73; tel. 6-63-10. • No. 285: Kosmonavtiv St., 47-b; tel. 6-45-20.

TRANSPORTATION

Train station: ploshcha Heroyiv Stalinhrada; information: tel. 004; **tickets:** tel. 7-29-43.
Bus terminus: Kyivska St., 6; tel. 5-12-69.
Airport: village of Havryshivka; information: tel. 2-28-08; 2-77-44.
International Connecting Flights Agency: ploshcha Gagarina; tel. 2-56-60.

AUTO SERVICING

Autoservis: Vatutin St., 172; tel. 7-79-96.

TOURING HISTORIC CITIES AND VILLAGES

ANTOPOL

Village, Tomashpolsky district.

PALACE, 19th cent. Built in the Classical style, in a park which occupies an area of 30 ha.

BUSHA

Village, Yampilsky district, on the Bushanka River, located 20 km from the district center.

CRYPT CHURCH, 6th-7th cent. Discovered in 1883 by the archeologist and ethnographer V. Antonovych. Located in clefts of a cliff overlooking the Bushka River. Unique interior relief compositions and inscriptions have been preserved.

POKROVSKY (PROTECTION OF THE BLESSED VIRGIN MARY) CHURCH, 17th cent. Built on the ruins of a former (1616) monastery. Destroyed by the Ukrainian Kozaks in 1648-1654. Rebuilt in 1787. The Pokrova church and cells (1787) and the bell tower (1908) have been preserved.

USPENSKA (DORMITION) CHURCH, 1757. Built on the site of the Troyitska (Holy Trinity) Church. Repaired in 1851. Paintings from the 19th cent. have been preserved. Rebuilt in 1978-1979.

TOWER, 17th cent. Part of the Busha fortifications. Rebuilt in the 19th century.

GONTIVKA

Village, Mohyliv-Podilsky district, on the Lozova River, 22 km from the Mohyliv-Podilsky railway station.

Monument to Ivan Gonta, the leader of the Haydamaky, 1968. Sculptor: I. Honchar.

KARMALYUKOVE (until 1955 — Holovchyntsi)

Village, Zhmerynka district, 8 km from the Serbynivtsi railway station.

Monument to Ustym Karmalyuk, popular Haydamaky chieftain who was born in this village, 1965.

KHMILNYK

City, on the Southern Buh River, 67 km from Vinnytsya.

First mentioned in written sources in 1368. City residents took part in the peasant-Kozak uprisings led by Nalyvayko (1594-1596) and Pavlyuk (1637), in the liberation war of 1648-1654, and in the peasant uprisings led by U. Karmalyuk.

Khmilnyk is known as a health resort; the radon-rich mineral waters are widely used in cures. A branch of the Ukrainian Scientific Research Institute of Resorts and Physiotherapy is located in the city.

PALACE, 1911-1915. Designed by I. Fomin as a palace-park ensemble. Includes a defense tower (1534) that stood on the "Black Route" by which the Tatars would invade Podillya. (Shevchenko St., 1).

USICHENNYA HOLOVY SV. IOANA PREDTECHI (BEHEADING OF ST. JOHN THE BAPTIST) ROMAN CATHOLIC CHURCH, 1603. Built in the Baroque style. Repeatedly damaged during the 17th cent. Substantial repairs were made to the building in 1728. Twentieth-century wall paintings have been preserved. (Shevchenko St., 3).

LYADOVA

Village, Mohyliv-Podilsky district.

CLIFF MONASTERY, 11th-19th cent. This complex of structures is situated on a mountain plateau above the Dnister River. In the first half of the 18th cent. a Basilian monastery was located in the grottos. The monastery was closed in 1795. The monastic complex consists of three crypt churches: Usichennya Holovy sv. Ioana Predtechi (Beheading of St. John the Baptist), St. Paraskeva Pyatnytsya, and St. Antoniy Pechersky (St. Anthony of the Caves).

MOHYLIV-PODILSKY

City, on the Dnister River, 154 km from Vinnytsya.

MYKOLAYIVSKY (ST. NICHOLAS') MONASTERY, 1754. Brick. In 1885 the church was enlarged. A historical-ethnographic museum is located on the premises. (Ploshcha Chervona, 4).

CHURCH OF ST. PARASKEVA; BELL TOWER, 1775. A wooden structure typical of the church architecture of Podillya. Oil paintings from the early part of the 20th cent. have been preserved. (Barny St., 16).

HEORHIYIVSKA (ST. GEORGE'S) GREEK CHURCH AND BELL TOWER, 1808-1819. Built by the architect I. Freiwald in the Classical style. Interior oil paintings from the early part of the 20th cent. have been preserved.

MUROVANI KURYLIVTSI

Town, 23 km from the Kotyuzhany railway station.

PALACE, 1805. Owing to its architectural construction it is known as the "Versailles of Podillya." Situated in a landscaped park and designed by D. Mikler. The palace was rebuilt in the 1960s. Fortifications dating to the 16th cent., including an underground casemate, have been preserved.

NEMYRIV

City, 45 km from Vinnytsya. First mentioned in written sources in 1506, i.e. in the decree of the Tatar Khan Mengli Ghirey. The inhabitants of the town took part in uprisings led by S. Nalyvayko. In the period of the liberation struggle from 1648 to 1654 the town was liberated by M. Kryvonis and I. Gonta. After 1797 it became part of the guberniya (province) of Podillya.

Nemyriv. Resort "Avanhard."

PALACE, 1897-1917; PARK, 19th cent. Built in the Neoclassical style by the architects H. Hriner and Ye. Kramarzh. Has a portico with four columns. Since 1921 it has been used as a recreation facility. Reparations to the building were made in 1956. The palace is surrounded by a park occupying an area of 85 ha. containing more than 80 species of trees and shrubs. (Shevchenko St., 13).

NOVA HREBLYA

Village, Kalynivka district.

MYKOLAYIVSKA (ST. NICHOLAS') CHURCH, 1701. A brick structure built in the Late Classical style. Nineteenth-century wall paintings have been preserved. Substantial reparations to the building were made in 1860.

RUDANSKE (formerly Khomutyntsi)

Village, Zhmerynka district, 18 km from the Kalynivka-1 railway station.

The S. Rudansky Memorial Museum. Located in the house where the poet was born.
Monument to S. Rudansky, 1969.

SHARHOROD

City, 90 km from Vinnytsya.

MYKOLAYIVSKY (ST. NICHOLAS') MONASTERY, 18th-19th cent. The ensemble of buildings includes the Mykolayivsky Cathedral (1829), built in the Classical style, an entrance wing with a bell tower (18th cent.), a walled tower (18th cent.), estate buildings.
KOSTEL NEPOROCHNOHO ZACHATTYA DIVY MARIYI (IMMACULATE CONCEPTION ROMAN CATHOLIC CHURCH), 1627, 1791. Built in the Baroque style.

Sharhorod. Mykolayivsky (St. Nicholas') Monastery, 18th-19th cent.

SYNAGOGUE, 1589. A brick structure. Decorative fragments dating to the 17th-19th cent. have been preserved on the pillars.

TULCHYN

City, 82 km from Vinnytsya.
First references to the city date to 1607-1609. The population took an active part in the liberation war of 1648-1654 and the peasant uprisings of 1768 known as "Koliyivshchyna."

PALACE (old), 1757. Designed by the French architect Lacroix. The grouping of buildings, including a theatre and other structures, is one of the better examples of the Classical style in Ukraine. Almost all the interior decorations were destroyed during the period of Soviet rule. Reparations to the palace were begun in 1975. (Leontovych St., 8).

PALACE, 1782. A small structure, built in the Early Classical style. (Lenin St., 8).

USPENSKA (DORMITION) CHURCH, 1789; **BELL TOWER,** 19th cent. A brick structure, built in the Classical style. (Gagarin St., 13).

The Ethnographic Museum with a monument to the composer M. Leontovych is located in the city.

VERKHIVKA

Village, Trostyanets district.

PALACE, 19th cent. Situated in a landscaped park occupying an area of 30 h. The palace and entrance gates are built in the neo-Baroque Romantic style. The park is a well-organized complex of formal gardens. An agricultural college has been located here since 1932.

VORONOVYTSYA

City, Vinnytsya district, on the Voronka River, 24 km. from Vinnytsya.

PALACE AND PARK, 18th cent. Built in the Early Classical style. Sections of the park surrounding the palace have been preserved. The palace houses a school and the Museum of Aviation History.

Tulchyn. Palace, 1757.

Volyn Region

Northwest Ukraine. Lies between the Polissya lowlands and the Volynian plateau. Climate: moderate-continental. A region rich in lakes (more than 220), forests, rivers. Chief river: the Prypyat with its tributaries.
Created in 1939. Area: 20,2 thousand sq. km. Population: 1,076,000.

History

This territory was settled in the Late Paleolithic Age. More than 160 monuments of the Paleolithic and Mesolithic Age are preserved. The earliest of them is the settlement of Rosten in the Lyuboml district. The East Slavic tribes of Duliby, Buzhany, and Volynyany lived here in the VII-X centuries. In the 10th cent. the Volynian land, whose name derives from the city of Volyn, was part of Kyivan Rus'-Ukraine. In 1199 it formed part of the Galician-Volynian Principality, whose population waged a struggle against the Mongol-Tatar hordes.

In the early part of the 14th cent. Volyn formed part of the Lithuanian state, and after the Union of Lublin in 1569, belonged to Poland. From 1793, Volyn, comprising the Izyaslav and Volynian viceregency, came under Russian imperial rule (1793-96). Volyn became a province (guberniya) in 1797.

From 1921 to 1939 Volyn was under Polish rule. Centuries of national and social

Zymne. Svyatohirsky (Holy Mount) Monastery, 15th-20th cent.

oppression, particularly during the period of Soviet rule, left a tragic imprint on the Volynian land. Hundreds of cultural monuments were destroyed. Throughout the centuries the Ukrainian population of Volyn fought against oppression. The most vivid example of this struggle is their active participation in the national-liberation wars of 1648-54 and in the Haydamaky Movement. Significantly, it was in Volyn that the Ukrainian Insurgent Army (UPA), which fought against both the Germans and Muscovite-Communist totalitarianism, was formed in 1942.

PROMINENT INDIVIDUALS

BORN IN THE REGION:

A. Krymsky (1871-1942), Orientalist, literary scholar, b. Volodymyr-Volynsky, died in prison. • **Ye. Sverstyuk** (1928), literary scholar, b. in the village of Siltse, Horokhivsky district.

LUTSK

Regional center on the river Styr, 470 km from Kyiv. Population: 214,500. Telephone code: 033.

Lutsk (Luchesk) is first mentioned in the Hypatian Chronicle in the entry for 1085. There are several theories to explain the origins of the name: according to one, the name derives from the word "luka," meaning a bend in a river; other theories indicate that it derives from Luka, the name of a chieftain of the Duliby, an East Slavic tribe. In the mid-12th cent. Lutsk was one of the largest cities in the Galician-Volynian Principality.

During the 13th and 14th cent. an icon-painting workshop was located in Lutsk. The most famous monument from this period is the icon of the Volynian Blessed Virgin Mary, first discovered in

Lutsk. Castle (center), 13th-14th cent.

the Pokrova Church (Protection of the Blessed Virgin Mary). The Lutsk brotherhood played a major role in the development of culture and education, whose members founded a school and the first printing house.

Lutsk was sacked and razed to the ground in 1240 and 1500. Under Lithuanian rule the city was considered the second state capital. In 1429 a conference of European monarchs was held here, during which the question of defending Europe from the Tatar onslaught was discussed. During the 15th and 16th cent. the city was one of the centers of international trade in Ukraine.

In the 19th cent. teaching institutions, schools, a private boarding school, and a gymnasium were established. The poetess, Lesya Ukrayinka, spent her childhood years here (1878-81).

CHURCHES, HISTORICAL AND ARCHITECTURAL MONUMENTS

POKROVSKA (PROTECTION OF THE BLESSED VIRGIN MARY) CHURCH, 15th cent. Reconstructed in 1873-76. Its oil paintings were restored in 1932 and 1966. The magnificent icon of the Volynian Blessed Virgin Mary, a rare masterpiece of the 13th-14th cent., originally hung in the church. Today it is found in the Museum of Ukrainian Art in Kyiv. (Danylo Halytsky St., 12; trolleybus No. 1, 6).

SVYATOTROYITSKY (HOLY TRINITY) CATHEDRAL, 1752-55. Originally a monastery of the order of St. Bernard. Rebuilt as a cathedral in 1877-79

LUTSK

B̄ Volyn'tourist Amalgamation

▣ Hotels:
  1 Ukraïna
  2 Luts'k
  3 Svitiaz' Tourist Hotel

🍽 Restaurants:
  1 Skhidnyi
  2 Svitlofor
  3 Teatral'nyi
  4 Volyn'
  Note. Restaurant Ukraïna is attached to the hotel of the same name

🚃 Railway Station

🚌 Bus Station

🛒 Market

🗿 Monument to Lesia Ukrainka

🏛 Architectural monuments:
  1 Building of the former Trinitarian Monastery, 18th c.
  2 Bell tower, 1536
  3 Lutsk Castle (ensemble of 14th—19th century buildings)
  4 Building of the former Jesuit Church, 1610

🎭 Theaters:
  1 Taras Shevchenko Theater of Music and Drama
  2 Puppet

🎵 Philharmonic Society

according to the designs of the architect, Rastrukanov. The paintings were executed by the Czech master F. Paralak and the artist, L. Spaska. (Ploshcha Teatralna).

DOMINICAN MONASTERY, 1390. Originally a wood structure, it was reconstructed in stone in the 18th cent. The monastery was liquidated in 1847. A military hospital began operating in the former monks' cells. Today the building houses technical and artistic artifacts. (Kafedralna St., 19; trolleybus No. 1, 6).

KHRESTODVYZHENSKA (ELEVATION OF THE HOLY CROSS) CHURCH, 1619. One of the earliest examples of the transition from wooden to stone architecture. Its design combines the traditions of ancient Ukrainian, folk, and Renaissance architecture. In 1702 the poet D. Bratkovsky, was buried in the church crypt. In 1890 the church was rebuilt following a fire. Was rebuilt several times afterwards. (Danylo Halytsky St., 2; trolleybus No. 1, 6).

JESUIT MONASTERY, 16th-17th cent. Architects: J. Briano, V. Hizhytsky, Y. Uminsky.

BASILIAN MONASTERY, 17th cent. Part of the complex of the Khrestodvyzhensky (Elevation of the Holy Cross) Brotherhood. Founded in 1624. (Hertsen St., 5).

THE TOWER OF THE CZARTORYSKI PRINCES, 15th cent. The castle was built in the 14th cent. Only the keep and part of the wall have been preserved.

BRIGITTINE CONVENT, 1624. Built on the site of a castle dating to the 16th cent. Damaged in a fire in 1724. Restored and partially reconstructed. In 1846 the convent was closed and a prison established on its premises. Eventually a music institute was founded here. (Kafedralna St., 16; trolleybus No. 1, 6).

BUILDING OF THE FORMER SYNAGOGUE, 14th-15th cent. Sustained damage during 1941-44. Restored in 1981. (Danylo Halytsky St., 33; trolleybus No. 1, 6).

LUTSK CASTLE, 13th-14th cent. A fortified structure with three towers: the Passage, or Tower of Lyubart, who was the ruler of Lutsk (1340-80), the Styr, or the Tower of Svydryhaylo, and the Vladycha. In 1987 a bell museum was established in the Vladycha Tower. Construction on the castle was begun during Lyubart's rule and completed during the rule of Svydryhaylo (1430-1452). Restored in 1977. (Kafedralna St., 1; trolleybus No. 1, 6).

HULEVYCH BUILDING, 16th cent. A unique example of residential architecture. Halshka Hulevychivna (1575-1642), one of the founders of the Kyivan Collegium, was a member of the Hulevych

Lutsk. Castle, 13th-14th cent.

Lutsk. Monument to Lesya Ukrayinka, 1977.

family. (Kafedralna St., 23; trolleybus No. 1, 6).

VAULTS OF THE OLD CITY, 16th-18th cent. Underground labyrinths in the vicinity of Kafedralna Street, Danylo Halytsky Street, and others. Excavations were begun in 1970. More than 50 subterranean sites were discovered, containing a large number of household artifacts, implements, etc. A prison complex with an isolation cell was discovered beneath the Roman Catholic Church of SS. Peter and Paul. According to legend, the subterranean passages linked Lutsk with the neighboring villages of Shepel, Zhydychyn, Olyka, and others. (Trolleybus No. 1, 6).

MONUMENTS

Lesya Ukrayinka, 1977. Sculptors: A. Nimenko, M. Obezyuk. Architects: V. Zhyhulin, S. Kilesso. (Teatralna Ploshcha).
Lesya Ukrayinka, 1965. Sculptor: L. Muravin. (In the Lesya Ukrayinka Central Park of Culture and Recreation).
T. Shevchenko, 1964. Erected near the Building of Culture of the Hnidavsky Sugar Plant. (S. Korolyov St., 10).

MUSEUMS

Museum of Regional Ethnography: Chopin St., 20; tel. 4-25-91. • **Art Gallery:** Kafedralna St., 1; tel. 2-30-75. • **Lesya Ukrayinka Museum** (in the Lesya Ukrayinka Pedagogical Institute): Vynnychenko St., 30. • **Historical-Cultural Reserve:** Zamkova Ploshcha; tel. 2-34-32.

THEATERS, PHILHARMONIC

T. H. Shevchenko Musical-Drama Theater: Teatralna Ploshcha. • **Puppet Theater:** Kryvy Val, 18. • **Philharmonic:** prospekt Voli, 46.

HIGHER EDUCATIONAL INSTITUTIONS

Lesya Ukrayinka Pedagogical Institute: Vynnychenko St., 20. • Industrial Institute: Lvivska St., 75. • Teacher Upgrading Institute: Vynnychenko St., 27.

LIBRARIES, ARCHIVES

O. Pchilka Regional Research Library: Chopin St., 11. • Regional Childrens' Library: prospekt Voli, 37. • Young Peoples' Regional Library: prospekt Voli, 2. • Regional Medical Library: Suvorov St., 1. • Regional State Archives: Veterany St., 21.

PARKS

Lesya Ukrayinka Central Park of Culture and Recreation: prospekt Voli, 13; tel. 4-81-44. • Park (dedicated to the 900th anniversary of Lutsk): 17 Veresnya St., tel. 5-40-01.

SPORTS COMPLEXES

Avanhard Stadium: prospekt Prezydenta M. Hrushevskoho; tel. 4-01-37.

HOTELS

Ukrayina: Slowacki St., 2; tel. 4-33-51; 4-33-55. • Luchesk: Vidrodzhennya St., 1; tel. 5-29-95; 5-29-96. • Svityaz: Naberezhna St.; tel. 4-34-81; 4-90-00. • Lutsk: Krylov St., 1; tel. 2-34-39, 2-34-51. • Dynamo: Danylo Halytsky St., 33; tel. 2-41-06.

RESTAURANTS, CAFES

Volyn: prospekt Voli, 42; tel. 4-11-38. • Teatralny: Lesya Ukrayinka St., 67; tel. 2-52-04. • Ukrayina: Slowacki St., 2; tel. 4-33-30. • Luchesk: Rivnenska St., 89; tel. 5-25-68. • Svityaz: Naberezhna, opposite the City Council; tel. 4-92-53. • Svitlofor: Striletska St., 45; tel. 4-00-80. • Dorozhniy: prospekt Voli, 42; tel. 4-24-67.

STORES

Centralny Univermah (Department Store): prospekt Voli, 1. • Garrison Univermah: prospekt Prezydenta Hrushevskoho, 1. • Znannya Bookstore: prospekt Voli, 41. • Mystetstvo (Art): Lesya Ukrayinka St., 11.

BANKS

National Bank of Ukraine (Regional Branch): Plekhanov St., 4; tel. 2-34-18.

TOURISM

Inturyst-Lutsk: Slowacki St., 2; tel. 4-47-58. Package excursions and special trips arranged throughout Volyn.
Volynturyst: next to the train station; tel. 3-15-14.
Suputnyk-Volyn: Chopin St., 1; tel. 2-47-01.

POST OFFICE, TELEPHONE

Main post office: Pershe Travnya St., 19; tel. 2-43-12.
Telegraph: Pershe Travnya St., 19; tel. 2-50-12.
Fax: prospekt Peremohy, 2; tel. 4-10-50.
Communications point: prospekt Voli, 14; tel. 2-70-44.

MEDICAL SERVICES

Emergency: tel. 03.
Pharmacies: No. 65: prospekt Voli. 3; tel. 2-48-98. • No. 134: Kyivska Ploshcha, 7; tel. 9-30-53.

TRANSPORTATION

Train station: ploshcha Vokzalna; tel. 005.
International Exchange: Vynnychenko St., 2; tel. 9-73-10.
Airport: village of Krupa; tel. 006, 056, 4-61-47.
Bus station No. 1: Konyakina St., 39; tel. 004; 4-60-48; 4-11-67.
Bus station No. 2: Lvivska St. 148; tel. 6-14-70.
Taxi reservations: tel. 058.

AUTO SERVICING

Autoservice: prospekt Engelsa, 145; tel. 5-00-62.

TOURING HISTORIC CITIES AND VILLAGES

BERESTECHKO

Village, Horokhivsky district, 25 km from the Horokhiv train station.

Became the site of Ukrainian pilgrimage after the battle of Berestechko, June 18-30, 1651, which took place between the armies of Ukrainian Hetman B. Khmelnytsky and the Polish King Jan Casimir III. In 1846 Berestechko was visited by T. Shevchenko who recorded the events of 1651 in the poem "The Field of Berestechko" and "Beyond the Ravine."

Berestechko. Church-Monument of the "Kozak Grave," 1914.

TEKLA'S CHAPEL, 17th cent. According to legend, the chapel was built on the graves of 500 girls, tortured to death by the Tatars in Berestechko.

TROYITSKY (HOLY TRINITY) ROMAN CATHOLIC CHURCH, 1765. A painting of the battle of Berestechko was executed in 1853 on the outside wall. Constructed in the Baroque style; alongside it is an 18th-century bell tower.

THE STONE PILLAR, 16th cent. Erected on the grave of O. Pronsky.

KAMIN-KASHYRSKY

City, on the river Tsyr, 150 km from Lutsk; a railway station. Approximately 7000 inhabitants.

First mentioned in written sources in 1196, when the Volynian Prince Roman Mstyslavovych, built a fortress on this site.

ILLINSKA (ST. ELIAS') CHURCH, 1700. Wooden. Was completely rebuilt in 1886 in a style reminiscent of Muscovite architecture.

RIZDVA BOHORODYTSI (NATIVITY OF THE HOLY MOTHER OF GOD) CHURCH, 1723. Has features of the Baroque style. Reconstruction in the 19th cent. divested the church of its characteristic forms of folk architecture. Paintings of the 17th-18th cent. have been preserved.

KACHYN

Village, Kamin-Kashyrsky district, situated near Kachynsky Lake, 7 km from the Soshychne railway station.

USPENSKA (DORMITION) CHURCH, 1589. Wooden. An example of northern Volynian folk architecture. Renovated several times. Paintings and carvings of the 17th-19th cent. have been preserved in the church. Restored in 1971.

KOLODYAZHNE

Village, Kovelsky district, 8 km from the Kovel train station.
THE WHITE HOUSE, 1949. A memorial museum-estate dedicated to Lesya Ukrayinka (1871-1913), where the poetess lived on and off during the period from 1893 to 1907.

KORTELISY

Village, Ratnivsky district, 10 km from the Kovel-Brest autoroute.

MEMORIAL COMPLEX, 1980. Erected in memory of the inhabitants of a village who were executed by the Germans in 1943. Sculptor: A. Oliynyk; architect: A. Komyeyev.
Museum of Village History, 1980. Opened simultaneously with the memorial.

LYUBOML

City, 127 km from Lutsk; a railway station. Population: 7000.
First mentioned in written sources in 1287.

HEORHIYIVSKA (ST. GEORGE'S) CHURCH, 16th cent. Built at the foot of the ramparts at the behest of the Volynian Prince Volodymyr Vasylkovych. In the church paintings dating to the 19th cent. are preserved.

TROYITSKY (HOLY TRINITY) ROMAN CATHOLIC CHURCH, 1412. Originally built in the Gothic style. Restored in 1971-75.
BELL TOWER, 1640.

Lyuboml. Heorhiyivska
(St. George's) Church, 16th cent.

MYLTSI

Village, Starovyzhivsky district, 13 km from the railway station of Nesukhoyizhe.

MYKOLAYIVSKY (ST. NICHOLAS') MONASTERY, 16th-19th cent. Wooden. An important monastery in Volyn, it had its own school in the 17th cent. The monastic complex includes the Mykolayivsky Church (St. Nicholas') (1542), a bell tower (1901), the prior's house (18th cent.) and monks' cells (18th cent.). **ONUFRIYIVSKY (ST. ONU-PHRIUS') CHURCH,** 1723. Originally a chapel. Substantially renovated in the 18th cent.

NOVY ZAHORIV

Village, Lokachi district, 30 km from the Horokhiv railway station.

ZAHORIVSKY MONASTERY, 16th cent. Y. Kondzelevych worked here in 1796. In 1943 a famous battle was fought near the monastery between a formation of the Ukrainian Insurgent Army and the Germans, including the Polish collaborationist police. A commemorative plaque was erected in honor of the heroes.

Nyzkynychi. Uspenska (Dormition) Church, 17th cent.

NYZKYNYCHI

Village, Ivanychi district, 12 km from the Ivanychi railway station.

USPENSKA (DORMITION) CHURCH, 17th cent. The sarcophagus and marble bust of A. Kysil (1599-1653), a civic and religious leader, as well as frescoes dating to the 17th cent. have been preserved in the church.

OKHLOPIV

Village, Horokhiv district, 6 km from the Stoyaniv railway station.

MYKOLAYIVSKA (ST. NICHOLAS') CHURCH, 1638. A typical example of a stone structure with features germane to the tradition of Ukrainian wooden architecture. The church was partially rebuilt in the 19th cent.

OLYKA

Village, Kivertsivsky district, 9 km from the Olyka railway station. First mentioned in the Hypatian Chronicle in the entry for 1149.

CASTLE, 1564. One of the first square-shaped defensive bastions in Ukraine.

*Okhlopiv. Mykolayivska
(St. Nicholas') Church, 1638.*

Survived many sieges from 1591 to 1648. Was renovated in 1883. Descriptions of the castle from 1686 and 1737 are extant. Occupies 2.7 hectares. Renovated in 1976.

TROYITSKY (HOLY TRINITY) ROMAN CATHOLIC CHURCH, 1635-40. Architects: B. Molli and Ya. Malivern. The church was decorated with sculptures and carvings by M. Erlenberg. The church complex includes a bell tower (1635-40), towers (1635-40).

PETROPAVLIVSKY (SS. PETER'S AND PAUL'S) ROMAN CATHOLIC CHURCH, 1450. The oldest Roman Catholic structure in Volyn. Rebuilt in 1612.

PIDDUBTSI

Village, Lutsk district, 12 km from the Kivertsi railway station.

POKROVSKA (PROTECTION OF THE BLESSED VIRGIN MARY) CHURCH, 1745. Stone, with nine cupolas. Constructed in the Late Baroque style with details typical of the transition to the Classical style.

SHATSK

Village, Lyuboml district, 33 km from the Lyuboml railway station.

Shatsky National Park, 1983. Area: 32,500 hectares Encompasses Lake Svityaz, the largest of Ukraine's many lakes.

"Shatski Ozera" Tourist Base. On Lake Svityaz. Open in spring and summer; limited operating season in the winter.

"Lisova Pisnya" Sanatorium. Situated on Pisochne Lake; open year-round.

VOLODYMYR-VOLYNSKY

City on the river Luh, 80 km from Lutsk. Population: 41,200.

A former political, economic, and cultural center of Kyivan Rus'-Ukraine. The first mention of the original name of the city of Volodymyr appears in the chroni-

*Piddubtsi.
Pokrovska (Protection of the Blessed
Virgin Mary) Church, 1745.*

cle "Tale of Bygone Years" for the year 988. Became the capital of the Galician-Volynian Principality in 1199. During the 12th-13th cent. was one of the centers for trade between Rus'-Ukraine and various European countries. Destroyed by the Tatars in 1240. In 1256 the Tatar Khan, Kuremsa, tried to capture this city-fortress. Volodymyr was one of the centers of early Ukrainian writing. The eminent chronicler, Nestor, visited the city. The art of bookbinding was well developed here. The most distinguished monument of the times is the Galician-Volynian Chronicle, compiled during the 13th-14th cent. Schools began to be founded from 1577. In the 18th cent. the Volodymyr Collegium was one of the largest in Ukraine.

In 1795 it came under Russian rule and was renamed Volodymyr-Volynsky. The population suffered greatly from cholera epidemics in 1831 and 1837, and from fires in 1833, 1853, 1855.

CHURCHES, HISTORICAL AND ARCHITECTURAL MONUMENTS

USPENSKY (DORMITION) CATHEDRAL, known as Prince Mstyslav's Church, 1160. The sole monument of ancient Ukrainian architecture in Volyn which has been preserved to the present day. Its structure is similar to the architecture of the Kyrylivska Church (St. Cyril's) in Kyiv. It collapsed in 1829. During 1896-1900 was rebuilt according to forms prevalent in the 12th cent. The cathedral complex includes a house with bell tower (1494), restored in 1969-1971, walls with a gate (17th cent.)

VASYLIVSKA (ST. BASIL'S) CHURCH, 13th-14th cent. A typical structure of Ukrainian architecture reflecting the emergence of a national art. Reconstruction in 1900-01 changed its original appearance.

EARTHEN RAMPARTS OF THE CASTLE, 10th-14th cent. Remains of an ancient city of Kyivan Rus'-Ukraine of the 10th cent., founded on this site by Prince Volodymyr the Great, after whom the city of Volodymyr was named. In the 17th and 18th cent. the castle falls into ruins and loses its strategic significance. Only the 9-10 meter-high ramparts, which encircle a square of 3 ha have been preserved. (Prykordonna St., 3).

MYKOLAYIVSKA (ST. NICHOLAS') CHURCH, 1780. Designed as a chapel. In 1800 it was renamed a cathedral.

SS. JOACHIM AND ANNA ROMAN CATHOLIC CHURCH, 1752. Built on the site of a wooden Roman Catholic church in the Baroque style. (Heroyiv St., 1).

Volodymyr-Volynsky. Uspensky (Dormition) Cathedral, 1160.

RUINS OF THE DEFENSE RAMPARTS OF THE DYTYNETS, 10th-12th cent.

ZHYDYCHYN

Village, Kivertsi district, 7 km from Lutsk.

ZHYDYCHYNSKY MONASTERY, 13th cent. According to the Hypatian Chronicle, in 1277 the Galician-Volynian King Danylo, came here to pray. Yuriy, the son of B. Khmelnytsky, lived here in 1662 as the monk Hedeon. The monastery complex includes: the Mykolayivska (St. Nicholas') Church (1723), bell tower (18th cent.) and the Bishop's residence (1723).

ZYMNE

Village, Volodymyr-Volynsky district, 7 km from the Volodymyr-Volynsky railway station.

SVYATOHIRSKY (HOLY MOUNT) MONASTERY, 15th-20th cent. Built as a defense post above a steep precipice overlooking the river Luh. First mentioned in 1458. Restored in 1899 according to the designs of the architect M. Kozlov. Also rebuilt were the bell tower, the Uspenska (Assumption) Church and the crypts Varlaamska Church and school were built. The monastic complex includes: the Uspenska (Assumption) church and crypt, 1495-1550. Rebuilt in 1898-1900, sustained damage in 1943; the Troyitska (Holy Trinity) Church, 1465-75; the Refectory-type Church and five defense towers. The monastery was restored in 1975.

Zakarpatska Region
(Transcarpathia)

Located in the geographical center of Europe and bordering on Romania, Hungary, Slovakia and Poland. The region occupies the southwestern part of the Ukrainian Carpathian Mountains and the neighboring northeastern central Danubian Lowland.

The territory is mountainous and hilly, and is covered with deciduous and coniferous forests, and Alpine meadows. The highest point in the region is Hoverla (2061 m) in the Carpathian Mountains. In the lowlands are fertile fields, orchards and vineyards. The climate is temperate-continental with a comparatively long spring, cool summer, warm fall and mild winter.

The country is dissected by numerous rivers. The largest are the Tysa, Borzhava, Tereblya, Rika, Uzh, and Latorytsya. There are several small mountain lakes of post-glacial origin. The most important is Lake Synevyrsk (989 m above sea-level).

More than 360 varieties of mineral waters have been discovered and researched. These waters are used in the treatment of various ailments of the digestive and circulatory systems, and physio-therapy. There are 10 sanatoriums in the region. The best known are Karpaty, Sonyashne Zakarpattya, Polyana, Kvitka Polonyny, Perlyna Karpat, and Shayan. To serve the needs of travelers the Latorytsya tourist complex in Mukacheve, 10 tourist centers with 9 branches, and three mountain shelters operate in the region. They can accommodate a total of 4,000 people. There are also 12 ski trails in the area.

Established in 1946. Area: 12,800 sq. km. Population: 1,279,00.

History

Near the village of Koroleve in the Vynohradiv district the remains of one of the largest and oldest settlements in Ukraine founded 500,000 years ago have been excavated. "Stoyanky" (dwellings) dating to the early Paleolithic Age have been un-

Uzhhorod. Mykhaylivska
(St. Michael's) Church, 1777.

Transcarpathia. Lake Synevyr Tourist Co.

earthed in Uzhhorod, Mukacheve, Berehove, and Khust. Near the villages of Hlyboke, Huta, and Kamyanets in the Uzhhorod district the remains of settlements from the Mezolithic Age have been excavated. More than 30 Neolithic remains, 80 from the Copper and Bronze Age, and many Iron-age settlements have been unearthed. Slavic tribes arriving from the territories of present-day Volynia settled here in the 1st cent. A.D. In the 9th-10th cent. the Transcarpathian region was part of Kyivan Rus'-Ukraine.

In 896 Hungarian nomadic tribes began migrating over the Carpathian Mountains to the lands near the Danube River. In 1867 Transcarpathia became part of the Austro-Hungarian Empire; after its fall in 1918 the region was incorporated into the Czechoslovak Republic. Transcarpathia became independent in 1938. Hungary occupied Transcarpathia in 1939 by the terms of the Munich Agreement. In October 1944 Transcarpathia became part of the Ukrainian SSR.

PROMINENT INDIVIDUALS

BORN IN THE REGION:

Y. Bokshay (1891-1975), artist; in Kobyletska Polyana, Rakhiv district. • I. Chendey (1922), writer; in Dubove, Tyachiv district. • V. Grendzha-Donsky (1897-1974), writer, political leader; in Volove (present-day Mizhhirya). • A. Patrus-Karpatsky (1917-75), writer; in Terebovlya, was imprisoned. • A. Shtefan (1893-1986), educator, social and cultural leader, president of the Parliament of Carpathian Ukraine (1939); in Poroshkovo, Perechyn district. • A. Voloshyn (1892-1945), president of Carpathian Ukraine (1939); in Kelechyn, Mizhhirya district, died in a Soviet prison.

BURIED IN THE REGION:

Y. Bokshay (1891-1975), painter; in Uzhhorod. • Y. Fentsyk (1844-1904), writer, educator; in Uzhhorod. • M. Luchkay (1789-1843), historian, linguist; in Uzhhorod.

UZHHOROD

City and center of the Transcarpathian region, on the Uzh River. Population: 125,000. Telephone code: 0312.

Uzhhorod was mentioned in the chronicles as early as 872. The city name Ung is mentioned in the Hungarian Chronicle "Gesta Hungarorum" as the residence of the Slavic Prince Laborets, who was executed by the Hungarian army in 896 on the bank of the Svirzhava River (today Laborets River is in eastern Slovakia). The city has changed names several times: it has been called Ongvar, Hungvar, Unguyvar, and Ungvar. The city of Uzhhorod was protected by a mighty fortress. In 1080 the armies of the Polovtsian Khan Kutesko devastated the entire region, but were unable to capture the fortress. During the Middle Ages the city was destroyed many times in the wars between the Habsburgs and the Transylvanian Principality. In the 11th-13th cent. Uzhhorod was under Hungarian rule. In 1648 a thousand-man detachment of Kozaks arrived, escorting the emissary of B. Khmelnytsky to the Transylvanian King Rakoci.

In 1919 Uzhhorod became the center of Transcarpathian Rus', under the rule of Czechoslovakia; in the fall of 1938, the capital of Carpathian Ukraine, and in 1949, the center of the Transcarpathian region of the Ukrainian SSR.

In the mid-17th cent. a Jesuit College and gymnasium were relocated here from the town of Humenne (today in eastern Slovakia). Later, the gymnasium became the main middle-level educational institution in Transcarpathia. During the next century theological seminaries and teacher-training colleges were established here.

From 1921 to 1930 a National Theater flourished in Uzhhorod. In 1945 the University of Transcarpathia was founded.

CHURCHES, HISTORICAL AND ARCHITECTURAL MONUMENTS

KAFEDRALNY SOBOR (CHURCH), 1646. Originally a Jesuit Monastery, it was designated a Ukrainian Catholic Cathedral in 1773. During the Soviet era the cathedral was transferred to the Russian Orthodox Church. Today it is once again a Ukrainian Catholic Cathedral. (Kapitulna St., 9).

HORYANSKA ROTUNDA, 12th cent. Built in the shape of a hexahedron with walls 2-2.5m thick. Ornamentation dating to 1360-70 have been preserved.

CASTLE-FORTRESS, 10th-16th cent. Built on the site of the palace of the ancient Ukrainian Prince Laborets. Its original appear-

Kafedralny Sobor (Church), 1646.

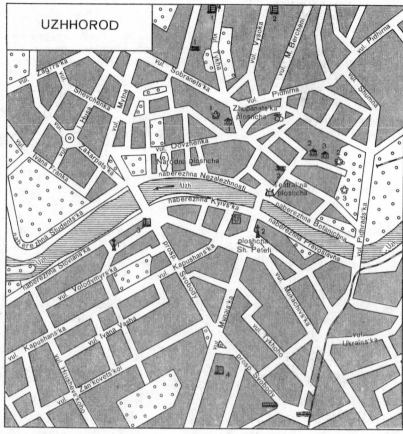

UZHHOROD

Hotels:
1 Svitanok Tourist Lodge
2 Druzhba
3 Uzhhorod
4 Zakarpattia

Restaurants:
1 Kosmos
2 Edelveis
Note. Restaurants Druzhba, Uzhhorod and Zakarpattia are attached to the hotels of the same names

Railway Station

Bus Station

Market

Monuments:
1 Writer Ievhen Fentsyk
2 Poet Sándor Petőfi

Architectural monuments:
1 Building of the magistracy, 1809
2 Cathedral, 1646
3 Castle, 16th c.

Museums:
1 Art
2 Local Lore
3 Folk Architecture and Life

Music-and-Drama Theater

Philharmonic Society

ance was restored in the 12th cent. Today it houses the Regional Museum and Art Gallery. (Kapitulna St., 33).

NEVYTSKY CASTLE (ruins), 13th cent. (Dobryansky St., 3).

FORESTRY BUILDING, 12th cent. The birthplace of the Hungarian poet I. Dendesi (1629). (Diyendeshi St., 8).

MONUMENTS

S. Petefi. In the city-center. (Ploshcha Petefi).

M. Luchkay Tomb. The grave of the 19th cent. linguist and historian. (Tseholnyanska St., in the center of the city).

Horyanska Rotunda, 12th cent.

MUSEUMS

Regional Museum: Kapitulna St., 33; tel. 3-44-42. • **Museum of Folk Architecture and Folkways:** Kapitulna St., 33-a; tel. 3-63-52. • **Art Museum:** ploshcha Zhupanatska, 3; tel. 3-70-81. • **M. Luchkay Memorial Museum:** Druhetiv St., 74; tel. 3-26-04.

THEATERS, PHILHARMONIC

Ukrainian Music and Drama Theater: Tolstoy St., 12; tel. 3-60-14. • **Puppet Theater:** ploshcha Teatralna, 8; tel. 3-43-38. • **Philharmonic:** ploshcha Teatralna, 10; tel. 3-23-22.

HIGHER EDUCATIONAL INSTITUTIONS

University of Uzhhorod: Pidhirna St., 46.

Castle-Fortress, 10th-16th cent.

LIBRARIES, ARCHIVES

Regional Library: prospekt Svobody, 16; tel. 3-41-40. • **Library of Uzhhorod University:** Kapitulna St., 9; tel. 3-63-95. • **Municipal State Archive:** ploshcha Zhupanatska, 3; tel. 3-33-79. • **Uzhhorod District Archive:** Korzo St., 10-a; tel. 3-51-02.

PARKS, BOTANICAL GARDEN

Bozdoshsky Park: Slovyanska and Studentska Naberezhna St. • **Pidzamkovy Park:** A. Voloshyn and F. Tikhy St. • **Alpinarium:** city-center. • **University Botanical Garden:** A. Voloshyn and F. Tikhy St.

SPORTS COMPLEXES

Tysa Sports Complex: Hay Hohola, 7.

HOTELS

Zakarpattya: ploshcha Kyryla i Mefodiya, 5; tel. 9-71-40; 9-75-10; fax: 3-50-31. • **Druzhba:** Vysoka St., 12; tel. 3-32-32; fax: 3-24-90. • **Uzhhorod:** ploshcha Khmelnytskoho, 2; tel. 3-50-60. • **Sport:** Profspilkova St., 4; tel. 4-33-44.

RESTAURANTS

Edelweiss: Voloshyn St., 26; tel. 3-60-62. • **Zakarpattya:** ploshcha Kyryla i Mefodiya, 5; tel. 9-71-40. • **Druzhba:** Vysoka St., 12; tel. 3-32-32.

STORES

Suveniry Zakarpattya: Korzo St., 10. • **Khudozhniy Salon (Art):** Voloshyn St., 18-a. • **Univermah "Ukrayina:"** ploshcha Kyryla i Mefodiya, 4. • **Kobzar (books):** ploshcha Koryatovycha, 1. • **Market:** Fedynets St., 21.

BANKS

National Bank of Ukraine (Regional Branch): Pushkin St., 1; tel. 3-31-32. • **Transcarpathian Commercial Bank "Lisbank:"** Zhovtneva St., 32; tel. 3-31-01, 3-25-39. • **Commercial Cooperative Investment Bank "Koopinvestbank:"** Hoyda St., 10. • **Joint-Stock Commercial Bank "Zakarpattya:"** Mukacheve, Myru St., 40.

Hotel Druzhba.

TOURISM

Inturyst: ploshcha Kyryla i Mefodiya; tel. 9-71-95.

Suputnyk: ploshcha Khmelnytskoho, 21; tel. 3-55-58.

Svitanok Tourist Base: Koshytska St., 30; tel. 3-43-09.

Zakarpatturyst: Krylov St., 10; tel. 3-40-06.

Travel and Excursion Agency: Sobranetska St., 152; tel. 4-20-21, 4-20-51.

Excursion routes: Architectural Monuments of the 12th cent., Horyanska Rotunda (take bus No. 2 at ploshcha Petefi, final stop), Nevytsky Castle (Dobryansky St., 3, bus to the Kamyanytsya bus-stop).

Hotel Berkut.

POST OFFICE, TELEPHONE

Main post office: ploshcha Poshtova, 4; tel. 3-20-41.

Central Telegraph: Naberezhna Nezalezhnosti St., 4; tel. 3-21-22.

MEDICAL SERVICES

Emergency: tel. 03.

Pharmacies: Korzo St., 6; tel. 3-40-37. • Ploshcha Koryatovycha, 2; tel. 3-43-62. • Prospekt Svobody, 18; tel. 3-40-62.

TRANSPORTATION

Train station: Statsiyna St., 9; tel. 3-23-00.

Ticket office: Tolstoy St., 31; tel. 93-20-40.

Bus Station: Uzhhorod-1: Statsiyna St., 2; tel. 3-40-07.

Bus Station: Uzhhorod-2: Dobryansky St., 3; tel. 3-70-04.

Ticket office: Tolstoy St., 33; tel. 3-31-55.

Airport: Sobranetska St., 145; tel. 4-29-74.

Airline Ticket Office: Tolstoy St., 33; tel. 3-42-65.

CONSULATES

Consulate of the Hungarian Republic: Sorokrichchya Zhovtnya St., 56; tel. 2-16-78.

AUTO SERVICING

Autoservis: Krasnodontsiv St., 20; tel. 3-42-54.

TOURING HISTORIC CITIES AND VILLAGES

BEREHOVE

City, 72 km from Uzhhorod. Population: 31,000.

In 1237 the hordes of Khan Baty so devastated the town that the Hungarian king was forced to resettle people into this town from neighboring villages and mountain settlements. The town was ruled by Serbian and Transylvanian kings and Hungarian feudal lords. In 1566 the town was plundered by the armies of the Turkish Sultan Suleiman I.

The Transcarpathian Agrarian Production Scientific Research Institute is located in the region and one of the largest gold deposits in Ukraine is located here.

GOTHIC CHURCH (Roman Catholic), 15th cent. In nearby Chepivka village.
HRAFSKE PODVIRYA (COUNT'S COURTYARD), 1629.

KHUST

City, 100 km from Uzhhorod, on the Rika and Tysa Rivers. Population: 35,400. Established in the 11th cent. In 1329 Khust was designated a crown city. The city was destroyed many times by the Tatars and the Turks. In January 1919 at the All-Carpathian Congress it was decided to unite with Ukraine. In 1938 Khust was the Capitol of independent Carpathian Ukraine. In March 1939 the independence of Carpathian Ukraine was proclaimed in the city.

CASTLE, 11th-12th, and 14th-16th cent. (Ruins). Located on a hill. In 1769 during a storm lightning ignited the gunpowder and caused an explosion which demolished the majority of the buildings.

YELYZAVETYNSKA (ST. ELIZABETH'S) CHURCH, 14th cent.

Monument to O. Dukhnovych (1803-65). A writer and civic activist who was born in the village of Topolya in the Pryashiv region (now part of Slovakia).

REGIONAL MUSEUM.

CARPATHIAN NATURE PRESERVE, 1968. Near the Dolyna Nartsysiv massif (Valley of Narcissus). Contains a unique collection of narrow-leafed narcissus. At

Khust. Castle Ruins, 11th-12th cent.

Synevyr Lake.

the end of April the valley is covered with a carpet of these snow-white flowers. There are also rare varieties of narcissus, such as the Saffron, Heifel, and other varieties.

MIZHHIRYA (until 1953 — Volove)

Village located in a mountain hollow, 154 km from Uzhhorod. Nearby are the Kamyanka (1587 m) and Kuk (1365 m) mountains. Population: 12,000.

Early documents refer to the village in 1415 as one of the properties of the Hungarian feudal lords.

The Mizhhirya and Karpaty tourist centers are located here. Excursions to Lake Synevyr, called the "marine eye of the Carpathian Mountains," and the Tereble-Ritsk Hydroelectric Station, which joins the waters of two rivers in one four-km tunnel are very popular. Hiking excursions to the Borzhava meadow located on a plateau, the Shypot Waterfall, the Forestry Museum in nearby Synevyr village are among the local attractions. The Verkhovyna Health Resort is located in the village of Soyma: the local mineral water is used in the treatment of gastro-intestinal, liver, and rheumatic illnesses.

MUKACHEVE

City and district center, railway station, 40 km from Uzhhorod, on the Latorytsya River. Population: 90,000.

First mentioned in the "Gesta Hungarorum." The city was founded in the 9th cent. as a military fortress and settlement of the White Croatians. In the 10th-11th cent. it was part of Kyivan Rus'-Ukraine. After the region was captured by the Hungarians, it became their fortress. In 1086 it was devastated by Polovtsian tribes and in 1241 by the armies of Khan Baty.

In 1281 the Galician-Volynian Prince Lev Danylovych extended his rule over parts of Transcarpathia, including Mukacheve. Within 40 years the city was once again under Hungarian rule. In 1393 the Hungarian king presented Mukacheve to the prince of Podillya F. Koryato-

Mukacheve. Mykolayivska (St. Nicholas') Monastery, 1806.

vych, who established a monastery, fortified the fortress and encouraged commerce. In the years 1938-44 Mukacheve was under Hungarian rule. In 1944-92 it was part of the Ukrainian SSR.

CHURCHES, HISTORICAL AND ARCHITECTURAL MONUMENTS

Mukacheve. Church, 1777.

**MYKOLAYIVSKA (ST. NICHOLAS')
CHURCH AND MONASTERY CELLS,**
1806. Established by Prince F. Koryatovych. Originally a wood structure, the monastery was rebuilt in stone in 1772 in the Baroque style. (Pivnichna St., 2).

PALANOK CASTLE, 14th-17th cent. Former residence of Prince F. Koryatovych. The massive walls of the castle, described in numerous legends and tales, withstood many enemy attacks. The castle is being restored. (Zamkova Hora).

BILY BUDYNOK (WHITE BUILDING) PALACE, 15th-18th cent. Belonged to the Counts Shenbons. Rebuilt in 1746-48 in the Baroque style. Richly ornamented, with a beautiful portal. (Myru St., 28).

KARPATY RESORT, 1890. Former hunting castle of the Counts Shenbons. Located 7 km from Mukacheve.

CASTLE, 14th-15th cent. In the center of a park. A two-storied structure with embrasures, towers, and underground passages.

The Palanok Castle is now a History Museum.

AUTO SERVICING

Ukrinteravtoservis: village of Chyna; tel. 6-22-90.

RAKHIV

City and district center on the Tysa River, 209 km from Uzhhorod. Population: 16,400.

First mentioned in documents dating to 1447. The original settlers were peasants from Galicia (Halych) and Transcarpathia. The Opryshky Movement under the leadership of O. Dovbush, I. Pynti, F. Boyko, and I. Pysklyvy was widespread here. Today this is a popular tourist destination.

The T. Shevchenko Monument and Regional Museum are located in the city.
CARPATHIAN NATURE PRESERVE, 1968. Composed of three complexes, two of which cover the Chornohora range (containing the highest peaks of the Carpathians reaching 2061 m). There is an Alpine belt of vegetation, with a large collection of rhododendrons.

SOLOTVYNA

Village on the Tysa River, between the Skalvan and Mahura mountains, 25 km from the Tyachiv railway station.

The village boasts a unique health establishment: the Republican Hospital for the treatment of allergies, the buildings of which are located in underground salt mines. Asthma and other respiratory illnesses are treated here.

SVALYAVA

City on the Latorytsya River, 72 km from Uzhhorod. Population: 19,800.

First mentioned in 12th cent. documents. Until 1264 the city was part of the Galician-Volynian Principality. Later, it belonged to numerous Hungarian feudal lords. The noble family of Count Shenborn-Buchheim ruled the city for two centuries.

Today Svalyava is a spa area, with approximately 100 mineral springs, approximately one-third of the total number of springs in Transcarpathia. The Polyana, Kvitka Polonyny, Sonyachne Zakarpattya resorts, the Choven children's resort, Kryshtaleve Dzherelo and Kvasny Potik sanatoria are located in the area.

Three companies produce 85 million bottles of mineral water of the Polyany Kvasovoyi and Luzhanska varieties.

MYKHAYLIVSKA (ST. MICHAEL'S) CHURCH, 1588. A wood structure (Village of Bystry).
History Museum.

TYACHIV

City and railway station on the right bank of the Tysa River, 136 km from Uzhhorod. Population: 12,700. The Uzhhorod-Rakhiv autoroute goes through Tyachiv.

Founded in the mid-13th cent.

Monuments to T. Shevchenko and L. Koshutov, one of the leaders of the revolution in Hungary of 1848, are located here.

Rakhiv. Marker for the geographical center of Europe.

Svalyava. Mykhaylivska (St. Michael's) Church, 1588.

CARPATHIAN NATURE PRESERVE, 1968. On the Uholsko-Shyrokoluzhansky Massif. Features stalactite caves (Molochny Kamin and Hrebin). Druzhba, the deepest shaft in the Carpathian Mountains contains unusual stalactites and stalagmites.

VILKHOVYTSYA

Village, 13 km from Mukacheve, 3 km from Chynadiyevo.

MYKOLAYIVSKA (ST. NICHOLAS') **CHURCH,** 18th cent. A wood structure.

Zakarpattya Sports Base: Mukachevska St., 3; tel. 2-33-35.

VOLOVETS

Village and railway station, 115 km from Uzhhorod, at the foot of the Play and Temnatyk mountains. Population: 7,000.

First documented references to the village date to 1433.

The Play Tourist Center is located in the village.

POKROVSKA (PROTECTION) CHURCH and **BELL TOWER,** 18th cent. Located in the village of Kanora.

VYNOHRADIV (until 1946 — Sevlyush)

City and district center, 100 km from Uzhhorod, at the foot of the Chorna Hora (Black Mount), on the right bank of the Tysa River. Population: 26,800.

After the arrival of the Hungarians in the Transcarpathian region inn the 10th-11th cent., a border fortification was built to defend the area from attacks by the Pechenegs and Polovtsians. In 1241-42 the settlement was destroyed by the armies of Khan Baty. The first documented references to Sevlyush date to 1262. The city was ruled for several centuries by the Hungarian magnates, the Pereni.

Monuments to T. Shevchenko, A. Makarenko, and I. Reves are located in the city.
KANKOV CASTLE, 13th-14th cent. Ruins.
FRANCISCAN CHURCH, and **MONKS' CELLS,** 14th-15th cent.
PALACE OF COUNT PERENI, 15th cent.

Zaporizhzhya Region

In southern Ukraine. The region is primarily steppe flatland, bisected by the Dnipro River. In the south it borders on the Sea of Azov. The climate is temperate-continental. Hot, dry winds (sukhoviyi) blow almost every summer; severe rain storms occur periodically.

Established in 1939. Area: 27.200 sq. km. Population: 2,116,000.

History

Settlement of the territory began in the early Paleolithic Age, as attested by remains uncovered near the village of Fedorivka in Zaporizhzhya district. Near Zaporizhzhya seven settlements from the late Paleolithic Age have been unearthed. More than 100 monuments from the Bronze Age have also been excavated.

In the 7th cent. B.C. the lands north of the Black Sea were ruled by the Scythians, who established their capital, Scythia, on the banks of the Dnipro River.

In the 4th cent. A.D. the country was conquered by the Huns, in the 6th cent. by the Avars, and in the 8th cent. by the Khazars. After the destruction of the Khazar Khanate in 966 by Kyivan Prince Svyatoslav, the Pecheneg tribe represented the greatest threat to the region. From the mid-11th cent. the steppes near the Sea of Azov were controlled by Polovtsian tribe.

After assembling on Khortytsya Island in the early 12th cent. the Ukrainian princes destroyed the Polovtsian tribes on the Molochna River. Soon after, the Ukrainian state suffered renewed attacks by the Tatars. The armies of the Ukrainian princes reassembled on Khortytsya Island and on 16 June 1223 were defeated on the

Zaporizhzhya Region.
Khortytsya Island.

Kalka River. A part of the population of the Azov steppes was enslaved by the Golden Horde and the Crimean Khans.

The Kozak movement arose in the late 15th cent. Khortytsya became the base of the Zaporozhian Kozaks and an important center of Ukrainian statehood. The Kozaks constructed "zasiky," defensive obstacles formed by felled trees with sharpened branches facing the enemy; hence the term Zaporozhian *Sich.* In 1554-55 D. Bayda-Vyshnevetsky built a castle on Small Khortytsya Island, which later became part of the Kozak fortifications system.

In late January 1648, after the defeat of a government outpost near Khortytsya Island, Hetman Bohdan Khmelnytsky launched his anti-Polish war. The Kozaks attained decisive victories in battles fought near Zhovti Vody and Korsun.

The Zaporozhian Sich was the key center on the crossroads of several important commercial routes: the "route from the Varangians to the Greeks," the Muravsky, Chorny (Black), and Chumatsky (Salt-Carters') routes.

The Tsarist government refused to tolerate the free-thinking Kozaks and in July 1775 Russian troops under Gen. Tekeliy, on the way home from the Turkish front, destroyed the Zaporozhian Sich.

The region has many historical monuments. There are several hundred burial mounds, called kurhans, scattered throughout the region and they are considered the most unusual monuments of ancient Ukraine. Settlements dating to the Paleolithic and Mesolithic Ages have been uncovered near the villages of Fedorivka and Petro-Svystunovo in the Zaporizhzhya and Vilnyansky districts, respectively (45 km from Zaporizhzhya). In the Dnipro, Molochna, and Berda River Basins more than 20 Neolithic monuments have been unearthed. The most unique sacred place is the Stone Barrow near Melitopol (30 km). In the central part of the steppe are numerous immense sandy pits three ha in diameter; images of sorcerers, bulls, horses, deer, fishing nets, and footprints are carved on the stone walls of the grottos.

Archaeologists have also uncovered 120 monuments of the Copper and Bronze Ages.

Scythian remains have been unearthed near Kamyanka-Dniprovska and Velyka Znamyanka. In Melitopol district many Sarmatian burial grounds have been excavated.

PROMINENT INDIVIDUALS

BORN IN THE REGION:

P. Hryhorenko (1907-87), human rights activist, general; in Borysivka, died in the U.S. • **N. Makhno** (1888-1934), Ukrainian anarchist leader; in Hulyaypole. • **O. Slastion** (1822-1933), painter, ethnographer, art specialist; in Berdyansk.

BURIED IN THE REGION:

Y. Hladky (1789-1866), the last chieftain of the Zaporozhian Sich; in Oleksandrivka. • **O. Ivchenko** (1903-68), aeronautical engineer, academician; in Zaporizhzhya.

ZAPORIZHZHYA (until 1921 — Oleksandrivsk)

City and regional center, along the Moscow-Simferopol autoroute, railway junction: Moscow-Simferopol and Donbas-Kryvbas. Population: over 800,000. Telephone code: 0612.

The city was founded on 26 August 1770, the date of construction of the Oleksandrivsk Fortress. Some scholars have suggested that the city was founded in 1554-55, when a fortress was built on Khortytsya Island, or even earlier — in the late 11th cent.

The hydro-electric station built on the Dnipro River divided the city in two. Its construction launched the Zaporozhian Industrial Complex, which comprises approximately 300 industrial establishments.

Khortytsya Preserve, located in the middle of the Dnipro River in the south-western part, belong to the city.

CHURCHES, HISTORICAL AND ARCHITECTURAL MONUMENTS

SEREDNIY STOH UROCHYSHCHE (SURVEY MARK). A settlement dating from the 4th-2nd cent. B.C. to the 1st cent. A.D.

BURIAL MOUNDS. At Bryanska, Borodynska, Istomin, Lakhtynska, and Selyshchna Streets.

ANTHROPOMORPHOUS STELA, 3rd-2nd cent. B.C. Stone statues of the 15th-8th cent. B.C. (Nemyrovych-Danchenko St., 46-a).

KOZAK FORTRESS, 15th-18th cent. On Mala Khortytsya Island.

KHORTYTSYA, 1965. A historical-cultural preserve. First mentioned as St. Gregory's Island in the mid-10th cent. It was an important Kozak bulwark against various invaders. Remains of the Zaporozhian stronghold have been preserved at Sovutyn Rock. The Zaporozhian Kozaks launched their anti-Polish rebellions from here. Destroyed by the Russian armies in 1775.

SVYATOMYKOLAYIVSKY SOBOR (ST. NICHOLAS' CATHEDRAL), 1886. Erected on the highest point in Upper Khortytsya.

ZAPOROZHIAN OAK TREE. A 700-year-old tree: it is 36 m high and its trunk is 6.5 m in diameter. (Verkhnya Khortytsya near Zaporizhzhya).

MONUMENTS

B. Khmelnytsky, 1965. Sculptor: F. Zaytsev. (Khortytsya Island).

T. Shevchenko, 1964. Sculptor: I. Shmulson. (Kolektyvna St.).

A. Vinter, 1966. Academician who directed the construction of the Dnipro Hydroelectric station dam. Sculptor: A. Allakhverdyants. Architect: A. Zavarzyn. (Vinter Blvd.).

Hotels:
1 Kolos
2 Dnipro
3 Zaporizhzhia
4 Pivdennyi
5 Teatral'nyi
6 Ukraïna

Khortytsia Tourist Lodge

Restaurants:
1 Berizka
2 Rosiia
3 Lahti
4 Pivdennyi
5 Khortytsia
6 Dubovyi Hai
Note. Restaurants Dnipro, Zaporizhzhia and Teatral'nyi are attached to the hotels of the same name

Railway Stations

Bus Station

River Port

Monuments:
1 At the Grave of the Unknown Soldier who saved the Dnipro Dam
2 M. I. Glinka

Monument of Glory to the soldiers who forced a crossing over the Dnipro in November 1943

Wonders of nature:
1 Catherine's Chair Rock
2 Evil Rock
3 Sich Gates, Snake Cave, Black Rock

Museums:
1 Khortytsia Island, historico-cultural preserve
2 Art Museum
3 Museum of Local Lore

Theater of Music and Drama

Philharmonic Society

MUSEUMS

Regional Museum: Chekistiv St., 29; tel. 64-39-12. • **Art Museum:** 40 rokiv Radyanskoyi Ukrayiny St., 76-d; tel. 34-06-32. • **Museum of 1905 Revolution:** Vasylyev St., 15; tel. 96-53-07. • **Khortytsya Island State Historical-Cultural Preserve:** tel. 52-51-88. • **Zaporozhian Kozaks Historical Museum:** Khortytsya Island; tel. 52-72-34. • **Museum of Folk Creations and Ethnography:** Gorky St., 38; tel. 64-17-54.

THEATERS, PHILHARMONIC, CIRCUS

Music and Drama Theater: Lenin St., 41. • **Youth Theater:** Tsentralny Blvd., 4. • **Puppet Theater:** Hohol St., 60. • **Philharmonic:** Lenin St., 183. • **Circus:** Rekordna St., 41.

HIGHER EDUCATIONAL INSTITUTIONS

University: Zhukovsky St., 66. • **Industrial Institute:** Lenin St., 226. • **Machine-Building Institute:** Zhukovsky St., 64. • **Medical Institute:** Mayakovsky St., 26.

LIBRARIES, ARCHIVES

Scientific Library: Lenin St., 142. • **Science-Technical Library:** Lenin St., 77. • **Medical-Science Library:** Chervonohvardiyska St., 38. • **Youth Library:** Lenin St., 210. • **Children's Library:** Sportyvna St., 14. • **Androsov Central Library:** Dzerzhynsky St., 51. • **Regional Archive:** Ukrayinska St., 48. • **Municipal Archive:** Lenin St., 164.

SPORTS COMPLEXES

Metalurh Sports Training Center: Tyulenin St., 13; tel. 32-15-13. • **Motor-Sich Sports Complex:** Ivanov St., 24; tel. 61-46-17. • **Metalurh Stadium:** Sportyvna St., 21; tel. 2-52-18. • **Yunist Sports Palace:** Peremoha St., 66; tel. 33-50-81.

HOTELS

Dnipro: Lenin St., 202; tel. 33-04-45; 34-26-60. • **Pivdenny:** Pravda St., 53; tel. 33-23-82; 33-24-18. • **Ukrayina:** prospekt Lenina, 162; tel. 34-66-73; 64-36-52. • **Teatralny:** Chekisty St., 25; tel. 64-24-38; 64-36-52. • **Inturyst:** prospekt Lenina, 135.

RESTAURANTS, CAFES, BARS

Zaporizhzhya (in the Inturyst Hotel): Lenin St., 135; tel. 39-94-12. • **Berizka:**

Sorok Rokiv Radyanskoyi Ukrayiny St., 55; tel. 33-01-13. • Dnipro: Lenin St., 202; tel. 33-15-36. • Zaporizka Sich: Khortytsya Island; tel. 52-81-42. • Zoloty Kolos: Rekordna St., 6; tel. 2-56-61. • Kozachy Dozor: Simferopolske shosse, 1; tel. 95-41-31. • Khortytsya: Khortytsya Island; tel. 60-53-78. • Rosiya: Chubar St., 2-a; tel. 32-68-13. • Chervony Kamin Pyvbar: Kamyanohorska St., 4; tel. 33-34-35. • Cocktail Bar: Shchaslyva St., 5; tel. 52-14-09. • Vernissage Cafe: Lenin St., 181; tel. 2-6-17. • Karlson: Malynovsky St., 13; tel. 96-38-12. • Marichka: Lenin St., 42; tel. 64-66-86. • Slavutych: Matrosov St., 23; tel. 33-71-55. • Khortychanka: Zachynyayev St., 2; tel. 57-83-10. • Chay: Lenin St., 189; tel. 2-66-79.

STORES

Ukrayina: Lenin St., 147. • Pravoberezhny: Vinter St., 30. • Verkhnya Khortytsya: Istomin St., 15. • Podarunky (Gifts): Lenin St., 148. • Suputnyk: Anholenko St., 13. • Budynok Radio: Lenin St., 133. • Budynok Odyahu (Clothing): Lenin St., 53. • Budynok Vzuttya (Shoes): Tsentralny Blvd., 3.

BOOKSTORES

Slavutych: Lenin St., 232. • Suchasnyk: Lenin St., 151. • Kobzar: Lenin St., 150. • Burevisnyk: Kosmichna St., 112. • Lehenda: Lakhtynska St., 6. • Dumka: Kremlivska St., 2.

BANKS

Ukrainian National Bank (Regional Branch): Dzerzhynsky St., 23; tel. 64-27-60. • Commercial Bank "Avtozazbank:" Lenin St., 8; tel. 64-22-82, 64-22-64. • Commercial-Joint Stock Bank "Slovyansky:" Elekrozavodska St., 3; tel. 52-13-25, 52-20-39. • Commercial Bank "Tavrydabank:" Melitopol, Marx St., 10; tel. 4-22-87, 4-32-44.

TOURISM

Inturyst-Zaporizhzhya: Lenin St., 135; tel. 33-05-54, 33-25-56.
Zaporizhturyst: Sorok Rokiv Radyanskoyi Ukrayiny St., 51; tel. 33-03-54.
Travel and Excursions Agency: Lenin St., 153; tel. 34-80-73.
Local Excursions: "The Monuments of Zaporizhzhya;" "Kozak Glory" (to Nikopol, the grave of Kozak's chieftain I. Sirko, departing from Khortytsya Island); Khortytsya Preserve (walking tour); "Around Khortytsya" (by ship), "Kozak Routes" (Khortytsya Island).
Included in the tours: "Journey to Kozak Country" (equestrian show) and other equestrian demonstrations.
A visit to the Orlovsky racehorse-breeding farm.

Zaporizky Shchedry Vechir: sampling of Ukrainian Christmas dishes in the Intourist national hall; includes a concert program.

POST OFFICE, TELEPHONE

Central calling point: Lenin St., 133; fax: 34-35-91.
Post Office branches: Lenin St., 186; tel. 33-12-22. • Pivnichnokiltseva St., 26; tel. 95-52-07. • Zadniprovska St., 11; tel. 42-14-22. • Lenin St., 144; tel. 33-61-05.

MEDICAL SERVICES

Emergency: tel. 03.
Pharmacies: Sorok Rokiv Radyanskoyi Ukrayiny St., 51; tel. 34-90-57. • Lenin St., 58; tel. 64-19-04. • Radhospna St., 36; tel. 95-53-23. • Pivnichnokiltseva St., 6; tel. 95-65-78. • Lenin St., 110-a (children's pharmacy).

TRANSPORTATION

Railway station "Zaporizhzhya-1:" tel. 005; 64-39-17; 69-12-53.
Railway Station "Zaporizhzhya-2:" tel. 64-21-67.
Bus Terminus No. 1: Lenin St., 22; tel. 64-26-57; 33-20-65.
Bus Terminus No. 2: Rekordna St., 37; tel. 34-57-36; 33-20-65.
Zaporizhzhya River Port: Hliserna St.; tel. 64-15-30; 69-52-09.
Lenin River Port: Leonov St., 1-a; tel. 2-60-55; 2-02-09.
Airport: tel. 64-25-65.
International ticket office: tel. 64-47-59.

AUTO SERVICING

Avtoservis: Avramenko St., 2; tel. 61-87-11.
Autoroute Service Complex: village of Mykhaylivka, Vilnyansky district, 1017 km Moscow-Simferopol autoroute; tel. 34-96-71; village of Yakymivka, 1173 km Moscow-Simferopol autoroute.

TOURING HISTORIC CITIES AND VILLAGES

BERDYANSK (until 1841 — Berdy; in 1939-58 — Osypenko)

City on the shores of the Sea of Azov. Population: 140,000.
The sea port was established in 1825-30. After the railway was extended to Chaplino station the city became an important commercial-trade center in the Azov area.
Berdyansk is a resort center: it has six health resorts and a boarding house. Miraculous cures have been attributed to the effect of direct sunlight on the water and mud of the surrounding estuaries.

Hotel Berdaynsk: Dyumin St., 55/23; tel. 3-66-69; 3-56-04. (From the railway station by bus No. 5 and 17 to the Rynok stop. From the airport, bus No. 7, to the Rynok station).
Travel and Excursion Agency: Michurin St., 95, tel. 4-17-28.
Arranges various excursions: "Historic Sites of Berdyansk;" "The Berdyansk Peninsula;" "Flora and Fauna;" "Aquatic Life in Berdyansk Bay."

HULYAYPOLE

City in the Haychur river valley, 8 km from the Hulyaypole railway station.
In the summer of 1919 the army of the Ukrainian anarchist Nestor Makhno (35-50 thousand men) camped here. His forces played a decisive role in battles fought in southern Ukraine.

HULYAYPILSKY REGIONAL MUSEUM: Lenin St., 79; tel. 4-13-54.

MELITOPOL (until 1842 — Novooleksandrivka)

City on the Molochna River. Population: 175,000.
Novooleksandrivka was founded in the late 18th cent. when Kozak runaways settled near Pishchana Mountain. The Scythians and the Greeks lived here and founded the town of Melita in the 1st cent. A.D.

MELITOPOL KURHAN (Burial mound), 4th cent. B.C. Excavated in 1954. Two burial vaults have been found: one contained the remains of women; in the other vault — the remains of a Scythian nobleman. Approximately 4,000 gold ornaments were also unearthed.

ST. ALEXANDER NEVSKY CATHEDRAL, 17th cent. A former Armenian church.

CEMETERY CHURCH of USIKOVNENNYA HOLOVY IOANA PREDTECHI (BEHEADING OF ST. JOHN THE BAPTIST), 1905. Built in the basilica style.

Melitopol Regional Museum.
Travel and Excursion Agency: Lenin St., 137; tel. 2-04-29.
Itinerary: Kamyana Mohyla Architectural Preserve.
Hotel Melitopol: Peremohy St., 3; tel. 4-21-93; 3-11-04. (From the train station, buses No. 1, 7, 17, 23 to the Sverdlov stop).
Commercial Bank "Tavrydabank:" Marx St., 10; tel. 4-22-87; 4-32-44.

PRESERVES IN THE REGION

KAMYANI MOHYLY (STONE GRAVES), 1924. A branch of the Ukrainian Steppe Preserve, between the villages of Rozivka Zaporizka and Nazarivka, Donets district. Situated on 456 ha of pristine steppeland.

KOSA OBITOCHNA (SPIT). A Ukrainian state nature preserve since 1980. 10-15 km from the city of Prymorske.

LARGE AND SMALL KUCHUHURY (MOUNDS). State Ornithological preserve (1974), an archeological monument. Comprises 13 islands of the Kakhovka Reservoir, 12 km from the Tavriysk railway station, 400 ha, of which 60 ha are dry land. A stopping point for migrating birds and the largest breeding grounds of rare types of fish.

STAROBERDYANSKY FOREST PRESERVE, 1846. Established by I. Kornis. 18 km from Melitopol, covers 1132 ha of forest and contains 150 varieties of trees, 50 species of birds, and over 40 animal species.

ALLEY OF CHESTNUT-TREES. Petrovsky Forest. Approximately 60 chestnut trees more than 100 years old and 300 m high grow here. (Near Vilnyansk railway station, on the Moscow-Simferopol line).

Zhytomyr Region

It is situated in the north, in two topographic-climatic zones: forest and forest-steppe. In the south, within the boundaries of the Dnipro Upland, the region is heavily dissected by ravines and river valleys. This region is rich in mineral resources and has over 200 small rivers. The main river is the Teteriv, a tributary of the Dnipro. Population: 1,507,000. Area: 29,900 sq. km.

History

The territory of this region was settled in the Early Paleolithic Age. Living quarters of the original settlers have been unearthed on the left bank of the Svynoluzhka river and near Radomyshl. Samples of the material culture of this era have been excavated, as well as the remnants of tent homes.

At the beginning of the new era various Slavic tribes, such as the Derevlyany, the Zhytychi and others lived here.

The Ukrainian national-liberation war of 1648-54 is an integral part of the history of the Zhytomyr region, which provided Hetman B. Khmelnytsky with four Kozak regiments.

During World War II this heavily-forested region became a base for Ukrainian forces, in particular the Organization of Ukrainian Nationalists and the Ukrainian Insurgent Army, who were engaged in armed resistance against German and Soviet troops.

Zhytomyr Region. Hansky Palace in Verkhivnya, where Honore de Balzac visited.

PROMINENT INDIVIDUALS

BORN IN THE REGION:

G. Conrad (1857-1924), English writer; village of Terekhove in the Berdychiv district. • **B. Lyatoshynsky** (1895-1968), composer; Zhytomyr. • **N. Matviyenko** (1947), singer; village of Nedilyshche in the Yemilchynsky district. • **I. Ohiyenko** (1882-1972), Metropolitan of the Ukrainian Greek Orthodox Church in Canada, historian, prose writer, translator; village of Brusyliv in the Korostyshivsky district; died in Canada. • **O. Olzhych-Kandyba** (1907-44), poet, one of the leaders of the Melnyk faction of the Organization of Ukrainian Nationalists; Zhytomyr; died in a German concentration camp. • **O. Shtul-Zhdanovych** (1917-77), political leader, head of the Melnyk faction of the Organization of Ukrainian Nationalists (OUN); village of Lopatychi; died in Canada • **L. Ukrayinka-Kosach Kvitka** (1871-1913), poetess, civic activist; Novohrad-Volynsky.

BURIED IN THE REGION:

T. Rylsky (1841-1902), civic activist; village of Romanivka in the Popilnyansky district.

ZHYTOMYR

Regional center, 135 km from Kyiv, located on the shores of the Teteriv River and its tributary, the Kamyanka. Telephone code: 0412.

The city is believed to have been founded in 884. This period in history is linked to a legend about Zhytomyr. A soldier from the retinue of the Kyivan princes, who founded a settlement on the steep bank of the Kamyanka River, considered the nucleus of the future city. Other theories concerning the origins of the city name refer to possible derivatives from two word combinations: "to measure rye" or "to live in peace." The city was razed to the ground several times, once by the armies of Khan Baty in 1240.

Preobrazhensky (Transfiguration) Cathedral, 1864.

CHURCHES, HISTORICAL AND ARCHITECTURAL MONUMENTS

HORODYSHCHE. Situated on the shores of the Kamyanka River, this town is an archaeological monument of the second half of the first century. Built by early Iron Age tribes.

PREOBRAZHENSKY (TRANSFIGURATION) CATHEDRAL, 1864. Built on the site of a Basilian church (1771). In 1847 a new building for the cathedral was constructed in the old Byzantine style. The cathedral is 53 m high. (Ploshcha Peremohy, 14).

CHURCH OF PRESVYATOYI BOHORODYTSI (HOLY MOTHER OF GOD). One of the oldest churches in Zhytomyr.

MYKHAYLIVSKY (ST. MICHAEL'S) CATHEDRAL. Belongs to the Ukrainian Autocephalous Orthodox Church.

ST. SOPHIA ROMAN CATHOLIC CATHEDRAL, 1737-51. Built in the late Renaissance and Baroque styles. The cathedral was substantially rebuilt in the Classical style in 1801. A bas-relief portrait of Yu. Zarembsky, the renowned pianist and composer, adorns one of the cathedral pylons.

St. Sophia Roman Catholic Cathedral, 1737-51.

MONUMENTS

T. Shevchenko, 1981. Sculptor: B. Kalovsky. Architect: P. Biryuk. (the corner of Shevchenko and Berdychivska Streets).

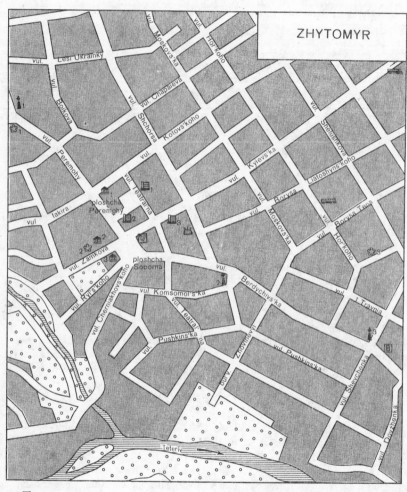

ZHYTOMYR

🅱 Excursion office

🏨 Hotels:
 1 Zhytomyr
 2 Mykhailovhrad
 3 Zhovten

🚃 Railway Station

🚌 Bus Station

🕴 Monuments:
 1 Writer Vladimir Korolenko
 2 Spacecraft designer Sergei Korolev
 3 Taras Shevchenko

🏛 Architectural monuments:
 1 Cathedral, 1866—1874
 2 Roman Catholic Church, 1744
 3 Magistracy, 1789

✿ Museums:
 1 V. Korolenko Literary-Memorial
 2 Local Lore
 3 S. Korolev Memorial

🎭 Ukrainian Music-and-Drama Theater

🎵 Philharmonic Society

A. **Pushkin,** 1899. Sculptor: H. Olishkevych. Architect: M. Betaki. (Zhovtnevy Blvd.).

S. **Korolyov.** Sculptor: O. Oliynyk. Architect: A. Korneyev. (Maydan Rad).

MUSEUMS

Museum of Regional Ethnography: ploshcha Zamkova, 1; tel. 37-29-65. • **Space Museum:** Franko St., 18; tel. 37-26-53. • **V. Korolenko Literary-Memorial Museum:** ploshcha Korolenka, 1; tel. 22-16-31. • **Pictorial Art Museum:** suburban village of Kmytiv. • **Nature Museum:** Komarov St., 18; tel. 37-44-15.

THEATERS, PHILHARMONIC

Ukrainian Musical-Drama Theater: ploshcha Soborna, 6; tel. 37-23-13. • **Puppet Theater:** Mykhaylivska St., 7; tel. 37-47-61. • **Philharmonic:** Pushkinska St., 26; tel. 37-42-68.

HIGHER EDUCATIONAL INSTITUTIONS

Pedagogical Institute: Velyka Berdychivska St., 44. • **Agricultural Institute:** Zhovtnevy Blvd., 9. • **Zhytomyr Campus of the Kyiv Polytechnical Institute:** Chernyakhovsky St., 103.

LIBRARIES

Regional Scientific Library: Engels St., 4; tel. 37-84-32. • **Regional Youth Library:** Kotovsky St., 9; tel. 37-40-21. • **Central Municipal Library:** Kyivska St., 74-a. • **Music and Theater Library:** Teatralna St., 20-a; tel. 37-51-61.

PARKS, BOTANICAL GARDENS

Central Park: Zhovtnevy Blvd., 37. • **Hydropark:** Chernyakhovsky St., 107. • **Botanical Gardens:** Korolyov St., 39.

SPORTS COMPLEXES

Central Stadium: Paryzka Komuna St., 30-a; tel. 37-25-33. • **Spartak Water Rowing Center:** Hydropark; tel. 24-19-70.

HOTELS

Zhytomyr: ploshcha Peremohy, 6; tel. 22-86-93. • **Mykhaylovhrad:** ploshcha

Peremohy, 2; tel. 22-56-45. • **Zhovtnevy:** Kyivska St., 10; tel. 22-56-45. • **Yalynka:** prospekt Myru, 34; tel. 20-65-18.

RESTAURANTS, BARS

Zhytomyr: ploshcha Peremohy, 6/2. • **Smolensk:** Mykhaylivska St., 6. • **Yalynka:** prospekt Myru, 30. • **Polissya:** Kyivska St., 197. • **Kokteyl-bar:** prospekt Myru, 30.

STORES

Central Department Store (univermah): Kyivska St., 25. • **Budynok Vzuttya** (Shoes): Kyivska St., 61. • **Yantar** (jewelry): Kocherha St., 6. • **Druzhba** (books): Kocherha St., 6.

BANKS

National Bank of Ukraine: Hohol St., 5; tel. 37-28-15. • **Komertsiyny bank "Polissya" ("Polissya" Commercial Bank):** Kyivska St., 5; tel. 37-04-91. • **Komertsiyny bank "Ahropostachbank" ("Ahropostachbank" Commercial Bank):** 1 Travnya St., 65; tel. 34-45-59, 37-04-23. • **Komertsiyny bank "Olevsky" ("Olevsky" Commercial Bank):** Dzerzhynsky St., 17; tel. 2-35-49.

TOURISM

Zhytomyr-Turyst: Velyka Berdychivska St., 63; tel. 34-05-85.
Inturyst: Kyivska St., 9; tel. 22-05-27.
Planeta: Kyivska St., 9; tel. 22-05-27.
Merkuriy: Komsomolska St., 8; tel. 22-07-70.
The Zhytomyr Travel and Excursion Bureau suggests several itineraries: bus trips to sites associated with Honore de Balzac, who spent time in the region; the village of Kopyshche, which was burnt to the ground during the war; the village of Kodnya, which the Ukrainian national poet, Taras Shevchenko and other literary figures visited for its historic association with the Haydamaky Movement in Ukraine.

POST OFFICE, TELEPHONES

Main post office: Kyivska St., 16; tel. 37-34-05.
Central calling point No. 1: ploshcha Peremohy, 7/1.
Central calling point No. 2: Moskovska St., 13; tel. 37-15-13.

MEDICAL SERVICES

Emergency: tel. 03.
Central emergency station: Velyka Berdychivska St., 36; tel. 37-51-58.
Main pharmacy: ploshcha Soborna, 4; tel. 37-44-46.

TRANSPORTATION

Train station: ploshcha Pryvokzalna, 3; tel, 36-14-83; information: tel. 005.
Main bus terminus: Kyivska St., 67; tel. 36-24-82.
Advance bus tickets for inter-urban travel: Kyivska St., 42; tel. 22-73-55.
Suburban bus terminus: Gorky St., 20-a; tel. 37-84-45.
Zhytomyr Airport: Kyivska St., 150-a; tel. 36-14-46; fax: 36-12-52.
Advance air tickets: ploshcha Peremohy, 5/36.
Taxi reservations: tel. 058; 37-05-81.

AUTO SERVICING

Avtoservis: Lenin St., 297; tel. 36-04-71.

TOURING HISTORIC CITIES AND VILLAGES

ANDRUSHIVKA

City located 47 km from Zhytomyr. First mentioned in 1683.

PALACE, 19th cent. Situated in a park, the palace belonged to M. Tereshchenko. Built in the French Renaissance style. Was somewhat rebuilt in 1975.

BERDYCHIV

City located on the shores of Hnylopyat River, 44 km south of Zhytomyr.

The territory was settled as early as the 2 cent. B.C. Bronze Age settlements and remnants of two settlements of the Chernyakhiv culture have been unearthed. In June-July, 1648, a detachment of rebels led by M. Kryvonis inflicted heavy losses on the Polish army near Berdychiv, which was later captured by the Kozaks. In 1703 Kozak forces under colonel S. Paliy of Fastiv distinguished themselves in several battles near Berdychiv. By the second half of the 18th century Berdychiv had become one of the largest trading centers in Ukraine. In the fall of 1846 T. Shevchenko visited this city.

CARMELITE MONASTERY, 16th-18th cent. Built on the Hnylopyat River on the site of a sixteenth century castle. In 1627 the monastery of the "barefoot Carmelites" was founded. In 1648 the armies of B. Khmelnytsky captured this monastery-castle, which was closed in 1792. A historical museum has been located on the premises of the monastery since 1925. In 1941 it was burned to the ground and executions of civilians took place on its site. Restoration work on the monastery commenced in 1958. (Kosohorska St., 17).

ST. VARVARA (ST. BARBARA) ROMAN CATHOLIC CHURCH, 1826. Major repairs were undertaken in 1857. The French writer, Honore de Balzac, married Evelina Hanska in this church.

MARIYINSKY (BLESSED VIRGIN MARY) ROMAN CATHOLIC CHURCH, 1634, 1739-54. Built in the Baroque style. The interior paintings were executed by the Italian artist, V. Frederice. During World War II the church burned down and was later restored.

KODNYA

Village in the Zhytomyr district, 3 km from the Kodnya railway station. Its history is connected to the Haydamaky Movement in Ukraine known as the "Koliyivshchyna" (1768). Tsarist armies captured Haydamaky rebel detachments led by M. Zaliznyak and I. Gonta and a mass execution of the rebels of "Koliyivshchyna" took place in Kodnya (approx. 3000 Haydamaks). Also executed were several well-known Kozak minstrels, whose songs of freedom were an important source of inspiration for the Ukrainian peasantry. In 1846 the Ukrainian national poet, Taras Shevchenko, visited the village.

CHURCH OF RIZDVO BOHORODYTSI (NATIVITY OF THE BLESSED VIRGIN), 1841; **BELL TOWER,** 1865. Built in the Late Classical style. Twentieth century wall paintings have been preserved.

Kodnya. Church of Rizdvo Bohorodytsi (Nativity of the Blessed Virgin), 1841.

BURIAL MOUND. The mass grave of approximately 3000 Haydamaky rebels executed in Kodnya in 1768.

Monument to T. Shevchenko. Made of Polissian granite.

Historical museum. Contains relics of Kozaks and Haydamakys who struggled to attain liberty for the Ukrainian nation.

KOROSTEN

An ancient city of the tribe of Derevlyany, situated on the shores of the Uzh river, 87 km from Zhytomyr.

Mentioned in the "Tale of Bygone Years" as an inaccessible fortress that towered over granite cliffs. Renowned for its association with Prince Ihor and Queen Olha. According to an ancient legend, the Derevlyany, incensed by Prince Ihor's unjust struggle against them, destroyed his army. His wife, Princess Olha, revenged her husband's death. The ancient chronicle recounts how she devised a crafty plan to burn down the city. Many remains of the material culture of the past have been preserved, including "Olha's Baths" situated on the Uzh River, and a burial mound. According to legend, the Kyivan prince's warriors were buried here. The history of the Derevlyany tribe is displayed in an exhibit in the local historical museum.

KRAYIVSHCHYNA

Village in the Volodarsko-Volynsky district.

MYKHAYLIVSKA (ST. MICHAEL'S) CHURCH, 1757; **BELL TOWER,** 1854. A wooden structure.

LYUBAR

Village, district center, located on the shores of the Sluch River, 80 km from Zhytomyr and 24 km from the Pechanivka railway station.

BASILIAN MONASTERY, 1666. A Ukrainian Orthodox Monastery of St. George, subsequently converted to a Basilian monastery. A school was founded here in 1775, with an enrollment of 450 students. Substantially renovated in 1888.

NOVA CHORTORYYA. Village in the Lyubar district, 108 km from Zhytomyr and 12 km from the Pechanivka railway station.

PALACE, 19th cent. Located in a landscaped park occupying an area of 70 ha. Was rebuilt at the turn of the century. Its interior decorations — stained glass windows, bas-relief, and paintings, are noteworthy. Parts of the palace are built in the Baroque, Renaissance, and modern styles.

NOVOHRAD-VOLYNSKY (until 1796 — Zvyahel)

City situated on the banks of the Sluch River, 87 km from Zhytomyr.

First mentioned in the Hypatian Chronicle for the year 1257. Belonged to the Galician-Volynian Principality. The remains of an ancient fortress recalling the exploits of the Kozak detachments of Severyn Nalyvayko and Maksym Kryvonis are located on the rocky river bank.

Novohrad-Volynsky is the birthplace of the Ukrainian poetess, Lesya Ukrayinka. The building in which she was born has been preserved.

Every year "Lesya's Roots" and "Lesya's Pleiades", popular literary-artistic festivals, take place in the city.

Lesya Ukrayinka's building. The birthplace of the poetess.
The L. Ukrayinka Literary-Memorial Museum. Displays artifacts from the life of L. Ukrayinka and the Kosach family.

OLEVSK

Village located on the Ubort river, a tributary of the Prypyat, 180 km from Zhytomyr.

MYKOLAYIVSKA (ST. NICHOLAS) CHURCH, 1596. This brick structure is an example of sixteenth century Ukrainian architecture. Enlarged in the 19th century.

OVRUCH

City, district center, situated on the left bank of the Noryn river, a tributary of the Uzh river, 127 km north of Zhytomyr.

First mentioned in the "Tale of Bygone Years" for the year 946.

Olevsk. Mykolayivska (St. Nicholas') Church, 1596.

VASYLIVSKA (ST. BASIL'S) CHURCH
OF THE BASILIAN MONASTERY, 1190,
1909; MONASTERY STRUCTURES, 1907-
09. The church of Prince Ryuryk Rostyslavo-
vych (baptismal name: Vasyliy). Erected on the
site of a wood church built in 997 by Prince Volodymyr Velyky (the Great). Destroyed by the
Lithuanians in 1321. By 1842 the church was in
ruins. In 1907-09 the church was restored according to the designs of the architect A. Shchusyev. Fragments of ancient frescoes have been
preserved in the church. A Basilian Convent was
built during the restoration. (Proletarska St., 2).

Tryhirya. Preobrazhensky
(Transfiguration) Church,
1854-73.

TRYHIRYA

Village in the Zhytomyr district.

TROYITSKY (HOLY TRINITY) MONASTERY, 15th cent. Founded by Volodymyr, Prince of Zhytomyr, on a rocky massif above the Teteriv River. Was the
second most important monastery in Ukraine, after the Pochayiv Monastery. Was
rebuilt in wood in 1613, and in brick in 1839. The monastery complex includes the
Preobrazhenska (Transfiguration) Church (1854-73), and cells (1782).

VERKHIVNYA

Village in the Ruzhynsky district, 15 km from the Brovky railway station.

The first documented reference to the village appears in 1600. Its history is intimately linked to the French writer, Honore de Balzac, who twice made lengthy visits
to Verkhivnya, where he worked on his play "The Stepmother", a novel, and his
multi-volumed masterpiece *The Human Comedy.*

PALACE, 18th-19th cent. The palace, surrounded by a landscaped, eighteenth
century park, is one of the most important palace-park architectural ensembles to be
built in Ukraine in the Classical style. Owned by the Hansky family. The palace
complex includes a Roman Catholic church (1810). Balzac lived here from 1847 to
1850. Restored in 1970-75.

Balzac Museum, 1959. Established in the Hansky palace, the former residence
of the great French writer. The museum contains books used by Balzac.

REFERENCE

Government

Supreme Rada: 252019, Kyiv, Hrushevsky St., 5.

Council of Ministers: 252008, Kyiv, Hrushevsky St., 12/2; tel. 293-52-27.

SELECTED MINISTRIES

Communications: 252001, Kyiv, Khreshchatyk St., 22; tel. 229-12-71.

Culture: 252030, Kyiv, Franko St., 19; tel. 224-49-11; 226-26-45; fax: 225-32-57.

Defense: 252005, Kyiv, Bankivska St., 6; tel. 291-54-41.

Economy: 252008, Kyiv, Hrushevsky St., 12/2; tel. 293-61-41.

Education: 252001, Kyiv, Khreshchatyk St., 34; tel. 226-32-31; fax: 226-33-23.

Environment: 252001, Kyiv, Khreshchatyk St., 5;
tel. 226-24-28; 228-40-04; fax: 228-06-44.

External Economic Relations: 252053, Kyiv, Lvivska Ploshcha, 8;
tel. 226-27-33; 212-54-23; 212-53-59.

Foreign Affairs (MZS): 252018, Kyiv, Mykhaylivska Ploshcha, 1;
tel. 212-86-60; fax: 226-31-69.

Health: 252021, Kyiv, Hrushevsky St., 7;
tel. 226-22-05; 293-61-94; fax: 293-69-75.

Investments and Construction: 252008, Kyiv, Sadova St., 3;
tel. 293-26-89; 292-04-70.

**Protection of the population from the after-effects
of the accident at the Chornobyl Nuclear Power Station:**
252196, Kyiv, ploshcha L. Ukrayinky, 1; tel. 226-30-67; 296-83-95; 296-86-77.

Youth and Sports: 252023, Kyiv, Esplanadna St., 42; tel. 220-02-00; 220-14-61.

AGENCIES

Ukrainian National Information Agency (Ukrinform): 252001, Kyiv,
Khmelnytsky St., 8/16; tel. 226-32-30; 229-81-52; fax: 229-24-39.

COMMITTEES

Tourism State Committee: Yaroslaviv Val, 36; tel. 224-81-49, 212-55-70.

State Customs: 252055, Kyiv, Politekhnichny Provulok, 4-a;
tel. 446-92-41, 274-81-94.

Social welfare: 252005, Kyiv, Bankivska St., 6.

Shevchenko State Prizes: 252008, Kyiv, Sadova St., 3; tel. 293-07-62.

National Olympic Committee of Ukraine: 252023, Kyiv, Esplanadna St., 4; tel. 220-02-00; 220-13-09; fax: 220-95-33; telex: 13-18-66 Tennis.

Writers Union of Ukraine: 252024, Kyiv-24, Bankova St., 2 tel. 293-45-86; 293-95-52

STATE COMPANIES

Radio and Television Company of Ukraine: 252001, Kyiv, Khreshchatyk St., 26; tel. 228-33-33; 226-31-44.

Foreign Tourism Joint-Stock Company: 252034, Kyiv, Yaroslaviv Val, 36; tel. 212-55-70; fax: 212-46-24.

SELECTED STATE INSTITUTIONS

"Book Palace": 253094, Kyiv, prospekt Gagarina, 27; tel.: 552-01-34.

General Procurator: 252601, Kyiv-11, MSP, Riznytska St., 13/15; tel. 226-20-27; 290-10-20.

Religious Affairs Council: 252021, Kyiv, Hrushevsky St., 14; tel. 293-23-94.

Supreme Court: 252601, Kyiv — 24, MSP, Orlyk St., 4; tel. 226-23-04; 293-33-13.

Republican Center for Exhibitions and Markets: 252085, Kyiv, prospekt Hlushkova, 1; tel. 261-74-24; fax: 261-76-77.

Political Parties of Ukraine

DEMOCRATIC PARTY OF UKRAINE (DPU)
Tel. 216-85-91; 293-75-56

GREEN PARTY OF UKRAINE (PZU)
Kyiv-70, Kontraktova Ploshcha, 4, Hostynny Dvir; tel. 417-02-83.

LIBERAL PARTY OF UKRAINE (LPU)
340037, Donetsk, Kirov St., 147-a.

PARTY OF THE DEMOCRATIC REBIRTH OF UKRAINE (PDVY)
Kyiv, Instytutska St., 27/6, suite 31.

PEASANT PARTY OF UKRAINE (SelPU)

PEOPLE'S PARTY OF UKRAINE (NPU)
Dnipropetrovsk, Naberezhna Lenina St., 1; tel. (0562) 58-80-32.

"RUKH" POPULAR MOVEMENT OF UKRAINE (NRU)
Kyiv, Shevchenko Blvd., 37/122; tel. 224-91-51; 216-83-33; 274-20-77.